Jill Bowen is a well-kn   ~~~malist who has written for
major Australian newsp   ears.
Since 1978 she has wo   alian
Stockman's Hall of Far   ional
board of directors.

KIDMAN
The Forgotten King

Jill Bowen

Angus&Robertson
An imprint of HarperCollins*Publishers*

To my parents,
H. A. (Ted) and Mabs Bowen –
with great affection

Angus&Robertson
An imprint of HarperCollins*Publishers*, Australia

First published in Australia by Angus & Robertson Publishers in 1987
A&R Imprint Lives edition 1992
Reprinted in 1993, 1994
This A&R Classics edition 1995
Reprinted 1996, 1997, 1998 (twice), 1999
by HarperCollins*Publishers* Pty Limited
ACN 009 913 517
A member of the HarperCollins*Publishers* (Australia) Pty Limited Group
http://www. harpercollins.com.au

HarperCollins*Publishers*
25 Ryde Road, Pymble, Sydney, NSW 2073, Australia
31 View Road, Glenfield, Auckland 10, New Zealand
77–85 Fulham Palace Road, London W6 8JB, United Kingdom
Hazelton Lanes, 55 Avenue Road, Suite 2900, Toronto, Ontario M5R 3L2
and 1995 Markham Road, Scarborough, Ontario M1B 5M8, Canada
10 East 53rd Street, New York NY 10022, USA

National Library of Australia Cataloguing-in-Publication data:

Bowen, Jill, 1943– .
Kidman, the forgotten king.
Bibliography
Includes index
ISBN 0 207 18968 4.
1. Kidman, Sir Sidney, 1857–1936. 2. Cattle trade – Australia – Biography.
3. Cattle trade – Australia – History. 4. Ranchers – Australia – Biography.
I. Title.
338.7636213092

Cover photograph by kind permission of the Mitchell Library,
State Library of New South Wales.
Printed in Australia by Griffin Press Pty Ltd on 80gsm Econoprint

10 9 8 7 6   99 00 01 02

Contents

Acknowledgements

WITH NO PAID secretary or researchers to help with the workload associated with this book, the assistance of many people should not go unnoted. They gave their time and effort and some went to great lengths to help provide material ranging from the whereabouts of former Kidman employees who could be interviewed, to letters, documents, newspaper reports, station records and photographs.

Within the Kidman family, I would particularly like to thank Sir Sidney Kidman's eldest grandchild, Joan Hopkins, of Adelaide, and her husband, Neil, both for their hospitality and for Joan's willingness and thoroughness in producing everything she could that might be likely to assist. I am sorry that another of Kidman's grandchildren, Isabel Lee, and her mother, Muriel Kidman, did not live to see this book completed, for they both helped me as much as they could. I am grateful also to Isabel's younger sister, Anne Abel Smith (now Fidock), and to Jean Reid, John Ayers Jnr (the current principal of Kidman Holdings) and John Kempe (now retired from that company).

Information from R. M. Williams, Ken Brass, Trevor Sykes, Martin Summons, Dame Mary Durack Miller, Roger Steele, Vern O'Brien, Bobbie Hardy, Rob Dempster, Russel Ward, Ken Kidman, Bob Kidman, Peter Bridge, Sandy Yarwood, Noni Farwell, David Ross Coles, Alex Stewart, Colin Adams, Dick Condon, Godfrey and Mary Turner, Mike Cummings, Graham Peart, Jock Makin, Tom Cole, Hayden Murray, Ranald Chandler, Elizabeth Warburton and Hugh McConnell led to progress in my research, usually via a hunt in the archives.

I am particularly grateful to the Westpac Banking Corporation for allowing me to do research in the old Bank of New South Wales Archives at Pyrmont, Sydney, and to senior archivist Clive Smith and Lynne Milton. In the Northern Territory, Ruth Dickson and Ian Sutherland were a great help at the Australian Archives. Within the Business and Labour Archives at the Australian National University, Canberra, Pennie Pemberton, Maureen Purtell, Colleen Pritchard and Michael Saclier all gave me a helping hand. I did such a long stint at those archives that visitors assumed I was a member of staff! The same solid support was given at the Charles Rasp Library, Broken Hill.

I travelled, where necessary, to pursue research ... frequently to Adelaide where I stayed with Don and Pauline Tilmouth; in Canberra I received hospitality from Bruce and Dorothy Davis, in Bourke from Dudley and Susie Dunn, in Alice Springs from Leslie Oldfield, and in Darwin from Liz Dumont and Clyde Adams My thanks to those people.

For their help in supplying the photographs that were required for this book, I would like to thank Martin Brannan Snr, Keith Stevens, Sean Tilmouth, Alan Barton and members of the Kapunda Historical Society.

This book would not have been written had it not been for the enthusiasm shown by businessman Dick Smith for the project. It was undertaken at his instigation and I thank him for providing a generous sum towards the research costs. I also thank him and his wife, Pip, for an airlift to Alice Springs where I did research.

I do remain most grateful to everyone who helped me with this project and for the unstinting spirit in which the help was given. The last to pitch in with her help — and certainly not the least — has been the editor appointed by Angus & Robertson to steer the manuscript into a book. *Bene laboramus una!* Thank you, Jacquelin Hochmuth, for your meticulous care. I consider myself a lucky duck that you were given the project.

J.B.

Introduction

I DIDN'T ASK to write this book. I was asked *if* I would write it. I have never flinched from a challenge but this represented a great departure from the newspaper and magazine journalistic work to which I had been accustomed for some twenty years.

In January 1984, when I was given ten days to make up my mind, the front pages of newspapers were thick with stories about the Big Wet and the chaos created as the "inland sea" swamped four states and the Northern Territory. They were the type of rains that Sidney Kidman would have loved, rains that brought down his "three rivers". I took the monumental rains as a good omen. I said "yes". There have been many times I have regretted that decision. Since I started my research it has taken more than three years of my life to punch this project to a conclusion.

I did not know anything about Sidney Kidman when I undertook to write about his life, except that his was a well-known name in the outback. I had not learnt about him at school or university.

Friends asked if I saw myself as "starting from scratch like some sort of amateur detective". I suppose that was one way of looking at it. Rather, I saw Kidman's life as a jigsaw puzzle. I was starting with an empty frame, with not even a huge pile of irregular, jumbled pieces to fit together correctly; but no pieces at all. Collecting these pieces has proved extraordinarily difficult.

I had assumed, incorrectly, that a man such as Kidman would have left a substantial repository of papers, documents and letters — or that the surviving members of his family would hold these. This was not so. It was little short of a shock to have Kidman's great-grandson John Ayers Jnr, the principal of Kidman Holdings today, unlock the safe in his premises in North Adelaide and say, "Go for your life. Don't think you'll find much there of any use to you." I didn't. It should be said that he was as helpful as he could have been.

After that I did become something of an amateur detective ... there was a mystery to solve and nothing much to go on. A lot of people helped. And I remain extremely grateful to all of my fellow amateur sleuths who were drawn into the case and endlessly supplied bits and pieces of information they felt might help.

I grew despondent when on so many occasions I came to a dead end. The answer was to leave that line of investigation and to concentrate on fresh leads. Many times a "dead end" could be "revived" later when new evidence surfaced. I was never short of others' opinions whenever and wherever I raised the name Sidney Kidman, but opinion was never the solution to the problem. Facts were needed to solve the case.

With so little to go on initially, I used Ion Idriess's book *The Cattle King* (Angus & Robertson, Sydney, 1936) as a guide. It did provide clues which led me around archives and libraries. Sometimes I got results; sometimes I was on a wild-goose chase.

I was often asked in the course of writing this book: "Why are you doing it when Ion Idriess has already done it?" The Idriess account of Sid Kidman's life has usually been accepted as gospel. However, some people claim it is "a bunch of rubbish". So, when puzzled people asked why I was writing a further book, I told the truth: "Well, fifty years after his death I have been given the job of reassessing Kidman's life." Some people said, "Good on yer," while others said, "Pity help you!" Others volunteered, "You'll just be rewriting the Idriess story..."

On that last score I do beg to differ. The more jigsaw pieces I found, the less reliable the Idriess story became, dwelling so very much as it did on the early part of Kidman's life and focusing so little on his final twenty-five years when he assumed great power and status and seemed to be constantly enmeshed in controversy.

Idriess told the story of the "Cattle King" in a very romantic and literary, rather than factual, way. Sid Kidman did *not* spend the greater part of his life swaying off into the sunset — or somewhere else — with his bum firmly planted in a saddle. Certainly he may have preferred the bush, but he was equally at home in city hotels and in business and bank boardrooms where he was instantly recognised, instantly respected and sometimes feared. And not just within Australia. On all of his overseas trips (and he made many) the red carpet was rolled out for him, and in England and the United States he was given the kid-glove treatment.

It is wrong to wrap up Sidney Kidman as simply "a cattle king". That is to overlook his massive horse sales and his considerable interests in sheep and wool.

It is wrong to assess him as just "a grazier". He was more than that. That description overlooks his business interests in foundries, shipbuilding, roadbuilding and water-conservation works and his £8 million proposal for railway construction.

Sid certainly didn't believe in putting all his eggs into the pastoral basket. But these other aspects of his life have rarely been mentioned before.

There are so many other myths about him — stories put around so often they are held to be true — that he didn't swear, drink or smoke, that his wife was a demure little "Scotch" woman (she was Scots and later grew to enjoy drinking his Scotch), that he sacked employees for lighting pipes or cigarettes with matches rather than campfire embers, allegations of meanness . . . the list goes on and on.

One thing held to be true by so many people is that Kidman carved out his own good fortune without so much as a helping hand from anyone else. I have not found this to be the case and suggest that if his immediately elder brother, Sackville Kidman, had not died prematurely, this book — and even the Idriess account — may not have been written. Until almost the turn of the century it was Sackville who called the business shots; it was his hand that "steadied the lead". In the partnership between the two brothers, Sack was the delegator and Sid was the doer. It was Sack's death that forced Sid to swing out of the saddle and become a desk jockey. Sid Kidman moved into a business whose base had been built up soundly by his elder brother.

Sack's death was a crucial turning point in Sid's life. Sid could have chosen to remain a drover and dealer in stock. Instead he elected to plug on and achieve, or try to achieve, their ambition on his own. And that was to establish a chain of stations that were almost drought-proof, places that when linked together would provide a substantial water supply, with the possible bonus of regular water and feed from floodplains when the "three rivers" came down. He spent his life locked in a battle with the land — and against drought.

Whether or not he succeeded the facts assembled in this book will allow readers to judge for themselves.

At the time of writing this Introduction, once again there are ominous signs. A severe rural crisis is forcing people to sell their machinery or their farms because of debt, just as they were almost 100 years ago in the 1890s. It was similar unfortunate business circumstances that enabled the Kidman brothers, Sackville and Sidney, to start buying up, in a big way, the initial links in what was to become a most amazing chain of stations. I cannot help feeling that the wheel has turned full circle.

Jill Bowen
March 1987

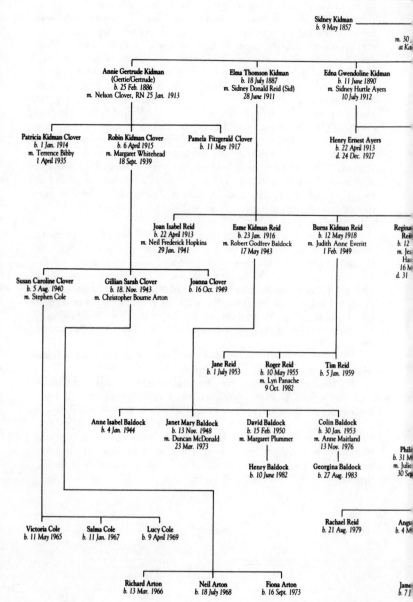

Sidney Kidman
b. 9 May 1857

m. 30
at Ka

Annie Gertrude Kidman
(Gertie/Gertrude)
b. 25 Feb. 1886
m. Nelson Clover, RN 25 Jan. 1913

Elma Thomson Kidman
b. 18 July 1887
m. Sidney Donald Reid (Sid)
28 June 1911

Edna Gwendoline Kidman
b. 11 June 1890
m. Sidney Hurtle Ayers
10 July 1912

Patricia Kidman Clover
b. 1 Jan. 1914
m. Terrence Bibby
1 April 1935

Robin Kidman Clover
b. 6 April 1915
m. Margaret Whitehead
18 Sept. 1939

Pamela Fitzgerald Clover
b. 11 May 1917

Henry Ernest Ayers
b. 22 April 1913
d. 24 Dec. 1927

Joan Isabel Reid
b. 22 April 1913
m. Neil Frederick Hopkins
29 Jan. 1941

Esme Kidman Reid
b. 23 Jan. 1916
m. Robert Godfrey Baldock
17 May 1943

Burns Kidman Reid
b. 12 May 1918
m. Judith Anne Everitt
1 Feb. 1949

Regina
Rei
b. 12
m. Jea
Ha
16 M
d. 31

Susan Caroline Clover
b. 5 Aug. 1940
m. Stephen Cole

Gillian Sarah Clover
b. 18. Nov. 1943
m. Christopher Bourne Arton

Joanna Clover
b. 16 Oct. 1949

Jane Reid
b. 1 July 1953

Roger Reid
b. 10 May 1955
m. Lyn Panache
9 Oct. 1982

Tim Reid
b. 5 Jan. 1959

Anne Isabel Baldock
b. 4 Jan. 1944

Janet Mary Baldock
b. 13 Nov. 1948
m. Duncan McDonald
23 Mar. 1973

David Baldock
b. 15 Feb. 1950
m. Margaret Plummer

Colin Baldock
b. 30 Jan. 1953
m. Anne Maitland
13 Nov. 1976

Phili
b. 31 M
m. Julic
30 Sep

Henry Baldock
b. 10 June 1982

Georgina Baldock
b. 27 Aug. 1983

Rachael Reid
b. 21 Aug. 1979

Angu
b. 4 M

Victoria Cole
b. 11 May 1965

Salma Cole
b. 11 Jan. 1967

Lucy Cole
b. 9 April 1969

Richard Arton
b. 13 Mar. 1966

Neil Arton
b. 18 July 1968

Fiona Arton
b. 16 Sept. 1973

Jame
b. 7 J

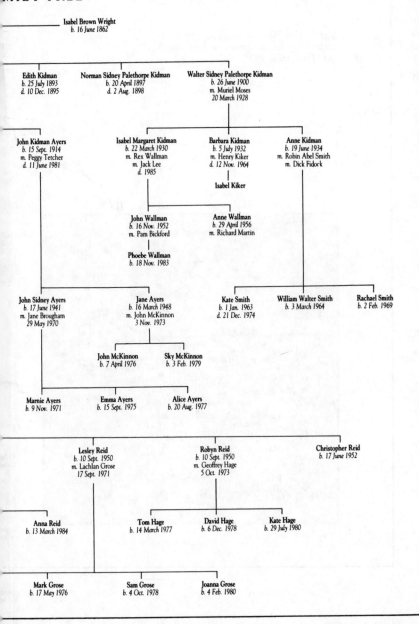

MILY TREE

Isabel Brown Wright
b. 16 June 1862

Edith Kidman
b. 25 July 1893
d. 10 Dec. 1895

Norman Sidney Palethorpe Kidman
b. 20 April 1897
d. 2 Aug. 1898

Walter Sidney Palethorpe Kidman
b. 26 June 1900
m. Muriel Moses
20 March 1928

John Kidman Ayers
b. 15 Sept. 1914
m. Peggy Tetcher
d. 11 June 1981

Isabel Margaret Kidman
b. 22 March 1930
m. Rex Wallman
m. Jack Lee
d. 1985

Barbara Kidman
b. 5 July 1932
m. Henry Kiker
d. 12 Nov. 1964

Anne Kidman
b. 19 June 1934
m. Robin Abel Smith
m. Dick Fidock

Isabel Kiker

John Wallman
b. 16 Nov. 1952
m. Pam Bickford

Anne Wallman
b. 29 April 1956
m. Richard Martin

Phoebe Wallman
b. 18 Nov. 1983

John Sidney Ayers
b. 17 June 1941
m. Jane Brougham
29 May 1970

Jane Ayers
b. 16 March 1948
m. John McKinnon
3 Nov. 1973

Kate Smith
b. 1 Jan. 1963
d. 21 Dec. 1974

William Walter Smith
b. 3 March 1964

Rachael Smith
b. 2 Feb. 1969

John McKinnon
b. 7 April 1976

Sky McKinnon
b. 3 Feb. 1979

Marnie Ayers
b. 9 Nov. 1971

Emma Ayers
b. 15 Sept. 1975

Alice Ayers
b. 20 Aug. 1977

Lesley Reid
b. 10 Sept. 1950
m. Lachlan Grose
17 Sept. 1971

Robyn Reid
b. 10 Sept. 1950
m. Geoffrey Hage
5 Oct. 1973

Christopher Reid
b. 17 June 1952

Anna Reid
b. 13 March 1984

Tom Hage
b. 14 March 1977

David Hage
b. 6 Dec. 1978

Kate Hage
b. 29 July 1980

Mark Grose
b. 17 May 1976

Sam Grose
b. 4 Oct. 1978

Joanna Grose
b. 4 Feb. 1980

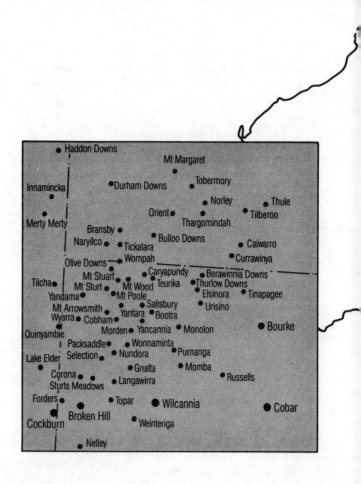

Stations that Sidney Kidman owned,
controlled or had an interest in, from 1890
until his death in 1935.

Prologue:
A Wild Birthday Party

THE OLD MAN in the grandstand edged himself forward in his seat as the first buckjump rider exploded into the arena. A mighty roar went up from the crowd. The old boy grinned as he recognised the inimitable riding style of George Crombie. Crombie would handle this outlaw.

But it was impossible to concentrate on the rider. The scene was almost total chaos. He knew that his boys were putting on a turnout to celebrate his seventy-fifth birthday, but he hadn't expected anything like this. Adelaide had gone mad. His son-in-law Sid Reid had pledged a bush rodeo with the cream of his stockmen and managers pitting their skills at buckjumping, steer-riding and broncoing. It was good of the boys to come to town and put on this bush-inspired public party. He'd had no hand in the thing at, all, except to insist that if the public was to have a look in, then a small entry fee could be levied. The money could go to the Australian Inland Mission. It should help them along a bit — if the gate-keepers had been able to collect the money. The man who could estimate most accurately the numbers in a mob of cattle couldn't come to grips with the numbers in the vast mob of people. Someone had said there were more than 50,000 crammed in and around Jubilee Oval — a fair slice of them had behaved like stampeding cattle and knocked over the fences to get into the ground. A further 10,000 were reported to be lowing fractiously in the streets outside because they could not gain admittance. From where he sat, he could see hundreds of people standing on the roof of a building on the south side of the arena. The massive trees in Frome Road were thickly infested with people hoping for a vantage point...men in dark suits and hats who, for all the world, looked like perched crows. What a turnout. How his boys would cope in keeping the show rolling was anyone's guess. The crowd had surged so far onto the arena as to leave virtually no space for a performance. He could see some men on horseback trying to

OVERLEAF:
At Jubilee Oval, Adelaide, part of the enormous crowd presses forward during the bush rodeo held for Sir Sidney Kidman's seventy-fifth birthday. (The Kidman family)

1

edge the crowd back. It seemed to be in vain. The loudspeakers started blaring, "We want to give you the best show we can but it is impossible if you hinder us by closing in on the horses. Get back! Get back! Or the show won't go on!"

Inspector J. R. Johns, in charge of the police arrangements, shared the anxiety about how the show would go on. The day for him had started quietly enough: the first Saturday in spring and the weather looked a bit on the crook side for the Sidney Kidman rodeo that afternoon. Oh well, it would probably mean a smaller crowd and less men rostered for the job. He reassessed the position mid-morning after a call from the Tramways Trust. Enormous numbers of people were converging on the rodeo. Special trams would be running from every suburb. Ticket-sellers weren't due to open the gates until 1 pm, but Johns decided to dispatch men to Jubilee Oval, Frome Road and North Terrace earlier than intended. Traffic would have to be kept moving and a big crowd would mean a field day for Adelaide's well-known pickpockets.

Arriving at 12 noon Inspector Johns sensed trouble. A crowd of 2,000 was outside the gates. Within fifteen minutes, the crowd had almost doubled. He couldn't believe the swarm before his eyes. Minute by minute it intensified. He hollered at his two mounted men to keep the queue in check, saw that his five motor traffic outfits hadn't a hope in hell of coping, and that his twenty foot-police made no impression whatsoever. An SOS went out for reinforcements. Superintendent McGrath and Inspectors Miller, Howie and Church and a dozen more traffic outfits were allocated. It would take them a while to get there. Everything for a mile or so around was chock-a-block. Trams and cars couldn't move for people, and people couldn't move because the gates weren't open. Inspector Johns fixed that quickly. People streamed into the oval, but not quickly enough for the crowd outside. Mob thinking took over. One in — all in! A section of the crowd hurled its combined weight against the fence and the scramble was on. Women and kids went under in the surge. Order had to be restored somehow...

It was Kidman's roughriders who took the initiative. If mounted police were needed, then they had their horses and weren't averse to cracking a stockwhip. Their rodeo performance started early that day as they shot into the crowd on their horses in their uniform specially created for the occasion: long boots, cream jodhpurs, blue shirts and stetson hats. They patrolled the broken-down fence and kept the mob moving in an orderly fashion, just as they could a mob of cattle. "Blowed if I thought S.K.'s party would kick off like this," Bert Carr, Kidman's manager at Nundora, yelled to Pierce "Barbed Wire" Edwards, the manager of Norley. "Just keep the pikers moving, Bertie boy," Edwards replied.

The presence of the Kidman men in their midst had a settling effect on the crowd outside the grounds. Inside, where the mob was yarded, it was a different story. No one, it seemed, knew when enough was enough. The ground was over-stocked long before the gates could be closed. With every seat taken, spectators took to the roofs of buildings. They shinned up fences and trees, until tree branches broke under their weight and a roof partially caved in, taking a number of people with it. It was some time before first aid could be given to those who fell through the roof and inside the building. The building was locked and no one could find the key. The St John Ambulance Brigade found itself, as had the police force, caught short. The brigade had assigned only twelve volunteers for duty. An urgent radio broadcast appealed for as many members as possible to hotfoot it to the ground to attend to the fainting and the injured, whose problems ranged from fractured skulls to cuts from broken glass and bad burns sustained when several people fell from the roof of a building and collected electric light wires in the process.

Things were warming up rapidly. The Kidman stockmen and managers attempted an official ride past the grandstand where the boss sat, with Archie McLean dipping the flag in salute. Good formation wasn't the order of the day with the horses fractious and edgy, and quite unused to such a seething mass of humanity at close quarters.

"We could have our hands full here today, Daddy," John Brooke, the manager of Mundowdna Station, muttered to George "Daddy" Hooper, manager of Diamantina Lakes in the Channel Country.

"Didn't come this far to cop an accident," Daddy Hooper muttered in reply.

"None of us did," chipped in Ernie Spencer, the manager of Quinyambie Station, "but get a feed of this crowd. Didn't know there were that many in Adelaide. They'll have to get back. It's bloody dangerous..."

"On top of that, fellas," said Charlie Smith riding in the contingent, "take a look at the weather..." South Australia has always had the lowest rainfall of any state in Australia and the grey skies overhead looked poised to pour.

"Quit worryin'," said Ernie Spencer. "Can't think of a better birthday present for the boss than if it pelts with rain..."

Down at one end of the arena another young man was having a hard time of it. Reg Williams, who made pack saddles for the Kidman empire, was in charge of the bucking stock and having a difficult time handling the horses. A bush rodeo devotee, in thirteen years' time he would go on to form Australia's professional rodeo outfit, the Australian Rough Riders Association. Like everyone else he was staggered by the boisterous, overwhelming crowd and not surprised

when one of the first horses let into the arena bucked briefly and spectacularly, then galloped straight into the crowd knocking people right and left. A woman with a young baby was knocked unconscious and her baby sent flying 15 feet away. Stretcher-bearers carted both to the casualty room. Alerted to the danger presented by pressing so closely on the arena, the crowd grudgingly moved back. Within a short time there was further chaos: a buckjumper hurtled his rider into the air and the horse tore along the length of the oval, kicking and plunging at its dangling reins, and straight into the crowd. Kidman men mounted on stockhorses galloped towards the outlaw to head it off, but not before people picked themselves up crushed and bruised. Police reinforcements and mounted stockmen had to force the crowd back further before the steer-riding could take place with any reasonable degree of safety. It took half an hour to force the crowd back behind the arena fence. The Kidman riders took every precaution against crazed steers (well equipped to gore people) plunging into the crowd.

A small nucleus of steers was taken to the middle of the arena in an attempt to ensure that if a roughrider was tossed, his beast would seek the security of the herd — bovine rather than human. But again, stressed by the vast crowd, animal behaviour worked to the contrary. Steers tore straight for the crowd — miraculously headed off at crucial moments by daring, slick-riding stockmen. The crowd roared to each thrill.

When the cattle drafting was under way and the combined nerves of the contestants, the police and the organisers were still under pressure, the day was saved (or ruined, depending on people's viewpoints) by the weather. It poured, driving the vast crowd to run for shelter, if indeed there was anywhere they could run. Collectively stupid, the crowd ran across the arena while an event was still being staged — mounted horsemen, steers and people met in collisions that were spectacular. The St John Ambulance worked to a frenzied pace.

The large squads of police, soaked through and with raw tempers after prolonged hours of crowd control, lined up for hours of overtime. Ditto the tramdrivers and conductors. If the crowd had

---

OPPOSITE:
Archie McLean, who led the march-past of Kidman employees. (Stockman's Hall of Fame)

OVERLEAF:
Eric Skett horsing around at the rodeo, with onlookers (from left) Charlie Smith, Mick Cusack, Arthur West, Wattie Johnson and Pierce Edwards Jnr. (Stockman's Hall of Fame)

caused chaos getting into the ground, it also caused chaos getting home. Several hours after the rodeo ended the City Watchhouse was flat out with calls about people who hadn't returned home. The police asked if enquirers had checked the hospitals. The switchboard of the Adelaide Hospital remained jammed for some time. Wards and beds filled up with accident victims.

Adelaide's paper, the *Mail*, in its edition on the day, 3 September 1932, plastered the incident-stacked afternoon on the front page and elsewhere. Headlines screamed "Rodeo outlaws plunge into crowd", "Spectators rush arena", "Police powerless", "Fine show marred". Inspector Johns was quoted as saying it was the most amazing crowd he had ever seen and the stiffest job he'd ever had to tackle as a member of the force. Elsewhere, what was being said is easy to imagine. In clubs and at Adelaide establishment dining tables the larrikinism of the whole affair was soundly condemned; around suburban kitchen tables youths, husbands and brothers recounted what they'd seen, heard and done and how close they'd come to disaster.

As a climax to the whole shemozzle, Sir Sidney Kidman, in whose honour it had all taken place, hosted a dinner at Adelaide's Oriental Hotel for his stout-hearted band of managers and men, who, aside from Mick, one of his Aboriginal roughriders from Macumba Station (whose leg was badly jammed into a post in the steer-riding event), had all escaped unscathed. His men excelled at roughriding almost every day of the week. The enormous crowd and the significance of the occasion aside, such a bush sports carnival wasn't nearly as appealing to them as the splendid dinner in a swish hotel hosted by their boss as a return thank you. It was almost more nerve-racking to get tarted up in their best bib and tucker and front the hotel than it was to perform at a rodeo. Kidman's men were more likely to return home and talk about the dinner menu — something on a culinary scale of which they rarely partook.

At the dinner, the president of the South Australian Legislative Council, Sir David Gordon, presided as chairman. Kidman's wily pastoral inspector and travelling manager, Ted Pratt, proposed the toast to Sir Sidney. "No one," he said, "who has worked for Sir Sidney could ever say he had a better boss." Applause thundered.

Rather than let Pratt steal all the limelight, those managers ably equipped to get up and say a few supporting words did so: John Brooke, of Mundowdna Station; Archie McLean, of The Peake and Stuart's Creek; Ernie Kempe, of Macumba and Eringa; Pierce "Barbed Wire" Edwards, of Norley and Bulloo Downs; George "Daddy" Hooper, of Diamantina Lakes; and the somewhat dour W. I. J. Foulis, of Corona.

Sir Sidney had a few words to say himself. He was glad to

announce that the Australian Inland Mission was better off by more than £1,000 as a result of the rodeo (around $25,000 by today's standards and it would have been significantly more if everyone had paid at the gates instead of breaking down fences and barging through; it should also be remembered for anyone assessing the donation value that the entry fee struck had been but a small amount to aid a good cause and not the standard rate of entertainment prices of the day). Sir Sidney could not overlook the splendid work undertaken by the St John Ambulance men. For their wonderful efforts he announced that a donation would also be forthcoming to the association by way of thanks, to assist the ambulance in its work.

The population of Adelaide in 1932 was just on 300,000. One-sixth of that population had turned out for Sidney Kidman's seventy-fifth birthday party. Anyone still short on a mental picture of the chaos it presented might care to bear in mind Sydney's population of more than 3 million in 1984. If one-sixth of Sydney turned out for an event there'd be half a million people scrambling for entry and vantage points. That is exactly how it struck Adelaide on 3 September 1932 when the rodeo was put on...the turmoil was formidable. It still remains the largest public birthday party ever put on in Australia to honour a private citizen. Australia had seen nothing like it before and we are never likely to see it happen again.

The date is sadly significant. Exactly three years later in Adelaide huge crowds would turn out again to honour Sir Sidney on 3 September 1935. They would be far more orderly as they lined the streets in thousands with many weeping openly. The cry could hardly go up: "The Cattle King is dead. Long live the King!" Sid Kidman — greatly lamented and in some cases detested — was gone. One thing was certain; there was no one who could take his place. More than fifty years later there still isn't, and the odds are there never will be.

OVERLEAF:
Kidman employees, relatives and friends at the 1932 rodeo (from left): back row — John Horsley, Harry Wyatt, Jose Milne, Bill Ferber, Phil Gourlay, George Crombie, Frank Wastell, Sack Kidman, Mr Warner, Bill Mudge, Alf Raw; second row — H. J. Bird, Ernie Kempe, Harry McCullagh, George "Daddy" Hooper, John Brooke, Arthur West, W. I. Foulis, Hugh Davis, Jim Wright, Sid Ayers; third row — Con White (standing), Walter Kidman, Archie McLean, Sir David Gordon, Sir Sidney Kidman, Rev. John Flynn, Sidney Reid, Ted Pratt, Pierce D. Edwards Snr; front row — John Ayers Snr, Mick Cusack, Ernie Spencer, Wattie Johnson, Bert Carr, Charlie Smith, Eric Skett, Pierce D. Edwards Jnr, Burns Reid; children — Reg Reid, Robin Clover. (The Kidman family)

1

From White House to Log Cabin

THE KIDMANS of South Australia can trace themselves back to 1465 in the reign of Henry VI, when John Kidman's will was proved at Norwich, England. He left his soul to God, his body to be buried in the churchyard at the Blessed Virgin Church, Hemsby, and money for the maintenance of the lights on the church's high altar plus a fee for the vicar, Sir John Knight, to celebrate Holy Communion. Sidney Kidman, a descendant of the Suffolk side of the family, left a lot more than that, including a reputation that has constantly aroused debate, if not argument.

The name Kidman is Saxon and was originally written as Caedmon. In 1663 the Kidmans were granted a motto, crest and coat of arms: *Deus et patria*, to which Sidney Kidman probably added, 250 years later, the word "drought".

Sidney Kidman's grandfather, George Kidman, was a yeoman farmer at Kelsale, Suffolk, where he had 160 acres of green and shaded land. The farm was (and still is) known as the "White House", a legacy of the small farmhouse it had when George bought it and which he rebuilt in white brick. A sportingly inclined man, George Kidman was fond of hunting and entertained many hunting and shooting parties in his new house. One of the old-timers in the Kelsale district in 1927 (when he was 90 years old) told the rector of the parish a yarn about Kidman's grandfather. The old-timer's father had worked on the Kidman estate and returned home one day, startling his family by saying that Master Kidman had shot one of the beaters. The fact was that a few stray pellets had peppered him, but he promptly fell to the ground as dead, whereupon Kidman rushed up to him and said, "Damn it, you old fool! You are not killed, are you? Here's a pound." Whereupon the "dead man" seized that considerable sum of money and made off home!

Kidman's grandfather was a man of means. He married Sarah Whitehead, a widow with two sons. She was a handsome woman with bright, dark eyes and dark hair, and they had one son, George Kidman. When Sidney's grandfather died in 1846, aged 66, his will described him as "George Kidman of Yoxford in the county of Suffolk, gentleman, then residing at 56 Upper Brook St, Grosvenor Square, London". In his will he left his widow, Sarah Kidman, £40 a

14

year out of his estate at Kelsale, and his son, George, all his real estate.

The one son of Sarah's second marriage, George Kidman, was 29 years old when he married Elizabeth Mary Nunn at St Mary's Parish Church, Bury St Edmunds, in 1848. On the wedding certificate he is described as a gentleman of Kelsale, County of Suffolk, the son of George Kidman, gentleman. Elizabeth Mary is described as the daughter of Frederick Nunn, a Suffolk farmer.

They lived on their estate at Kelsale and had two sons, George, born in 1849, and Frederick, born in 1850. But by 1851 George Kidman had made up his mind to take his wife and young family to South Australia. The reason for the move is not known, but it is said that hard times brought on by the Napoleonic Wars played a hand in it. In any event he left the White House in Suffolk for a log cabin in Adelaide and arrived in 1851 without capital. After staying briefly at Norwood, George set up as a farmer on more than 50 acres of leased land at the corner of Montacute and Marybank Roads in Payneham, Adelaide, growing crops, breeding pigs (for quick money) and running a few cows. The rate records, which start in Adelaide in 1854, show him as being the holder of the land, which included a small house and 5 acre garden and vineyard. Two years later, the Payneham Rate Assessment book still lists George Kidman as being the occupier in a wooden house of three rooms, a stable and a barn.

George had been busy and working hard — in other areas too. His two sons born in England, George and Frederick, increased to three with the birth of Thomas on 29 March 1853, and four with the birth of Sackville, born on 25 March 1855 (the children's paternal grandmother, Sarah, in her young days had been in the household of the Earl of Dorset whose family name is Sackville). Another son, Sidney, was born on 9 May 1857. Their father George was a popular and hard-working community-minded man. This was proved early in 1858, when in March he received thirty-nine votes entitling him to election as one of the three councillors on the Payneham District Council.

The road that went by his farm was the only access to the abattoirs and took a heavy amount of local traffic. George Kidman put it to Council that the road be kept in better condition. He may well have wished that he hadn't because it killed him. In May that year it was resolved that Councillor Kidman "be empowered to repair the Montacute Road and cross road near his house at an expense not exceeding five pounds". In June, Councillor Kidman was "empowered to employ four drays for three days filling ruts on the Montacute Road". During the bleak weather that prevailed at the time, he succumbed to bronchitis and died a few weeks later on 17 July 1858. A death notice in the *Adelaide Observer* lists him as being

highly respected and his death much regretted and the *South Aust-tralian Register* mentions him as "George Kidman, in his 39th year, of Glen Stuart, Fifth Creek, and formerly of Kelsale, Suffolk, leaving a wife and five children".

Mrs Kidman's grief was magnified by the fact that a sixth child was on the way, and on 19 September 1858 Charles Kidman was born. Widow Kidman had six sons all under the age of 10 to look after. Her plight was considerable. She notified her family in England and faced up to the day-to-day battle of keeping her small estate going. It was impossible on her own. She sought help from the Starr family who lived at Thorndon, less than a mile from her property. The Starrs' son, Stephen, was sent to help her with the farm work.

Elizabeth Mary Kidman was in her mid-thirties and the farmhand Starr, half her age. No doubt there were anxious family conferences in Suffolk as to what could be done for Elizabeth Mary and her six boys, and the decision taken was that they would be better off in Australia as long as they could be sustained while the boys were young. Later, perhaps, they could all return to England if she wished. Her father, Frederick Nunn, a man of comfortable wealth, made immediate arrangements to send steady financial benefits to his daughter. She received an annual sum of £140, as well as the finance to enable her to build a suitable home, a two-storey brick house with a galvanised iron roof and generous back verandah (still standing today).

In 1862 Mrs Kidman received the news that her father had died on 18 April at Bury St Edmunds. He had remembered her and her boys generously in his will; Mrs Kidman felt both lonely and abandoned.

For better or for worse, Elizabeth Mary Kidman at the age of 38 married the farm-hand Stephen Starr on 25 September 1862. She was pregnant at the time. Their first child, a girl, Phyllis Ellen Starr, was born on 26 April 1863.

Elizabeth's second marriage was a total disaster. Starr was a drinker, a brawler and a no-hoper who was hauled before the courts on more than one occasion. In 1864 he faced a charge of insolvency, at which his wife was subpoenaed to give evidence. The accountant's report said of him:

> The Insolvent is described as a farmer. He married in September 1862 and was himself out of debt; his wife owed about £40 and was in possession of an income of about £140 p.a. The Insolvent

---

OPPOSITE:
Elizabeth Mary Kidman née Nunn, Sid's mother. (Joan Hopkins)

has since held three farms successively. His occupation however, appears to have been confined to cultivating the land, for he does not account for the produce of any crop. He has lived on his wife's income, his debts, and the sale of a few loads of wood. There are no books.

In giving evidence, his wife said, "I have received remittances generally in March and September and if I was hard up for a pound, Mr Williams (Thomas G. Williams, of North Kensington, Adelaide, her trustee) would oblige me with one." Part of her difficulty, she said, was that when a draft of £80 was sent she lost £40 in legacy duty, causing her to apply to her brother in England for an advance on the next remittance, which was always promptly sent. At the time of the court case she said, "I have no money now except what I work for." Her work would have been manual: tending the grapes in the vineyard (perhaps even making wine), and looking after the vegetable garden, the orchard and a few cows.

Starr was gaoled for a month for contracting debts without any reasonable expectation of being able to pay them and for wilfully concealing the true state of his affairs by omitting to keep proper books of account. His liabilities were not huge, but they were impossible for him or for his wife to meet. They were £187.16.6.

One piece of her court evidence was hardly destined to promote marital happiness between Elizabeth and Starr. In fact, it shows the contempt she had for him less than two years after their marriage: "I have seven children, one by my present husband. I refuse to pay my husband's debts. My money belongs to my children."

Stephen Starr did not own the three farms cited in evidence but worked them as a paid employee, so he was of little or no help to Elizabeth Mary on her own place. That he returned to her house intermittently is obvious: two more children were born between 1863 and 1868, Octavia and Alice Mary Starr.

In 1868 Stephen Starr was back in court again for drunken brawling and belting a policeman who tried to control him in a fracas at the Walkerville Hotel. Six desperately awful years came to an end, much to Elizabeth Mary Starr's relief, when Starr abandoned her.

No doubt the sadness and unpleasantness of the second marriage and a drinking, brawling stepfather had an impact on the Kidman boys. One by one (and as soon as possible) they left home at an early age: first George and Frederick, then Thomas and Sackville, all determined to find work and send money home to their mother. Sidney Kidman was a 5-year-old boy when his mother remarried. Forced to grow up and spend his formative years with a belligerent stepfather probably caused him more distress than some of the older boys. Certainly Sidney Kidman did not know his father, who had died when Sidney was 14 months old.

There was no local school at Athelstone until 1872, so Sidney Kidman received whatever schooling he did at a little private school not far from his home, where the teacher was Miss Ellen Packham. Folk memory (strong enough in the area for it to be right) is that he "learnt a bit of readin', writin' and addin' up but hardly enough to amount to millions".

Kidman himself was to say later: "I was an uninteresting kid and I don't remember doing anything remarkable at Bagent's school." Whenever he did attend, it provided a welcome respite from an unhappy atmosphere at home. Certainly by the time he was 12, in the style of his elder brothers, he was working at Dean and Laughton's saleyards. He slogged long hours for 5 shillings a week working with stock delivered by incoming drovers. Most of his money was handed over to his mother.

It is certain that he frequently questioned the drovers, for the most part affable men, for news of his brothers, George, Fred, Tom and Sack. A year later he had sufficient confidence in himself to shove off and join them. One local history suggests that terror prompted him to leave home after he was caught up in the tom-foolery of a rock-throwing contest while wagging school. It is alleged that a badly aimed rock missed its target and crashed through the window of a nearby building. Fearful of a beating from strict parents when he arrived home, Sidney decided to run away north. The story is unlikely. His stepfather had left his mother by that stage and, if he was working full time at Dean and Laughton's saleyards, then his school days were behind him. More probably he just wanted to put Adelaide behind him and go and work with his brothers.

In the thousands of press interviews he was to give later on, whenever journalists asked for a rundown on his life, Sidney Kidman started by giving his birth date in 1857. The next reference invariably related to 1870, the year he left home. He avoided mentioning anything about his life in the intervening years. He never alluded to his parents or his formative years.

He never saw his mother again after he left home. After George Kidman's death, life had dealt her nothing but a series of back-handers and struggles. Elizabeth Mary Kidman Starr died on 23 June 1873 at the age of 49. Her son Charles was with her at the time. Her death certificate cites a "disease of the liver" as the cause. Her second husband, Starr, mourned her not at all. He was living at Melrose at the time and working as a teamster. He instantly married a girl aged 17 and later (in the 1880s) became the proprietor or lessee of a hotel at Wirrabarra. The three young girls were taken in by Eliza Starr, Stephen Starr's unmarried sister.

Under the terms of Elizabeth's father's will, executors were directed to "set apart the sum of £4,000 and to lay out the sum in their names [Mary and her six sons] on such investments as cash under the control of the Court of Chancery may be invested upon or in preference or guaranteed shares...and to pay the annual income thereof to my daughter, Mary Kidman for her separate and un-alienable use during her life notwithstanding any marriage she may contract and after her decease to pay and divide the capital of the said sum of £4,000 and the securities for the sum unto and equally among all her children who shall attain the age of twenty one years or be married." The six Kidman boys and three Starr girls were all beneficiaries.

Plagued by money worries after the death of George Kidman in 1858, Elizabeth Mary Kidman had been too reduced financially to afford a headstone for his grave at St George's Anglican Church, Woodforde. He still lies there in an unmarked grave. It has often been said to Sid Kidman's discredit that, despite the enormous amount of wealth he was to make, he didn't spare just a little to put up a headstone for his father who, in leaving his English "White House" for an Australian log cabin, provided the launch pad for him to achieve all he did. Certainly if Sidney had been born in Suffolk, he would never have gone on to control an area of land equivalent to that of England, Scotland and Wales, which he succeeded in doing in Australia. Queen Victoria, so concerned with empire building and preservation herself, wouldn't have tolerated a bar of it!

2
Off to a Runaway Start

AROUND 1870, Sidney Kidman left home without his mother's consent or knowledge. It is highly unlikely that he got away to a Tom Mix start — clambering from his second-storey window, across a galvanised verandah and dropping neatly into the saddle of his horse waiting below, although the story of an upstairs exit via the roof has been put about a lot in the neighbourhood. Kidman was a strapping young fellow at the age of 13 and the din he would have made would have wakened his mother — if not the dead! Any secrecy relating to his departure ended one day later. By then he had bought a horse for 50 shillings and stayed overnight at the Exeter Hotel, Rundle Street, which was owned by friends of his mother.

In his first day of travel he made it to Kapunda, a distance of 50 miles. It was a thriving town, the legacy of the discovery of copper in 1842 by Francis Dutton and Charles Bagot. He put up at the Prince of Wales hotel and the 5 shillings he had set out with was reduced to 1 shilling after he had paid the overnight tariff for himself and his horse.

He continued pressing north, and here my account must differ from an earlier one given by Ion Idriess. Idriess claimed that at Mount Bryan Kidman met Harry Russ and Charlie Hames, who had come from Mundi Mundi Station to the Burra for rations and were about to return. The young Kidman boy had met them at the Adelaide saleyards months earlier, when they had travelled down with a mob of Mundi Mundi cattle. They asked where Kidman was going. He told them he was intent on meeting up with his brother George, who was working in the Barrier region (better known today as Broken Hill). The two men confirmed that George Kidman was working at Poolamacca Station with a droving plant, suggested that the boy had a long ride ahead and could string along with them, but that his horse looked more fit for the boneyard than the journey that lay ahead. If the young boy would mind their dray, they'd take his horse off and give it a feed. Kidman obliged, but the men were a long time returning and when they did, they were drunk. They had sold his horse for 10 shillings and spent the proceeds on booze in a rough bush pub. It caused Kidman, in cold fury, tears stinging his eyes, to utter, "I'll never drink. So help me God, I won't."

It is unlikely that this happened. South Australia was a small colony at the time (184,000 people). The two men knew the boy and they knew his brother George. The other Kidman brothers who had also left home, Frederick, Thomas and Sackville, were working in the same area as George at the Barrier. They were big, burly men. Sackville Kidman stood 6 feet 7 inches in his "stockinged feet". The two men replenishing stores would hardly risk stealing a horse from a younger Kidman brother and blatantly swilling the proceeds in a bush pub. Horse thieves in Australia may not have been strung up as they were in the United States at the time, but the belting that Russ and Hames would have received at the hands of the older Kidman boys (sooner or later) didn't bear thinking about.

The Idriess account has young Kidman (minus a horse) trudging on to Mundi Mundi Station with Hames and Russ. Russ was sent on further business to Poolamacca Station and agreed to take Kidman with him, on a 60 mile stage, with Kidman (at least) riding this stage on a horse courtesy of Hames (a horse that was on loan only). Idriess had Russ and Kidman nearly dying of thirst, threatened by dingoes and so down on tucker as to be forced to stone, stun and kill waxbill birds, roasting them on the campfire and eating everything — legs and all, except the tiny burnt beaks. It is a fairly dramatic final stage to Poolamacca, one that Kidman never alluded to in hundreds of press interviews later in his life.

Ion Idriess wrote of Kidman's life in the 1930s. But as early as 1903, when Kidman was receiving generous press attention, he said, in the *Adelaide Observer* of 5 September, "I think I was 13 when I decided to clear out. I got hold of a cheap horse and bound for nowhere in particular, and with practically nothing on my back and no money in my pockets, away I went. I rode to Kapunda. I earned a few shillings there and then I went on to the Burra. If I remember rightly, it was there that I swapped my horse with a bit to boot. I gradually worked my way north until at last I struck the Barrier."

One thing is certain: when he reached Poolamacca, he was not received with open arms by brother George. He received a severe tongue-lashing and was ordered to return home. It was pointed out to him that with the four eldest sons away from home and working (and sending money to their abandoned mother), a fifth brother was hardly required. He would be more nuisance value than anything else. His duty was at home with their youngest brother, Charles, and three infant stepsisters.

Sid Kidman stood his ground and refused to return. Until George could find suitable work for him, young Kidman stayed with German Charlie, who ran a nearby grog shanty. Kidman became the odd-job boy around the shanty, swinging the axe on the wood heap, caring for horses. He tackled everything enthusiastically and was often tipped small amounts by passing patrons for looking after their horses well. Kidman was a pleasant-mannered fellow who was never idle. In his spare time he made greenhide hobbles for sale or would seize upon a hat with a hole or tear in it left around the place and mend it for resale.

German Charlie quite liked the young fellow and admired his sense of industry. What Kidman admired about German Charlie is less certain. He thought of him as an amiable rogue. Charles Carl was his correct name and he appeared around Menindee, New South Wales, in the 1860s, setting up his grog shanty at Campbell's Creek tributary near the Poolamacca homestead in 1867. It was a typical grog shanty, serving the needs of drovers, teamsters, prospectors and other travellers. Drunken brawls were commonplace. Men went on the ran-tan, ran amok, some even died. And it's said that German Charlie kept a watchful eye on the less competent of his drinkers with a grave ready-dug for their reception if the worst seemed likely — especially in searing summer heat. It is not surprising, considering the snake juice dispensed to them. More than half the contents of a flagon of spirits would be removed, topped up with water and, to restore colour to the adulterated drink, old clay tobacco pipes were boiled and the nicotine-laced water added along with a dash of turps. If the beer went flat, it gained an unexpected froth from a bar of soap shaken up in the keg. An old bushman, interviewed in the course of research for this book, maintains that things have improved since. "We've got bush champagne today," he said. "Metho and Epsom salts. If you want pink champagne, whack in a slug of beetroot juice!"

German Charlie's shanty was a hive of activity — if not iniquity — and he was widely hailed as a celebrity among the settlers in the district, certainly for his capacity to outsmart the law. When a one-legged traveller left the shanty without paying the account, German Charlie tailed him and caught him. In a fit of rage he chopped the man's wooden leg in half. Charged with assault, he success-fully pleaded "not guilty" on the grounds that he was merely cutting dry timber on Crown land.

Kidman made the most of the time he spent in the rough and raucous grog shanty working for German Charlie. He looked and he listened and he learnt, and he'd politely engage drovers, teamsters or travellers in conversation. He was always interested in what they had to say. Much of the conversation related to who was travelling where and with what small mobs of cattle, where work prospects were good, and where they were not. Men talked of expansion: the start of the construction of the telegraph line across the continent from Port Augusta to Darwin, the move west of the Darling into the semi-arid "corner" area, the push across Queensland to wild country of the Cooper, Diamantina and Georgina rivers, and intermingled with all of this talk was water — or the lack of it. What the travellers had to say was not bush-bar gossip, but information gained first hand.

Kidman absorbed it all and observed a lot — wheeling, dealing, cheating and cheque busts. All said, the short time staying with German Charlie Carl had been interesting. Kidman was a lot wiser — about everything. German Charlie had not paid him, but had given him his keep and a roof over his head until his brother George found work for him. He was popular with the men who called by the shanty in the time he was there. Some accused him of being "tinny", no doubt in his capacity to earn a few pence here and there from various travellers. He acknowledged such remarks with a smile.

When George Kidman returned he outlined the job he'd found for his brother: shepherding stock for Harry Raines at 8 shillings a week. George was moving on with a droving plant elsewhere. He dropped Sid off at Harry Raines's camp with a small blanket, a quart-pot, a knife and fork, and two greenhide straps to roll his swag.

Working for Harry Raines was tough. Unforgettably tough. It had a lasting impact on Kidman and, in later life, when journalists asked him to stir his memory embers and talk of his first intro-duction to the bush, he spoke of his work with Harry Raines: "Harry Raines and his wife made out from Swan Hill and just squatted down in a dugout on a creek in the Barrier area. He had no station, only a bit of a yard and no rent to pay and he bought 500 sheep off Corona Station when E. L. B. Dickens [the son of the famous novelist] was manager and had 200 or 300 goats, and that is how he started.

"I got a job with him at 8 shillings a week to do as I was told. I used to sleep in the dugout, the coldest shop I was ever in. In those days people did not have big swags and a lot of bedding but just a rug. That was all I had. I had to get up early, as it was the only chance to get warm, and hunt up the saddle horses.

"Sometimes I would mind the goats and sheep and have a look for any stray cattle or sheep for Harry. He would say they were his; it was all open country. After the big drought broke in 1869 a lot of cattle came over from the Flinders Ranges and any that Harry could get belonged to him. I was sent away with a bit of a rug and a little tucker in my swag to look for them scores of miles away."

When not out on his own, Kidman shared the work around the rough camp with an Aboriginal called Billy. For warmth at night, Kidman and Billy huddled together under the thin rug, with the Aboriginal's dog. Their rations were 8 pounds of flour a week, 2 pounds of sugar and 1 pound of tea; the flour was riddled with weevils and grubs after six months of transport. Despite sieving, the flour never baked hard. Billy supplemented their diet with possums and an occasional fish from a waterhole. The bond of friendship between the two became strong. There wasn't time to talk as they worked, but at night around the campfire it was question and answer time — Kidman asking the questions and Billy providing the answers. Billy became his tutor in bushcraft and Aboriginal lore, and Kidman, with a thirst for this knowledge and a retentive memory, was an excellent student. There were light-hearted moments when they chiacked around, but in the time they worked together Billy contributed much that was to be invaluable to Kidman later. There was little that Kidman could contribute in return...a scant knowledge of city life in Adelaide...snippets from his limited schooling. But he did offer friendship and respect — a respect for the Aboriginal people he would maintain for the rest of his life.

Kidman became such a promising young bushman that Raines put him "on loan" to other new settlers filtering into the area. Raines described him as "the kid who knows his way about". He rode hundreds of miles for the "claypan squatter" Raines. He came to know the country like the back of his hand. He engaged any newcomers in conversation, enriching his knowledge further on where they had come from and why, which way they had taken, the feed conditions and the water, who else they had met en route... All this information made a further deposit in his memory bank. At the same time, the coins in his small leather pouch were increasing. There was nothing on which to spend the money, but while at Menindee travelling for Raines, Kidman outlaid a large amount for a handsome shawl for his mother, which he packaged carefully and sent to Adelaide with a droving outfit.

"A boy's first thoughts should always be for his mother," he was to tell employees (particularly young, unmarried men) later on, checking the ledgers to see how much of their wages they retained and how much they sent home. If, in Kidman's opinion, a young boy was not sending home a suitable proportion of pay to his mother, he would be "advised" as to where his first responsibility lay and to correct the situation.

No doubt the presence of Mrs Raines reminded him of his own mother. He was always glad to get back from a long ride to her cheerful presence. She was a typical outback pioneer woman. She toiled as hard as any man and sang as she went about her work. It was in the Raines's bough-shed camp that the benefits of thrift were driven home to Kidman. Mrs Raines saved everything, never knowing when it would come in handy. Bags were treasured for patching pants and providing thread. Containers were saved for quandong (or wild peach) jam.

In the quandong season, Kidman became her willing servant. "Billy and I used to go to Langawirra, 25 miles away, to get a load of quandongs for Mrs Raines to make jam. It was a great place for them. She would take the stones out, string the fruit up to dry and use them when she wanted to make quandong jam which is very nice. That was the only luxury we had in Harry Raines's camp," Kidman said.

Work with Raines terminated abruptly with the arrival of Abraham and Matilda Wallace. Wallace had selected the land and arrived to take it up, furious to find the nomad squatter Raines using it.

"There was a great row when they met about Harry being on the country that Wallace had taken up," Kidman said. "Abe was one of the best-known men in that country because he was so tough and daring. He was hawking on the Darling first around Wilcannia when stations were few and far between. He'd been dealing in sheep and making good money before he took up the selection, which he called Sturt's Meadows. He put a well down, built a house and settled there. Harry Raines was hunted out. It left me without a job so I went to Mount Gipps Station where I got 10 shillings a week which was a rise in pay."

Harry Raines selected land at Mootwingee and prospered, as did Abe Wallace on Sturt's Meadows, despite early misadventure with Aborigines.

"When Abe was away on a trip, the blacks stuck up Mrs Wallace and stole a lot of rations," Kidman said. When Wallace returned to his homestead and plundered stores, he showed the type of daring of which Kidman spoke.

"Abe had a heavy, long sword in his possession and off he set to the blacks' camp." He sought the big, fat king, Cheeky Jacky, who had led the attack and found him naked, lying face down in a sound sleep after a big feed.

"Without saying a word," Kidman continued, "he dived it into his ribs three or four times. The blackfellow ran for his life and was not seen again for months. It frightened the lives out of all the blacks and they were very good to the Wallaces after that."

Other reports of this encounter suggest Kidman was wrong in one detail — it was the Aborigine's big, blubbery backside where the bayonet hit home. The shriek he gave lifted cockatoos out of trees.

After a year away from home, Kidman, aged 14, packed his small swag and walked to Mount Gipps Station, where he was hopeful of getting work. Mount Gipps, covering about 1,400 square miles, was in the heart of the Barrier Range and the biggest station in the area. His luck was in. He was paid 10 shillings a week as a rouseabout.

3
Benefits of Getting the Sack

CAPTAIN CHARLES STURT had explored the Barrier Range in 1844–45, and at the time the land west of the Darling was occupied by various Aboriginal groups. They included the Bulalli, Barkinji and Wilyakali tribes, and at places like Mootwingee (green grass) and Euriowie (brackish water) they expressed their primitive art in the form of rock carvings and ochre work.

In the 1850s, squatters moved into the west Darling district, taking up land with Darling River frontages and then spreading out to the Barrier Range in the 1860s, a movement that gained momentum after the great Darling flood of 1863–64, which left the area lush with feed. A land scramble resulted, led by Riverina families and Victorians. By 1865 the Mount Gipps Station was in the hands of Victorian wool-broker Hastings Cunningham and W. Macredie. Several years later it was a flourishing station with a homestead, men's quarters and outbuildings of mud and stone. It employed forty men, among them Sid Kidman's three brothers. The ledger's wages sheet shows four Kidmans on the books in 1872. Sackville Kidman worked for 15 shillings a week as a water drawer; Fred Kidman, at £1 a week for general services; George Kidman, as a boundary rider for £1 a week; and Sidney Kidman, at 10 shillings a week for general services. Their brother Tom, moving independently of them, was engaged in similar work in South Australia.

Time at Mount Gipps for Sid Kidman was short and sweet, a treat after the rough existence eked out with Harry Raines, with good, solid tucker, and a bed to sleep in. It was hard work from dawn until dark, running the horses up in the morning with the blacks, drawing water, carrying drills to well-sinkers, and riding for days around the big unfenced station moving mobs of sheep onto fresh feed. But for Sid Kidman it bristled with excitement. After the isolation in which he'd worked for Raines, Mount Gipps pounded with activity: it was more like a tiny town. He was the baby in an outfit of burly, experienced men who, as frequently as they could, made him a target of humour and jest. Every bush jape ever invented was worked on "the kid", including those with elements of danger when he was dared, taunted or told to try his luck aboard outlaw horses. They laughed at his busters; he grinned at their laughter, dusting himself down for another go. He never once complained or whinged to his older brothers. He took what was dished out to him — usually with a smile. He was a hard and willing worker and soon acknowledged as a "kid who didn't shirk and could pull his weight".

Exposed to every facet of station life, he learnt how a well-run place ticked over. He learnt from the station men. He may have had little in the way of formal schooling, but at Mount Gipps, in eighteen months, he crammed in additional bush learning. He asked questions, questions and more questions (always choosing his moment carefully) of men at the station and visitors to it. He had a way about him when he asked questions that caused people to reply gladly. Others asking similar questions might have been seen as stickybeaks and given a raw reply, but everyone answered the Kidman kid because he was so sincere. Older men may also have been flattered by being asked to impart their bush knowledge and skills.

The Kidman kid saw the less desirable aspect of station life as well: short-fuse tempers that led to flying fists and filthy mouths. He made himself scarce when fights were on. He saw enraged men vent their anger on both horses and dogs, beating them unmercifully and blaspheming while they were at it. Kidman kept his lips buttoned. He heard men swear their heads off when things went wrong on a job. He didn't know why. All the swearing in the world wasn't going to make things right. Swearing, he decided, was a useless expenditure of energy. He made up his mind not to swear, a resolution he kept to the point that Melbourne cattle auctioneer Harry H. Peck, in writing his memoirs sixty years later, referred to Kidman as "the cleanest-mouthed man I ever met. Not once did even a solitary damn escape his lips." Kidman had his own form of cussing. People who incurred his displeasure were referred to either as "jolly beggars" or "jolly tinkers".

It has often been said, to the point that it is held to be true, that throughout his life Kidman didn't swear, drink or smoke. The only truth here is that he did not swear. It didn't make him Robinson Crusoe; there were many others at the time who didn't hold with bad language, religiously minded men who observed the third commandment. Kidman's personal discipline not to swear came into prominence later when he became a public figure. He didn't swear himself, and he didn't like it in others, particularly employees, and anyone with a foul mouth didn't stand much chance of getting a job at his Currie Street, Adelaide, offices or from his station managers.

At Mount Gipps in 1873, a new chum came seeking a job, a young Scotsman called George McCulloch. George Urquhart, the overseer, put the boy on at £1 a week, 10 shillings more than Kidman was receiving — and Kidman had toiled hard and faithfully. Kidman's nose was somewhat out of joint. He mentioned the matter to a young stockman, Philip Charley, and to George Lind, the bookkeeper, who sympathised. Kidman was widely liked at the station by all the men, who encouraged him to front the overseer and ask for a rise. It was not one of their bush japes — urging Sid on and hoping to see him end up in hot water. The japes had long ceased. But that was the result. The stern overseer, who had never warmed to Sid, gave him the sack instead!

Kidman took it on the chin and took the wages owing him. He had indulged himself a bit when he first landed at Mount Gipps (not surprising after the deprivations at Harry Raines's camp) and had eaten up much of his wages in jam. Jam at the time was 2s. 6d. a tin and Kidman hoed into it with such enthusiasm that, in some weeks, he effortlessly devoured four tins. It didn't take him long to cure himself of that habit.

He took his leave of Mount Gipps; George McCulloch's arrival was partially responsible for it. Their paths would cross again a decade later when McCulloch was manager of Mount Gipps. Kidman would also brush again with Philip Charley, the young stockman, George Lind, the bookkeeper, and George Urquhart, the overseer, and another Mount Gipps employee, a boundary rider called Charles Rasp. More than a few bob would be at stake — more like a few million pounds.

Browned off, Sid rolled his meagre possessions in his swag and set off walking to German Charlie's grog shanty, about 20 miles north at Poolamacca. Fifty-five years later he said, "Getting the sack was the best thing that ever happened to me." One seriously doubts this, but the abrupt termination of work at Mount Gipps forced him into a new phase of life, one that gave him experience in several new areas and one in which he became an independent operator.

"I made for a ram shepherd's camp the first night and had the bad luck to find he had moved on. I spent the night out in the open with no matches and no food, and the following day arrived at German Charlie's.

"The Barrier Ranges were noted as the home of all the rogues and horse stealers in Australia and it has often been said that German Charlie was in the habit of stealing other people's horses and killing their cattle, but I say he did not do it and I worked for him.

"German Charlie was a well-known man in the early days at the Barrier and he gave me £1 a week to look after his cattle and deliver meat to outlying camps," Kidman said.

German Charlie Carl traded in beef as a sideline to the activities of his grog shanty, a log hut outfitted with bullock hide hammocks stretched over frames of axe-hewn mulga.

Kidman was happy with the job, which had given him a wage rise and the freedom to tail the few hundred head of cattle in the

unfenced hills, which by this stage he knew like the back of his hand. He worked the cattle on his own. He may not have liked the lone-liness, but he made it "work for him". With no distraction, his total attention was taken up with the cattle. He learnt to recognise in-dividual animals, their behaviour patterns, the leaders and the stirrers, and to spot mob thinking. In his spare time he wasn't idle, making greenhide hobbles, and plaiting whips and halters, which he sold to travellers at the grog shanty. When he was delivering meat by packhorse to the scattered well- and tank-sinking camps, he forced himself to memorise every feature of the land and bush through which he travelled.

From time to time (to liven the area up and to boost profits) German Charlie hosted a race meeting, which was always advertised on the q.t. Kidman was given the job of riding hundreds of miles in all directions to inform men — with the exception of the squatters, who detested such occasions, when men upped and left and often didn't return for a week after a bout on German Charlie's snake juice.

Kidman only ever attended one such spree (at which he rode a winner and received £10 prize money). He saw the dills that men made of themselves and the damage they did to themselves and others when in the grip of the grog, and he avoided the louts and roisterers, talking instead to the men who'd come along for the sport itself rather than the booze. What these men had to say was always of interest: the push west of the Darling into the semi-arid corner, the move in Queensland towards the little-known country of the Cooper, Georgina and Diamantina, the implications of the telegraph line that now stretched from Port Augusta to Port Darwin (it was rumoured that gold had been found when some of the post holes were sunk), and the areas where money was to be made. The country's railways, still in their infancy, stopped well short of out-back settlements. Good money could be made from transporting goods. Quicker money could be made from gold, and the possibility of finding gold (or, if not gold, some other mineral) was a constant topic of conversation.

There had been a white quartz rush in the Mundi Mundi area close by a few years before, which had amounted to absolutely nothing, and things looked set to move in the Cobar district where Hartman and "Campbell" (not his real name) had discovered copper.

OPPOSITE:
Staff of Mount Gipps in 1873 (from left): standing — *George Lind, Philip Charley, Sid Kidman*; seated — *George McCulloch, George Urquhart.* *(Photographer: J. H. Nixon)*

There was talk of silver slugs being found at Thackaringa, not far from the South Australian border. It was a time of great expansion, and expansion meant money for those who could capitalise on it.

Kidman did. His bush experience landed him another wage rise — £2 a week — as a guide to the overlanders taking up new country. At the completion of his pilot work, he saw no reason to return to German Charlie empty-handed. In the Wilcannia area he picked up a mob of horses at a cheap price. They were taken by German Charlie and sold at a high profit, with a healthy commission going to Kidman. It was the first time that Kidman had operated independently in buying stock. He liked both the feeling and the result. It was something to be repeated as often as he could. The chance was denied in the short term, when he was thrown out of a job again. Dry times seized the area. Grass withered. Waterholes dried up. His job with German Charlie's cattle came to an end when Charlie Carl was forced to send his stock elsewhere in order to save them.

Kidman, with £200 saved, decided to go in for transport and bought a small team of bullocks to transport food supplies at £2 a ton (from Menindee 80 miles away) for German Charlie and other station-owners in the area. He learnt the bullocky's art quickly. There was no shortage of work and drought quickly forced up transport prices. Recalling those days, Kidman said, "I went loading from Wentworth to Menindee to Wilcannia. During the drought people were paying £15 a ton for carting from Wentworth to Menindee and £25 from Menindee to Wilcannia. Willie Maiden (later the original owner of the South Mine at Broken Hill — he bought it from his brother-in-law George White for £500) was also carting and loading to Wilcannia at £25 a ton. Flour was from £50 to £75 a ton."

Despite the good money, it was slow going. Kidman seemed to be on the sideline while activity bristled around him. Delivering a load to Wilcannia, he sold the bullock team at a profit when he heard that a copper rush had been confirmed at Cobar. A rush meant an instant tent town and men who needed to be fed. Being in at the start was bound to be interesting and there was bound to be a quid in it for him.

In 1869 two Danes worked their way north from Hay, New South Wales, well-sinking and always on the alert for any new presence of minerals. One was Thomas Hartman, who had run away to sea to escape compulsory military training, later becoming a miner in the California gold rush and then travelling to Australia to join the Bendigo–Ballarat rush. At Bendigo he met a fellow Dane who called himself "Charles Campbell"; his correct name was Ferdinand Emelius Kempf. He was a professional man experienced in engineering, surveying and architecture.

Hartman and "Campbell" were travelling with a stockman, Gibbs, and an Aboriginal tracker. Between well-sinking work, while camped at a waterhole, they were convinced they were in copper-bearing country because of the ochre used by the Aborigines in the area to paint their bodies. Their calculation was correct. They took samples of the ore to a Cornish woman on a property 50 miles away (she had worked at the Cornish mines), and she confirmed the richness of the ore. Claims were staked and registered, and the following year Hartman and "Campbell" returned to the area to send a dray of copper ore to the river ports and then by steamer to South Australia's copper smelters.

The find led to the setting up of another frontier canvas town, Cobar, which was a roar of activity by 1875, with furnaces demanding 50,000 tons of wood a year to keep them rolling. The place was thick with promise — and problems. The mines were far from railways, and the cost of carting copper by horse and bullock to the nearest port or railhead was high. As the mines were in dry country, the cartage of copper was impossible in almost drought conditions when the grass withered on the plains and the mud baked in waterholes.

Young Sid Kidman, then 18 years of age, was drawn to the activity less on account of the minerals than the opportunity it brought for stock and transport. Miners would have to be fed, and stock would also be needed for work and for transport. Sid camped in a prominent spot and the morning after he arrived busied himself cutting down saplings for a bough-shed shop. He had £250 at that stage, so he was in a fair position to set up as a butcher — a most welcome one where the miners were concerned — but one of the drawbacks, as Sid quickly found out, was having to ride 80 miles to Wynbar Station to get beasts. His first buy was two head of stock for £8 each. They had to be driven the return 80 mile trip.

Recalling his Cobar days, Sid said, "I didn't stick at it long. I had to pay too stiff prices for the cattle and had to go too far for them so I chucked the business. I had a bit of a lean-to with a roof made of bushes and the meat was hung on hooks."

Sid paid cash for his purchases, but when the miners he supplied came with pitiable tales and asked for "trust" (credit) he gave it to them. And not a few of them left the place — or tried to leave it — without offering him any payment. "Some of those miners were pretty tough, I can tell you," Sid said. "I got tired of them trying to bolt without paying their debts. I would serve them once a fortnight and they would try to get away.

"I had to follow some of them of 20 miles. I would head them off and return by the back road to Cobar and run right into them. I would say to them, 'Where have you been? You are going away without paying,' and they would always have an excuse ready. 'We would give you a cheque but you can't give us any change,' they would say. But I always took the precaution of having plenty of change on me.

"Another fellow and I had just about all the trade at Cobar before it grew into a big town. I went in for transport as well and had a dray or two and used to get a fellow to drive them loaded with copper to Bourke 100 miles away for £2.15.0 a ton.

"At this time Cobar was all open country in all directions and there were a number of miners and other people about but there was no flour, tea or sugar to be had. I got a horse and went to Condobolin on the Lachlan and bought some bullocks, tea, sugar and other rations. At Cobar I sold the sugar at 1 shilling a pound, the salt at 6d. a tin, the small tins of jam at 2s. 6d. each and the soap at 5 shillings a bar. I didn't know much about trading then or I would have bought tons more.

"I was still doing this while I was butchering. I saw water go to 1 shilling a bucket and flour to £10 a bag and £100 a ton."

Sid worked ceaselessly and, when he had made a profit that pleased him, he took all of his cattle hides from his butchering business, loaded them up and carted them to Menindee, 450 miles away, and shipped them by steamer to Adelaide, something that gave him a further tidy sum. He had more than £350 when he left Cobar.

At Menindee it was only by coincidence that he ran into his elder brothers, George and Sack, who were travelling with a mob of stock to Adelaide. An extra hand was needed for the trip on wages of 25 shillings a week. Young Sid made sure he got the job. Why travel to Adelaide at his own expense if he could get paid for going there? He could live on his wages and keep his savings intact. The Kidman boys took the mob south, stopping for a welcome break at Kapunda where Sid met and was greatly taken by a fetching young girl called Isabel Wright. He pledged to call and see her the next time he passed through Kapunda.

In Adelaide he used his savings to buy sixty horses, and he returned to the bush with them knowing there would be a demand for them. He was proved correct and sold them for a total of £800, and while at Bourke he bought another mob, for which he paid £120. By quick resale he made a profit of about £300.

"Later," Sid said, "I got a billet along the road with a chap named Denny Blake who was in charge of a mob of bullocks. We got into a row for being on a creek at Koonoona. The Hon. John Lewis bought 100 of them at the Burra for around £10 and more than 50 were sold at Kapunda and the rest in Adelaide.

"I went back to Menindee on more horse dealing and bought 60 or 70 from George Miller at Redan. I made a good sale of a couple at

Terowie and then Bill Player, who then kept the pub at Marrabel, bought two or three. I camped with them at Kapunda for two or three days [no doubt again visiting Isabel Wright] and then brought them on to Adelaide through the back lanes to Boase's Bazaar, where I sold them for up to £38 each. I no longer had any teams. I sold them to the mines when I left Cobar."

After his sale at Boase's Bazaar in 1880, Sid returned to the bush, again dealing in horses, and spent some time attached to a circus — not as a performer (although his horsemanship would not have failed him in that regard), but as a creditor.

"Jimmy Ashton's it was," Sid said. "He was always travelling about but never had much money. I sold him some piebald horses and we went from Morgan to Wentworth, Pooncarie, Menindee, Wilcannia, Louth, Bourke, out to Cobar and then back to Louth. We had to swim the horses over the Murray and go after them. On top of selling Ashton the horses I bought some horse feed for him and I was in deeper straits. Anyhow, he had a wonderful night at Louth; made about £150. He paid me the whole lot that he owed me and I cleared."

Not every one of Sid's dealing transactions made a profit. Occasionally his dealing resulted in a loss when he arrived on the scene with horses to find a town or area over-supplied. It strengthened his resolve never to regret a loss, but to think more nimbly in the future to ensure that it didn't happen again.

In 1881 the rush was on again, again in western New South Wales to Mount Browne, where gold was discovered in the remote area near the stony desert where the borders of New South Wales, South Australia and Queensland meet. People poured out of the river ports of Bourke and Wilcannia intent on scratching a fortune from the ground; in many respects, the scene at Mount Browne, and later at Tibooburra when gold was discovered there, was one of despair. There was barely enough fresh water for men and horses to drink let alone to wash the auriferous dirt.

Sid Kidman was still steeped in horse dealing at the time, and he was based for a while at Wilcannia, where he had teamed up in a partnership with Bill Emmett (also known as Hammett), a well-known horse dealer. The basis of the partnership was that Emmett travelled widely, buying up horses, and Sid was to look after them on the selection at Wilcannia, while also buying and selling locally.

Cobar had taught young Kidman two valuable lessons: one was the value of credit where the miners were concerned, and the other was the benefit of getting in early at any new burst of activity in the outback. There were no prizes for those who came late — or last. Sid suggested to his partner that again they look at transport and rations for the new diggings, and Sid's job with the horses was farmed out to someone else as he hurried to acquire a table-top wagon stocked up with rations and headed for Tibooburra, 35 miles south of the Queensland border, where he set up the first ration store. The store was an instant success and Sid made repeated trips with provisions, also securing another table-top wagon to carry the swags and goods and chattels of the intending miners trudging to the fields — at £2 a piece.

Recalling those days, Sid said, "The place was desperate for water but there was a place known as Chinaman's Well which was of great benefit at the height of the Mount Browne gold boom. Everyone lived on that water. It was a wonderful well around which Chinese gardeners had about an acre and a half under vegetables which they sold to the diggers.

"I was in partnership with Bill Emmett for a few years. He was the greatest dealer that ever existed on the Darling. If he thought he could sell a horse he would ride 50 miles and go without breakfast, dinner or tea.

"He would have his pockets bulging with cheques and notes for months and months but had no system whatever. He made a lot of money and fooled it away. When we were at Wilcannia he used to live in a dugout and I lived in a tin hut.

"He would get up at daylight and make a fire, boil a pannikin of tea, cut a piece off a pig's jaw, grill it and eat it with a piece of damper. When he finished he would smack his lips and say, 'Well, I call that a nice meal.' He lived like a blackfellow yet he was thankful for anything he got. That taught me to be thankful too. You might wonder where he got the pigs' jaws from. He bought about 150 of them. They came up in drays from Sydney and were bad six months before he got them. I told a boy to throw them down a dry well, not before a fellow had come to the camp one day and Bill had sold him one for 5 shillings. What do you think of that?"

The lack of water at the Mount Browne and Tibooburra gold-fields made them tragic places with miners working in temperatures that, during one year, were over 100 degrees continually for six months. Men were stricken with sandy blight and died of typhoid and dysentery. In three years the area produced about £80,000 of gold but at such an alarming cost in money, health and life that men were retreating rapidly by 1882. Again, Sid and his partner had made a handsome profit on the ration store and also with their horses at Wilcannia where, at times, they ran up to 800 and often received high prices for them from the agents or representatives of the Cobb & Co. coaching line. Often they were half-broken colts that were sold by Kidman and Emmett to the coaching business for £15 each on the basis that "the youngsters would soon learn".

His brief partnership with Emmett was not only a profitable one for Sid, but also an educational one. The man was an expert on horses. What Sid didn't know about horses he learnt quickly: how to judge and assess horses singly or in mobs; how to sum a horse up at a glance; and which types of horses were eagerly sought for coaching work. It was a time of learning for Sid just as Cobar had been with his butchering when he became proficient in estimating the weight of the beast on the hoof and, by comparison, its cut-up weight. It later enabled him to estimate, within a few pounds in weight, the saleable weight of undressed beef. Thirty years later when Sid was in Sydney, the following snippet found its way into one of the newspapers:

There is no nasty pride about one of our millionaires, anyhow. I was imbibing in the Winter Garden of the Australia the other night and at a table nearby sat Cattle King Kidman with a number of affluent-looking friends.

Presently a bell boy ushered in one of the completest, old bush whackers I have seen. With his vast, pale, fur-like whiskers waving in the breeze, the ancient hurried up to Kidman, his gnarled hand outstretched and on his lips the glad words, "Ow are yer? Don't yer know me?" Kidman allowed his fin to be waved up and down but obviously didn't recognise the oldster and bluntly said so. Quoth the visitor, "Don't yer remember *Cobar?*" "Yes," said Kidman, "I was butchering there." "Exactly! And I was one uv yer butchers!"

The light of recognition filled the cattle monarch's eyes. He pump-handled the aged product of the wilderness with utmost heartiness, bought him liquor and plunged into conversation. It struck me that not every millionaire would publicly recall a town by the fact that he had butchered there nor be so obviously and simply glad to meet an indigent old employee. Take it for all in all, the episode rather raised my opinion of bullock Czars.

4
Isabel

ALMOST THIRTY YEARS before the discovery at Cobar, copper had been found at Kapunda in South Australia by Francis Dutton and Charles Bagot. Convinced that the characteristic green among some rocks was copper, they kept their 1842 find a secret until an 80 acre section of land was bought for £80. A trial shipment was sent for evaluation. Its high grade attracted an excellent price, and Cornish miners resident in South Australia were brought in to get things going.

South Australia, the only colony without any convict settlement, was predominantly favoured by English and Scottish settlers who had capital to invest and expand. They quickly gained control of both pastoral and commercial interests. That was certainly so at the copper town of Kapunda, which flourished quickly to the point that, in the census year of 1871, it had 2,273 people, with a further 2,190 in the nearby area, a bigger population than Port Adelaide and Gawler. In 1866 the District Council and the town's football club (Australian Rules) were found. It was one of the first football clubs formed in Australia. In 1868 John Costello overlanded 200 horses from Queensland and sold them in Kapunda: that was also a first.

Small wonder that HRH Prince Alfred, Duke of Edinburgh, visited the town in 1867 to see the mines at work, but no one had advised the Kapunda miners of the specific purpose of his visit, and they had all been given the day off to see him. People jostled for prime viewing-spots on the balcony of the Lord Palmerston Hotel, paying the staggering sums of 7s. 6d. on the balcony and 3s. 6d. on the roof. Overnight the Prince was the guest of Kapunda businessman Andrew Thomson. The band from the Prince's ship, the *Galatea*, played in Thomson's illuminated gardens.

Along with members of the Dutton family of Anlaby, Jenkin Coles, Charles Bagot and H. B. Hawke, Andrew Thomson, a 34-year-old Scotsman, was an influential force in Kapunda, helping to build up the town's commercial strength and forging and financially backing new businesses, including that of the stock agents and auctioneers Liston and Shakes, which became Shakes and Lewis and then Bagot, Shakes and Lewis.

After Prince Alfred's visit, Andrew Thomson wrote to a relative in Scotland, Ann Wright, a widow with one child. He urged her to consider the benefits of Kapunda and to migrate with her daughter. Prospects were better than those where she lived in Alloa, the biggest town in the smallest county in Scotland. Ann Wright (née Ann Thomson of Droughty Ferry) had married ship chandler John Wright at Dundee in 1859, and they had one child, Isabel. John Wright died when the girl was an infant. Taking her Kapunda kinsman at his words, Ann Wright left Alloa, Clackmannan, on the River Forth, for Australia. There was no half measure about her departure: she persuaded her mother and sixteen other members of her family to go with her. At Kapunda the affluent businessman Andrew Thomson took Ann Wright and her mother and daughter under his wing. Fortune smiled on Ann Wright, who married David Will, a widower with children. David and Ann Will had three further children: Wally, Edith and Violet.

Young Isabel Wright was 8 years old in 1870 when the family contingent arrived in Adelaide. She grew up in Kapunda, a bright child with a passion for books, learning and embroidery. A devout young girl, she taught scripture at Sunday School and later became a schoolteacher. Despite the fact that Isabel had arrived in Kapunda at the same time that Sidney Kidman had left it as a 13-year-old boy, they met almost ten years later. The meeting did not change the course of his life, but ultimately only his status as a bachelor.

Kidman's lack of formal education worried him not one iota. Towards the end of the 1870s, when he was in his early twenties, he was somewhat shocked to find out there were young men of his age who were still continuing their learning at schools and colleges and who had never worked. Miss Isabel Wright, the young lady to whom he had taken a fancy in Kapunda in South Australia, had told him so. She already taught at the Congregational Church Sunday School at Kapunda and had her heart set on becoming a fully fledged schoolteacher as well.

There was quite a bit, it seemed, to this business of learning. She had spoken of other languages, such as the writing of Latin and the speaking of French, which left Kidman totally unimpressed. Why, they had a wonderful language in the Queen's own English and he could see no reason to contemplate any other. She spoke of the great works of poets and playwrights. Great scholars, she said, knew them by rote. Had she not read one to him? It was about a woman dressed in white who'd floated down a river on a barge and died on the way to a place called Camelot. The verse was a dreadful bit of goods, according to Kidman, and the writer had it all wrong. Rivers shouldn't be associated with death. They were a mighty life force. Anyway, he had no desire to learn by heart great chunks of poetry.

Of what possible use could they be to him? But he would like to know more about rivers, especially Australian rivers, where no woman in her right mind would deck herself out in white and float off in a boat to die. If that was education he would kindly pass, except on the matter of Australian geography. Miss Wright had pledged to have a series of maps for him to look at the next time he went through Kapunda. They'd go over them and talk about them and he knew he'd be the wiser for it.

Water was everything in the bush: if you had it, you lived; if you didn't, you died. It came from rain. The rain filled the rivers, which meant good times for stock. Drovers were always on the lookout for a thunderstorm. They followed them wherever they could to pick up good feed on the way to market. But there was more to it than rain and rivers. Kidman could remember his amazement, while on a horse-buying trip north, in coming across a small belt of good country. They were dry times elsewhere, and the grass was scarce and withered. But from the top of a ridge he saw a flat, riddled with fat stock grazing on good green herbage and grasses, yet he knew that no rain had fallen in the area for some time so how could this be so? He rode to find out. The luxuriant country was hemmed in by ridges. He continued towards giant gums, which pinpointed a creek, yet it also had been dry for some time. Where the creek cut through the flat, its banks were shallow. It could only mean one thing — floodwaters. A flood of fair force had come down quickly and the banks had been unable to contain the water. It had spilled out all over the place until it exhausted itself, hence the verdant pastures.

The discovery shook him a little, to the point that he stopped in his tracks and boiled the billy as he thought the matter over further. Perhaps he was wrong? Perhaps there was some other explanation? He dismissed the theory quickly. He knew the country as well as, if not better than, many other bushmen, but this was the furthest north he'd ever travelled and he'd not struck country like it before. If it was floodplain country, then how many other similar patches were studded around the creeks that fed into the rivers and around the rivers themselves in that Queensland, South Australia and Northern Territory border country? Any man holding property around such rivers had a second chance — a wonderful bonus. As well as the local rain, when the rivers came down from the north they would not only fill the waterholes, but also deposit a generous expanse of water anywhere they broke their banks and the country was low-lying. Why, you could have floodplains stretching for 20 to 30 miles and

OPPOSITE:

Miss Isabel Brown Wright of Kapunda, South Australia. (Isabel Lee)

green feed to carry through while neighbours elsewhere were suffering drought conditions.

He reflected that perhaps his discovery was not so amazing and that men were aware of these facts already. Drovers spoke of large stations that had been taken up in the remote region that saw people pressing further north-east into the corner of South Australia and almost to the very corner of south-west Queensland. The floodplains would be of great benefit to them, but they were in such an isolated position they would need crack drovers and men who knew the whims and ways of the country to travel the stock the long distance to market, and fat stock 1,000 miles away from a market were useless unless the drovers could get them there, not only alive, but also in prime condition for sale. One thing was certain: if you owned, controlled or had an interest in a large number of stations along the bulk of the rivers and creeks that made the floodplains possible, you'd be doing all right. You could stage cattle towards a market and also maintain condition without moving off your own land.

But all this would be to no avail unless the price at market compensated for the effort. Kidman had been caught on a couple of occasions with mobs of horses and cattle that had not reached the expected price at market. He'd been caught out in Cobar when the time and effort expended in 80 mile trips just to buy cattle for his butchery at the new mining settlement hadn't given him the return he'd hoped for. More than time and effort would be involved with these floodplains stations. There would be a risk factor as well. What if the big rivers didn't come down from the north? That would leave you stranded — high and dry. So what were the odds with these rivers? How reliable were they? He'd have to ask around a bit. Not only that, but he would have to apply himself to the matter as well and make a point of riding further into Queensland to scout out these rivers and creeks and their floodplain potential. The return trip south would be equally interesting — another discovery trip to see just how cattle might be staged towards a market. It had already been done once. He knew that, but the risk had been tremendous and the drove had been illegal, which was putting it mildly.

Harry Redford's cattle thieving feat would go down in history as the world's greatest and most successful cattle rustle. In 1870 he stole 1,000 head of cattle from Bowen Downs, a vast central-western Queensland run, and headed off with them into uncharted country. He intended pushing them 1,000 miles to Adelaide over wild country that ten years before had claimed the lives of explorers Burke and Wills. Foolishly, he had allowed a pure white imported bull to remain with the mob. He traded the bull off at the first opportunity, an act he was later to regret.

Redford had staged the cattle south-west out of Queensland and into South Australia through country that was unknown, arid, semi-desert and desert to Lake Blanche, where he accepted the sum of £5,000 for the entire mob. It was a staggering amount of money at the time.

Redford and his two accomplices headed straight for Adelaide — money burning holes in their pockets — before the theft was discovered on Bowen Downs and police set off in pursuit. Redford was long gone when the weary hunters, hardly able to believe that he had pushed the herd so far and through such impossible country, staggered into Adelaide. In pursuing him, the posse did come across the white bull, which was later used as evidence against Redford.

He was ultimately arrested and committed for trial at Roma, Queensland, in 1873. Despite the fact that one of his accomplices had turned Queen's evidence and confessed the entire story, Redford was let off scot-free. The jury, after all, had been composed of admiring stockmen who'd sat riveted to their seats as the dramatic stock theft unfolded in the courtroom. To them, Redford was less a criminal than he was a hero. They had no compunction in acquitting him and when the trial judge, Judge Blakeney, thundered, "I thank God, gentlemen, that the verdict is yours and *not* mine," hats hit the roof. As a result, the Queensland Supreme Court suspended the holding of further jury trials in Roma for two years and Parliament passed a Brands Act, introducing a new system of registering stock that would make successful theft on Redford's scale almost impossible to repeat.

Kidman was but one of hundreds of stockmen and drovers who had heard the tale retold and re-embroidered and relived around campfires. To him it now had a new significance that so few — if any — of the others had been able to grasp. They were always too busy thrilling to the yarn to consider restaging it themselves — only legally, of course. Any recounting of the Redford tale around a campfire always ended the same way, with plenty of thigh-slapping, hooting and laughter and with someone always tossing in: "It's not what you're allowed in life but what you can get away with!" It left Kidman wondering: could you get away with it, droving cattle down a new, risky (if not dangerous) "back corridor"? Others were taking the obvious routes to markets, and for that he could not blame them.

Kidman didn't know too much about the markets in Brisbane, Sydney and Melbourne. The horses and cattle he'd been associated with were, for the most part, traded in Adelaide. And here was a new route to Adelaide — for anyone bold enough to give it a try. It could only be brought about in conjunction with a number of things: floodplain country, excellent drovers — men of Harry Redford's calibre — and an agreeable market.

The discovery of the patch of floodplain country had not been lost on Kidman. How many other bushmen had traversed such lush spots and merely spoken of them in an offhand way whenever weather and conditions were discussed as a "spot of country in good heart" without realising the wider relevance — that if as many as possible of these "spots of good heart" were linked together under common ownership, a chain could be formed with each good link taking stock further towards a market? Such stock, in good times, would fatten all the way. In bad times? It didn't bear thinking about...

Pausing to investigate fully the first piece of floodplain country he ever encountered was to have a long-lasting influence on the fortunes of young Sid Kidman. It was certainly something to keep in mind. There was little, next to nothing, he could do about it as a 22-year-old youth, albeit a lucky one. Under the terms of his maternal grandfather's will he had recently received the sum of £400 when he had turned 21 years of age.

He'd really forgotten that he had turned 21. He had no mother, no father to remind him. His brothers were scattered everywhere. His twenty-first birthday went unheralded and was of no account to him, until he reached the Barrier on a trip south and brother Sackville presented him with a letter advising him of the legacy and requesting that he proceed to Adelaide to sign a few papers. On the way, at least, he would see Miss Wright at Kapunda. He hoped they would not quarrel. He delighted in her company, but not when she rode roughshod over him in this business of learning and education. She had asked him about his mathematics, and he had replied that he knew his sums and times tables. She found him faultless in those, but explained other dimensions of mathematics — algebra where 2x equalled 4y. Kidman could not have given a tuppeny hoot. She also spoke of geometry and angles. The only angle he was interested in was the angle of the sun or the angle of the man with whom he was dealing in stock: the angles of the sun he knew and the angles of dealing he was working out fast, and it seemed to him that they had nothing to do with straight lines and where they intersected, but rather supply and demand and being in the right place at the right time.

Miss Wright, he believed, was someone who liked him and was prepared to help him. The maps she had pledged to get would be of use, and she could explain them fully to him. The lessons he wanted from her were indeed those of the vast Australian outback, particularly those Queensland rivers, the Cooper, the Diamantina and the Georgina, that could make a "back corridor" possible for droving stock and, for any man who wanted to take it further, a chain of stations incorporating as much of that floodplain country as possible.

Now there was a bold dream for anyone of gumption and vision...but perhaps he was figuring wrongly? Certainly Harry

Redford had got through with stock successfully, but did that mean it could be done time and time again? As for the chain idea, stations so far were held by numerous different individuals. Not one family or company had bought up vast tracts of land...

Anyway it was an intriguing idea and an intriguing area of country — so isolated and so little known about it. In any event, he'd have a yarn to Sack about it at the Barrier on the way through, and at Kapunda he would talk about it some more with Miss Wright as they went over the maps. There was something else he wanted to talk to her about too. Miss Wright, he felt, could be his Miss Right. He didn't want to rush things, but in time to come, when he was in a better financial position, he'd like Isabel Wright to become Isabel Kidman.

5

The Greatest Deal

IN THE EARLY 1880s Australia was swept with an air of robust optimism. In thirty years the population had grown from 400,000 to 2,500,000, most of whom were Australian-born. The visiting novelist Anthony Trollope remarked that Australia was like a young whale that had risen at last from the depths and was beginning to blow. A new sense of nationalism was fed by expanding development works in irrigation and railway construction and by new enterprise in burgeoning cities.

It wasn't simply the vastness of the country that inspired faith in its potential. Certainly the pastoralist and the wheat grower, in spite of the hazards, had proved that the land could produce wealth, and of land there was plenty. Not much of it that was useful remained for the little man. Although theoretically the land had been unlocked, the original squatters and their descendants by one means or another had contrived largely to thwart the aims of free selection. Large tracts of land were still held by hard-headed men who had found ways of converting their leaseholds to freeholds.

Significantly, they did not automatically own what was underneath the land, and by 1880 Australia had become a burrower's paradise. The prospect of gold drew men almost anywhere, and the Barrier Range (700 miles west of Sydney and 280 miles north-west of Adelaide) was as remote and forbidding as any area in which people sought their el dorado. The Barrier Range was one of stark, barren hills, monotonously surrounded by saltbush plains. It had an average yearly rainfall of 9 inches. The squatters' push west of the Darling was accompanied by paddlesteamer traffic on the river, enabling supplies to be shipped. The area was essentially, until the late 1870s, a remote pastoral one and the haunt of cattle duffers, where more than one bushranger dallied for a portion of his career.

In 1867 an abortive white quartz rush took place at Poolamacca sheep station in the centre of the ranges. The reported gold discovery proved to be a hoax perpetrated by a shepherd employed at the station, and interest in the district as a source of minerals waned.

In 1876, Charles Nickel and his mate McLean discovered silver–lead ore while well-sinking at Thackaringa sheep station, 5 miles east of the South Australian border and 25 miles south-west of the present city of Broken Hill. The Pioneer Mine, the first to operate in the Barrier Range, was set up by Paddy Green, a Menindee store-keeper. Green raised 36 tons of ore, had it carted to Burra and sent to England. Unfortunately it was jettisoned on the voyage when the ship met difficulties. Soon after, he sent off a further 100 tons, which fetched £16 a ton. The ore contained 65 per cent lead and 35 ounces of silver to the ton, so despite the heavy cost of raising it, and freighting it to the coast and then to overseas smelters, it gave Green a clear profit margin.

The rush to Mount Browne for alluvial gold in 1881–82 briefly diverted attention from this discovery, which intensified later as prospectors realised there might be no payable gold to be found in the Barrier Range area, yet outcrops of ore and slugs of silver were found to contain chlorides of silver of startling richness. Some of the stuff assayed in Adelaide produced as much as 18,000 ounces of silver to the ton. Since silver was worth nearly 4 shillings an ounce, the pickings were superb. The area rippled with excitement and it can scarcely be wondered that the station hands of the district caught mining fever.

It caught on at Mount Gipps Station, where Sid Kidman had been happily and briefly employed a decade earlier, before he was sacked after a dispute over wages. The overseer, who had hired George McCulloch on higher wages, knew on which side his bread was buttered. George McCulloch was the nephew of Sir James McCulloch, a former premier of Victoria and principal of McCulloch, Sellars and Co., which owned the 1,400 square mile run. In 1875 George McCulloch had taken over the management of Mount Gipps from his cousin, William Findlay. He was noted for his impatience with prospectors and anything else that disrupted the pastoral routine on the large holding, the main feature of which was a 150 foot high "broken" hill that stretched for 2 miles.

By 1883 Charles Rasp had joined the station hands at Mount Gipps as a boundary rider on £1 a week — an unlikely person for such a job. He was by training an edible-oil technologist, and he had more than a passing interest in the broken hill, the black-clad crest of which he'd had ample opportunity to investigate. On 5 September 1883, convinced that it was rich not in silver but black oxide of tin, he took into his confidence David James (contracted to sink dams on Mount Gipps) and his offsider, James Poole, and they pegged out 40 acres of the blackest part of the hill, registered their claim with the mining warden, Richard O'Connell, and then, not without some trepidation, reported what they had done to the boss, George McCulloch. McCulloch, annoyed on the one hand yet anxious on the other to be a party to any major discovery, suggested that a wider syndicate be formed to draw in resources to prospect a greater part of

the broken hill. McCulloch nominated himself along with Rasp, James and Poole, George Urquhart (the sheep overseer), George Lind (the storekeeper and bookkeeper), and Philip Charley (a station hand) — an unusual combination of seven at a time when landholders tended to keep a distance between station hands and themselves. Six additional leases were pegged out and the seven claims registered as Blocks 10–16, running almost the full length of the 2 miles of the broken hill.

Each member of the syndicate undertook to contribute £70, a considerable amount at the time. They each provided £1 a week to cover the rent for the leases, amounting to £74 a year. McCulloch must not have been very optimistic or he would have drawn upon his uncle's wealthy firm to finance the venture. The money also provided for the first shaft to be sunk.

The first venture undertaken by the Broken Hill Mining Company was disappointing. By some ill chance a shaft was put down on perhaps the poorest part of the lode and only low-grade carbonate of lead was discovered on the surface. The money raised had been spent. Shares in the mine began to change hands. Lind sold his interest to McCulloch, and Rasp bought out Urquhart for £10. McCulloch, wanting to make a quick killing, and finding three syndicate shares too risky to hold, tried to interest a casual station bookkeeper, Alfred Cox, in a one-fourteenth share for £200. The visitor haggled over the price, offering only £120 and challenging McCulloch to a game of euchre to see if the price was £200 or £120. The stakes were probably never higher in a card game, unbeknown to the players. Cox won. He left Mount Gipps with a priceless share. McCulloch lost a share that six years later would have returned him nearly one million times as much.

Despondent at the initial result, James Poole went on with his dam-sinking. It was surer than mining anyway. Water was of greater importance at the time. They were drought years around the Barrier Range and the pall of death was everywhere. On Kinchega Station 30,000 sheep died. Their carcasses were piled in heaps and the stench of burning flesh and wool engulfed the countryside.

Using his combined knowledge of stock and the country, Sid Kidman, then aged 27, put his bush skills to good use in the the drought years. They were the first he had to work as a drover moving stock to markets. He succeeded in bringing down, with minimal loss, whatever stock could travel. He drove to the Barrier area where his

OPPOSITE:
Sid Kidman in the 1880s. (Photographers: Hammer & Co.; source: Joan Hopkins)

brother Sack was now based. An influx of mining hopefuls created a local market for meat, and there was always Adelaide as well. With an ear always alert to information, he was aware of the silver stirrings in the Barrier.

In his own words, Kidman said, "About this time Broken Hill was beginning to move along. After the drought I went to Cobham Lake Station and bought 900 cows and bullocks — all they could muster out of 10,000 — at £3 a head.

"I travelled the cattle via Broken Hill and sold them at the Burra. On the way I met Jim Poole, who was a partner with David James, sinking a tank at the Nine-Mile, which is a few miles from where Broken Hill now is."

Poole filled in the ex-Mount Gipps station hand with news of the silver syndicate struck up by the Mount Gipps seven (all of them known to Kidman) and offered him a slice of the action. Kidman recalled, "I gave Jim Poole ten of the culls for a one-fourteenth share in the Broken Hill and also left ten bullocks to be broken in. The culls were worth about £60. I paid a £6 call to sink Rasp's shaft, the first shaft that was ever sunk at the Barrier." On Kidman's part this is incorrect. The first shaft on Block 13, Rasp's shaft, had already been sunk and yielded disappointment. If he had included the word "successful" in relation to the "first shaft sunk at the Barrier", it would have been accurate.

Kidman was annoyed in time to come at the story that was put around that he had bought a one-fourteenth share in Broken Hill for ten working bullocks. Numerous journalists recounted such a story, including Ion Idriess. Working bullocks were valuable in those days and Kidman resented the insinuation that he parted with ten of them for the share. He claimed the share was offered to him at £60, for which he gave only ten store bullocks worth £6 each.

The Adelaide Stock Exchange was not formed until 1887 (at a time when Broken Hill was fast becoming famous) and before then shares were bought and sold in the streets, in private offices and along the tracks. Kidman's record of the transaction, dated 28 July 1884, at Silverton, New South Wales, stipulates: "I have this date sold M James Poole 10 stears branded. Dceriptions [a list then stated how they were marked on the near rump, off rump and 'ribbs']...10 head in all for value receved in considration of 1/14 in Broking Hill mine on Mt Gipps."

Kidman went on to the Burra with his mob and afterwards visited Kapunda for the pause that refreshed, to see Miss Isabel Wright, the girl he intended to marry. On the return trip to Broken Hill in the rickety red Cobb & Co. coach, Kidman talked animatedly with a fellow passenger, a man called Harris, a sharebroker.

"I told him I had a one-fourteenth share in Broken Hill which I would sell for £150, a one-twenty-eighth in the Bobby Burns, for which I wanted £250, and a mine called Dunstan's Reef, for which I asked £200," Kidman said years later.

"In twelve months the Bobby Burns was not worth much; while I was in Queensland they carted Dunstan's Reef into Broken Hill for flux and Harris sold my one-fourteenth share in Broken Hill to Bowes Kelly and Wetherby for £150 but I received only £100. Bowes Kelly and Wetherby made a fortune out of the share."

Stories have circulated that the cheque was a dud and that Kidman was ultimately lucky to get £100 for the share. The truth was that the cheque was sound but that the agent Harris took £50 as his commission.

The date of the transaction of Kidman's purchase of the one-fourteenth share is of great interest. It was July 1884. In September, only two months later, a geologist, Norman Taylor, reported that the broken hill ridge contained the most extraordinary and largest lode he had seen anywhere. Ironically, around the same time the young jackeroo Philip Charley picked up some rich silver chloride out of a carelessly dumped pile of carbonate of lead alongside the initial Rasp's shaft. Chloride assaying 600 ounces to the ton was recovered.

It is ridiculous of Idriess and other journalists to suggest that "young Kidman was quite satisified with his first and only mining venture" and that "stock always claimed his heart rather than mining". It was not his first and only mining venture, and he was far from satisfied about the outcome. Kidman was essentially a trader and a dealer. He had always worked with stock but made money on the side wherever he could. Certainly he had made a quick £40 on this transaction, but what he stood to make if he could retrieve that share didn't bear thinking about. Desperately he tried to get it back. The matter was touch and go. He wrote from Broken Hill instructing the agent Harris *not* to sell, but letters crossed in the mail, one advising him that the sale had been effected and enclosing a cheque for £100.

Kidman confessed on several occasions, "How hard I tried to get that share back. But I could not. After that little romance I went away into Queensland again to buy cattle out on the Mulligan at Sandringham Station. I went into partnership with my brother Sackville and remained so until his death."

His quest for a quick quid had let him down badly and it would be forever drummed into him. No doubt that monetary thinking along the lines of "a bird in the hand is worth two in the bush" did influence him at the time, in view of his thoughts of marriage with Isabel Wright. Kidman did not dismiss the matter lightly with the words "after that little romance" which perhaps was a customary term then for a mishap or misadventure. Out of curiosity, he maintained a constant interest in the affairs of BHP until the day he died, ever running his glimmers over the finance columns to see how things were faring and what his one-fourteenth might have been worth. Today, if he had kept the one-fourteenth share in BHP and subscribed to the various issues along the way, it would have been worth (in April 1986) $666 million.

No wedding bells rang out for Kidman and his girl when they were married at Kapunda on 30 June 1885. Despite Isabel Wright's strong association with the Congregational Church, there was no church ceremony. She and Sid were married at the house of Mrs Will, Isabel's mother, by the Rev. W. Fernie, with an overwhelming number of Isabel's friends and family present. It had to be the case, no matter how many guests attended, as the only member of Sid's family at the wedding was his younger brother, Charlie.

Their marriage certificate is a sea of misinformation, with both spelling and factual errors, joining together "Sydney Herbert Kidman, 28, bachalor, cattle dealer and the son of John Kidman" and "Isabell Brown Wright, 23, spinster and daughter of John Wright dead". Standing out impressively on the slim sheet of formality are two signatures, those of the bride and bridegroom. The small spidery handwriting of the minister and witnesses and the pen that dipped to jot the sundry details is dominated by the large, bold and flourishing signature of Sid Kidman and the equally positive, firm signature of Bel Wright. Perhaps it was symbolic of a union that was to last fifty years.

During their courting days, Sid wrote Bel no long, or even short, romantic letters from the bush. When it came to the skill of writing, he could go little beyond his strong, bold signature. At 28 he was a man of straight, plain talking. He was also a confident man, but his confidence fell short when it came to putting pen to paper. He knew how to speak words but not how to write them. His spelling was notorious. He was able to improve on this somewhat over the years, largely because of the help of his schoolteacher-wife. Just as he was keen to learn and absorb factual information in the bush, pot-shotting questions at anyone who could provide the answers, he was equally keen to be Bel's oldest-ever student at home, where question and answer time was probably par for the course over a drink of tea.

After years of rolling up for impromptu visits at Kapunda, idling for a day or two, then returning to the bush, Kidman asked Bel to marry him in 1884. There was never any question that there was any other woman in his life. In the bush he worked either solo or in the company of men and often far removed from towns and the social life they afforded. It was something he did not consciously seek, unlike many men who couldn't wait to bust a cheque in favour of a pub, grog tavern or on a fling with a bit of skirt whenever and wherever they could find it.

In all likelihood Sid was not the only man who paid attention to Bel Wright, a good-looking, educated girl, well-respected in Kapunda because of her connections, status as a teacher and work within her church. But it was the raw, humorous, good-looking bushman whom she favoured most. Typical of the era, he did not propose marriage until he considered he was in a sound financial position to support wife and family. By 1884 Kidman knew that droving and dealing with cattle, sheep and horses was a good wicket on which to bat, and there were moves to expand into coaching.

An aspect of marriage that came as a shock to Kidman was something as simple as a house. For fifteen years, more than half of his life at the time he was wed, he'd not lived in one. He said, "I never knew what it was to be in a house until I was married. I was more used to sleeping blackfellow style with a fire at my head and feet and one each side of me."

A house was a first priority for his wife, and he gave her the best possible. Bald Hill, Kapunda, (so called because of the absence of trees around it) was their first home. It was a Victorian bluestone place with a few outstanding features that lifted it out of the ordinary class. It was a large family house for the day, but not quite grand enough to be called a mansion. Yet it purported to be more than it was with its turreted entrance porch, and central mansard roof section capped with a widow's walk that gave access to viewing long distances. It would have cost him a few bob.

They lived at Bald Hill for fifteen years. Isabel coped with long spells of time on her own, for Sid was away more often than he was at home. However, his short stints at home became productive ones. Their first child, Annie Gertrude Kidman (better known as Gert), was born on 25 February 1886. A second child, Elma Thomson Kidman, arrived on 18 July 1887, and they took out the hat trick with a third daughter, Edna Gwendoline Kidman, on 11 June 1890. Four of Kidman's brothers, George, Sackville, Thomas and Charles, managed to produce nineteen sons between them (as well as a good sprinkling of daughters), causing Sid perhaps some disappointment when his fourth daughter, Edith Kidman, was born on 25 July 1893. Little Edith caused more than disappointment: she brought alarm and grief, dying in infancy on 10 December 1895.

Kidman was jubilant on 20 April 1897, when his first son, Norman Sidney Palethorpe Kidman, was born — a happiness that was short-lived. The boy died at the age of 16 months on 2 August 1898.

On 26 June 1900 a second son was born, Walter Sidney Palethorpe Kidman. He was watched over with every care. Bel was 38 when he was born — not too old to try again should anything happen to this son, but anxious that no misfortune should befall the boy to the point that he was perhaps over-protected and cosseted.

If there were sad years within the marriage, they were those that saw the death of two infant children. Such sadness never departed but it was considerably eased when Walter arrived. Bel Kidman bore the loss of her children stoically. She most certainly was not the "sweet Scotch lass", "the little bride" of whom others have written. The only truth here is that she was Scottish.

She was able to survive Kidman's long absences from home because she was not dithering and dependent. She was an immensely capable woman, fired with a strong, if not dominant, spirit. Fiddling and diddling at home with housewifely matters was not to her liking, nor were small, screaming, dribbling, teething children who constantly needed monitoring. Bel Kidman appreciated her children (and grandchildren) more when they were older, toilet-trained, at school and able to converse with her intelligently.

Her eldest grandchild, Joan Hopkins, of Adelaide, said, "Neither grandpa nor grandma were emotional people. He was always the same. He laughed easily — always the same pleasant gentle laugh and smile. Gran wasn't emotional at all. She could sit up in the back of a car and go over a precipice without batting an eyelid. She didn't spoil you, not Gran. She wasn't the cuddly or lovable type but we didn't dislike her. She would have rather gone out into the garden for the day than minded small kids. She was not tall and as she got older she got heavier, especially under the chin, which we referred to as Gran's 'pelican pouch'."

Muriel Kidman, Sid and Bel's daughter-in-law, endorsed those comments: "Was she good looking? No. She was pretty when she was younger and when I knew her she was plump with double chins. He was tall and she was tiny and round by comparison. She didn't like looking after kids. She'd have preferred to have done a hard day's ironing. But I was very fond of her, as I was of him. They were a devoted couple."

Unquestionably Sid and Bel's was a happy marriage. According to Joan Hopkins, "He worshipped her. She was never part of the background of his life but instead an equal, competent partner. He consulted her about everything. They made decisions together. If she advised against anything, he did not go ahead with it."

The ceremony at Kapunda in 1885 provided the double harness that linked them for more than half a century. It was special in another way. It was the only small, quiet important celebration in their lives. From then on, family weddings and other important occasions were marked with bigger, grander gatherings, to the point of civic receptions and official banquets, both in Australia and overseas.

In 1935, during an interview on cattle prices, dealing and the market, Kidman was asked: "What's the greatest deal you ever made?" It didn't take him long to answer the journalist. His eyes lit up as he did so and he answered unexpectedly, "My wife. She's been my mate for fifty years!"

6
The Long Paddock Years

B Y 1885 THE BROKEN HILL area was firmly established as
Australia's principal mineral field. Kidman may have failed in
retrieving his one-fourteenth share in the Broken Hill company, but
its success meant opportunities for him in another direction, as had
Cobar with copper and Mount Browne with gold. The influx of
people required both transport and tucker, and Kidman was in an
ideal position to provide both.

The headquarters of the Kidman stock-dealing operations was at
Silverton. It was run by Sack Kidman, enabling the brothers to be
instant suppliers of meat to the miners. Sid worked as the roving
partner, attending to buying and droving and any other business
that would make money; one such operation was running mail
coaches. He tendered successfully for the running of a mail coach
from Terowie, South Australia, to Wilcannia, New South Wales,
(about 350 miles). It made good business sense. Apart from droving
sheep and cattle, Kidman was regularly travelling to Bourke and
buying horses on the Barwon, McIntyre and Bogan and bringing the
mobs of more than 250 down to Liston and Shakes to sell in
Adelaide. On one occasion, finding no ready market for the horses,
he applied for the Terowie—Wilcannia mail run. It would mean a
useful outlet for the horses.

The ink was barely dry on the agreement when Kidman was
approached to sell out. "Without putting any horses on or starting
operations I sold the contract to George Rayner for £600 and he sold
it to Hill and Co. and, owing to Broken Hill breaking out, it was one
of the most profitable mails Hill and Co. ever carried," Kidman said.
"They charged £5 from Terowie to Silverton and the coach often
used to carry twenty-five passengers. Hill and Co. made about £6,000
a year from the contract. My idea in getting the contract in the first
place was to use the horses I could not sell."

Just as he had done with his Broken Hill share, Kidman, some
might say, had done the wrong thing again with his first mail
contract, unloading it too quickly at too small a profit. But he made
an instant profit on the deal with a big mob of horses still intact that
were sold elsewhere at a profit. Yet it prompted him to think about
the wisdom of getting back into the cut and thrust of the transport

business as a sideline to stock dealing and he approached Jimmy Nicholas about forming a partnership. Jimmy Nicholas had gone to work for Cobb & Co. at Wagga Wagga in the early 1870s as a 12-year-old lad. His father, a successful mining speculator in the early days of Victorian gold, had depleted his fortune and ruined his health, which forced the boy into early work to help support the family.

"My father had been a good horseman and taught me to ride and drive well so I naturally turned to Cobb & Co. for a living, starting at the bottom as a groom and working my way up," Nicholas said.

"The six men associated with Cobb & Co. then were Alick and John Robertson, John Wagner, Walter Hall, James Rutherford and a Mr Whitney. I never knew much about Mr Whitney. Rutherford, Wagner and Hall were supermen who would have been great at any calling they took up. The two Robertson brothers were more of the office type, good financiers but not nearly the ginger in them the other three men had. They came across from America, where they'd had experience with Wells Fargo and Company, when they saw the possibilities coaching offered with the gold discoveries. In the 1860s they dissolved the partnership. Jim Rutherford and Walter Hall took New South Wales as their base for operations and traded as Cobb & Co., Rutherford and Hall proprietors, Sydney, and the two Robertson brothers and Jack Wagner retained the Victorian portion, trading as Cobb & Co., Robertson and Wagner proprietors, Melbourne.

"The two firms were known as Victorian Cobb and New South Wales Cobb. Victorian Cobb did nearly all the Victorian coaching. They crossed the Murray at Echuca and ran all the western portion of New South Wales out as far as Tibooburra. New South Wales Cobb did the balance of New South Wales and were largely interested in the Queensland Cobb & Co., which was another registered company. These three companies created the precedent that a coaching company, to pay, must have all the traffic or nothing. They could not divide the passenger traffic with any other firm on the road. Consequently when any other person got any of their mail contracts and they could not deal with him at a satisfactory price, they at once commenced operations to run him off by cutting the passenger fares down to something ridiculous, sometimes carrying the passengers for nothing. Some of these feuds lasted for years, but usually the new contractor, without any previous knowledge or experience of mail contracting, found out he had got his contract too low and either forfeited or made some arrangements for Cobb to carry out the contract for him.

"I was driving out of Wagga for them when I was 15 and drove for the two firms for ten years around western New South Wales and on the network of roads New South Wales Cobb had in the New England area, but after the years I'd spent on the hot Riverina plains I couldn't stand the New England cold and cleared back to the Darling and drove from Wilcannia to Mount Browne.

"I left the Cobbs in 1884 and went with one of their managers, Mr G. A. McGowan, who had obtained an interest in a mail contract running from Wilcannia to Terowie in South Australia. He only kept the line for a short time and then sold it to John Hill and Co., the big South Australian coaching firm, and I drove there for a year. [This would indicate that Kidman sold the run to McGowan and partners who sold to Hill and Co.] Then another driver named O'Neil and myself started mail contracting. We were fairly successful and in 1887 Sid Kidman bought O'Neil out, and he and I carried on mail contracting for a good many years, running into big contracts at times. We traded as Kidman and Nicholas and our operations ran into all states except Victoria but much the biggest in New South Wales and Western Australia. Sid and Sack Kidman held a half interest in the firm and I the other half. They very rarely came amongst the coaching, as their business of stock dealers kept them busy in another direction."

The agreement was that the Kidman brothers would supply the horses and that Nicholas would handle the day-to-day running. The partnership was tough enough not to be bullied by Cobb & Co. It stayed on the road to become Cobb & Co.'s most formidable opposition. Some people, initially, were dubious as to whether Kidman and Nicholas would make a go of it.

Nicholas said, "I was regarded as 'one of Cobb's old drivers' and Kidman as 'a cattle dealer'. It's true that I was one of Cobb's old drivers, but I'd spent most of my life involved in the coaching business and had thoroughly studied it in all its branches, so if I didn't know enough to run a coaching firm after seeing both the best and the worst coaching in Australia then I must have been a booby indeed.

"Regards Sid Kidman, I don't think Australia has seen many men as smart as he was. We were young fellows together and great pals. He was one of the nicest men you could meet. He was a great horseman and would ride or drive anything and was probably Australia's best judge of a bullock. He could hop off the top rail of any yard onto any bullock, ride him around, slip off him onto the top rail well before the bullock knew what had happened. He would buy and sell anything from a pocket knife to a station, and one deal did not disturb him a bit more than another. He is one of Australia's supermen. I never saw him drink, swear or lose his temper. He could box, if necessary, as well as the best of them and was not a bad poker player, but five bob rises were his limit. I think that he — with those few different characteristics in his favour — and I with my considerable knowledge should have been able to run a successful coaching enterprise."

They did. "We ran a line with horses from Morgan in South Australia to Cobar in New South Wales. It connected up with the South Australian and New South Wales railways and was about 620 miles long. It passed through Renmark, Wentworth, Pooncarie, Menindee, Wilcannia and Cobar. We ran along the Murray and Darling rivers for about the first 500 miles and then out across to the Sydney railhead at Cobar, some 150 miles from the Darling. Another road we ran was from Booligal on the Old Man Plains through to Tibooburra passing through Mossgiel, Ivanhoe, Wilcannia, White Cliffs and Milparinka with a branch running down to Tarrawingee. A third was from Broken Hill to Wentworth (200 miles) and a fourth from Broken Hill to Menindee (75 miles). Another of our lines was from Farina, South Australia, to Cordillo Downs, Queensland, a distance of 400 miles and yet another from Hergott (now Marree), South Australia, to Birdsville, Queensland. The Bourke to Wilcannia contract we had once or twice but sold it to the original contractor, the Morrison brothers.

"These different lines ran into something more than 2,000 miles of coaches. Some services were run three times a week, others twice and some, once a week. It took some 1,400 horses, 40 coaches and 150 men to run these services properly."

Most of the coaches were the American thorobrace type (a standard type used for coaching throughout Australia), with some ritzy numbers too. "They were the English style De Luxe Jack coaches," Nicholas said. "They were a class of coach sumptuously upholstered and, although swung on the leather thorobrace springs, they were not placed on rockers but the body of the coach was made half round the shape of the rockers and ran on same. This made them much more comfortable riding, but they were a great deal heavier and mostly used for coaching royalty or governors with about six or seven picked horses to draw them."

Kidman and Nicholas employed only first-class drivers, many of them former horse and bullock teamsters. Kidman often swung aboard the coaches himself when he wanted to go on a stock-buying trip from Broken Hill. He never travelled as a passenger but always up front and often took the ribbons, but only ever in short bursts, because of his capacity to either doze or fall into a sound sleep at a moment's notice, and driving required both skill and constant vigilance.

"There were hazards," said Nicholas. "Old-time Victorian drivers used to say that the glue pot on one of the Victorian roads was, in winter, the worst bit of road in Australia. But on the Old

Man Plains in winter, at a place called Holy Box change near Mossgiel (on the 300 mile stretch from Echuca to Ivanhoe), there were numerous places of the glue pot calibre. Lakes and swamps were all filled and creeks all flooded and the following conversation between groom and driver frequently took place on a dirty night: 'Any news of the Willandra crossing?' from the driver. 'Yes, the water is still rising. It is now half a mile wide and there are ten or a dozen teams stuck there. They have had to doublebank each wagon across with forty or more horses on them. The road is ripped to pieces so look out, but the teamsters sent word to say they have a team of horses ready to pull you through if you get anchored there tonight.' In winter this Willandra (about 6 miles from the Holy Box change) was a rotten place. Passengers who had heard the conversation between driver and groom would get a nervy feeling up and bombard the driver with all sorts of questions as to what was going to happen to them. If the coach got stuck in the Willandra, how were they going to get on? Would they have to spend the night on the coach or would there be a buggy there to get them to dry land? Was there any danger of the coach and all being washed away with all hands drowned? The poor old driver, already loaded himself with doubts of really what was going to happen, had to allay all their fears by saying that everything would be all right and they need not be afraid. Generally the horses, used to the mud and slush and bog of the plains (if not busted), would scramble through somehow. Coaches were built for that special type of work — low and strong and very hard to turn over, so while they kept on their wheels the horses would tug them out by their own volition."

The success of the company destroyed the monopoly bid by Cobb & Co. on coaching, and Kidman and Nicholas became second to them in overall coach work in Australia, a fact that greatly worried Sid's brother Sackville. Expansion meant heavy costs and there were times when Sid, ever intent on good bargains and dealing, arrived at Broken Hill with big mobs of sheep unexpectedly. It sent Sack into bursts of rage. If no market could be found for them there would be no money and Sid's reckless buying could bring them all to ruin. Sackville Kidman shrewdly watched the Adelaide market (and later the Sydney and Melbourne markets) so that, if Sid glutted the Broken Hill market, Sack could rail the surplus to Adelaide via the line from Cockburn on the border, which saved a long, slow droving trek. Then a new market presented itself.

Gold was found in 1888 in the Pilbara in Western Australia and then, in 1891, in the Murchison River and in 1892 at Coolgardie. The stampede to the west was on and boats were jam-packed because there was no railway. Again transport and tucker were essential requirements for the new goldfields and the Kidman brothers moved in quickly. They pioneered attempts to ship meat from Port Adelaide to Western Australia to supply the goldmining population; in the first two steamer loads nearly half the cattle were lost. Better organisation reduced the losses for future shipments, which also included pigs and sheep. Others tried to horn in in a similar way but the Kidman brothers' superior knowledge of stock availability and trading gave them a keen business edge. In Western Australia the firm of the Emanuel brothers and John Forrest acted as their agents. The scream was on for transport as well, and in 1894 Jimmy Nicholas went west to expand the coaching business.

"We had tendered for all our New South Wales mail contracts again and there seemed to be some chance of certain mail contracts on existing routes falling through. At Southern Cross, Western Australia, I went to a meeting of the Coolgardie Coaching Company and got them to give me a month's option over their coaching plant from Southern Cross to the goldfields. We intended buying them out for £5,000, and, when I got back to the hotel after the meeting, there was a wire from Kidman saying our tender had been accepted for all the western portion of the New South Wales mail contracts. So it was a case of abandoning the option on the CCC lines and hurrying back east to get several hundred horses, coaches, plant etc. ready to start our new contracts by New Year's Day. I told the CCC people I'd be back to deal with them as soon as I sold some of our less suitable routes, which I did, but it took me longer than I thought.

"By then the railway had been opened to Coolgardie and the Coolgardie Coaching Company had registered the firm and named it Cobb & Co. Ltd. There were six members in the company — Charlie Saw, William Marwick, Billy Milne, Wilkinson, Jack Day and another. They were the originals of Cobb & Co. Ltd in Western Australia, and some of these members sold out to others."

Instead of paying £5,000 for the business, the price had doubled when, in June 1896, Kidman and Nicholas made them an offer of £10,000 for the entire twenty-four shares in the company on a walk-in-walk-out basis. "They accepted — all but Jack Day — so we let him keep his shares and bought him out about a year later. The deal was a good one. We got our money back in seven months."

This was at the time of the boom days when money was no object where transport to the goldfields was required. Coaches were run from Coolgardie to Kalgoorlie, Bulong, Ejudina, Broad Arrow, Paddington, Menzies, Niagara, Mount Malcolm, Mount Morgans, Laverton, Leonora, Lawlers, Wiluna, Black Range and Mount Magnet.

Sid and Sack's youngest brother, Charlie Kidman, went west to help with the operation, and the company, which retained the old name of Cobb & Co., rolled along making good profits, especially when fresh rushes were about and plenty of people were travelling. The coaching operation became so vast that Nicholas, too, headed west to handle the show in Western Australia. "I question if any other road had its big daily traffic carried better than the Menzies to Malcolm and outback was carried," he said. "Our coach arrived at Menzies regularly at night with twenty to thirty passengers and twice a month, in addition to this load, we had from half a ton to a ton and a half of gold on her. The combined coach route–mail subsidies eventually yielded £40,000, but there were big expenses in the early days of Coolgardie and Kalgoorlie and other goldfield rushes, owing to the water supply being mostly obtained from condensers. Our water bill alone was not less than £5,000 a year.

"In 1896 Kidman bought a station in the MacDonnell Ranges — Owen Springs — at a ridiculously cheap price. It had about 4,000 horses on it. But we found that, against mustering the horses, travelling them down 400 miles and then railing them another 1,000 miles or so, we could buy a more suitable animal in the districts our coaches were running through.

"New South Wales Cobb amalgamated with some brothers named Morrison in the network of mail contracts that went west from Dubbo and out onto the Darling at Bourke and as far down as Wilcannia, Milparinka and back Cobar way. We got practically all of their contracts on one or two occasions, but they finally got our lot because, in 1897, we sold them all our coaching plant, including horses in one line. We had been established in Western Australia for more than one year and were not sorry to have a good cleaning up over East."

In the west, the "wobblies" kept clattering and bowling along and making money for Kidman and Nicholas — something of a saving grace in the Depression of the 1890s and bank crashes that had the eastern colonies in a vice-like grip. But the great gold boom saved Western Australia, and Kidman, once again, had been clever enough to muscle in on its activity and had done quite well — in fact very well. The sale of the eastern coaching routes and mail contracts didn't worry him at all. In fact, he deliberately wanted to off-load them. There is no record of the sum that was received for their sale, but it was a large amount — just what he wanted to enable him to go "station shopping". He was in the black while others were in the red, and many properties were available at bargain-basement prices. It was time to get moving with his long-cherished dream of a chain of stations. He'd worked towards this goal for twenty years.

For the twenty years leading up to 1895 Sid Kidman worked "the long paddock". He was constantly on the move and home for him was anywhere in Australia where he slung his hat or dumped his swag. His marriage and the buying of a stylish home at Kapunda changed little in his life. Kapunda provided him with a base, where he spent as much time as possible between excursions in the backblocks. He was constantly droving, dealing and trading in horses, cattle and sheep (and anything else that would make some quick money on the side). Mostly he was successful, but sometimes there were reverses, when he took a financial hiding. He learnt from his mistakes and adopted a philosophic attitude. Regret, he decided, was a useless emotion. If you couldn't rewrite the past the answer was not to worry about it.

It made him happy to see his brothers frequently and work with them when possible on droving and horse-buying trips: George, Fred, Sack and young Charlie. In 1880 Sack became the manager of Sturt's Meadows for their old friend Abraham Wallace (who'd taken up the place ten years earlier and hunted Harry Raines, the illegal squatter, from it). Wallace was going overland to stock a new station, The Elsey, in the Northern Territory and Fred Kidman was in Wallace's camp. The first cattle had gone into the Northern Territory only in 1872, with D'Arcy Wentworth Uhr, and Wallace was one of the early pioneers. He arrived at The Elsey Station in April 1881, with about 1,500 head of cattle and some good horses. Misfortune struck on the way. Fred Kidman was drowned in the distant Kimberleys while crossing the flooded Fitzroy. It was said that he had 100 gold sovereigns with him at the time he was drowned, but only Fred's body was recovered; the money was not to be found.

It seems less a case of what Sid Kidman did than what he didn't do in the "long paddock" years. "I got up big mobs of horses and Liston Shakes and Co. sold them in Adelaide. Some lots averaged nearly £20 a head. I paid no paddocking from Terowie. I just let the horses pick along the road. Sometimes if I could not sell them I'd buy up another 100 in Adelaide and head the lot back to sell in Wilcannia and Queensland. My attention was always turned to cattle. Once I bought a mob at Kalara on the Darling and brought them to Adelaide and lost £100 on them. Still, I thought I would have another try and purchased another lot from Hector Norman Wilson on the Paroo. Mr E. M. Bagot sold them at the old corporation yards, and I lost another £100. There was a bit of a drought on, so I went back to Wilcannia and bought 50 tons of chaff at £10 per ton. I went away for about three months and when I returned I sold it for £30 a ton. I bought 100 bags of oats at 10 shillings and sold them at £1. The

---

chaff I purchased at the New South Wales weight, 2,240 pounds to the ton, and sold at the Adelaide weight of 2,000 pounds. In those days chaff was up to £35 per ton and flour was sold at from £50 to £75 a ton. That was before the railway of course, when people were dependent on the steamers.

"I travelled the 'three rivers' in Queensland, selling and buying cattle and camping out and was content wherever I was. Many persons would have been miserable if they had been in the predicament I was once in on Cooper Creek, when I was going to take fifty camels from Nockatunga to go to Western Australia. I was travelling up the Cooper in flood time. The Afghan I had with the horses got lost and I was two days from Nappa Merrie to Tanapara on the Wilson. I had a horse and a pair of hobbles. I was two days and a night without anything to eat and no blankets. I rode through floodwater for about 100 miles. When I was within 6 miles of Nappa Merrie, a wild duck flew up from its nest and I found nine eggs. I hobbled the horse and lit a fire. As a rule, I never carried matches but as good luck would have it I had them on this occasion. I roasted the nine duck eggs and had a good feed. I never want to eat nine roasted duck eggs again after fasting for two days!

"I often swam the Queensland rivers just by hanging to a bullock's tail, and the most remarkable thing I have seen or heard was when I discovered a man on an island near Bulloo Downs. The shearers' strike was on and he'd cleared out. Rain had fallen in torrents and on one night 10 inches was recorded. All the creeks were running in flood. This chap got onto a peak or some sort of island and water surrounded him and he was stuck there for forty-two days living on pigweed and such stuff. He was just about done for when my blackfellow found him and said, 'Him bullock! Live on grass!' and the poor fellow did look like a skeleton. He was in such a plight because he could not swim.

"He had tied his blanket to the top of a tree to attract people, but everyone missed him. He had written a letter to his mother to tell her he had died of hunger. Fortunately we found him and he did not die. He was the poorest man I have ever seen — just like a piece of rubber. We tied him up with a stirrup leather and had a job to get him over the creek which was running very fast. He camped with Charlie [Kidman's blackfellow] and me that night and all he could say was 'Johnny cake'. We took him on to Bulloo Downs.

"About three months later a man came into my shop at Broken Hill and said, 'Do you remember me, Mr Kidman?' 'I do not,' I replied. 'Don't you remember rescuing a man who had been six weeks on an island?' he said. I said, 'You are not the man, are you!' He said, 'Yes, I am.' He was quite fat. I never saw or heard of him again.

"I reckon I have travelled the biggest mob of cattle. Once we sent

3,300 from Rocklands to Bulloo and we had to work them in two mobs. Another time I had 25,000 wethers on the move at once and that is nearly a record.

"I was nearly killed once. We were loading cattle for the west at Port Adelaide and I fell down the hold and was knocked about a bit, but otherwise have not received more than my share of cuffs from Nature," Kidman said.

The mining boom at Broken Hill locked Sid and Sack into closer business arrangements as partners in the coaching and mail contracts enterprise and a butchery set up to serve the needs of the miners. It sprang up immediately as a bough-shed butchery at Silverton, the original "silver city", 15 miles away from Broken Hill. Later the brothers operated in Gipps Street, Silverton, as S. Kidman and Co., wholesale and family butchers. But the 'S. Kidman' stood for Sackville and not for Sidney.

Sack Kidman had never travelled far from the Barrier area. He had married Anne Matilda Bartlett and had six children: Florence, Frederick, Anthony, Hurtle, Elsie and Bessio. Sack was a giant, 6 feet 8 inches in boots, good looking and amiable, and only disposed to rant and roar against brother Sid when he speculated in too risky a fashion with stock. Sack guided the day-to-day operations, which saw business grow, but on several occasions Sid, buying big lots of stock at bargain prices (and without paying enough attention to the markets for them), arrived at Broken Hill to a furious reception from his brother. Such reckless stock gambling could have wiped them out. It was usually Sackville who sorted out the messes when they occurred. Sackville Kidman was a shrewd man and had been better educated than his brother Sid.

Elders handled the business for them both as bankers and stock and station agents. The Elders Adelaide records in the late 1880s and the 1890s show the Kidman account as one of the busiest, along with that of Faiz and Tagh Mahomet, who were in a similar line of business. Their first account was as S. and S. Kidman (Sid and Sack), and the 1889 ledgers show they were dealing in a big way, paying £250 border tax on each mob of 10,000 sheep and £75 border tax on every 300 cattle. Large numbers of stock were handled from Chowilla, Bulloo Downs, Sturt's Meadows, Milo, Mount Arrowsmith, Naryilco, Comongin, Retreat, Thargomindah, Elsinora, Innamincka, Coongie and Sandringham stations. They were chipped by the Treasury in Sydney for non-payment of rent on a homestead lease in the Broken Hill area. (Under the 1884 New South Wales Land Act, the area of a homestead lease was not less than 5,760 acres and not more than 10,240 acres, and the lessee was required to enter into possession ninety days after the surveyor had marked out the boundaries and obliged to live on it for six months of the year during the first five years and fence it within two years.) The accounts show that S. and S. Kidman were also paying £549 rent on Queensland country.

Sidney Kidman had an account with Elders on his own: that of Thule Station, a small 71 square mile, unwatered run of open mulga flats and ridge country not far from Charleville, Queensland. He acquired the small holding in 1887 from William Kilgour and, curiously, it began at the north-west corner of the You Can't Lick It run. The rent on Thule was £45 a year. In the same year, Kidman acquired Cobbrum, an 83 square mile adjoining run, and then Thule and a part of Cobbrum were consolidated with a third run, Oblong, to become Elverston in April 1890. Sid Kidman held Elverston until 1893, when he transferred it to William Rooks, of Adavale. It was the first country Sid acquired on his own.

In 1891 the brothers transferred their butchering business from Silverton to Broken Hill and incorporated their youngest brother, Charlie, into their dealings. Charlie had been living at Silverton and had his own account with Elders as C. N. Kidman. Little brother Charlie didn't lack for shrewdness either, to the point of being a rip-off man. On 8 July 1891, C. N. Kidman paid through the Broken Hill branch of Elders £1,600 for the purchase of W. A. Grunike's butchering business. On 23 September 1891, he sold Sack and Sid a half share (one-quarter share each) for £2,200. In various months in 1891 S. and S. Kidman were in debt to Elders for £16,000 — a considerable amount of money in those days — and Charlie Kidman's C. N. Kidman account was also in debt. Interest charges from Elders were 8 per cent while other customers were levied 3, 4, and 5 per cent. The following year things hadn't improved much, with the Kidman brothers in debt to £10,000 and still paying 8 per cent. The debt was reduced dramatically at times by amounts of £3,000 when big mobs of sheep were sold. The interest charge was dropped to 7 per cent in January 1893. The impression from the Elders ledger books is that the Kidman brothers were high-risk customers and that Elders were acting as a high-risk finance company in handling their business. Small wonder that Sackville raged whenever Sidney went off half-cocked on large and dubious stock dealings. The accounts relate only to stock dealing and not the coaching business which, as it expanded to four states, absorbed money in big costs. The accounts show two things. If, after several years in a successful partnership, the Kidman brothers were in something of a stretched financial position in the early 1890s, it is hardly likely that they would have waded in for major station purchases before then. The accounts also show that, by the early 1890s, they did hold some land in New South Wales around Broken

Hill and in Queensland, thereby dismissing the myth that Owen Springs was the first piece of country Sid Kidman took up. The first piece was the tiddler Thule, which perhaps was an ominous beginning, bordering as it did on the You Can't Lick It run.

7

The "Chain-of-Supply" Strategy

BY THE MID-1890s, when he was almost 40 years old, Sid Kidman had become a "computer on horseback". He had amassed the most tremendous amount of knowledge on the Australian outback, not that anyone meeting him would have known: the homespun, knockabout bushman kept the knowledge stockpile closely unto himself. Certainly the "young kid who knew his way around" the back of New South Wales in the 1870s sufficiently well to be a guide to the overlanders had become a mature man who could manoeuvre confidently around the back country anywhere, particularly in South Australia and Queensland.

From the moment he had spied that first piece of floodplain country, he had spent fifteen years investigating the floodplains scene. It would be impossible to estimate how much time had been spent in the saddle and how many thousands of miles he had ridden in that time — always on stock-dealing business, of course — checking on floodplain country in good times and in bad.

The coastal regions had never interested him at all, until his wife pointed out that they should. He could well recall her first geography lesson. It dealt with the Great Dividing Range: any rain that fell on their eastern side found its way into gullies and rivers that led to the Pacific Ocean. Anything that fell to the west found its way into an inland river system. Her finger had scooted across the map pointing out how the system worked in New South Wales — how the Macintyre, Gwydir, Castlereagh, Macquarie and Bogan rivers were linked to the Darling. But it was the less reliable inland river system in Queensland to which Sid gave rapt attention. She could point to the western fall of the Great Dividing Range where the Thomson and Barcoo rivers started flowing south-west to join Cooper Creek which, just 100 miles north of the New South Wales border, turned west into South Australia, expending itself before reaching Lake Eyre. A low range of hills 300 miles south of the Gulf of Carpentaria gave a starting point to the Diamantina. Rain on the southern side of the hills kicked the river off. It ran roughly parallel to the Thomson River, which became Cooper Creek, but traversed drier country, crossing the South Australian border further west in the Queensland "corner" before flowing into Lake Eyre. The southern falls of the

Barkly Tableland were a starting point for the Georgina River, its many feeders reaching back into the Selwyn Range behind Cloncurry and Mount Isa, draining the western side of the table-land and moving south close to the Northern Territory border to fill Lake Machattie and swinging west to join the Mulligan, a narrow watercourse fringing the Simpson Desert. There was also the Bulloo River, rising up in central Queensland and flowing south-west for about 400 miles to flow into the Bulloo Lakes near the New South Wales–Queensland border.

The area in the far south-west corner of Queensland, watered by the Cooper, Diamantina and Georgina, would later be known as the Channel Country. Kidman calculated it to be almost 60,000 square miles of flat plains subjected to periodic floods. Its annual rainfall varied from 10 inches at the top end to half that amount near the South Australian border. The monsoon rains could be guaranteed to start the headwaters of the three rivers flowing each year and yet, as he had observed, a heavy, wet monsoon season combined with falls of rain in the Channel Country itself created flood conditions when the rivers and their complicated network of gutters, minor channels and billabongs oozed and overflowed onto the extremely flat land, producing, in due time, rich fattening grasses and herbage. It was a superb natural irrigation system, but it did have a major drawback: the seasons were erratic and floods could not be relied upon every year. Even in a normal year Kidman had seen the rivers as dry, sanded beds for several months — but at least topping up many deep and permanent waterholes. In years of extreme drought, it would be a place of abject misery and death. The harsh, isolated country offered a tremendous challenge to anyone prepared to run the seasonal gauntlet.

Sid had travelled it all frequently enough, noting how the Queensland–South Australian border fairly accurately marked the limit of good land. In South Australia, Innamincka Station on Cooper Creek and Clifton Hills with its fattening swamp on Goyder's Lagoon on the Diamantina had some first-class grazing land, but closer to Lake Eyre the sandy soils were marginal. He noted how the alluvial plains began on the Cooper south of Windorah, Queensland, spreading out for 30 or 40 miles — that, as his wife had explained, was wider than some parts of the English Channel. It nourished Durham Downs, Karmona, Nappa Merrie and Innamincka.

The Diamantina sustained Diamantina Lakes Station and Davenport Downs, as well as Monkira, where he'd seen floodplains 60 miles wide. There was also Durrie Station, Roseberth and Pandi Pandi. Farrars Creek, to the east of the Diamantina, watered Currawilla and Palparara. Below Boulia, the Georgina provided good floodplains at Marion Downs, all the way to the 100 square mile Lake

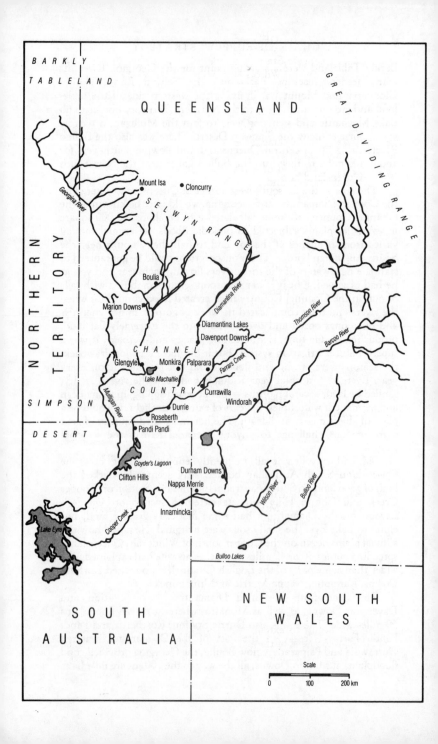

Machattie on Glengyle Station. Similar alluvial plains dissected by channels existed on the Wilson and Bulloo rivers.

Sid knew that the floods came down between January and March, and he'd seen the miraculous change as the floodwaters receded, leaving an inland sea of green grass springing up — pepper and button grass, Flinders, couch, wild sorghum, cane grass and Mitchell grass. But if the floods came later, in March or April, the green sea was usually one of clover. The annual grasses matured quickly, so much so that by the end of winter they dried off rapidly and blew away; the soil cracked and remained that way until the bountiful blessing of floods once more. Yet, even in a poor season, Kidman had found that what dry grass or bush was about was sweet. It was not sour country. Cattle were able to do well on it, where they'd go poor on sour country even though the grass was feet high.

Rain in the north would bring down the Diamantina and Georgina; rain in the north-east, but to the west of the Dividing Range, would bring down the Cooper. Rain in both places would bring down all three rivers and their tributaries, and the Channel area would be lush and verdant without so much as a drop of rain falling on it.

Additionally, a major discovery would help to make the area more reliable and the dream he was nurturing a sounder proposition. It was now possible for water to gush from the very interior of the earth — artesian water they called it. A flowing bore had been sunk at Kalara Station near Bourke, New South Wales, in 1878. This was the first tapping of the Great Artesian Basin, the largest in the world, which covered 600,000 square miles, mostly in Queensland, but extending into New South Wales, South Australia and the Northern Territory. Kidman was fascinated by the process from the outset and excited by further developments, which, by 1884, saw the New South Wales government start sinking bores along roads and stock routes, and with such success that places hitherto impassable through lack of water were now opened up. Kidman had marvelled when the dry track from Wanaaring to Milparinka had been made passable, thanks to this underground water. And Queensland's first gusher had flowed at Barcaldine in 1888. Remote New South Wales and Queensland saw the greatest development of windmill-powered bores and they varied in depth from 10 feet to 7,000 feet. It augured well for the "three rivers" country. In fact, a man taking it up in time to come might find numerous such bores to supplement what Mother Nature had to offer.

The hand of progress was evident elsewhere. By the 1860s railways had begun to extend inland, and by the 1880s the great decade of development of these lines had arrived. Harry Redford in his cattle rustling escapade of 1870 may have set out from central

Queensland obliged to drove the stock almost to Adelaide, but twenty-five years later the railways had snaked out, certainly to Oodnadatta in South Australia, which afforded trucking facilities from Hergott Springs (later to be called Marree) or Farina. It meant that drovers would have to stage cattle down the Birdsville Track or back corridor area to the railhead. For a large, continual operation there was still a problem. If the going had been stiff, stock would need a bit of a breather, a break where they could spell for a bit and put on condition. Kidman believed he had found such a place called Mundowdna. It was centrally located between Hergott and Farina, and had some reliable watering and, equally importantly, good feed. It was about 1,000 square miles, studded thickly with edible bushes and grasses. To make the whole show work, such a depot would be needed, in fact, it was essential to what he had in mind.

He had not been slack in studying up on his markets. Adelaide was still the obvious one, but preferably *not* in competition with everyone else. If you had a monopoly on that "three rivers" or Channel Country (or at least a big stake in it), plus the advantages of the railways and a fattening depot at Mundowdna, you could virtually control that market. Brisbane, Sydney and Melbourne would provide alternatives. And why stop there? Apart from the domestic market, there was the overseas market, with people crying out for meat on the other side of the world. Periods of beef gluts and scarcity were not infrequent; a shortage of beef would mean high prices at home, and, even with a glut, there could be high prices for exported meat. It was all thanks to the refrigeration business that had been backed by Thomas Sutcliffe Mort. It was a remarkable process that meant meat from Australia could be sent 12,000 miles to England. Kidman could recall some early worries with it in the late 1870s, when talk outback around the campfires said it would never succeed. But it certainly had, and Australia had pioneered the world in this new development. The first cargo of Australian frozen beef and mutton arrived in London aboard the *Strathleven* in 1880 in a very satisfactory condition, and shipments had been sent regularly since.

What he had in mind was an operation on a vast scale. Knowing what was going on at any one place at any one time would be important, particularly in regard to feed and water requirements, what other drovers were on the road with mobs, how large the mobs were, and which markets they were headed for. There was a way around that, too. Letters would be useless, but there was no reason why drovers couldn't use the good old "singing wire". These telegraph lines were a mighty thing. Sydney, Melbourne, Adelaide and Brisbane had been connected for about thirty years and then they'd pushed them inland. The big show here was the one that stretched from Port Augusta to Darwin. He could remember that opening for business when he was a 15-year-old boy. He didn't understand then and he still wasn't quite sure how messages could travel along a bit of wire suspended on poles, but the fact remained that it could be done. He recalled his wife saying how costly the Overland Telegraph Line had been — nearly £500,000 to put up the wire and the 36,000 poles that carried it. The interesting thing was that it didn't stop at Darwin — a cable went under the sea to England, meaning a quick means of communication with that country. It would be up to the drovers to get a message sent from the nearest telegraph office to the office at Broken Hill, where Sack was based and could make the decisions.

There wasn't an area where Sid hadn't done his homework. The grand overall plan required a chain of stations on the three rivers that were linked to a droving route, rail transport and markets, markets that could be played to best possible advantage. It also required good, reliable men sending a constant stream of information through the telegraph system. It would also, as Sack had suggested, require a few bob. Sack had advised him to put that thought in his pipe — and smoke it.

Others who have studied Kidman's life have insisted for fifty years that Owen Springs was the first place Kidman acquired and, more importantly, have stipulated that he took it up much earlier than he did. The date of 1880 is frequently mentioned. But at the age of 23 Kidman was in no position to buy land, not even on a half-share basis with William Coombs for £1,000, which is the story so frequently told that it is held to be true. It knocks Kidman's image around somewhat that it is not so — the young boy who'd hit the big league when just into his twenties and who bought up with the bravado of a seasoned pastoral hand. Historians point with authority to 1886 as the date when Kidman obtained Owen Springs. It is impossible. The property was firmly in the control of someone else at that stage.

Writers have claimed that, when Kidman took it up, it was 2,200 square miles in area. Again the image of the zealous fellow acquiring such a big land slice is dashed. Owen Springs was less than a third of that size when it fell into Kidman's hands. It has also been said that he bought Owen Springs as the first link in his massive pastoral chain. He did not. Owen Springs was bought for another reason entirely, and the chain Kidman so keenly desired concerned station link-ups along the Cooper, Diamantina and Georgina rivers. What *can* be said of Owen Springs is that, when Kidman did buy it, it was his first venture as a landholder into the Northern Territory and he bought it to make quick, and he hoped big, money from it.

Owen Springs on the Hugh River, south-west of Alice Springs, was the second pastoral lease in Central Australia (Undoolya was the first) and was taken up by William Gilbert for his father, Joseph Gilbert, who died in 1884. The station was closed down and the stock sold to the pioneers of Bond Springs. In 1886 Sir Thomas Elder restocked Owen Springs with horses and cattle and ran it as an outstation of Mount Burrell, further to the south-west. Charles Gall was the manager of Mount Burrell for Elder after his purchase of the station in 1885 from Gilmour, Hendry and Melrose, who ran 1,000 cattle and seventy horses on it.

The centre had, by this time, earned a good reputation as horse-breeding country and it was Elder's intention to breed horses for the Indian Remount Service — ultimately a failed enterprise for him. But his intentions were clear. In 1887 he placed a further 110 horses on Mount Burrell and imported two Suffolk Punch stallions from England. Owen Springs was carrying 1,500 to 2,000 horses and 1,000 cattle by 1890. Elder had only mediocre results with his remount venture, and he sold the stock from Mount Burrell and Owen Springs at a loss in 1893 and abandoned the leases in 1894, after losing £40,000 in eight years. The two pastoral leases — each of 300 square miles — were auctioned in 1895, and Charles Gall (Elder's former manager) became the lessee, the lease commencing on 1 July 1895. He died on 12 January 1896, and the property passed to his family, to John Gall of Cantara, and by 20 August 1896, Sidney Kidman of Kapunda, South Australia, was the stockholder owning the station.

Kidman would not have bought Owen Springs without first riding there and seeing what it had to offer. The answer was horses — almost unlimited — and a fine stamp of a horse to boot. All that remained was to convince brother Sack that it was a good deal on which they could not lose. The horses could be incorporated into the coaching business operating in four states or else sold at a profit. Sack was convinced. Although Sid Kidman's name is the only one appearing on the lease, Sack was also a partner. They went shares in it, just as they went shares in everything else. Sid himself said, "With Owen Springs, my brother Sack stood in with me." The price they paid was £1,500. Their coaching partner, Jimmy Nicholas, asserted, "There were 4,000 horses on Owen Springs when Kidman got it." It amounted to a very nice return after a small outlay and a lot of hard work. Sid went to Owen Springs to supervise the muster and take an active part in it himself. It was a time-consuming job. There were no fences, so few of the horses had known the branding iron, let alone bridle or saddle.

When heavy trucking costs from Oodnadatta threatened to take the cream off the profit, Sid and Sack looked elsewhere for their coaching horses, staging the Owen Springs horses south when conditions and the markets were best. They did not bolt at the project in one fell swoop. On one occasion Sid Kidman arrived at Oodnadatta with 500 horses. They were in poor condition through drought and a scarcity of feed on the way to the railhead. They were too poor to truck and such as would have reached market would not have fetched enough to pay their freight. Under these circumstances Kidman offered the 500 horses to his men in lieu of wages, an offer they scornfully refused. Accordingly, he had the horses branded with a number 9, turned them loose and paid his men with his cheque. A year later he mustered the horses and brought them to Adelaide. They were fat. There had been a good season, the grass was knee high and the "number nines" fetched at public auction from £25 up to £39 a head. Yet the year before he'd refused to pay 25 shillings freight on them because they would not have fetched that price per head at auction.

That was only 500 of the Owen Springs horses. If they'd fetched the lower amount of £25, it meant £12,500. If only half of the 4,000 Owen Springs horses had realised £25 when Kidman dovetailed them into similar markets, he would have made £50,000 — not a bad clean up for him and Sack on a £1,500 outlay. They probably wished an Owen Springs would drop into their lap every week.

Of the holding itself Kidman said, "There's always plenty of water thereabouts. It doesn't take much rain to make the creeks and rivers run up there, as the range country is pretty rough. There are some big springs to the north of the hills and, though there is bad country to be found between Hergott Springs and the ranges, on the whole it is surprisingly well watered for stock of all kinds — including sheep."

Kidman made money from his first Northern Territory station and, despite his notation of its suitability for all stock, his love affair with Owen Springs was fleeting. Once it had served its purpose, he transferred it to the Willowie Land and Pastoral Association Ltd on 10 July 1901, holding it for just five years. Had it been construed as either a first or an important link in a chain, he would have held on to it.

Curiously, he had a change of heart about Owen Springs towards the end of his days. Just as it was one of the first stations he bought, it was also one of the last. One of the Kidman family companies, Oakden Hills Ltd, bought an enlarged Owen Springs (900 square miles) in 1930. The company still held the station at the time of Kidman's death but the second time around Owen Springs brought neither the joy of a well-planned coup nor big money. It brought nagging troubles.

The Kidmans' first major property acquisition was Cowarie Station in South Australia, about 50 miles north-east of Lake Eyre. It was taken up in 1895, the year before Owen Springs. August Helling pioneered Cowarie in 1875, and the Kidmans, who were second, were joined subsequently in the partnership (or at least Sid was) by Edward (Ted) Pratt, a man who later figured prominently in the Kidman pastoral empire as a most efficient, and some would say tough and cunning, travelling manager.

Kidman kept his grip on this station until his death, and in 1905 Mayoh Miller and William Coulthard, both of Kapunda, South Australia, were issued a forty-two year lease on a block at Cowarie, transferring their lease to Kidman and Pratt in 1914. The Mayoh Miller–Coulthard lease is interesting. Both were Kapunda businessmen, no doubt very well known to Sid, and it was Mayoh whom Kidman asked to join him in a partnership towards the end of the First World War in a venture to build wooden ships, to combat war shipping losses, and to transport goods to England.

Cowarie was on Derwent Creek, an erratic watercourse struggling north-west to meet the lower Diamantina and the last outpost on the river before it exhausted itself into the desert sands bordering Lake Eyre. In a kingdom of sand, it was a glimmer of hope for spelling cattle on their trek down from western Queensland runs, with its substantial boomerang-shaped waterhole screened by coolabahs and wattle. It was almost on the edge of civilisation, teetering on the outskirts of the Simpson Desert.

Owen Springs was the second station purchase and, in the nineteen months following, Sack and Sid Kidman bought up quickly elsewhere. Just how quickly is evident in a letter written by Sackville Kidman to his cousin Fred Nunn in England. The letter, dated 31 March 1898, shows that the small holdings around Broken Hill had been increased to bigger holdings and that a number of other stations were in their hands as well. The letter reads:

Dear Fred,

Your very welcome letter of 11th January to hand. I was very sorry to hear of your Father's death, in fact I did not know that any of my Uncles were dead until I received your letter. I should very much like to hear from my Aunt Phyllis and any of my cousins.

You say Fred that your Father lost all his money and property before he died. I was surprised to hear that as I did not think he was a man to speculate. One thing worse than all for you Fred was losing your poor wife and your children being left without a Mother.

You say you would like to get your boys out to some new country. There is no doubt as soon as they are able to look after themselves we could either give them something to do or get them into something out here. As for yourself, we might be able to get you a billet as a bookkeeper but I cannot promise until I have written to my brothers as my brothers Charlie, Sidney and myself are partners and trade as Kidman Brothers.

Since you left Australia we have had many ups and downs but I think we are in a fair way of doing well now at Broken Hill. We have a small run of about 40 thousand acres within 10 miles of Broken Hill where we graze stock. We have another place about 10 thousand acres within 85 miles of Broken Hill towards the Queensland border and we have another station Alton Downs 240 miles from Broken Hill on the Queensland border and in Queensland we have Tickalara Station (700 square miles of country with 22,000 sheep, 600 head of cattle and 600 horses).

On the Herbert River in Queensland we have Annandale and Roseberth, two cattle stations with about 10,000 head of cattle and 500 horses, and joining these two runs in South Australia we have Hatton [Haddon] Downs and Pandi Pandi Stations with about 5,000 cattle and 300 horses and on The Clayton Station 25 miles from Hurgert [Hergott] Springs we have about 200 square miles with a quantity of stock on it and about 100 miles further north we have Cowrie [Cowarie] Station with about 2,000 cattle and about 200 horses. In the Northern Territory about 1,000 miles from Adelaide we have Owen Springs Station where we breed a number of horses. On this run we have about 3,000 horses and 2,000 cattle and we have sent some of our horses from this place to the Indian Market as a trial shipment.

We have a very large mail coaching plant in Western Australia and our coaches and buses run all over the gold fields in the name of Cobb & Co. Since the gold fields broke out we have shipped to Western Australia thousands of sheep and cattle and also a number of pigs and other produce from the Eastern States.

Of course in all our different branches of business we employ considerably over 100 men and boys. I manage the Broken Hill part of the business, my brother Sid, the South Australian Branch and Charlie the Western Australian Branch and I reckon if we have as good luck for the next five years as we have had for the past three, we should be independent.

My brother George was very lucky at the first of the Broken Hill Mines and made a lot of money out of shares in fact I believe he was worth about £30,000 but worse luck, he has lost it all again speculating in other shares.

My brother Tom is fairly well off as he has some very good property in the Mt Gambier district of South Australia. He is not wealthy but comfortably off.

My brother Fred I have not seen for years but he is the black sheep and squanders all he earns.

Fred, old man, I look forward to taking a trip home to England some day to see you all if you do not come out to Australia.

Of course, Fred, if you or any of your family come to these Colonies, we will do whatever is in our power for them but as far as our work is concerned it would be principally station work and travelling with the stock from one place to another.

You might show this letter to my Aunt so that she may see that we never wasted what her poor Father left us.

Sackville Kidman wasn't word-perfect in letters, but he was streets ahead of Sid. The letter has only one puzzling overtone: the reference to brother Fred, who had certainly died several years earlier en route to The Elsey. While Sack Kidman may have had a genuine wish to take a trip home to the old country to see everyone, he was denied his chance. Less than a year later, on 10 March 1899, Sack died unexpectedly from peritonitis. He was 43 years old.

It left the Kidman ship without a captain, or an anchor. Whereas Sid was always on the move, Sack had stayed put in the Barrier region, becoming well-known and well-liked, and was hailed as a solid citizen. *The Critic*, on 15 April 1899, said of him:

The somewhat sudden death of Mr Sackville Kidman, which occurred at Broken Hill, will cause at least a passing spasm of regret amongst sporting men throughout Australia, for'"Sack", as he was popularly known, was intimate with every man of any weight in the sporting world. He was associated with the Hill from its opening, established the first line of mail coaches prior to the opening of the tramway. In pastoralist circles he was one of the best known and most successful men in Central Australia. On the outbreak of the Westralian goldfields he succeeded to the management of the Barrier business vacated by his brother Charles N., with whom Darcy Uhr, formerly a sub-inspector of police in Queensland, joined in the butchering business, since established as one of the best on the field. Like his brother, Sackville was a lover of the horse, and his colors were always up in the meetings at the Hill, and in the district.

Sid Kidman didn't score a mention. In a fully fledged obituary that appeared on 8 July 1899 in *The Critic*, the distinct impression is given that Sackville held the reins in the brothers' business affairs.

In the memoirs of Broken Hill one of the most respected names is that of the late Mr Sackville Kidman. A native of South

Australia, he commenced life as a drover of cattle, and by remarkable energy and industry, lived to become the possessor of enormous interests throughout the whole of Australia. For years he drove cattle from various parts of Queensland, over the borders of New South Wales, selling them in the best market and accumulating a fortune by sheer perseverance and endurance. In this way he gained some knowledge of the pastoral country which surrounds the Barrier, and for some time he was engaged as manager of Sturt's Meadows Station, about 50 miles from Broken Hill. When Silverton started Mr Kidman opened a butchering establishment there, but afterwards sold it, and with his brother Mr Sidney Kidman went again to Queensland, where he bought cattle and sheep and extended his trade in the southern colonies. Taking up some homestead leases in the Broken Hill district, they established large interests there, and did a considerable trade in cattle with butchers of the Barrier. When Broken Hill became a township, Messrs Sackville and Sidney Kidman, in conjunction with Mr Chas N. Kidman, another brother, set up in business there as butchers. The growth of their business has been one of the features of the commercial history of the Barrier. They have now a large establishment in Argent Street, and several smaller ones around the district, and their trade is very extensive. The Kidman Bros afterwards took up a number of mail contracts, which were gradually increased until they now carry mails throughout many parts of the colonies. Some idea of the extent of their operations in this direction may be gathered from the fact that they have had 1,000 horses working on their mail coaches, whilst their yearly income from the government upon these contracts has amounted to £10,000. When the Westralian boom took place they shipped a large number of their best horses to Western Australia, where they established an extensive carrying business under the well-known title of Cobb & Co. They have drawn as much as £12,000 annually from the Westralian Govt. The firm of Cobb & Co. consisted of Messrs Kidman Bros, James Nicholas and J. Day. Before the railway opened this coy had the mail contract between Menzies and Kalgoorlie at £3,300 per year — about the highest-priced contract in Australia. It is an interesting item that they have paid as much as £500 per month for water, and £1,000 per month for horsefeed. The firm do a big trade in cattle with Western Australia, and have a number of butchering establishments in that colony. It is estimated that they ship about 1,000 bullocks every month to the West. To the commercial man, these figures alone would appeal very strongly, but they by no means represent the limit of the operations of Messrs Kidman

Bros. They have large interests in big station properties in N.S.W., S.A. and Q., and breed horses, which are shipped to India and other countries. It is astonishing when one contemplates the enormity of Messrs Kidman Bros' dealings in stock. At times they have as many as 10,000 head on the road at once. They deal in sheep and cattle, with buyers in every colony, and as breeders of prime stock the names of the firm are known throughout Australia.

It may be understood by the foregoing remarks that the life of Mr Sackville Kidman was marked by stupendous energy and enterprise. He was a man who made many friends by reason of his kindly nature and bluff, outspoken manner. On the 10th March last he died, respected and beloved by all who knew him. Long before Broken Hill was known, he had gone to the Barrier, and there were few old residents in those parts who did not know him. For a few years he had worked on Mt Gipps Station, the birthplace of the original B.H. Syndicate, and afterwards at Sturt's Meadows, where his services were alike appreciated. Mr Kidman was at one time in business with his eldest brother at Tintinallegay, on the River Darling, but in '79 he left there to return to Sturt's Meadows. Mr Wallace, the owner of Sturt's Meadows, has been known to remark, "If there was one man in the world to whom I would have given my last drop of heart's blood it was to Sack Kidman. His men say they have not lost a master, but a brother or a father." It will thus be understood how genuine has been the grief felt at the death of Mr Kidman. His widow has been the recipient of expressions of sympathy from numberless friends.

It is said that Sack's death caused antagonism within the family in the who-got-what department. Speaking about it in 1985, Thomas Bray Kidman, of Penola, South Australia, a grandson of Thomas Kidman (Sid's elder brother), said, "Sack Kidman was the brains behind the Kidman Brothers of Broken Hill. It was he who acquired the land-holdings close to Broken Hill so he could always feed the miners. He'd had earlier foresight when the gold rush started in Western Australia. He sent his brother Charlie Kidman and nephew Charlie Kidman (who got the nickname "W. A. Kidman" — he was Tom's second son and Sid's nephew) to start butchershops at Boulder, Kalgoorlie and Coolgardie.

OPPOSITE:
A newspaper advertisement for the Kidman Bros butchershop. (Charles Rasp Memorial Library, Broken Hill)

"What really put the Kidman brothers on their feet was the big mine strikes at Broken Hill in the early days. Hundreds of miners were dying of lead poisoning. They wanted the mines ventilated and kept clean of lead. You only have to look at the Broken Hill cemetery to see how many died.

"Sackville decided to feed the striking miners with meat. He had Charles's [his brother's] backing, but cocky young Sid said, 'Don't feed the bastards.'* Sack replied, 'You're only the drover. Go and get 500 wethers from Corona and when you've done that, I want 200 fat cattle brought in from Momba.' Sidney told everyone that Sackville would go broke. 'I'm only droving them in for him,' he said.

"The strike was the longest in the history of the Hill, but Sackville saw it out. He even cut the meat up himself and made sure that the striking miners with big families got their fair share. That's where my father, Tom Kidman (Sid and Sack's nephew), came into it. He was 16 years of age and killing eighty sheep a day plus four bullocks and delivering them to the shop in Argent Street before the flies got around in the morning.

"After the strike, of course, the Kidmans had all the trade at the Hill.

"The day Sack died, Broken Hill stopped. The men walked off the mines to attend his funeral and wives (women did not attend funerals in those days) cried openly in front of the Kidman Brothers' butchershop in Argent Street.

"The Kidman brothers broke up the business when Sack died, and there was a hell of a row over Sack's estate between Sid and his brother Tom, who were executors of Sack's will. [This is incorrect. Sid was not an executor.] Sid really got his start proper out of Sack's estate. He got a couple of stations for next door to nothing from Sack's boys before Tom turned up, although Sid looked after Sack's sons later on, giving them responsible jobs in his pastoral business."

When things were squared up, Anne Matilda Kidman received the butchering business in Broken Hill, which her sons ran for her. Sidney retained most, if not all the properties — perhaps cutting in his sister-in-law and nephews with shares. What the youngest brother, Charlie Kidman, got is less certain. It is highly likely that he asked for money outright and perhaps settled for a few shares in stations here and there. Unquestionably Charlie Kidman was having a top time in Western Australia handling the coaching business with Jimmy Nicholas. They became horse-racing partners — an expensive habit into which Charlie Kidman plunged with gusto. He was also a

---

*I have accepted the comments of Mr Thomas Bray Kidman for this chapter but reject any suggestion that Sid Kidman used the word "bastards" in conversation. It may have been "tinkers" or "beggars" but it would not have been "bastards".

heavy gambler. Sid Kidman went on to incorporate as many of the family as possible into jobs within the company whenever the opportunity arose. But when Nicholas finally bought out Kidman from the coaching interests in Western Australia and Charlie returned east, Sid was wary of any further involvement with him in business. The young brother and formerly forceful young partner remained very much on the fringe of Kidman operations. He was less an asset than he was a nuisance factor, and Sid accommodated him with smaller responsibilities where there was least chance of his botching them.

It has been said that Sid's "disgust was great in 1900 when he found he had to start an office". Until then he is alleged to have kept every detail of his far-flung business either in his head or in his little black book and the pressure of business outgrew the little black book. It's rubbish. Kidman was forced to open an office in 1900 because, until 1899, his brother Sackville had run the entire show and plotted and guided the brothers' destiny. Sid then took over. If he was compelled to set up an office, he didn't see why it should have to be in Broken Hill. A room in the big, new mansion he was about to buy at Kapunda would suffice and would save money. Who would he get to run it? he asked his wife. She suggested Andrew Thomson, the now retired Kapunda businessman who had urged her mother to migrate to Australia. Kidman agreed, and, if Thomson needed extra help, there was always his wife's stepbrother, Wally Will.

One can ask: Had it been Sid Kidman who died in 1899, what would the obituaries have said? There is strong evidence to suggest they would not have been as glowing. This is largely because it was Sackville Kidman who was dominant in the partnership and responsible for the steps that led to business prosperity.

Curiously, again, for the brother to whom he was closest and owed so much, Sid Kidman did not find a few spare pounds to put up a headstone on his grave. Just as Sid didn't worry about his father, George, at Woodforde cemetery, he didn't worry about brother Sack, who still lies in an unmarked grave at Broken Hill.

8
Depression and Acquisition

THE WORLD HAD SLIPPED into a catastrophic business spiral in the early 1890s, with Europe and the United States tormented by what could only be termed a major depression. In the United States decades of lusty expansion were devastated by financial hurricanes. Businesses formerly prosperous went into the red; factories shut down; bankruptcies multiplied; wages were cut; workers by the millions lost their jobs and those with jobs faced the recurring nightmare of unemployment.

Australia, so dependent on the export market and with investment so largely dependent on British investors, could not continue to be unaffected by world trends. The long-continued expansion of the 1870s and 1880s had been based mainly on over-optimistic borrowing, both government and private, from British investors. For some years export prices had been waning, but, because of the development of new export industries (among them frozen beef and mutton) and the increase in total exports, Australia had been able to stave off the effects. Up until 1889, in spite of falling prices, heavy investment in land and building continued. At the beginning of 1889 the total advances of the Melbourne banks and finance companies alone amounted to £113 million. And in Melbourne, speculation was such that some central city real estate prices soared to levels higher than any reached again for almost fifty years.

In 1889, in view of the possible withdrawal of large British deposits, banks began calling up loans — particularly on pastoral properties. Many of the loans, secured on properties at a time of higher export prices, exceeded the current value of the properties themselves. As prices for wool, wheat and beef continued to fall, foreclosures and bankruptcies snowballed into financial panic. In 1893 most banks in Australia suspended payment and were reconstructed; many failed completely. People by the tens of thousands lost their life savings and their jobs. Many pastoralists found themselves unable to meet the demands made upon them.

Like generals whose supreme tactical opportunity comes when the battle is going badly, Sack and Sid Kidman had to wait for a time of financial and business disaster to come into their own as prominent pastoral holders. They had their "three rivers" and chain-of-supply stations worked out — the only thing holding them back was money. Sid, champing at the bit and wanting to make an earlier bolt, had been reined back by the more cautious Sack. Now, with the crash, people going under and banks wanting to off-load properties, they were there to be picked up at extremely cheap prices. The eastern states seemed to be riddled with pastoral properties in such predicaments, but the Kidman brothers ignored them all, no matter how tempting the bargain, unless they were of strategic importance to their overall plan.

Initially there was nothing — or little — in the way of comment as the Kidman brothers bought up their far-flung and isolated patches of land. But as they continued to acquire when others were forced to toss in the towel, resentment started to smoulder. Criticism came not from the "little" people of the outback, to whom the Kidman brothers were well known as fair dealers and employers who were willing to give a job to a good, capable man. It sparked in city circles, emanating from pastoralists over cap-in-hand discussions with bankers, chiefly in Sydney, among people whose western New South Wales holdings did not interest the Kidmans at all at that stage. They were men who'd controlled large stations, opting for a high standard of living and lavish hospitality, and who were often absentee landlords. They were guilty of overstocking, allowing rabbit infestations to go unchecked — the type who whipped around the bush driving spanking four-in-hands. They were well aware of the droving–dealing duo, and it seemed little short of preposterous that they were down and out or forced into lesser circumstances while the Kidman brothers were on the up-and-up and doing well. It didn't take long for the message to be put about that the Kidmans were "rising to better things through the misfortunes of others". An element of intrigue crept in. The Kidmans also didn't appear to be running the land in the accepted fashion. What they were doing smacked of straight-out stock dealing rather than the traditional methods of pastoralism. Perhaps they would be only flashes in the financial pan and go under themselves. The talk built up as the Kidmans continued to buy up.

In the troubled years of the 1890s, it was the bank Johnnies who held the trump cards, and they were more than happy to deal with the brothers. Within the banking fraternity it was agreed that the chief business was lending money, but perhaps they'd steeped themselves too heavily in pastoral matters and gone overboard where the bush was concerned (believing no doubt that the bubble would never burst) and now they wanted out. They sought to relieve themselves of properties at a time when the Kidman brothers offered themselves as likely buyers.

Speculation about their activities didn't worry Sack or Sid. They played the game very close. There is no record of their outlining their three rivers, chain-of-supply scheme to anyone. Trusted and competent drovers were recruited increasingly. The older and wiser among them perhaps had more than an inkling of what the Kidmans were setting out to do, but they were tight-lipped men who kept their opinions to themselves. Certainly the press caught up with them when they delivered stock to cities or major country towns, with pencils ready to flash vigorously over notebooks for reports of death or drama on long droves. More often than not they went away disappointed, construing the Kidman drovers an unnewsworthy lot. Their trips rarely resulted in stock losses of any note or adventurous dealings with the blacks, mainly because they were so competent, and journalists, seeing no hope of being able to dash off a story of some outback derring-do for their readers, resorted to small, if not dreary, reports of the country through which they'd travelled, and grass and water conditions. The drovers, when interviewed, confronted the same few predictable questions. It would seem that not a single press man ever asked them about the buying pattern of the Kidman brothers and what it represented. Many would have replied in any case, "Don't ask me. I just work for them." Had the question been put and but a few answered, "There's more to this than meets the eye. You mark my words, sonny Jim," an agile-thinking press man or two would have been on the Kidman doorstep at Broken Hill or Kapunda asking them to expound on their business operations and intentions. It doesn't seem to have happened. There is not a single piece of press publicity with even a mention of the Kidmans' plan to link backblocks. On the other hand, the question could have been put and either avoided or dismissed by Sack and Sid as being irrelevant or unimportant. In any event, there was no public airing of what they hoped to achieve or the grand plan they had in mind. Where they were buying up, they were going in as second and sometimes third owners, and the places in question could hardly be said to be in tip-top condition, as a result of overstocking and the dark, evil stain that was spreading throughout the country — the rabbit.

Five rabbits arrived with the First Fleet in 1788, probably Silver Greys, the tame, domesticated variety. Three belonged to the governor and two to the officers and men of the detachment. The lot found their way into the pot. Rabbits were further introduced to Sydney, Tasmania, islands about Bass Strait (as food for the benefit of stranded seafarers) and Melbourne. In 1884 Rabbit Island, off Wilson's Promontory, was abounding in rabbits, which afforded good sport and fresh meat to the whalers. In 1846 the *Port Phillip Patriot* reported that "numerous rabbits which have from time immemorial escaped from the hutches and clutches of the vendors in the market place, have taken refuge under the police office!"

At first, natural barriers confined the rabbits around Sydney and Melbourne: walls of forest hemmed them in; there were no suitable feeding areas; and carnivorous animals, native cats and dingoes, and carnivorous birds also threatened them. With no expanse of open land in which to spread, the rabbit could do little harm. But it got an opportunity when the clipper *Lightning* arrived in Hobson's Bay with twenty-four wild rabbits consigned to Thomas Austin, of Barwon Park, near Geelong. They were delivered within a few days and Mr Austin released them on Christmas Day in 1859 — without question the worst Christmas present Australia has ever received. They prospered in a way that first pleased, then amazed, then worried people. Within six years Austin had killed no less than 20,000 rabbits on his estate and estimated his remaining stock to be 10,000. Here at last was a breed that could thrive and multiply on a scale that no predator, man included, could hope to contain by means then known.

By 1878 his wild rabbits had spread north and west, invading South Australia and New South Wales, and by 1886, taking pastoralists by storm, had reached the Warrego and crossed into Queensland. By 1895 they'd arrived in Western Australia, successfully crossing 1,500 miles of Nullarbor Plain, much of which was waterless. By the turn of the century rabbits were devastating pastures across the country.

There was a pattern to the rabbit invasion. If fodder was sparse, it ate the lot. If it was plentiful and of good variety, it selected the best. The female rabbit had an uncanny knowledge of the plants richest in vitamins, which promoted not only her own health but produced large crops of young. Soon the heart was eaten out of the pastures with only poorer kinds of grass, herbage and weeds left for stock. Although land appeared to be covered with food plants of a sort, its value had decreased. It was possible to run only one sheep where, with the best of fodder plants, four could have been run with safety. The rabbit blasted the face of the land to such an extent that, with the advent of even an ordinary dry season, the country reached advanced drought stage almost immediately. Small wonder the rabbit was termed "the drought before the drought", or "the living drought".

The Kidmans must have taken the impact of the rabbit into consideration when devising their master plan. Their stock would be competing against the rabbit; then again, so would everyone else's. Sid, the more travelled brother of the two, had seen plagues before — mouse, rat and owl plagues. Often they disappeared as quickly as they'd sprung up, although this certainly wasn't the case with the rabbit. He'd noted with dismay how they ate the saltbush down to the very roots. He'd seen them dead 6 feet up trees, after a last ditch stand for survival while trying to get a little bit of herbage. Drought and dry times knocked them back a pace. The infestations weren't quite as bad far out, and perhaps improved rabbit-proof fencing might arrest their advance. He didn't know, but the only good rabbit was a dead rabbit, and when his daughters had asked for some "dear little rabbits" at Kapunda he'd belted the metal fly-swatter on the table in such exasperation as to take a chunk out of it. They could have some dear little ponies instead.

Rabbits, rumour and encroaching dry times notwithstanding, Sack and Sid started acquiring places. Cowarie in South Australia had come first, then Owen Springs in the Northern Territory in 1896. The same year they made a bid for Annandale, the most remote station in Queensland. They paid £5,000 for it and later consolidated it into a holding of 2,574 square miles. Its southern edge was the South Australian border; its western, the Northern Territory border. It had an extensive frontage on the Georgina River as well as two floodwater lakes that became immense patches of good feed when the water subsided. It was stocked with almost 5,000 cattle and hundreds of horses. The sale of the stock alone, despite the depressed prices of the 1890s, would have paid for Annandale, a dry slab of land that had been acquired cheaply. But with stock prices so low it is unlikely that the brothers sold off cattle at a time when fat cattle were fetching less than £1 a head and sheep as little as sixpence a head. Records show that cattle numbers on Annandale had doubled three years later.

Prices had improved somewhat by 1897 and the extent of the Kidman brothers' operations became apparent when just one drover, D. J. (Jim) Ronan, bought £44,000 worth of cattle on their account mainly in south-west Queensland; the highest price paid was £3.7.6 a head for 1,000 bullocks from Brighton Downs. Regardless of what may have been said in the cities, wherever Ronan travelled with a Kidman cheque book he was a very welcome man. Indeed Kidman presented a ray of hope in the economic gloom — his cheques were never dishonoured.

Ronan was instructed to "work the system" and recalled years later, "It meant travelling from Birdsville to Winton, Thargomindah to Camooweal and detouring to inspect cattle on the road, sometimes standing the horses up to 70 or 80 mile stages to meet mailmen with telegrams. They were sent 'collect' to John Barker in Adelaide, who was always in touch with Kidman. Some of the wires cost pounds and not shillings to dispatch, but I was always told to wire and not to write."

In 1897 they acquired Tickalara in south-west Queensland and almost on the New South Wales border. The 700 square mile holding was a smaller but strategic property where stock coming down from Queensland could be spelled before moving on into New South Wales and the Broken Hill market. In 1899 Sack Kidman listed Tickalara as having 22,000 sheep, 600 cattle and 600 horses. In South Australia, Haddon Downs and Pandi Pandi (313 square miles close to the South Australian border and directly south of Birdsville) and The Clayton (186 square miles and not far from Hergott Springs, later called Marree) were bought. In Queensland they acquired Kaliduwarry (800 square miles in the south-west and bordering on Dubbo Downs). They also bought Caryapundy, 326 square miles in the north-west of New South Wales, from Arthur Bartlett (related to Sack Kidman's wife, formerly Anne Matilda Bartlett) and moved Arthur on to Annandale to act as manager. In 1899 in South Australia they took up Mount Nor' West (800 square miles and to the west of Farina) and arranged to buy Dubbo Downs from the Union Bank of Australia Ltd for £2,100.

Dubbo Downs (886 square miles) was on the Georgina River in south-west Queensland, touching on two other holdings, Annandale and Kaliduwarry. Sack Kidman didn't live to see this transaction completed, as he died in March 1899. Dubbo Downs was transferred to Sack and Sid in 1902 from the Union Bank, and the interest of Sackville's executors, Thomas Kidman (his elder brother) and Phillip Jonas, was transferred to Sidney Kidman on 23 June 1903. On the same date the executors also transferred Sack's interest in Annandale to Sid.

Operating on his own in 1899, Sid Kidman took up 2,096 square miles of country in the north of South Australia adjoining the Northern Territory border. He stocked it with horses from Owen Springs and called it Eringa. Aside from the small holding of Thule (the 71 square miles that had been his first acquisition on his own in 1887), Eringa was the first big place he took up on his own and not in a partnership with Sack. It was of such significance to him that he named his house at Kapunda Eringa and later, when he moved from Kapunda to Adelaide, also named the new house there Eringa. But it was not to be one of his outstanding properties; it was closed down at least twice through drought and bad times while he held it. Perhaps the name Eringa became a close and constant reminder that he would always have to live with drought.

Moving in with a new partnership involving Western Australian station agent Isadore Emanuel, of Perth, and Alexander Troupe, a Sydney pastoralist, Kidman made arrangements in 1899 also to acquire Austral Downs, almost 800 square miles of country on the Herbert River in the Northern Territory. The property had its eastern boundary on the Northern Territory border. As the century drew to a close, Sid Kidman owned, controlled or had an interest in nearly 11,000 square miles of country.

Speculation about Sack and Sid's activities had increased in 1898 with the death of the noted pastoralist Jim "Hungry" Tyson, or "Hungry" Jim Tyson, another big landholder with interests in three states, and it increased further in 1899 after the unexpected death of Sackville Kidman. How would Sid Kidman go solo? No one had to wait very long to find out. The 42-year-old man, obliged to wait on the sidelines for so long, had been given the nod; he'd picked up the pastoral ball and was running strongly with it. A newcomer to the big game, he'd found form surprisingly well. On the opposing team, Mother Nature was about to bring him to the ground with a head-high tackle from her most intrepid front-row forward — Drought.

Thrown entirely on his own resources Sid Kidman continued to buy. Carcoory, 1,000 square miles on Listore Creek in south-west Queensland's Channel Country, was next. It adjoined Annandale, which touched on both Kaliduwarry and Dubbo Downs. It was 60 miles north of Birdsville and between the Diamantina and Georgina rivers. If both were to flood, stock would fatten well on Carcoory, but at the time of purchase (and Kidman paid Ronald McGregor £5,500 for the place) the waterholes were dangerously low. To avoid wasting extra money on managerial wages, Sid asked Arthur Bartlett, the manager of Annandale, to take Carcoory under his wing as well.

Money had to be found to finance the increasing purchases. Sid's buying pattern was to put down a deposit and then make an immediate start to pay off the balance by the mustering and sale of fat cattle on the new place. Profits from the sale of mobs of cattle and horses on other stations financed the remainder, as well as the results of standard stock dealing, by which Kidman would buy mobs of stock in the backblocks and then, confident he could make a quick profit on them, scramble to the nearest telegraph station and sell them over the wires, registering healthy gains that often stretched to thousands of pounds.

In this respect Sid was not a typical large pastoral owner and landholder. He did not live on one of his properties, and he did not live in a capital city directing his affairs from a large office. A small business office was run by Andrew Thomson in one of the rooms at Sid's home, Eringa, at Kapunda. Kidman was absent more than he was present, but he took no back-seat position in the running of his business; his was rather a backside view. The backside was generally in the saddle, somewhere in the Australian outback, buying, selling or delegating drovers or droving himself. No one knew where he'd bob up next, brandishing a cheque book, investigating conditions and checking with his men rather than on them. Had he had to check on them, he would not have given them jobs in the first place. He enjoyed the camp camaraderie, the swag, tucker and spirit around the fire and felt completely at ease with his men, black and white alike; where his men were concerned, the feeling was mutual.

His stockmen, drovers and recently appointed managers were not readers of daily newspapers. But the bush telegraph had its own special way of conveying news. The same Sid who'd worked with them or alongside them in the bush for a number of years had fallen on good times. It didn't seem to have changed him though. He wasn't bunging on any airs and graces — he was still slogging it out in the bush with the rest of them, and his sense of humour hadn't left him. In his early forties, Kidman was a big, tall fellow, sporting a moustache and thick, brown beard; the remainder of his swarthy face and arms were dark tanned. In anyone's book he was a good-looking cove. Stories were put around in later years that there was "a touch of boong" in Sid or "a whack of the tar brush" somewhere within the family. The "boong" accusations are definitely untrue. Some more remote members of the Kidman family allude to an earlier member of the family taking up with a Portuguese courtesan at the time of the Peninsular Wars in the early 1800s, but it can hardly be said to have affected Sid Kidman, whose grandfather George Kidman married the English widow Sarah Coules, née Sarah Whitehead. Their only son, George Kidman (Sid's father), was born in 1819 in England and married an Englishwoman. The "boong" story, perhaps sparked by Sid's great swarthiness, was given a helping hand by his lifestyle. It was acknowledged that he could "find his way around the bush like a blackfella", that he could "live off the land like a blackfella", that he was happier "sleeping blackfella-style around a campfire than dossing down in beds".

As his fortune improved he made no attempt to alter his lifestyle, which for the most part saw him away from home for long spells at a time and working on his own or with his men. If eyebrows were raised in the cities because of the irregularity of his way of life (which certainly wouldn't have bothered Sid), he found an esteem in the bush among his employees. Despite newfound wealth he remained the same homespun, hard-working Sid, seeking no special status, affable, amiable and expert enough to turn his hand to any job required in a camp — even camp cook, which happened on several occasions in camps other than his own. Sid could knock out a brownie, damper or Johnny cake with the best of them.

Men of his vintage, and those older who had worked with him for ten or twenty years either stock droving or dealing, were happy for his success: the bright young kid who'd made good and who in middle age showed no signs of altering on the strength of it. One wonders just how far he might have gone had newfound wealth brought about a change in his character — a dictatorial Sid issuing orders in an imperial way and distancing himself from his men? For the bush has always had its own way of dealing with tall poppies, and Kidman certainly would have been aware of this. Perhaps the frank boss-and-worker relationship was carefully cultivated and maintained on his part; if so, it shows an additional insight and cunning.

The big-scale enterprise towards which he was working depended not only on his "three rivers" and his "back corridor", but also on seasoned hands and men expert at shifting stock. He couldn't hope to do it all on his own, and any droving mistakes in dry times would be costly, so an integral part of his plan was employing men of the best skill and calibre. He knew the men he wanted, and although several of them had come across to him in 1898 when Hungry Jim Tyson had died, he'd be needing a lot more. So there was an extra point to his campfire yarning, when he was always on the alert for any likely new or younger fellows who showed potential. Sid was willing to give them a go. They could always take their talent and labour elsewhere — so there was no point in getting them offside. Kidman did make one thing clear — that there was no room in his outfit for anyone who was slovenly, sloppy or careless in their work.

Where the men were concerned it was apparent that Kidman wasn't running just any sort of show, but rather one where only top-notch hands had a look in; among those who qualified were drunks, lechers, those who had had brushes with the law and those who for one reason or another had changed their names. There were some who were intolerant of blacks, who were wantonly cruel to animals or who had foul mouths. But Kidman, while not admiring these things, couldn't afford to be choosy. "Men of saintly dispositions who were hopeless with stock would have been as useful to Kidman as a sore arse to a boundary rider or as good as tits on a boar pig," a former Kidman employee said. It should also be remembered they would have proved equally useless to anyone else wanting good stockhands. Kidman sought the man who was a cut above the rest; the man who, faced with a difficult situation, a challenge, an unexpected spot of bother, would think and tackle his way out of it — a man with a bit of extra heart — and guts. Men who delivered the goods. Incentives could help. Kidman had thought about that too: shares perhaps for station managers who worked for him and who made places pay; bonuses for drovers who could deliver exact numbers on time and despite long, dry stages. As the century drew to a close, the employment of his men, particularly those men who would be closest to him in the running of the operation, remained an important factor on his mind.

Sackville's death the year before had been a bitter blow; likewise the death of his infant son, Norman, the year before that. Now in 1900 he was blessed with another son, little Walter. Sid was 43 years old. What if he was to die unexpectedly as Sack had? He certainly didn't count on it, but nor had Sack. If Walter survived, and Kidman prayed he would, he'd need twenty-five years up his sleeve before he came good, whether Sid was alive or not. Sid's wife knew of his grand plans and had encouraged him openly to take them as far as he could. If he died suddenly, he could hardly expect Bel to hang onto the reins for twenty-five years. She'd have a go — it was in her nature. He reflected that she wouldn't make too bad a fist of it. But she wouldn't be able to handle things without the help of the experienced men Kidman was trying to weave into a fabric about him and so neatly that they would want to stay.

He'd seen Bel with her nose over her nice tapestries. They started off in little bits and ended up as big, fine pictures. All the stitching, she told him, had to be as neat underneath as it was on the top. Why worry, Kidman thought? Once the thing was dumped in a picture frame or made into a cushion cover or chair panel, you didn't see the underneath so it didn't matter. If the sewing on the top was right it still made a good picture. It is the way, perhaps, in which he saw his emerging pastoral empire — as a growing picture with the men providing the stitches. The more correct stitches, the better, but any crook needlework that crept into the back stalls didn't really count. Bel had said that a judge at a show wouldn't pass any tatting that shaped up that way. But Kidman had no intention of setting himself up as a judge where his "stitches" were concerned. That was something for a higher authority. Just as long as the stitching was right on the side that showed would be all that mattered to him. The other side of his men's lives was never important to him, just as long as it didn't interfere with the top side, the job side that produced the right result: just as long as the under side stayed under and the right side showed.

It must be said that a great number of people who worked for Kidman over the years made fine stitches in the pastoral tapestry; totally neat on both sides. It was these people who earned his lasting affection, especially the families who moved to remote frontiers in his employ, initially few of them, but later on many. On any inspection or droving trip he would linger longer in their homes, perhaps as a mark of respect to the women and invariably drawing a comparison between them and Bel. Bel was canny, competent — even tough, he supposed — and had things turned out differently would she have been able to stand life in the bush or cope as well as these women did? They could turn their hand to stock work as well as carving a home out of nothing, raising and educating children and enduring, enduring and enduring lives of hardship that would make their city sisters swoon. He didn't know whether Bel would be able to take it and it was never put to the test. But he doubted it.

He would, forever, whip his hat smartly off his head as a mark of respect to a good bush woman. He never, at any stage, considered the men who worked for him as "heroes" yet considered their wives and mothers in a heroine class all of their own. The meals he enjoyed around their outback tables — plain, straight, humble fare — would please him more than a handsome spread in a town or city hotel dining room. After tea the women were always asked to join him and the men in a few hands of cards, a simple pursuit at which he still loved to win, but he was a jovial loser when trumped by a drover or manager's wife.

It should be said that, where bush women were concerned, the feeling was not always mutual. There were limits to endurance and battling the odds. Small hand-made coffins were lowered with sad regularity into never-settling graves of sand. Plants and cuttings were carefully nurtured on long treks for the highly prized little garden that added both a softening and productive touch to the raw outback — gardens that flourished one year to wither the next or be lost under a drift of sand. The women blamed Kidman for it because they went with their men, and Kidman elected where the men should go.

From 1895 Sid and Sack had started employing people as the big pastoral plan began to evolve. Over a span of forty years, Sid would go on to employ thousands. There are no records to show what thoughts ever cruised through his mind at the earliest relating to boss–worker relations, whether, as has been said, he was as "cunning as a shit-house rat" in deliberately cultivating and maintaining a happy set-up in the bush with his amiable and knockabout presence or whether, as his good fortune took off, his simple nature saw no reason for change, seeking to roll along with the venture, still steeping himself as much as possible in the work and the way of life he loved. Perhaps the truth lies somewhere in between. Certainly his attitude from the beginning towards those who worked for him created something very special.

Mutual benefits ensued. Those who worked for him counted it as a badge of honour, and it would be said later, and repeated and repeated, that you were "entitled to walk tall if you worked for Sid" and that "a Kidman stockman was a Vesteys manager".

Longtime bushman–businessman R. M. Williams said in 1984, "Kidman carefully created his own position and tradition. The secret of his success lay in the selection of men who worked for him."

Jim Vickery, who in 1984 was the chairman of the South Australian Pastoral Board and director of Outback Management, commented, "A mysterious attitude existed among Kidman employees. It was not just loyalty but a savage loyalty that was not found anywhere else in any other pastoral companies. Employees couldn't have cared less working for other big concerns such as the Peel River Land and Mineral Co., Vesteys, Angliss, Beltana Pastoral

Co., Elsinora Pty Ltd, the Scottish Australian Co., and Australian Estates. They all owned strings of properties employing significant numbers of people yet never enjoyed the intense loyalty displayed by employees as did Kidman. Why it existed was never fully understood but it pervaded the entire Kidman organisation and men took an intense and lasting pride in being labelled as 'a Kidman man'."

Kidman business activity in Western Australia (the coaching business, the string of butchershops to accommodate the goldminers, and shipments of stock from the east to the west to provide the meat) had drawn Sid into contact with Forrest and Emanuel, an alliance of solid Western Australian and wealthy Jewish families with pastoral operations in the West Kimberleys and offices in Fremantle, where the company acted as Kidman's Western Australian agent. Kidman had already gone into partnership earlier in 1899 with Isadore Emanuel in Austral Downs on the Northern Territory and Queensland border, and no sooner had the partnership been formed than Emanuel contacted Kidman again.

Goldsbrough Mort wanted to off-load Victoria River Downs, said to be the largest pastoral property in the world. It was the size of Denmark and, with its subsidiary station, Carlton Hill, added, it represented 12,500 square miles of well-watered land, albeit in rough, wild country about 400 miles south of Darwin. Forrest and Emanuel's rivals, Connor, Doherty and Durack in the East Kimberley, were also interested in acquiring it, to the point that M. P. Durack went to Melbourne to see Goldsbrough Mort principal, J. M. Niall, to clinch the deal quickly.

Durack was informed that the rock-bottom price was £25,000. He offered £22,000 on behalf of his syndicate; £10,000 cash down and the balance payable in six to nine months. Niall finally agreed to the terms, but the C. D. and D. partners had a sudden change of mind and, stalling for time as they contemplated the offer further, proposed payment in four more widely spaced instalments. Haggling went on. Niall could not agree to the C. D. and D. terms and the syndicate could not agree to his. The matter was settled most happily for Goldsbrough Mort a few weeks later when Victoria River Downs was purchased at the higher price of £27,500 by a syndicate including Emanuel, Forrest, Kidman and G. S. Yuill, a director of the Adelaide Steamship Company.

Shares in the partnership were Forrest, Emanuel and Co., (eight-sixteenths), the Kidman brothers (four-sixteenths), G. S. Yuill (two-sixteenths), Robert Richards (one-sixteenth) and B. J. H. Richards (one-sixteenth). The deal was finalised within a few months of Sackville's death with Sid Kidman obviously talking the executors of Sack's estate, Tom Kidman and Phillip Jonas, into helping stake the one-quarter share. Niall again wanted £10,000 down in cash and the balance within six to nine months and Kidman, strapped for cash as a result of buying up so recently elsewhere, was barely able to afford his share.

The Victoria River Downs offer took Kidman by surprise. It had no direct relevance to his cherished chain, but from a trading and dealing point of view he found the property irresistible. There were an estimated 27,000 head of branded cattle on the place and, it had been said, twice that many unbranded. Kidman was taking the word of others on that. Victoria River Downs was one place of which he had no personal knowledge. The furthest he had been that way was to the Barkly Tableland buying stores.

There were aspects of the Victoria River Downs sale he didn't understand — so much land, so many cattle, so much reliable water and all at such a cheap price. On the other hand, the country was as wild as the tribal, cattle-killing Aborigines who menaced the place. The white cattle thieves were having a field day too; to boot, there were no fences. In fact, it was scarcely less dangerous than the Cape Colony, where war had just broken out between the Boers and the British.

When the war broke out in South Africa in 1899, all separate Australian colonies sent contingents; a total of 15,000 Australian volunteers went to fight. Back in Australia 3,750,000 people were steeped in patriotic frenzy. The war would mean a lively kick-along for Australian stock breeders and the new owners of Victoria River Downs had every intention of exploiting it. Western Australia also represented a good local market. By the mid-1890s, as a result of the gold rush activity and sudden influx of people, the west was able to absorb far more cattle than were being produced. That would be handy while it lasted — which wouldn't be forever, Kidman calculated. But if the cattle could be staged back east to markets, then Victoria River Downs would have jolly relevance to his chain of stations and "back corridor". But what a drove. What a trek.

Still, the Duracks had done it, setting out from Goulburn in New South Wales in 1867 to go to Thylungra on Cooper Creek, basing themselves there until 1883 and then moving on across the top to the more reliably pastured and better rainfall country of the Ord. The MacDonalds had done it too, again setting out from Goulburn in 1883 and making their run in one hit via Cooper Creek and Sid's three rivers country across the top to Western Australia, where they pioneered Fossil Downs Station, near the junction of the Fitzroy and Margaret rivers. Nat Buchanan, D'Arcy Uhr and Hughie Farquharson (among others) had moved big mobs across from Queensland to the other side of the country. If stock could be moved in that direction successfully, it ought to work just as well in reverse. The thought preoccupied Kidman. A shorter route would be better, but in twenty-two years no one seemed to have found one. Any direct line from Victoria River Downs back east to his three rivers was out of the question because of the Tanami Desert in the north of the Northern Territory and the Simpson Desert in the south. Kidman wondered about the Simpson (for reasons other than the shifting of Victoria River Downs stock). It was one place where he hadn't had a good poke around. He wondered if there was a way through it. He soon found out — the hard way.

Having supervised a horse muster at Owen Springs in 1900 and seen the men and horses started on their way south, Kidman decided to find out if it was possible to shift stock from the eastern fringes of the MacDonnells, south-east to his expanding chain in south-western Queensland. It would give him an alternative if it could be done. He set out on horseback and didn't get far. The Simpson, he found, was a small but deadly desert. He'd seen some dry country in his time but this took the cake — not a skerrick of water. Not a skerrick of hope. Only a fool would have persevered. He was forced to turn back. The exercise was not wasted. He now knew it was impossible to reach the three rivers from that position in the Centre. Stock from the Territory, with the exception of those on Austral Downs in the north, would have to go south along a secondary chain of stations extending from the Centre into South Australia. The railhead was at Oodnadatta, but the way progress was bowling along it would extend further into Central Australia. A wise man would have a secondary chain of stations planted conveniently around the path of the proposed railway. The sooner he got going on that idea, the better.

In a reflective mood Kidman rode south to Hergott Springs in South Australia, making himself a fine billy of tea from the train engine's boiler before he boarded. The other interesting aspect of the attempted crossing of the Simpson, he mused, would be that if he could take up the entire western area of the Georgina, he would have no neighbours.

He'd be glad to get back to Kapunda to see Bel and the children, and the Victoria River Downs partners had asked him to tee up a new manager for the large and unwieldy place. He'd have to be a top fellow and Kidman had wired Jim Ronan and asked him to meet him in Adelaide. Ronan was an exceptional fellow, and Kidman had taken exception to the way in which they'd first met near Broken Hill in 1886, when drover Ronan camped overnight with a mob of cattle and horses that couldn't resist a paddock of good, sweet herbage. He let the horses in at night to feed and had them out and the fence re-strained before daybreak. Kidman, riding hell for leather and carrying a heavy stockwhip, caught up with him soon after, or rather with his offsider, who was tailing the mob, and demanded an explanation for their trespassing.

"Don't ask me," said the offsider. "You see the boss." Kidman galloped on to Ronan demanding explanation.

"Don't ask me," said Ronan. "You see the boss."

"But that jolly tinker back with the packs said *you* were the boss," Kidman spluttered.

"That bloke," said drover Ronan of his offsider, "is the biggest liar on the Barcoo."

Kidman galloped back to have it out with him and, having got to the strength of the matter, left the offsider with the rejoinder: "If my jolly horse wasn't so blown I'd catch Ronan and use this [the whip] on him. You tell him the next time Sidney Kidman meets him they'll take tea together. They'll certainly take tea together."

That's exactly what they did do ten years later, when Sid and Sack started buying up and needed crack hands. Ronan was summoned to Kapunda, not particularly relishing the occasion. Kidman, upon meeting him, remarked: "You're the jolly tinker with the Welford bullocks who put his horses in my paddock back in '86. I promised you a drink of tea. We'd better go and have it," he added with a slow smile.

Ronan had performed well over the last few years. Using Annandale Station as a base, he had travelled the backblocks of Queensland buying stock for Kidman and consigning it to drovers; more often than not to Pat Kennedy. He could take on Victoria River Downs.

Kidman didn't get to the heart of the matter in a hurry, carting Ronan off to a horse sale at Adelaide's Barker Yards, where he bought two big draught geldings for shipment to the west. Turning to a couple of children, who could always be relied upon to be lurking around such places, Kidman said, "I want a couple of lads to take these horses down to the trucking yards."

"What's it worth, Mr Kidman?" the bigger of the group asked.

"What do you reckon is a fair price?"

"Two bob."

"For the pair?"

"No fear, Mr Kidman! Two bob each."

"Well now, I don't know where I could earn four shillings as easily as that . . ." Australia's emerging cattle king took a halter in each hand and started through the city streets, with Ronan walking with him and relieving him of one horse.

"Well, Jim," Kidman said, "when truanting boys ask two bob a horse for a walk to the railway yards, what would I have to pay you to take charge of Victoria River Downs?"

"Nothing less than 400 quid," Ronan replied. It was a substantial amount of money in 1900, but the job was a substantial one, and Ronan was the man he wanted for it.

"I've never been to the Victoria River area, Jim," Kidman said. "I'll come up and you can pay me to lead your horses around at two bob a time..."

Having the last word, as he had when he plundered Kidman's bit of good feed at Broken Hill in 1886, Ronan replied, "I've always found it's far easier to lose money than it is to make it, Mr Kidman."

9

A Backhander from Drought

IN THE THIRTY YEARS since he had left home, there had rarely been a day in Sidney Kidman's life when water — or the lack of it — hadn't been discussed. It is doubtful that he coined the phrase "There's always a drought somewhere in Australia", but it was one he was to repeat over and over again throughout his life, to the point that it was attributed to him. If he could have been prevailed upon to swear, diatribes of abuse would have been heaped on drought, yet all the swearing in the world wouldn't have helped things or made the dry times go away. In a strange way, drought was something he honoured, as soldiers in a battle might have a healthy respect for the fellow on the other side, or at least respect for the ability of the opponent. Kidman did not underestimate his foe. Had it not been for drought, his life would not have taken the course it did. Dry times had set in from 1895; the dry times, rabbit invasion and financial crashes all lumped together were the reasons he and Sack had been able to buy places so rapidly. It was a funny sort of a battle — drought enabling him to buy up when the one aim in doing so was ultimately to defeat it — a bit of a helping hand from the enemy.

Others had had a gutful and retreated from the fight between 1895 and 1900; in time to come, they would be classified officially as drought years, but Sid didn't see them that way. They were certainly dry times, and in evaluating his three rivers country, he saw dry times as being the normal condition and good seasons, the exception. They hadn't hampered him too much with his stock movements, but he didn't like the way things were shaping up. Stock movements were becoming limited and limitation meant loss.

A bunch of wires from Dick Townshend, Pat Kennedy, Arthur Bartlett, John Brooke, Ted Pratt, Pierce "Barbed Wire" Edwards and his brother Albert "Tie Wire" Edwards had reached Wally Will at the Kapunda office, reporting a very arid state of the country in south-west Queensland. Jim Ronan confirmed things. It was not a time to be dilly-dallying in Kapunda. His job was north with his men, and he made immediate arrangements to leave. Any chain was only as good as its weakest link. Kidman considered the chain he had formed so far to have no weak links — what it did have was thundering great gaps. The chain was by no means complete. He had plans to incorporate many other stations. Time seemed to have run out, at least where this encounter was concerned. Drought was dealing him a backhander when he wasn't quite ready for it, yet he refused to be pessimistic, clinging to his faith in the three rivers. Things couldn't go on the way they were. It had to rain somewhere, sometime, even if no rain fell at any of his eighteen stations. The bulk of his stations were linked to the three rivers, so that if it rained in the north of Queensland, the north-west or the north-east, the rivers would come down. Good rain elsewhere could still save the day. The best course to plot seemed to be to carry on as usual, hoping for that to happen.

He rode through Queensland towards his most northerly holding, Austral Downs, greeted only by hostile silence with the exception of the crows. He'd never seen the country looking as awful. The absence of birds was an omen of things to come. The country at Austral Downs, and even further north at Avon Downs, wasn't quite as bad. The problem to contend with at Avon was isolation. Stock couldn't be moved from the place because of dry times elsewhere. Banking on rain within the coming months, Kidman bought up 1,200 store bullocks (bullocks that would fill out and fatten within a year) at £3.10.0 a head and arranged with drover Joe "Gleeson" to lift them in twelve months and stage them down the Birdsville route to Carcoory, and from there he would have them droved through the South Australian corner to the railhead at Hergott Springs. In reality, Joe "Gleeson" was Joseph Dickson, who, because of either a run-in with the law, domestic or family troubles, had upped stakes in the Aramac area and gone to the more remote area of the Northern Territory to work. His father, John "Old King" Dickson, was a pioneer of the town of Aramac. He was a master baker who soon extended the business to include a butcher's shop and dairy. He was named "Old King" for his ability to put up his "dukes" in a fight.

Kidman arranged to buy 500 bullocks from Warenda, on the Hamilton River, western Queensland, from Elder Smith. Drover Jack Clarke was instructed to take them to Birdsville. Kidman's agent did not meet Clarke there, and a letter instructed him to go to the Andrewilla waterhole. Still there was no sign of Kidman's agent, and the South Australian customs officer demanded payment of £1,000 border duties, which Clarke had no authority to pay. Elder Smith was still the legal owner of the mob, and they were obliged to attend to the matter. Kidman advised that he would not take delivery of the mob unless it was delivered to Hergott Springs. The same letter also advised that in view of the drought it was pointless to come south. It put drover Clarke in a fix. If it was madness to go south, it was equally futile to return. Clarke sent a stockman ahead to look for water. Reliable waterholes were dry, but, finding some brackish water in a creek at the Potato Tin sandhills, he launched the mob off onto a

117 mile dry stage to Cooper Creek. The cattle were spelled at Mungerannie, and, to avoid travelling in the heat, they moved off camp at midnight. Towards midday disaster overtook them.

"The cattle were walking well," Jack Clarke recorded, "when a huge cloud reaching as far as the eye could see appeared in front of us. The bullocks walked quickly and were inclined to break into a run. We steadied and stopped them waiting for our packhorses to catch up.

"I said to Charlie Birkett beside me, 'Reckon that's rain or dust?'

"'I think it's rain,' he answered.

"'If it is we're blessed,' I said. 'If it's dust we're cursed.'

"A cool breeze blew up as if coming off rain. The bullocks had their heads up sniffing. Five minutes later we were smothered in dust. Horses, cattle and all turned their backs to the dust huddled together in a heap. You couldn't see your hand before you. When we looked at our watches we had to put calico around them and strike a match to see what time it was. Three hours later it showed no sign of breaking. We'd hobbled our horses where they stood and dropped the packs at their feet. Some of the packs were never found. They were buried in the sand. About sundown the dust slackened a little so we had to try to get the cattle to move.

"Seventy were smothered. The ones that lay down were smothered too. Then we got them to face the dust. Some would horn others that were struggling and dying. Their eyes were like balls of fire in the dust. They walked well for a couple of miles and then the dust came up as thick as ever and we were wound up in a knot again. We were all knocked up.

"Toward morning, the bullocks got restless. They tried to get away in the opposite direction. Some did get away, but I held what I could. The dust didn't break till the sun rose the next morning. We were then 17 miles from water. We travelled along in the terrible heat dropping the bullocks in little lots. When we came to the water we only had 75 head. The ones that got away had hit the Cooper 10 miles from where we were so I went back and tracked them up. It was hard to see the tracks in the dust. On the claypans between sandhills I managed to locate a few. They were walking, slowly, one behind the other, lost, half-blinded, heads hanging. I found another 30 head — 28 of them were dead in salt water. When we left the Cooper we only had 72 head out of 500."

Clarke, it would be said, was cruelly victimised by fate. Kidman refused to accept the cattle, and Elder Smith lost £4,000 plus the additional £1,000 pledged for customs duty. Sympathy went only one way — and not in Kidman's direction. If Elder Smith refused to pay the £1,000 customs duty, Clarke would be liable. Public opinion held that it was Kidman who'd done the dirty; he wasn't directly responsible for the dust storm, but he'd scraped out of the deal to best advantage. People sorry for Clarke, including fellow drovers and Kidman drovers, had a whip-around and realised £300 to assist him in his time of trouble after such an admirable effort. The money was not needed — and was returned — when Elder Smith met the £1,000 border cost. Quite a few people, hitherto Kidman stalwarts, were very unimpressed by the stand Sid took.

If public opinion reached him, it did not concern him. The gloves were on now and the fight against drought was on in earnest. No rains came, not anywhere, to relieve the south-west Queensland situation. No rivers came down. If remaining stock stayed where they were, they would die. If he attempted to move them, following the brief storms and seeking a spot of feed and staging them towards a market, it was likely they would die anyway. It was better to live in hope and do something than to sit back, do nothing and accept the situation. Managers were instructed to put any stock capable of travelling on the road and told that the wire service would be used to best possible advantage to advise them of rain, water and feed conditions. But what rain, what water, what feed? All news was bad news.

Almost the whole of Australia was affected by this drought, although not, Sid noted, the top end of the Northern Territory where Victoria River Downs, his eighteenth and last pastoral interest, was. The cattle there were as thick as thieves and even the thieves — black and white — working full bore wouldn't make a dint in them. There was no hope now in trying to stage them over with the east as dry as it was. Again, in isolation, Victoria River Downs would have to work out its own salvation in the west, supplying the market there and putting a few bob into the petty-cash tin, which was running low. In fact, it was low enough to start putting off men. Anyone not of vital importance on any of the stations was retained for as long as possible and then paid off, reluctantly, and on the basis that, when better times returned, jobs would be available again.

No one blamed Kidman for it. He'd kept things going and men on the books longer than they'd anticipated. Other pastoral outfits had started tightening up and shedding men well in advance. Still, they operated with a lot more "cream", "cream" that Kidman hadn't carried to date and never intended to. Kidman's was more of a lean concern, and when even the lean scheme of things was threatened, there was little other recourse. Stations were virtually closed down when drought conditions made it impossible for standard stock work

OVERLEAF:
One victim of the turn-of-the-century drought. (Bill Bennett)

to proceed. Sid was under siege with a handful of command troops out on the road with cattle; anything left behind would mean a feast for the crows.

Death was the daily news to hand. Western New South Wales offered no manoeuvrability. Young lambs were herded into pens and clubbed to death so that their mothers might live (bullets were too dear to be wasted). Where water did exist, anywhere, stockmen had the unenviable job of pulling rotting bodies clear in order that weakened stock, nearly on their last legs, might find a drink from the creek or hole, while goannas waddled about the smorgasbord of rotting flesh and bloated crows and kitehawks were barely able to launch themselves from the unlimited dining table to the lower limbs of trees for a brief respite.

Queensland was the worst hit — no rain fell, even on the coast let alone the interior region, to burble off his three rivers. In inland New South Wales, South Australia and Central Australia — the very area of all his properties with the one exception of Victoria River Downs — rainfall was less than 50 per cent of the average, and as far south as Victoria it was only 60 per cent in many parts. In New South Wales there were up to thirty-six successive drought months at numerous stations. The Territory and areas of Western Australia didn't seem to be as greatly affected.

No records exist of the losses sustained by Kidman in the drought years of 1900–1903. But 2,000 Rocklands bullocks put on the road from Carcoory did not find water or feed and every one perished. He sent 1,000 breeding cows towards Pandi Pandi, hoping for water and feed there. Every one perished. The Cowarie stock couldn't be budged. The areas around Broken Hill were bone dry and eaten out, even if he could have shifted stock there. Herds on the track from Annandale, Roseberth, Tickalara, Kaliduwarry, Caryapundy, Dubbo Downs and The Clayton were decimated. And Haddon Downs, Pandi Pandi, Mount Nor' West, Eringa and Austral Downs offered no hope. Kidman sold out his interest in the coaching business in Western Australia to Jimmy Nicholas in order to keep some cash in the till. There are no details to be found of the transaction in which, by now, Kidman had less than a 50 per cent stake. Nicholas held 50 per cent and Kidman's brother Charlie, who'd gone to the west some years before to keep an eye on operations, had a stake in the show as well and was having the time of his life in Western Australia, indulging in racehorse partnerships with Nicholas and kicking up his heels in drinking sprees associated with horse racing.

If Kidman didn't want to antagonise his workers, drovers or managers needlessly, then he didn't want to get on the wrong side of the family either. Charlie was still meant to be looking into and keeping an eye on the string of butchershops set up to look after the goldfields and checking with the agents, Forrest and Emanuel, on the Kidman stock movements. But since the recent Victoria River Downs partnership, Kidman could make a more direct check himself. His brother Charlie wasn't of much help.

If he was to divest himself of the interest in the Western Australian coaching activity, then he figured he could divest himself of Owen Springs, the Northern Territory station acquired initially for the big numbers of horses that could supply the coaches. When it hadn't worked out as a dovetailing operation, Sid had sold the horses off anyway and made a fine profit. In fact his horse profits had counted for a lot. After a final muster and movement of horses off Owen Springs, in 1901 he sold the station to the Willowie Land and Pastoral Association, having held it for five years. Even so, the money received from the two ventures wouldn't last forever, but they would tide him over a bit, and the last thing he wanted to do was to have to sacrifice his south-west Queensland country — any of it — although it was not a bumper of good to him at this stage. He pared off what he had to in order to provide the cash flow to survive.

There wasn't much point in staying with his men. They were spread here and there trying to get stock through. He would learn if they did; he would learn if they didn't. And bad news continued to follow him all the way to the Queensland coast. By then he knew the appalling state of his own properties, and the stickybeak in him wanted to find out just how bad everyone else's were. He rode across Queensland, envious of some of the bigger spreads at Richmond and Hughenden, and caught the train at Longreach for Brisbane. The country certainly changed as he nudged towards the coast. There was no point in envy. These places cost so much more. This wasn't where his life's work was. He could never have afforded a chain of these. Owners insisted these places had taken a belting from the drought. Kidman could only smile and shake his head. They looked like paradise compared with the stricken country of the south-west.

In Brisbane he was to see business friends of Forrest and Emanuel, and some leading men from various banks and pastoral companies. He absorbed Brisbane through the soles of his boots and soaked up the conversation in its streets and major meeting places. There was a lot of talk about nationhood, the war in South Africa, and the need to guard against migrants and coloureds who might threaten the standard of living. Talk of drought seemed to be well down on the list and, when people did mention it, the loss of the whole situation seemed to escape them in the same way that a description of someone else's pain does.

In a hotel dining room he heard the complaining voice of "an old duchess" raised in annoyance at the scandalous price of beef. He put down his eating irons and thrust aside his serviette, intent on giving the old boiler a piece of his lip about how men slaved in the outback and how a thirsting bullock sought water: how a weakened animal, struggling for a drink, caught a hind leg in a tree root, perishing over several days through lack of strength to escape it and ending with its neck stretched out at an unnatural angle and a blackened tongue lolling on the ground just inches away from water, an animal trying to survive only to get to market to accommodate her dinner table. Perhaps that would put her off her feed — and complaints. Goldsbrough Mort's J. M. Niall put out a hand to restrain him: "Don't do it, Kidman. Not worth it. Some people never understand. Why don't you take a trip home by steamer. Surround yourself with water. Forget about things for a bit..." Kidman could think of nothing worse. Water as far as the eye could see and all the wrong type. He might take leave of his senses, like one of his poor bullocks, and jump overboard into it.

"We can't have that," remarked the Bank of New South Wales's Queensland inspector, Mr Halloran. "We value you too much as a customer." Still smarting over the lack of city understanding of the drought problem and losses, he may have overlooked the banking compliment paid him.

His drought losses from 1900 to 1903 were enormous. Ion Idriess put cattle losses at 35,000. It ought to be recalled that Kidman had seventeen stations by then, not counting his interest in Victoria River Downs in non-affected country. He would only have had to have lost an average of 2,000 head from each place to have clocked up the loss. That estimate is far too low. Cattle men have since put the losses at twice that number — cattle that were stranded and left to die on various stations or that died on the way to markets.

The reduced numbers of cattle, Kidman's and everyone else's, that did find their way to markets naturally fetched a high price. If Jim Ronan had bought £44,000 worth of cattle for Kidman in 1897 (when a good bullock fetched just on £4), it is reasonable to assume that cattle in the 1901 to 1903 drought times fetched twice as much at city markets, or perhaps more. If Kidman did lose 70,000 head of stock over three years as a result of the drought, then it meant a financial loss of somewhere between £500,000 and £700,000. It was a monstrous sum in those days.

Earlier writers dealing with Kidman's life have suggested that the turn-of-the-century drought "sent him bust" and at one stage left him "without a shilling in the world", which amounts to a very loose handling of the facts. For that to have been a reality every station he owned or had an interest in would have had to have slipped through his fingers. And that did not happen.

He allowed only Owen Springs to go, which left him with a string of seventeen stations, most of which had taken a severe battering but remained intact. Owen Springs had served its purpose, repaying him with particularly good profits from the sale of horses. Just before Kidman off-loaded it in 1901, he held a final horse muster in which any suitable stamp of a horse was rounded up and headed south to Kapunda, which he then described as his "home town", although he rarely lived there for any length of time. The horses provided the nucleus of the first Kapunda horse sales, held in 1900, at which 350 went under the hammer. No records show the prices they fetched, but if they averaged £10, or higher, in drought times, then they accounted for a handy spot of cash up his sleeve at a time when he needed it most. Unquestionably the sale was a tremendous success; had it not been, he would have ditched the idea. But the initial Kapunda horse sale became the first annual Kapunda horse sale. The horse sales ran for thirty-six years, growing to the point where not hundreds but thousands of Kidman station horses were sold each year to an invasion of local, state, interstate and overseas buyers. The Kapunda horse sales were the biggest ever to be staged, not only in Australia but in the Southern Hemisphere. Establishing them was a shrewd move on Kidman's part, giving him an extra string to his financial bow at a time when things were grim with cattle, at least in the eastern states. In the north-west, at Victoria River Downs, manager Jim Ronan shipped 13,000 head of stock in four seasons, from 1900, when he was appointed by Kidman, to 1903. Given that they may have fetched £10 a head and that Kidman was a four-sixteenths shareholder at that stage, the money coming in from Victoria River Downs was a salve to the drought sores in the east. They were worsening considerably in 1900, but if the year had one bright note it could be said to have been on 26 June when Bel gave birth to their second son, Walter. Their first son, Norman, had died in 1898 aged 16 months. Three years before that their fourth daughter, Edith, had died aged 2 years and 10 months. Sid Kidman was jubilant at the birth of his second son, and he spent an increasing amount of time at home out of concern for Bel and the boy, and coming to grips with how quickly his three eldest daughters had grown up: Gertie was 14, Elma, 13 and Edna, 10.

The house at Bald Hill that Kidman had initially secured as the family home was quite a notable house in anyone's book. (One hundred years after he had moved into it, in 1985, it was still standing at Kapunda, a fine but isolated house on a hill with stables that were added later, in disrepair and with the big tract of land around it sprinkled with subdivision and For Sale signs.) As a salute to his family, and to Bel in particular for the help she afforded him and for tolerating his long absences, as a gesture to show his delight at the birth of Walter and perhaps as a compensating measure for the death of two other children, Sid decided that his growing family should have a bigger and better home.

At a time when others allege he was penniless he made a move to buy the biggest, grandest home Kapunda had to offer, and the town was not short on prestigious houses. Lanark House was built originally by Alexander Harvey Greenshields in 1879 at a cost of over £4,000. Greenshields, a native of Lanarkshire, Scotland, went to Kapunda in 1864 under engagement to Messrs Scobie and Thomson, large general storekeepers, one of whom was Andrew Thomson, a relative of Bel Kidman's mother. Greenshields stayed with the company for a while and then, in 1869, felt enterprising enough to break away on his own. He started up a drapery business, which was said to be the largest of its kind out of Adelaide. Ten years later he built Lanark House and, as the *Kapunda Herald* noted at the time, "a pound was not withheld by Mr Greenshields where it would add to the beauty or accommodation and the residence was regarded by those acquainted with its interior as one of the most convenient and comfortable homes in the northern districts". The grounds could only be described as magnificent. There was a principal conservatory and lesser conservatories catering for more than 5,000 potted plants, stables, sheds, ferneries, nursery gardens, kitchen gardens, an orchard, a rosery, shade houses, immaculate driveways and flower beds. The *Kapunda Herald*, waxing lyrical one year on a garden tour, commented: "The plants and gardens form one of the finest private collections in South Australia with popular and rare flowers of every shade and colour forming a thing of beauty which once seen is indeed a joy forever. Some chrysanthemums brought into the house for decorative purposes and on account of their special excellence, at once attract notice. A plant of Grandiflora, a rich ball of yellow, had fifteen blooms each measuring upwards of 1 foot in circumference; Madam Christine (pink) had flowers an inch or two bigger." The house itself had exterior stone walls 2 feet thick, more than twenty rooms, servants' quarters and two main entrances with magnificent hallways, one with a domed skylight.

Like her fellow Scot, Bel was a great garden lover. Kidman could think of no finer gift for her. It would suit him too, he supposed. With so many rooms in the place, one could become his office and save him a few bob and the bother of acquiring premises in Main Street, Kapunda. Also Lanark House and its extensive gardens occupied only part of a large area of land. Bel wouldn't grizzle, he figured, if the rest was turned into horse paddocks for his Kapunda sales.

In 1902 when drought was tearing away at his little pastoral empire, Sid felt confident enough to set up as a king in his own little Kapunda castle. The exact price he paid for Lanark House is not known, but it was more than £8,000, twice the amount it had cost Greenshields to build it twenty-six years earlier. Not content with buying it, Sid gave Bel her head to redecorate. She did so with great gusto. Bathrooms were torn out and refurbished with the most up-to-date fittings and £300 was spent on the installation of an acetylene gas system. To boot, there were gardeners, stablehands, and household help to assist Bel with the children and the cooking. It all spelt extra wages. The fact remains that if Kidman had been financially reduced he would not have entered into such a grandiose domestic buying spree, and the house at Bald Hill would have catered for the family needs for some time to come.

Sid squared up for the place in 1902; the family moved in, and he moved off on another trip north, but not before he'd given the new house a new name — Eringa. The choice of the name remains a mystery. It is not an Aboriginal word with a specific meaning; it may have had special relevance to him as the first big station he bought on his own and not in a partnership.

Bel's stepbrother Wally Will ran the office at the new house, taking care of the day-to-day matters, receiving the wires sent in by managers and drovers, and redirecting the news to Sid on his travels where possible. The extensive use of the telegraph, advising of conditions and rain, or the lack of it, on his stations, combined with his own outstanding knowledge of the far out country enabled Sid to make the best possible decisions about stock movements. Sitting in the office and fiddling with wires certainly put you in the picture, but the best way to get the complete picture was to go and see for yourself and get the news first-hand. He went by train to Hergott Springs and on by horse to visit his northern South Australia stations and those in the Queensland south-west corner. Calling at Carcoory and finding the same grisly, unrelieved vista of drought, he closed down the homestead.

Recalling the incident years later, Sid said, "Carcoory had about 4,000 cattle on it when I bought it. When I landed there in the drought I asked of a few fellows hanging around the homestead, 'How many cattle have you got left?' They said, 'Only two. We have killed one and the other is not yours.' They were just keeping a few horses together. I said to one chap, 'What are you doing here?' He said, 'I am the storekeeper.' 'What have you got in the store?' 'A bag of sugar,' was the answer. 'What!' I said, 'storekeeping on a bag of sugar?' I paid the lot off except Jim Jardine. The cook's wife came out of the kitchen wearing a silk dress. She had enough dough and flour all over it to make two dampers. The mail man was there and asked me if he could live in the place for 18 months. I agreed, providing he let me have all the fowls back. (But the next time I went there he had killed off all the fowls and the roof of the house had been blown off.) Well, I told Jim Jardine to load up the wagon and take the rations over to Annandale. Plenty of fellows would have gone stark cracking after a knock like this, but I kept going. There was no meat to be had for a feed so I shot cockatoos and stewed them down."

115

Sid was getting ready to move on from Carcoory when something happened that sent his crushed spirits soaring. An account of it is given in the records of the Dickson family, of Aramac, Queensland.

Joseph Dickson was known to Sidney Kidman as Joe Gleeson. Joe put a G in front of his mother's maiden name and made it Gleeson. He took delivery of 1,200 head of Avon Downs bullocks in the Northern Territory in 1901. Sidney Kidman gave Joe a twelve months' commission to take them to Carcoory. It was a disastrous drought and Joe battled with the 1,200 he was shepherding. He would watch for storms in the sky at night. They could be 50 to 100 miles away. He would make in the direction of the storms. In those days there were no fences and it was no problem to move in any direction.

Joe arrived at Carcoory when Sidney Kidman was there eyeing the dismal scene of cattle carcasses in the dried-up creek bed. Joe told him that his cattle had not had a drink for three days. "Never mind," Kidman said. "It might rain soon." Joe looked up. The sky was clear and bright and you could have fried an egg on a shovel quite easily from the heat. However, as they stood there talking, large black clouds began to appear and very soon large raindrops began to fall and then a torrent of water was racing down the recently dried-out watercourse.

Regrettably the Dickson records don't mention Sid's reaction — whether he tossed his hat in the air, shouted praises to God,

116

danced a jig with drover Gleeson or hurled himself full bore and fully clothed into the sudden stream. They do, however, mention Gleeson's reaction. Kidman's thanks were fulsome and his pledge of increased work at increased rates after such a memorable droving trip cut no ice with Gleeson. He wanted no focus put on the achievement and no recognition. According to the Dickson family records, "Joe never returned home to Aramac again. All communication with him was lost. Rumour has it that he died somewhere in Western Australia."

When conditions and feed improved the 1,200 bullocks were staged to Hergott Springs and trucked to Adelaide, where they fetched £12.5.0 a head. The skill and determination of one excellent drover gave Kidman almost £15,000, doing as much to lift his morale as his bankroll. Certainly drover Gleeson was not on his own, and Kidman's faith in hiring the best and most competent of men was rewarded time and time again during the drought years, as drovers did get through, though often with reduced numbers.

If Kidman's estimated 70,000 stock loss in the drought had been measured at the Avon Downs bullocks price in 1902, his loss would have been £857,500. It is impossible to gauge his losses exactly, but they were of such magnitude that people may have assumed, quite wrongly, that he was down to his last bob and out for the count. It is

ABOVE:
Lanark House, which became the first Kidman home called Eringa. (Kapunda Historical Society)

not so. Financially, he toughened out the drought and there were only two years, 1901 and 1902, when he was slowed down to the point that he could make no further pastoral purchases (and 1902 was the year he bought the Kapunda house Eringa). By 1903, still officially a bad drought year, Kidman was snooping around again and in a mood to buy — both stock and properties.

Kidman's banking records give another dimension to his position during the turn-of-the-century drought. His first recorded interview with the Bank of New South Wales was on 16 August 1901, when drought was costing him dearly with stock losses. The record of interview made by the Sydney manager of the Bank of New South Wales, Thomas Ivey, gives no indication of any grim financial position on Kidman's part. After a meeting with Kidman, Ivey noted in his manager's diary, "Sidney Kidman. Interview with him when he signed contract for purchase of 700 Carandotta bullocks. Mr Kidman said he has got on very well with Mr Halloran our Queensland inspector but he could not do business with Mr Roberts our Queensland station inspector. Mr Kidman said Mr Roberts was getting too old for the work. Informed chief."

The bank owned Carandotta Station (4,000 square miles of country on the Georgina River in south-west Queensland) and the bank manager did not question Kidman's capacity to buy 700 head of stock. There is also no suggestion that Kidman went to the bank cap in hand, in fact he appears to have been frank and open, to the point of being critical of bank staff. The fact that manager Ivey felt the need to "inform the chief" puts Kidman in the category of a customer who was a cut above the ordinary.

The drought may have halted him in his tracks temporarily when it came to buying up places, but while his own stock losses had been great they didn't stop him dealing in stock and buying up where he could, even as far away as the Barkly Tableland. The drought had not been as acute there; Sid had determined this for himself by riding there and having a personal look. His crack drovers were dispatched to the area to buy up mobs, where possible, with a cash deposit and the balance at three, six or more months after delivery. They then moved them across the top of Queensland to coastal markets. In 1901 Sid was buying 700 bullocks from a station in his three rivers country, which meant that Carandotta had not been knocked about so severely in the drought. Carandotta would be a handy fighting link in his chain if he could get hold of it, but why advertise that fact to the banking boys? What they didn't know wouldn't hurt them.

He continued to buy stock — from Rocklands, Alroy, Herbert Vale, Alexandria and Lake Nash — and was always a welcome customer whenever he or his drovers appeared. If Kidman didn't take their cattle, who else would, or could? And he didn't confine his interest just to cattle; he bought sheep as well. Big mobs were bought up at several shillings per head and resold, almost immediately through the telegraph, at twice or three times that amount. Kidman's word as a dealer was good, and in the depressing drought situation terms could be wangled in his favour: an agreeable deposit, which was often lower than the seller would have liked, and the balance spread over a period that was often longer than the seller would have liked. The tactics produced not a small amount of grizzling about flint-hearted Sid, but the more realistic among the sellers were also satisfied that they would get their money and that it was Kidman who was taking the risk. Once the stock was off their hands it was Kidman's job to get it to a market under appalling drought conditions or else resell the stock to his advantage. Sid proved to be pretty good at handling both, using his system of the telegraph to best advantage and, it has been said, instructing his drovers to pay the telegraph operators a little something extra for any information they could give about other mobs on the road — how big they were, in whose charge and where they were headed. It enabled Sid to make more favourable marketing decisions.

Things didn't always go Sid's way. Sydney bank manager Ivey's diary notes on 27 November 1901 state, "Chief declined to grant Kidman further extension of time for lifting Brighton bullocks but agreed to accept half cash and half at two months". And on 3 April 1902: "Re Carandotta sheep. Chief agreed to allow Sidney Kidman until 30th instant only to take delivery of the sheep purchased by him. Wired S.K. and the manager of Carandotta to that effect." Kidman's bid to stall for time and put off a deal for as long as possible or until it best suited him did not always work out.

Throughout 1902 and 1903 he continued to deal in stock in big numbers. Officially, 1903 was still a drought year, but in the north, isolated monsoon storms resulted in patches of feed and drovers followed the storms, while still contending with long dry spells.

Unquestionably Kidman made a considerable amount of money from successful dealing during the drought years, though small perhaps in relation to his staggering losses. Talking of two deals, he said, "I bought 3,000 5-year-old bullocks as fat as mud for £4 a head. I bought a lot of beautiful cows off Alroy Downs and Roxborough and dropped them at Annandale and that is how I stocked up Dubbo Downs again. I went to Glengyle, Camooweal and different places and all told got nearly 20,000 cattle. They were cheap and fat. I went into Townsville and saw my bank manager and then went down to Sydney where I met two well-known men. They asked me where I had been and I told them I had been out the back of Queensland buying up a lot of cattle very cheap. 'You had better let us in on them,' they suggested. 'Anyway,' I said, 'you give me £10,000 on them: I will put up another £10,000 and go back and buy more. If you don't come in, I am off to Melbourne tonight and then home to Kapunda.' They would not come in. I went home and in ten months I had made £40,000. That put me on my legs again."

While many went under, he remained buoyant, sufficiently so to be approached by the Bank of New South Wales in the middle of 1903 and asked if he would like to buy Carandotta. He shrewdly shrugged the matter off. The bank, in his opinion, had stipulated a sky-high price, which didn't suit him at all. Rather than admit that, he claimed he wasn't in a position to buy and had "every last six-pence invested and was in the process of restocking his runs". Again, Kidman was gambling — against the bank finding another buyer at such a lofty price. He wanted the station very much and was a dab hand at playing the cat-and-mouse game. He remarked to Bel, "If I hang around a bit and blow my nose I think they will come and tap me on the shoulder again."

While waiting for the shoulder tap he made as many enquiries as possible about Carandotta, and not openly. He found stock numbers on the property that pleased him; many were in a suitable condition for sale. Additionally there was a mob of bullocks on the road to market and 300 bales of wool on the way to London for sale. Carandotta was directly north of Dubbo Downs — a fair stretch mind you — but there were a couple of other places in between the two that he had his eye on — Sandringham and Glengyle — and why stop there? Monkira, Davenport and Diamantina Lakes would link up the chain effectively. Carandotta also had a subsidiary station, Walgra, which carried reasonable amounts of cattle, sheep and horses, not nearly the number the place had carried pre-drought but still very satisfactory. Going over the figures with Bel, he said, "It's better than a poke in the eye with a blunt stick."

Kidman was obliged to hang around blowing his nose for four months, in which time no suitable buyer could be found by the bank. When Carandotta was re-offered by Pitt, Son and Badgery for £65,000 on a walk-in-walk-out basis, Sid suddenly seemed to find the money that would clinch the deal. It was, he said to Bel, the "nicest Christmas present he could give himself that year" and the diary of Thomas Ivey on 28 December reads, "Chief agreed to extend time for payment by S.K. of £20,000 due on 3rd proximo on account of his purchase of the station to January 10. Interest to be paid from June 3 to date of payment of £20,000. See our letter to Pitt, Son and Badgery."

Sid had gambled successfully. The Carandotta wool sold excellently in London, and the mob of bullocks trucked to Sydney five days after he bought the place realised a record price. Jubilant, Sid set off on a personal inspection of Carandotta and one with a difference. He was travelling with his friend, Julius Grunike, a mate from the early days of Broken Hill when Sack, Sid and Charlie had bought out the Grunike butchering business in 1891. He urged Bel to go along as well. There was no point in holing up in Kapunda all of her days. He wanted her to see for herself the empire he was carving out. She might as well go along on her first inspection trip. If she didn't like it, she need not go again. Bel protested the silliness of launching herself into the saddle.

"No, no, no!" Kidman insisted, swatting flies with a vengeance on the verandah at Eringa, as they discussed the matter. They would do the trip in style — by rail or steamer to Brisbane, then out west by rail and then a buggy journey. Bel agreed and in the stinking hot summer month of January 1904 she found herself, all corsetted and correct, being pitched around in a buggy as the party set out from Hughenden, Queensland, to Carandotta.

At first she carried a parasol to shield herself from the sun, but when her arms started to ache she opted for the practicality of a big, wide-brimmed hat. Initially she was extremely interested in all her husband had to say, but he rarely seemed to stop talking about every single feature of the country...this place and that place...how badly they'd been affected by the drought...the stock they once carried and carried now...how much of it was also due to rabbits and overstocking...who owned various stations and what they'd paid for them...whether or not he had his eye on them. He seemed to know everyone they met along the way, or, more correctly, they seemed to know him. The trip was an eye-opener to Bel Kidman. This was where he truly *was* most at home. His enthusiasm and interest were unbounded. She also saw the compassionate side of her husband's nature where animals were concerned...the hat that was pulled from his head and filled with water and offered to a weak calf...his exuberance when he noted groups of cattle in good condition. "Bel," he bawled at his wife, "you should always drop your deepest curtsy when you see a fat bullock!" Out in the middle of nowhere Bel Kidman had no intention of alighting from the buggy and swooping into a curtsy. She couldn't in any case. Sandwiched between the luggage the party was carrying were three calves Kidman was attempting to save, and one of the calves was spreadeagled over the vast lace bedspread she was in the process of crocheting, part of it draped across her knees and the remainder around her feet. She understood the homage to which her husband was referring and acknowledged the remark with a deep bow of her head and a smile.

Bel Kidman couldn't bear to be idle. Sitting and swaying in the buggy and endlessly staring at mile after mile of country which, to her, was tedious, had little appeal. She was happier if her hands were busy, and she took to crocheting enormous lace bedspreads and tablecloths, still intent on taking in all that Sid had to say and pausing from her work when something of special significance needed to be pointed out. The white bedspreads rapidly became dark red or deep brown, depending on the dust kicked up in the country through which they were travelling. She carted them back to Adelaide with her in their filthy state, to avoid wasting water in the bush washing them, and they were boiled up in the copper until they emerged a bright shade of white. Her first trip outback, she insisted, was a productive one, as would be every trip in the future.

The visit to Carandotta proved more than agreeable to Sid. The manager appointed by the Bank of New South Wales, Jack Edge, was still in charge, and Kidman was delighted to find the place neat and orderly, with no signs of waste or rubbish. It didn't take him long to assess the capability of manager Edge, who was invited to stay on and manage Carandotta for Kidman at £100 more a year in salary and a bonus when the place started paying its way.

Edge asked if there were any special instructions, to which Kidman replied, "No. Just make the place pay, feed the men well and allow no waste. With the price of transport being what it is, no food and no goods should ever be wasted."

In Sydney, on their journey home, Kidman had a meeting with bank manager Thomas Ivey. Ivey's diary for 6 May 1904 states, "Long interview with S.K. when he settled with regard to Carandotta Station." Or had he really settled?

Back home in Kapunda, a reporter from the *Adelaide Observer* snared him for an interview and asked him two predictable questions: how many cattle he had and to what he attributed his success? Responding to the first, Sid said, "Without I settle down and get to figures I cannot tell you the number of cattle I have now. But I reckon that tonight I have 15,000 head on the move for different markets or different stations trekking from droughty spots to places of good feed," he answered matter-of-factly, for the first and only time. In later years he would be suitably vague when the question was put to him, either because it suited him or because his operation had grown so vast that he genuinely did not know.

To the second question he said, "I don't know. I was always dealing in horses. I have always taken care of little things and I don't think one can go far wrong who does. When I ride onto one of my stations I look at the small things. If the trifles are strewn all about then I know why that station is not paying its way. If the small things are let go amiss, so will the big things.

"People think I have been making money for years. They must remember that I held stations before the drought and held them all through. [This is not quite correct for he did off-load Owen Springs.]

122

I, however, took the precaution to handle my stock; to send those from the bad places to my stations that were better off." Carrying the interview ahead under his own steam, he added, "I am more pleased to talk to a man carrying a swag than to your politicians. The man who goes in for raising cattle or breeding horses cannot go far wrong, especially cattle. I have owned a racehorse or two, but don't care much for races. I don't mind what I do. I would just as soon have a good square feed at a station as sit down to the best spread at a hotel. I have a few irons in the fire. I go for cattle, horses, sheep; in fact, all sorts of stock. I still hold a mail contract or two, have an interest in several butchershops and grow wheat as well. Now excuse me, for here is the mail."

"Mr Kidman turned aside," the reporter commented, "and had to deal with nearly forty letters and run through a dozen telegrams which gives a fair idea of his daily correspondence." The journalist headed his little article: From Cowboy to Cattle King.

One of the letters Sid opened would have caused him to sigh deeply. It was a stiff note from the Bank of New South Wales. He had in fact *not* settled where Carandotta was concerned and the bank was taking a dim view of the situation. Sid guessed he'd have to get around to doing something about it, and sent them back a letter pledging to right the matter.

In Sydney, in his manager's diary, Thomas Ivey noted on 5 November 1904, "As requested in his letter of 27th ulto, Chief agreed to allow Kidman until February next to complete payment of in-stalment of £20,500 due 1st instant for purchase of Carandotta Station and stock. Proceeds of present wool clip to be applied towards payments of the instalment and 5 per cent interest to be charged on all monies overdue on 1st instant from that date until date of payment." The bank was proving that it could get tough, even with good customers. They'd had enough of the dawdling of the man currently tagged "Cattle King". The bank's attitude didn't perturb Kidman greatly. He'd square up when he felt like it.

A further entry in the Sydney manager's diary on 14 April 1905 stated, "Interview with S.K. where he said he was moving 40,000 sheep and 5–600 cattle south from Carandotta and that he would have the bank paid off for Carandotta by February next. Said he wanted to know what fats available at Brighton and would call on his return to Sydney from Bourke."

The bank, it would appear, was paid off in 1906 for the property he agreed to buy in 1903. The Carandotta purchase is indicative of the way he strung business out to suit himself. Adding to the bank's exasperation, no doubt, was the fact that, from 1903 to 1906, he entered into negotiations to buy up, or bought up outright, a string of several more stations to bolster his chain, while Carandotta was still not finalised. The Kidman way of doing business was by now becoming recognised in financial circles. He was as good as his word — in the long run — and in the meantime there was nothing much anyone could do to bring him to heel. He was such an important customer that everyone wanted his business and no one wanted to offend him.

10
A Non-stop Buying Spree

I N 1903, WITH CARANDOTTA in his clutches, Sid embarked on a buying spree that left Australia breathless and succeeded in arousing much comment overseas, certainly within the British Empire, in the Mother Country and the dominions, and in the United States, where people were slightly incredulous that land transactions of such magnitude were happening in some place other than their own country. Americans already cherished the notion that the biggest and best of everything took place in the U. S. of A. Nor, where Kidman was concerned, was the buying spree a spasmodic one. It would roll on, virtually uninterrupted, for twenty-seven years.

With the ink still wet on the Carandotta agreement, Sid made his twentieth major purchase. He bought Lake Albert in the Menindee area of New South Wales. He knew the area well from his early days at the Barrier and from his transport days. Lake Albert, which cost him £85,000, was never considered as a chain property, but simply a means to an end. He bought it from the trustees of the late Sir W. W. Hughes with a view to turning it over quickly. The South Australian government was interested in buying it from Sid Kidman, but didn't act speedily enough. Within a short time Sid sold two large blocks out of it. Mr W. Richardson, a well-known breeder and dealer, bought Warringee, the head station and portion of the Lake Albert run near Menindee (about 4,000 acres), and the second block was bought by Mr Bowman, of Poltalloch. In fact, within six months Sid had disposed of the entire property and stock and cleared £25,000 on the transaction.

A report in the *Pastoralists Review* in 1903 said, "Some folks say, 'What a lucky man!' Rather they should say, 'What a plucky man!' for while rich men stood by and looked askance at the estate, the cattle king who knows a lump of ground just as he knows the difference between a fat bullock and a giraffe, stepped in and did the business."

Pocketing the Lake Albert profit, Sid headed north again on a buggy trip with Bel. If he was a "Cattle King", then he was anxious for a few more little jewels for his crown. In one fell swoop he bought up Bulloo Downs, Glengyle and Sandringham in his precious three rivers country in south-western Queensland (all big, strong links in his main chain). In South Australia he bought The Peake, which, along with Coongie, added to his Central Australian chain. The transactions took his tally of stations to twenty-three. Kidman owned, controlled or had an interest in 11,000 square miles at the turn of the century, before the Victoria River Downs purchase (12,500 square miles) and Carandotta (4,000 square miles). On the debit side, 600 square miles went when he off-loaded Owen Springs, leaving him with 26,900 square miles before he went on his 1904 shopping spree. (The square mileage of Lake Albert has not been credited or debited to the 26,900 figure as he turned the station over so quickly, selling it almost as soon as he had bought it.) Glengyle, Sandringham and Bulloo Downs added another 12,098 square miles of country in Queensland, and The Peake and Coongie (Coongie was the flood-out section of Innamincka Station) brought another 7,597 square miles in South Australia, making Kidman a monarch of 46,595 square miles of territory when the 1904 transactions were completed.

Sandringham and Glengyle were the most important acquisitions. Sandringham joined Dubbo Downs and Glengyle; Glengyle adjoined Kaliduwarry and Annandale. The chain was considerably bolstered by these two for an outlay of some £50,000. Sandringham (3,068 square miles) was north-east of Bedourie on Palliou Creek and the Georgina ran through its eastern section, giving Kidman some floodwater country, and Glengyle (6,183 square miles) was on the Georgina and had deep, permanent waterholes. He had grand plans for both these places. They were reliable areas where stock from the Barkly Tableland, or even Victoria River Downs, could be droved and allowed to fatten on the hills and flats of lignum and saltbush. Artesian bores would be needed to shore up against any future dry times or drought.

Bulloo Downs (2,847 square miles), south-west of Thargomindah and on the Bulloo River, wasn't the place it had once been: overstocking, rabbits and the drought had taken their toll, but Sid felt sure the country would recover. The reserve price on it was £40,000 but his offer of £20,000 to Powers Rutherford and Co. was accepted. He asked one of his favourite managers, "Galloping" Jack Watts, to take Bulloo Downs under his wing in addition to nearby Tickalara. Kidman had loved the Bulloo Downs country in earlier days and wanted it because of its strategic importance. Cattle from Bulloo Downs could supply three major markets: Adelaide, Brisbane or Sydney.

Coongie (2,818 square miles) had also been knocked around in the last thirty years since Kidman had first become familiar with it; he almost flinched at the havoc caused by rabbits. Still, Coongie adjoined Innamincka Station and he had Innamincka in mind for later on. The Coongie property was owned by Norman Wilson's estate and Sid made an offer of £5,000 for it, which was refused. Normally he did the haggling. In this case it was the reverse. The trustees considered there were at least 2,000 head of cattle on the run and would not accept less than £3.5.0 a head. Kidman quite happily agreed to the offer, confident that Coongie, in its reduced state, had around 1,000 head. After the run was mustered and only 920 head of horses and cattle could be delivered, Sid paid out £2,990. Coongie provided a link between his northern South Australia stations and south-western Queensland holdings. The Peake created a new link in his Central Australian chain, which stretched down through South Australia. The Peake (4,779 square miles) was 200 miles south-east of Eringa. It was bought for £9,000 from John Bagot (with Kidman in partnership with a Mr Kempe), and, when Kempe died, Kidman purchased his share.

As well as the five stations bought in 1904, Kidman bought nineteen mobs of cattle from numerous stations: they tallied 23,516, for which he had outlaid £132,129.

With the demand for cattle tapering off in Western Australia, Kidman decided to get cracking on his idea to bring Victoria River Downs cattle back east. In 1903 Jim Ronan left Victoria River and the vast station was run temporarily by Tom Cusack until early 1904 when Richard (Dick) Townshend took over. Townshend had spent his life in the bush; in fact he started off droving for Sid Kidman down the Cooper. He was an extremely capable man — Kidman knew it and Townshend himself knew it, so if Kidman wanted to land him with such a demanding job he wasn't going to be shy in wage demands, having seen the way Ronan was able to get what he had asked for a few years before. Townshend wanted a 20 per cent increase on Ronan's salary and he got no argument from Kidman. His wages were £41.13.4 a month, an extraordinary sum for a manager at the time, yet Kidman was about to make some extraordinary demands of Townshend.

There were not a few doubting Thomases who felt that Kidman would come a cropper with the west-to-east move, which was teed up as soon as Townshend was appointed to Victoria River Downs, and he was instructed to get 1,000 head of cattle for Blake Miller to bring across. Whether the move succeeded or failed, it was another big first attempt in the Australian pastoral industry.

Kidman argued that there were cattle willy-nilly on Victoria River Downs. If the entire mob was lost, then it was a loss that could be tolerated. That was the worst that could happen, and he naturally hoped it wouldn't. At the best, Miller, a top drover, would get through. Kidman had every faith in Miller, one of his drovers who had successfully got cattle through to market during the worst conditions the turn-of-the-century drought had tossed up.

Balanced against that was the reputation of the dreaded Murranji Track, a 140 mile horror stretch from Top Springs to Newcastle Waters. Legendary drover Nat Buchanan had opened up the track in 1886, bringing cattle east-to-west, but not without great difficulty. The end result was hailed as a great droving feat. Could Blake Miller pull off the reverse journey? Kidman, reliably informed by the telegraph, knew that the summer rainfall in the area had been particularly good that year. He argued that it augured well. The trip was very much on Sid's mind in the next few months. Wires, sent wherever possible, had kept him informed of progress. It was a triumphant day when Miller brought the mob into Kidman's south-western Queensland country, for it paved the way for other Kidman drovers, Jumbo Smith and the Lewis brothers, to follow.

Kidman was in a rare state of excitement the day he tore open the wire at Kapunda. He flung aside the rest of the mail and raced from the house to flap the good news under Bel's nose. She was in the conservatory, watering-can poised over row after row of pelargoniums in pots. Sid ran so exuberantly that he did not stop at the door. He free-wheeled into the glasshouse colliding head-on with his wife, sending her flying, as well as the plants. Sprawled on the ground she offered her husband a baleful glance. "Oh, Sidney," she said. "Oh, Sidney..." Sid retrieved his wife from a very earthy situation with profuse apologies, at the same time shouting excitedly about Miller. It was just a small spot of domestic mayhem. Another more costly serve was just around the corner.

Kidman had faced drought and flood. In 1904 it was his lot to face fire. His house burnt down.

He always made a point of being home for Christmas with Bel and the children, in this case their third in their new home, Eringa. On New Year's Eve, a Saturday, in the morning Sid had spent some time in the office yarning about stock matters to A. W. Richardson, Elder Smith's manager at Kapunda, and was in the hallway with Bel seeing him off when he interrupted the farewell with "I can smell fire", and cast an intuitive glance at the skylight in the hall where smoke could be seen.

"Why, the house is on fire," Kidman shouted and raced outside followed by the others. He jumped onto the cast iron railing around the verandah, shinned up a verandah post and climbed over the verandah roof to the roof proper. He could certainly see the fire but couldn't reach it and, even if he could have, he could have done nothing as it would have been almost impossible at short notice to send him up buckets of water at such a height. Also, there was no fire hose on the premises.

He stood on the roof beefing out orders, yelling at 14-year-old Edna to look lively and get going on her bicycle to alert Foreman Cook at the fire station a mile away. He didn't have to tell Bel to smarten herself up and remove what she could from the house. She'd already broken into a run to retrieve her precious jewellery. Richardson sprinted back inside to shout to the house staff and children and to get them out. It was a sweltering hot day and there were strong winds. One of the gardeners ran to the scene tossing up a few heavy bags for Sid to try and beat out the flames. In the process he had a narrow escape and fell over backwards on the roof, saving himself, he said later, "by the skin of my teeth".

It took Edna twenty minutes to get to the fire station and the brigade turned out promptly at her summons, with Foreman Cook scoring points for quick thinking. On seeing a spare horse and dray in Main Street he decided to make use of it. He sent his men on with one reel and nabbed the horse and dray to return to the station to get a second hose. Driving hell for leather, he overtook the brigade wagon and helped it up the rise to the Kidmans' garden entrance. They got to work with alacrity, but from the start they were pitted against a task they had no hope of mastering. The place was a huge furnace. Volunteers had arrived at the scene. All available hose was put to work, but the pressure of the water wasn't all that it should have been. There was scarcely enough force to carry the water to the eaves of the house.

The fire had devastated the house so completely that there was almost nothing to save by the time the brigade arrived. Foreman Cook at one stage bravely entered the house to try to combat the fire and had only just stepped outside one of the rooms when the ceiling came down with a crash.

The Kidman family didn't stand around uselessly waiting for the bridgade to arrive. Bel and the servants made repeated trips into the house to get out as much as they could — clocks, vases, light furniture, some clothing and anything small they could pick up and run with.

No one gave a thought to the office, which was adjacent to the hallway and where the fire had raged initially and most fiercely. A few hours later the Kidmans stood in the grounds of their now less-than-magnificent home, with the dining room furniture, a fair proportion of Bel's wardrobe, Walter's rocking horse and assorted decorator items. No one thought to save anything of Sid's; he had nothing but what he stood up in and the children were no better off.

Reporting on the fire, the local paper, the *Kapunda Herald*, said, "The fight was kept up with great and constant vigour until the last little flame was extinguished and exhausted and perspiration and water-drenched men were relieved of work and went home for a well-earned rest and a change of raiment."

In typical Aussie fashion, quite a crowd had gathered to help fight the fire and try to assist in any way, even to the point of supplying food and drinks. The paper continued, "The men were liberally supplied with refreshments. Ladies in the neighbourhood very thoughtfully brought buckets of tea whilst there was also a supply of other liquids for those who preferred them."

"At one stage of the operation Mr Kidman was lost sight of and quite a sensation was being worked up," the paper added. Mr Kidman, it must be said, took the entire matter very calmly and couldn't even work himself up to have a drink of "other liquid". The following morning he and Bel escorted a party of press people through the ruins, and Kidman, it was noted, showed "great calmness, self possession and not the slightest sign of excitement in discussing the fire".

He corrected an erroneous impression that the fire had started because of a defect in the acetylene gas installation put in a few years before. "The pipes were not near where the flame broke through in the ceiling of the hall, the office and drawing room," he said. When it was suggested that a spark from the kitchen chimney, which was in proximity to the skylight, was the cause of the fire, Sid said it was unlikely as there had been no fire in the stove since breakfast time and the bath heater had not been used that morning. "I'm of the opinion that wind carried a spark either under the roof where it joined the skylight and set fire to some dry sparrows' nests or that the heat of the sun acting on the glass caused ignition of some inflammable material. I'm positive the gas was not the cause.

"When I went out and got on the roof and found I could do nothing, I thought the best plan was to start moving what furniture we could. This we did, but saved nothing to speak of when we had to stop on account of impending danger to life. With the exception of a few small things we have saved nothing, so fiercely did the fire spread throughout the place, but I am very thankful that it happened at a time when we were able to get the family out of the house," Sid told them. Bel, calm and collected, expressed her thanks that "the fire didn't happen at night time".

Remarkably the stables, storehouse, shade houses and conservatories (one of them 110 feet long) were not damaged, despite their close proximity to the fire and the strong winds.

Was the place insured? "I'm not aware of it," Sid said. "The wife will know." Bel had covered it with a modest £1,000 (the house was insured for £600 and the furniture for £400).

There was nothing left but the charred walls of Kapunda hardstone (the basement walls were 2 feet thick and the internal walls 1 foot thick and well-bonded) and blackened and twisted roofing-iron threatening any minute to fall or be carried away by the still strongly blowing wind. The verandah, which extended around three sides of the house, had been only marginally damaged as the station firemen and volunteers had successfully contained the flames within the house walls.

The year before, Bel had replaced the furniture the family had taken with it from Bald Hill with costly new furniture. It was all gone. The bathroom, redecorated with imported tiles and the most up-to-date fittings, was a wreck. Crystal doorknobs were melted to such an extent that they resembled large pieces of topaz. But she was more upset at the loss of several of her lovely paintings and Sid (although he had lost a handsome gold watch valued at 60 guineas) regretted more the loss of a piece of wood from the famous Dig Tree where explorer Burke had died. Kidman had souvenired it from the tree at Innamincka Station on his travels.

Bel, in a dignified manner, walked through the wreckage, her long skirt blackened to the knees as she swished around black charcoal; Sid was in the same suit he had worn the day before, currently the only one he possessed. He was quite unconcerned about his dress; his suit pants were studded with marks from battling the fire the day before. An extra innings of charcoal wouldn't make a whit of difference. The palms and backs of his hands were tender and showed signs of early blistering as he picked up and then hurled away bits and pieces, pausing for a while to try to identify them. Showing the press people where the office had stood, Kidman remarked, "I did make an attempt to remove some papers but a packet of cartridges started to explode and I had to retreat."

What would they do now, the press asked? Whimsically Kidman replied, "Oh, I don't know...buy a cheap place and live in Adelaide...," turning his back on them and continuing to sift among the ruins. Bel directed a grave stare at his back and gave her own view of things. Such was the affection they had for Kapunda that of course they would stay there, rebuild and possibly even add another storey to the house.

One reporter trailed off with Kidman as he hunted further within the wreckage of his office. Was he after some important papers, deeds or securities? "No," bawled Sid, somewhat exasperated, "it's my spurs I can't find!"

Sid shipped the family off to Henley Beach, a suburb of Adelaide, to live there while the house was being rebuilt. The Kidman girls — or at least Gertie and Edna — distinguished themselves by getting into a spot of trouble. Eyebrows were raised and teacups clattered in their saucers along with the gossip in Adelaide's drawing rooms when the Kidman girls indulged in mixed bathing.

Back in the bush, Sid entertained the men around the campfire at night with his story about the fire. "Boys," he said. "I don't have a roof over my head at Kapunda and I don't here either and I know what I like best. Fancy houses can get you into a lot of trouble..."

Between 1904 and 1906 Kidman forged ahead with his empire building, buying up another string of stations and ploughing improvements into those needing them. Money was not frittered away on titivating up homesteads, nor on yards and fences. His main priority was water and overcoming the lack of it. He attempted to whittle down some of the long, dry stages faced by his drovers and cattle with a succession of bores. Next time when drought hit, and he knew there'd be a next time (because the run of good seasons he'd had since the turn-of-the-century drought had ended wouldn't last forever), he would be better prepared to fight back. It was a case of striking while the iron was hot.

Monkira Station slipped easily into his hands. It was a very handy flood area of almost 2,500 square miles, fronting the Diamantina in south-western Queensland to the east of Lake Machattie, and not too far from his Glengyle, Dubbo Downs and Sandringham runs. Then Kidman turned his attention to Norley.

Norley was on an outside channel of the Bulloo River, 17 miles north of Thargomindah, and had been founded in 1864 by an Englishman, John de Villiers Lamb, who transferred his leases a decade later to another Englishman, William Naunton Waller. In 1886 Waller disposed of Norley to William F. Armytage for the large sum of £120,000. (Armytage must have been well-heeled; that same year he bought Thargomindah Station for £70,000 after its owner, Vincent James Dowling, met his death at the hands of hostile Aborigines, who speared him while he was mustering stock in the sandhills on what is now Wongetta Station.)

The number of cattle on Norley at the time was 38,441, and the waters they depended on in the almost 2,000 square mile run were the Bulloo River, Mooliania, Dewalla and Wommera creeks with Bullawarra Lake being a main watering point. It was probably the greatest number of cattle ever run on Norley. But Armytage did not prosper. The rabbits devastated Norley, which Armytage had overstocked. He managed to hold onto it throughout the drought years, but Sid Kidman knew that Norley's stocks had slumped so badly that, by 1902, it held only 200 head of cattle. The property fell into the hands of the Bank of New South Wales and was up for sale. The bank's Melbourne manager was handling the sale and Sid made a hurried trip to Melbourne with no appointment with the bank manager whatsoever. It wouldn't do for the bank to think he was overly eager to snap up Norley!

Arriving in Melbourne, he ducked in and out of the bank only to enquire of the bank messenger as to when the manager took his usual lunch hour, and Kidman made sure he was back in the vicinity of the bank for an "accidental" meeting as the manager returned from lunch. The contrived meeting happened according to plan and, after hearty personal greetings, Sid made as if to be off and on his way but the manager invited him to step up to the office for a bit of a chat about this and that. When they finished their yarn, Norley was safely in Kidman's hands and at a price that suited him — £25,000. Naturally Sid had wired Galloping Jack Watts to do a preliminary check on the place, and he had done some advance checking himself and found the reserve price of £30,000 not to his liking.

The bank manager was so elated at having pulled off such an unexpected coup that he insisted on having a gold pencil inscribed and presented to Sid as a memento of the purchase. It was Sid who laughed all the way from the bank as he and the manager went straight to a local jewellers. (Kidman later gave the pencil, inscribed with the word "Norley", to his daughter Elma, who gave it to her granddaughter Jane.)

Kidman was more than happy with the purchase. He knew the station then had 4,000 cattle and 500 horses. He also thought that, if a few bob and a bit of attention were ploughed into Norley, it would become a strong link in his chain. Naturally the job of manager went to Galloping Jack. He could take that under his wing along with Tickalara and Bulloo Downs.

Jack Watts was one of Sid's most loyal managers and also a trusted friend. He was born in Adelaide in 1872 and was working in the Thargomindah area in 1890 when he caught Sid's eye as a first-rate stockman. Several years later, when Sid started buying up places and sought the finest hands to run them, Galloping Jack Watts was one obvious choice. Galloping Jack ought not to be confused with Jack Watt who also worked for Kidman, but from the 1920s onwards. Jack Watt was born in Quorn, South Australia, in 1912 and started working for Kidman at the age of 12 at Cowarie and later managed the place.

Of Galloping Jack Watts, Kidman later said, "He takes as much interest in a station as if it is his own. He thinks nothing of riding from Bulloo Downs to Norley in a night — 100 miles. Jack is the lightest rider I have ever seen and is like a postage stamp on a horse. I have never been to Norley but that he would come to meet me. Once he came to the Paddy Paddy Plain 120 miles out to pick us up. He had wonderful ponies and would get fifteen or twenty in sometimes and change twice and fly for 100 miles or more in a buggy. I have never seen a more active man. I have seen him have two cups of tea and a cigar for breakfast and smoke the whole day long and eat nothing more."

Galloping Jack turned out to meet Sid when he arrived on his first inspection trip as owner, and he found a big contingent of Aborigines camped by the homestead waiting to see the "new pfella boss". They were led by "King" Tinder (also spelt Tindah).

"It was very dry when I first went to Norley," Kidman said, "and I said to Tinder, 'Cattle poor. Need big pfella flood to make 'em plenty feed jump up alonga bullock. What you make 'em big flood for?' Tinder said, 'I will make 'em £100 big pfella flood.' 'Too much,' I told him and then asked another fellow called Paddy what his price would be. 'Two pfella shillin'.' Tinder was doubtful and said, 'Paddy no got 'em rain stone. You got big pfella mob.'

"I gave three blacks some meat, flour, tea, jam and sugar and tobacco, and they were as pleased as if I had given them £500. They went up to a little waterhole on the creek and hammered away for three weeks. Sure enough, it started to pour.

"I think that Bulloo Downs and Norley had some of the finest blackfellows you could ever see in Australia. I was going along early one morning and saw some blackfellows rounding up bullocks. I said to them, 'What you bin do 'em alonga these cattle? You no shift 'em,' and they said, 'That one already belong 'em Bulloo Down. We go out, catch 'em, bring 'em back; too much 'em walk about this way,' and they would go out and get such cattle and take them back to Bulloo Downs. They were splendid chaps."

In recent times, a South Australian academic described Kidman's life as "a catalogue of crime" and alleged mistreatment of Aborigines. He was asked to put forward his views and evidence for this book yet chose not to do so. Records and interviews with many former Kidman employees and managers suggest that Kidman's attitude was the complete opposite. He had a great affection for the Aborigines stemming from his earliest teenage days in the Barrier area when his work mate, friend, guide and teacher was the Aboriginal boy Billy. There were two areas in which his thinking dovetailed closely with theirs: one was in the understanding of the land, and the second, the sense of humour both shared; it was a simple, childlike sense of fun. Kidman was at ease and happy in their company, a feeling that seemed to be mutual. But it is not to say that some Kidman managers, when Sid's back was turned, did not take a harder line with the Aborigines than the boss. In doing so, they ran the risk of offending Kidman, whose views on the Aborigines were clear-cut.

"I get on tiptop with the blacks," Sid said. "People don't properly appreciate the Aborigines. They are most useful on the stations if they are treated rightly. I feed, clothe and treat them well and pay some of them wages. I have given all my managers instructions that the blacks are not to be knocked about or interfered with. If they don't suit they are allowed to go and hunt game for themselves. I have never shot a blackfellow or hammered one in my life. A lot of people in the Gulf land and in the Northern Territory especially have treated the blacks very badly. I have known managers treat them disgracefully. In the far north people think they can treat them like goods and chattels. I think men who take the gins and live with them should be prosecuted. Lots of station managers have had gins living with them. This sort of thing leads to a lot of trouble.

"What I admire in the blacks is their love for the place in which they are born. If they are taken away from it, their sole thought, night and day, is to get back again."

Sid himself was always glad to get back to Norley whenever the opportunity presented itself, and both that station and Monkira were "special" to him because of two animals: the steeplechaser Bullawarra and the Monkira bullock.

When Kidman took over Norley he started to introduce new stud stock among which was the thoroughbred stallion Sir Simon. One of Sir Simon's progeny was Bullawarra (named after the main lake on the run). Bullawarra became a champion hurdler, the many successes in Victoria heading up to a win in the 4 mile Australian Steeplechase at Caulfield while carrying the daunting weight of 12 stone 11 pounds. In 1914 (although no longer owned by Sid) Bullawarra was sent off in the steamer *Runic* to tackle the Liverpool Grand National, a longer distance and then regarded as the world's greatest cross-country event, at Aintree. Sid was always very proud to say that he had bred and owned Bullawarra.

It was Monkira Station that turned off the Monkira bullock, which held the record for more than forty years as the heaviest bullock ever slaughtered in Australia. The bullock was bred by Smith, Debney and Co at Monkira and was slaughtered in Adelaide in 1894 by the butcher L. Conrad. Its live weight was 3,042 pounds and its dressed weight, 1,992 pounds. The bullock was sold and slaughtered a decade before Kidman had Monkira as a run but, nonetheless, his name became synonymous with "the Monkira bullock", and it must be said that Sid never went out of his way to correct any wrong impressions about the bullock. He liked being associated with the biggest and the best and to tell the press that "Australia's best and heaviest bullock had come from Monkira". In that regard he was quite accurate; he would have been more accurate had he said that it didn't happen in his time.

Monkira did continue to turn out beasts of enormous size while Kidman held it, animals of a size that astounded men at sales. One

---

OVERLEAF:
Bullawarra winning the 1911 Obi Hurdles in Melbourne. (Joan Hopkins)

Monkira bullock was so large as to not survive the journey to town to have a fetching photograph taken and statistics noted for the record before the slaughterer did his work. Allegedly it was heavier than the initial Monkira bullock, but the rail trip proved too much for it. It did not survive the 400 mile rail journey. Sid was sorry about that.

Delighted to have secured Monkira and Norley as little gems for his crown, Sid set his sights on Thargomindah Station in his Channel Country. There were some stations, he figured, that were about as useful to a man as pockets in his socks, but this wasn't one of them. It was 1,117 square miles on the Bulloo River and not too far south of Norley. It would provide another useful chunk in the chain.

Content in south-western Queensland for the time being, he moved into South Australia. He had had his eye on Macumba Station for a while. It would be a handy lump of territory in his Central Australian chain. It was 1,634 square miles of wild and unimproved country and fairly dry at most times. Yet the Macumba, part of the Alberga and Hamilton rivers, ran through it, and in exceptionally good floods it received waters from the Finke, Australia's most ancient watercourse. It would need bores to sustain it; he knew that and intended to act on it. Herb Foulis was given the job as manager; he was but one of many members of the Foulis family who would work for Sid for the next thirty years.

Mundowdna was his next acquisition. The 998 square mile holding in South Australia was of utmost strategic importance to him. It was a geographic gem because of its close proximity to the north–south railway. It wasn't so much a link in the big chain as it was a nerve centre — a trucking depot for cattle coming south from his Central Australian and south-western Queensland stations. Mundowdna would be a spelling and fattening depot where cattle, foot-sore or poor, could recover condition before being trucked to market from Farina or Hergott Springs. Many other mobs of cattle also arrived in the area constantly, to be trucked to market. Moving them in poor condition would certainly result in a loss. Sid would be more than happy to relieve the owners of them, at the right price, and fatten them himself at Mundowdna before sending them on to market as required. The asking price for Mundowdna, formerly a sheep run where the dingoes had had a field day, was £4,000. Kidman would have been prepared to pay that amount many times over for the important trucking depot it now provided for his chains. A first-class cove would be needed to manage it and Kidman gave the job to John (Jack) Brooke, who only ever worked for two men in his life; the first had been Hungry Jim Tyson and, on his death, Kidman had enticed Brooke into his operation.

Such was the movement of stock at this time from Victoria River Downs across to Queensland and New South Wales that Kidman extended his interest in the north when the Hon. John Lewis offered him a one-fourth share in Newcastle Waters, which Lewis held with his brother, Henry F. Lewis. It was on Newcastle Creek, south of Daly Waters, and was initially a 500 square mile run, for which the partnership paid rent of £25 a year. It later became a 3,847 square mile holding. By 1907 Kidman either owned or had an interest in twenty-nine stations, and they covered 58,691 square miles of country.

Kidman's extraordinary bout of buying attracted amazement in some circles, and criticism in others. Sid had no qualms about openly defending his interests. "Lots of people say I have been buying places and throwing the country up. I have been increasing rather than decreasing my holdings. I pay a higher rent in Queensland than I do in South Australia because the rainfall and carrying capacity of the country are better.

"I intend to keep the holdings I have and increase them if I am able to. If I can only make the rent on some places during the next few years I shall be satisfied. There is plenty of country on which I am not making rent. My cattle are increasing very fast and with a few good seasons I will be able to utilise all the country I hold. Still, I consider the country in Queensland is far superior to that in South Australia and most of my cattle are at present in Queensland. Anyone who has travelled through the western and south-western parts of Queensland must have seen the difference in that class of country to our north country.

"In Queensland the rainfall is much heavier and the natural waterholes, lakes and billabongs are much better than in South Australia. That means better grass. I consider one mile in Queensland will carry as much stock as six miles in our South Australian north country. But it pays to hold the country because, although there may not be water or grass on one place, there will be on another. Norley and Thargomindah are 1,600 or 1,700 miles from Victoria River Downs but, having scattered depots, I can always get into Sydney, Adelaide or Broken Hill with the cattle.

"What is going to be the salvation of Queensland is the great tract of artesian country and the number of bores being put down. There must be 1,000 bores with water running from 2 up to 35 miles. Everyone seems to be putting them down. When the drought comes again the losses will not be nearly as heavy as they have been in the past. I have just let four bores on Annandale and Sandringham. With labour and droving costs being so high, it has been very expensive to work these places but with one or two good seasons I reckon I will make them pay their way.

"The wages for men and output for running the places amounted to £21,578 in 1907. To that has to be added rations, rent and plant.

People think I have been making a lot of money. They make a mistake. My desire has been to build up a big herd of cattle. My ambition is not to be rich but to hold the largest herd of cattle in Australia, if not in the world, and the same with horses.

"Droughts might come along again as they have done before and give things a hit back but with the present prospects, I think I will attain my ambition."

11

"Knock 'em Down"

A S MUCH AS IT WAS important for Sid to know exactly what was happening on his outback runs and to be quickly and reliably informed of stock movements, it was equally important for him to keep tabs on the end result, and that meant regular attendance at the cattle sales, chiefly in Adelaide, but also in Brisbane, Sydney and Melbourne whenever possible. His presence invariably drew both comment and attention. "There he sits at the cattle sale watching the beasts as they are rushed into the ring," revealed a report in the *Adelaide Register*. "He knows them all by their brands. They are the geography of Australia to him."

What a characteristic man he is dressed in his grey-blue clothes and his felt hat turned up behind and pulled down over his forehead. His right foot is drawn up on the seat, the knee finding a lodgment in his armpit. His left leg is sprawled out somewhere. He looks the typical wiry bushman. His eyes have absorbed the weird and strange light of the bush.

The portcullis is drawn up and two bullocks are rushed into the ring and he starts bidding for them. When he sets his eye on a beast, he means to have it. If he thinks the auctioneer has not caught his bid he swings his arm like a windmill and yells out, "Ha!" He has the energy of a dozen men. He will jump down among the cattle, wave his handkerchief and draft them out.

Sometimes when they are selling a lot of pot-gutted, ridge-backed, shrivelled-up and nondescript beasts, he will drop his head on his arms and have a few minutes' sleep; but he knows by intuition when a good bullock is under the hammer, rubs his eyes, stretches his arms and wakes up. What do they think of him? Why, that he is a wonder. He has done many things but likes best being mixed up with cattle. It is his work, his play, his joy, his sorrow, his very life and he plays the game for all it is worth.

At the cattle sales on Monday a well-known man remarked, "Well, in buying those 20,000 cattle when he did Kidman has been the salvation of the beef trade here." Mr Kidman was in great heart on Monday. His pockets were bulging out with telegrams from all parts of the interior telling of great rains.

From Boulia in Queensland he received the following message: "Three in Bedourie, 5 Sandringham, 3 Carcoory, 2 Dubbo, 1½ Monkira and good reports from Camooweal." Another message told him that across the big stretch of country between Bourke and Windorah the fall had averaged 4 inches. Other gratifying reports came from Roxborough, Glenormiston, Marion Downs and elsewhere. The prices of store sheep and store cattle are going up and Mr Kidman is in the trade up to his neck.

Sid certainly was in the trade up to his neck and, at the sales, usually on the selling side of things, when he found no time to sprawl on a seat and indulge in forty winks. When his cattle were sold, he was on his toes on the rostrum, at the side of the auctioneer. It could be argued that he didn't need the services of an auctioneer, because he virtually sold his own cattle!

A further report in the *Adelaide Register* in 1907 said:

One has only to visit the market to realise how completely Mr Kidman has control of it. He can, by the nod of the head, say if the price of meat shall remain high or be reduced — if the butchers follow the market with corresponding movements in prices.

Mr Kidman stands on the rostrum beside the auctioneer and his eagle eyes scan the circle for bids so that between the two of them advances are never missed. He was in his usual place on Monday when about 300 of the 548 cattle yarded came from his paddocks and the speed at which lots were knocked down at his command was remarkable. Mr Kidman knows beforehand what every beast is worth to a shilling — he almost knows the value of each hair on their hides — and unless there is something exceptional about a bullock or a cow he gives no quarter to the auctioneer but simply says to the bidder, "It's yours," when he thinks such a course is desirable.

The market opened with some cows that did not come within the category of "prime stock"; but prices were exceedingly good and as soon as a certain price was reached up went Mr Kidman's pointer, directed towards the butcher who had given the winning bid. The spirit of liberality is by no means lacking in him for he could have secured higher prices for dozens of lots but he stopped the competition as soon as his estimate was reached.

"Nine ten did you say, Bert?" he asked when Mr H. Kither, the auctioneer for Messrs Bennett and Fisher, knocked down a cow to a butcher. "Yes," came the reply from both the auctioneer and the buyer. "Too much," said Mr Kidman, "not worth it. Let him have it for £9." For the next couple only £6.10.0 was offered, but this was refused because "the blooming train fares for these beasts come to nearly that!".

"When are you going to trot in the good stuff?" asked Mr W. Kither [a butcher related to Kither, the auctioneer]. "Here's a couple of beauties," said the jovial owner as a fine pair of fat monsters rushed into the ring. "Who's got 24 notes?" asked the auctioneer and Mr Kither and others replied at once, "I have!" But Mr Kidman had already caught the eye of the Rundle Street butcher and without waiting for the price to advance, as it undoubtedly would have, he bawled out at the top of his lusty voice, "They're yours, Kither. Hurry up there, boys. No time to waste today. Here's another couple . . ."

"Twenty-three," said Mr L. Conrad and the words were hardly out of his mouth when Mr Kidman nipped in the bud the appeal of the auctioneer for advances by shouting out, "Enough. They're yours, Conrad. Up with the gate. What about these?"

"Twenty-three," was all Mr Conrad could say before the excited seller stopped the proceedings again with: "They're Conrad's." For several minutes this sort of sale without competition went on with small butchers and others paying the same rate, "first come, first served" being the principle on which the negotiations were carried out.

"It's no good hanging on for another five bob or even a pound," said Mr Kidman. "When you reach the value I put on them you can have them. I won't run you up."

"We can't live at these prices," said Mr W. Kither when he paid £26.10.0 for a pair of upstanding animals, which probably weighed more than any other couple put in the ring, but the only satisfaction he got from Mr Kidman was, "You can take my word for it that my cattle today are the worst lot you'll see for the next three months."

Three beasts then entered the ring and the auctioneer asked, "What about £34 for them?" but Mr Conrad urged that £32 was plenty. "Alright," said Mr Kidman, "book them to Conrad."

During the sale Mr Kither talked to a few strangers to the market and was loud in his praise of the generous manner in which Mr Kidman treats the butchers who cannot afford to pay big prices. "He won't let them pay big prices," said the ex-alderman. "I've often heard him say to the auctioneer quietly, 'Take a pound off that. He can't afford so much,' or 'Take a pound off that, it's bought for a widow.' At every market he could get higher prices if he wanted to, but when he hears the bidding touch his level he is quite satisfied as a rule and down goes the hammer."

Another butcher observed that although the market

depended almost entirely on the Kapunda man he was by no means deserving of the condemnation which was usually showered upon him by the public owing to the prevailing impression that he is entirely responsible for prices remaining high. "As a matter of fact, if it was not for Kidman's action in letting cattle go without waiting for bidders to cease their competition, the price of meat would be much higher because we would have to pay more for our stock. He knows the exact value of every beast when it is driven into the ring as well as if he had put the animal on a weighing machine and as soon as the figure is reached, he stops the bidding and points out the buyer. At the same time, I think he knows what he is doing and the average works out satisfactorily. I suppose the average today will be about 32s. 6d. per 100 pounds."

Roughly speaking, Mr Kidman sells 15,000 every year in this state and the bulk of the cattle come from Queensland and the far north.

In the far north, his cattle were, as ever, on the move, and towards a market. Just how extensively Kidman was involved in stock operations may be seen by a 1907 report sent from Charleville, Queensland, on the movement of stock in the area, much of it destined to go south to Adelaide to enable him to maintain his control on the market. It read:

Charleville, August 20. — Glowing reports continue to arrive regarding the splendid rains on Mr S. Kidman's well-known Annandale depot on the Herbert River, near Birdsville. Twenty-three inches has been recorded on the run. This is a record for any border station. These excellent rains have occurred at a time when large mobs of cattle are coming in from Victoria River Downs in the Northern Territory.

The country is capable of fattening cattle in large numbers and the prospects of the season have been so good that Mr S. Kidman (the "cattle king") purchased 1,360 bullocks and cows brought in by Drover Prentice from Newcastle Waters for the Hon. J. Lewis. These cattle have now been released on Annandale.

Mr Kidman purchased from J. Lewis and Co., of Adelaide, 1,340 Newcastle Waters cattle brought in by Drover Turner. These have gone on Coongie Station near Cooper Creek for fattening purposes.

Drover Larkins has passed Urandangie with 1,200 Victoria River Downs bullocks for Birdsville district; owner, Mr S. Kidman. Twelve hundred Brunette bullocks have arrived at

Annandale in charge of Drover Starr; owner, Mr S. Kidman.

The following stock have left Coongie Station, Cooper Creek, to the order of the owner, Mr S. Kidman: — 450 cattle in charge of Drover N. Shaw, 450 cattle in charge of W. Vile, 500, E. Pratt.

Several mobs of fats are getting ready on Annandale run; also, 1,200 Noranside cattle in charge of E. Gaffney; Mr Kidman, owner, 600 Alroy cattle for Annandale, Burgess in charge and 2,000 Alexandria cattle will leave this week for Annandale, James Jardin in charge; Mr Kidman, owner. Three thousand bullocks will depart from Brunette Downs on 30 August for Annandale, P. Kennedy in charge; Mr S. Kidman, owner. Several large lots of cattle are leaving Wyndham to be shipped to Fremantle for Perth market; owners, Emanuel, Kidman and Troupe.

Drover Barnfield has just passed Urandangie with 1,200 Victoria River Downs bullocks for Birdsville; Mr S. Kidman, owner. Drover G. Hooper with 1,200 Victoria River bullocks passed Brunette Downs, Northern Territory, 1 August, destination Birdsville; Mr S. Kidman, owner.

Five mobs of cattle, all prime, from Victoria River Downs are travelling for sale down the Georgina; owners, Emanuel, Kidman and Troupe. The drovers in charge of these mobs report the track dry in parts. Five hundred fat cows and bullocks have just left Palparara for southern markets; Mr Kidman, owner. Four hundred and fifty fats are leaving Monkira for Adelaide; Mr Kidman, owner. Four hundred are leaving Annandale in charge of Drover Byrne also for Adelaide market; Mr S. Kidman, owner. Five hundred have left in charge of Gaffney for Adelaide; Mr Kidman, owner.

Permits have been granted by the stock authorities in this state for the great Kapunda horse sale. All the horses, except a small line, are the property of the "cattle king". The total number to be yarded will be 2,500. Five hundred and thirty now on way from Bulloo Downs, and 220 from Tickalara, 391 from Monkira and several mobs will be yarded at Kapunda from North Adelaide. Mr Kidman is owner of all lots.

Stock reports were listed with great frequency and this was but one in the year of 1907 which showed Kidman with 17,550 cattle all on the move for fattening or market (not counting those in which he had an interest with Emanuel and Troupe). The figure was nicely rounded up to 20,000, if his horses destined for sale at Kapunda were counted as well. The cattle numbers certainly took the limelight, but sometimes that changed: the limelight switched to his horses and the amazing way in which they were sold at his home town of Kapunda.

Once a year the Cattle King could lay claim to another title as well — that of Horse King of Australia. Kidman's annual Kapunda horse sales were the largest ever to be held in the country, with thousands of horses moved in a systematic way from his northern stations to go under the hammer of Coles and Thomas auctioneers (brothers-in-law).

This area of Kidman's life has often been overlooked — and quite wrongly — or never given the emphasis it deserved. The cattle markets could fluctuate daily, weekly or monthly, but an annual horse sale was a different proposition. He knew how many horses and what types he had on his various stations; he also knew the market requirements down south. Once a year he dispatched horses to fit that market, so the Kapunda horse sales represented an annual and, more importantly, a large and stable slice of income.

It has been said that there was no way the little town of Kapunda could have coped with thousands of horses dumped on its doorstep overnight as there were insufficient yarding facilities, and that only hundreds of horses were auctioned each year. Not so. The Kidman system was used. Station managers were wired to start a certain number of horses on a certain date so that many mobs were on the road travelling at the one time, often arriving within a day of each other. The sales started out in a smaller way and grew quickly to the point that they lasted a fortnight or eleven selling days, bringing Kidman amounts of around £33,000.

His first big sale was held in October 1900 when 350 horses were auctioned at the rear of the North Kapunda Hotel. Many people were sceptical and could not foresee that this was the beginning of a series of huge annual sales that would run for more than thirty years and attract buyers from all over Australia and throughout the world; in fact, they were to breathe new life into Kapunda with the mining boom over. The town benefited from the influx of buyers and Kidman's practice of charging admission, the proceeds going to local charities. The second year 400 horses were auctioned at the sale, with 1,000 head in 1902 and 1,230 in 1903. By 1905 the number was close to 2,000.

The initial sale prompted Norman Richardson to write: "Kidman's Kapunda horse sale revived many old memories for me. It was on 6 December 1880 that he brought his first mob of horses to Adelaide. They were sold at Formby and Boase's Bazaar in Currie Street and James Shakes of the firm Liston and Shakes was the auctioneer. There were about 200 horses in the mob which Kidman had brought from a New England station in New South Wales and they were branded TB on the near shoulder. The sale was most successful. I bought sixty-two horses at an average of £6.10.0.

"Sidney Kidman was a young and active man, and entering the

saleyard with a bridle in his hand, he would chivvy a horse and leap on and off its back and announce in a loud voice, 'That jolly tinker is broken in.'"

Sid hadn't changed much over the years. The sales gave him the opportunity to combine his "born dealer" and "head showman" gifts and none of the usual trimmings incidental to a fair were lacking. The sales were conducted in a carnival atmosphere with peanut and fruit vendors, hawkers selling frankfurters, and itinerant cheapjacks proclaiming their various wares in raucous tones. The place was thick with practical jockers and pranksters, and in the sale ring Sid's boisterous, chatty style and endless fund of humorous remarks kept the spectators in good spirits and constant roars of laughter.

Such was the quality of the horses that the Indian remount buyers felt compelled to attend. The Victorians who shipped to India were "Colonel" Steve Margrett, J. E. Robb, R. McKenna and Son, A. Glasscock and Son, and W. A. Jones Pty Ltd (who all shipped to Calcutta) and Bob and Theo Gove and the Baldocks (who shipped to Bombay). From New South Wales, H. Davis and Co. (formerly the Lyons Bros) attended, and from Queensland, Alan McPherson (who took over the business of J. S. Love). Davis and McPherson were also licensed exporters to India, along with Bob Skene of New South Wales and his father, Curtis, who took small teams of ponies (fifteen to twenty annually) for polo requirements in the State of Kashmir. George Medlow and Mick and Sam Rasheed attended. They were prominent South Australian horse dealers who sent occasional consignments to Western Australia but did *not* ship to India.

South Australian farmers, a strong German component among them, rolled up, as did farmers from Victoria's western districts — all wanting horses for drays, teams, buggies and stockhorses. Women were among the buyers wanting ponies and hacks (thoughtfully, one day of the sales was set aside as Ladies Day), as well as the Adelaide Suburban Tramway Co. and the Parkside Tramway Co.

If you could survive the Kidman sales, it was said you could survive anything.

The sales invariably opened with a few words from the boss after an introduction from auctioneer C. J. (Charlie) Coles. "I think you'll find most of what Charlie said is true," Kidman responded one year. "The mob we're dealing with is one of the largest ever yarded by any one owner anywhere.

"It's one of the finest lots I ever saw. They come from different parts of Queensland and Northern Australia and I don't think you'll find an old or blemished one among them. It's more expensive for me to sell 2,000 than 12,000. I have some of the best men in Australia and I want to acknowledge their assistance. So we won't haggle for a pound or two. You must bid quickly if you want a horse.

"When I rode through his town in '70 I only had one horse and he only had one eye and the only person I knew was myself!

"Today I'm the largest owner in Australia and I'll put up £50 for a hospital if it can be shown that any owner pays more rent than I do in Queensland and South Australia. Here," he said, handing up a document to the auctioneer, "I got a bill yesterday for £4,622 — rent for sixteen stations in Queensland and my expenses run into something like £50,000 a year. Now, what about getting down to work. These horses have no tickets on their tails. Let her go, Charlie!"

The speech was typical. The following year it ran, "You can't go into any yard in Australia and see thousands of horses equal to those I have for you. They are not bought up horses but horses from my own stations. You can rely on what we tell you about them. I would not tell you that a horse was a year older or younger than he actually is for £5 or £20. It pays a man to give an extra 10 shillings more here because he gets the accommodation he doesn't get in any other part of Australia.

"Coles and Thomas have the distinction of receiving more horses from a single client than are yarded for one man in any other part of the world. We don't come here to run them or jerk you along. I don't want the horses but the money as I have been spending a lot lately. (Laughter)"

Taking off his coat and straddling the rostrum he added, "In '70 I passed through the town with one horse with one eye and with 5 shillings in my pocket. Today I own more horses and cattle than any other man in Australia. (Cheers) I don't own much cash but plenty of country. Open the gate, Charlie, and let her go!"

And the next year: "I've been to sales in Queensland, New South Wales and Victoria, and I believe Kapunda is the daddy of them all. Go on, Charlie," he remarked to the auctioneer who handled the hammer, "I am here to sell horses and not to talk. However, as you know, I came through Kapunda many years ago with one horse that had one eye and now I own more cattle and horses than any man in Australia...," with a buyer interjecting, "Yeah, but Bill Burgess has the most ponies. (Laughter)"

"And, ladies and gentlemen," Kidman continued, "I don't swear and I don't drink and I don't smoke...," at which point someone was always waiting for him with: "Yeah, but you tell a heck of a lot of lies, don't you, Sid..."

People hooted, backslapped and fell about with laughter, including Kidman himself.

Strange and candid opening speeches they may have been, but it was clever sales strategy, putting people in a great frame of mind for buying and filling some with awe to the point that they bought horses just so they could say they "had one of Kidman's".

Someone, either the owner or a drover, seemed to know something about each horse as it came into the ring and the *Kapunda Herald* remarked, "...and though as time went on the strain on the auctioneer necessitated help from a brother artist, at no time did Sidney Kidman show signs of a failing voice, whip or lasso. The only break in his day's work was a few moments' adjournment beneath the auctioneer's box for the discussion of his lunch. That no accident occurred from kicking horses — at times there would be no less than three men in the ring 'demonstrating' — was more the result of luck than care. If any animal showed a desire to kick, it was encouraged to do so. If it looked like bucking, Sam, a black boy, or Kidman himself offered it every chance to display its powers. Seldom has a sale been conducted on such humorous lines; one is accustomed to the conventional funny remarks of the auctioneer but not to the owner assuming the role of circus proprietor, showman and general 'farceur'."

Bidding was spirited but equally spirited was the activity in the crowd, more often than not led by horse exporter Steve Margrett (dubbed "the Colonel" by Charlie Coles' brother, Ross, because of his dapper appearance).

A placard would suddenly appear on someone's back, saying, "For sale. Apply Charlie Coles," and the spectators roared with laughter. Gents who sat on the rails found their coat-tails tangled together with fishhooks. Men with a newspaper on their knees or in a pocket suddenly found it on fire. Crackers were put in the crowns of hats causing men to duck for cover when they went off. Pranksters (sitting in a higher position) produced handfuls of twigs and placed them into the brims and crowns of hats of men below. Fellows suddenly found their heads on fire. Or else a dreadful powder known as "cot-itch" was sprinkled down inviting coat necks from the rear. Stink bombs were lit. In fact, men behaved like outlandish schoolboys — but no one seemed to mind.

Kidman, either in the sale ring with the horses or in the auctioneer's box following the bidding, was never a sitting duck for these capers, but on one occasion the Indian horse exporters bribed a Kidman employee, Mickey Woods, with 10 shillings to put a packet of crackers in the boss's pocket.

"It just about blew his coat off...well, it blew the pocket clean out, anyway," said Norman Gurr, former Kidman drover and later manager of Clifton Hills.

It did more than that, according to a former Kidman manager, Jack Watt. "It damn near blew half his arse off!"

Kidman assumed the role of ringmaster during the sales. He took liberties with some of the wildest unbroken colts, proving, nine times out of ten, that he was the undisputed master of the situation. He kept up a running commentary on the age, class and qualifications of

the horses in between yelling at people in the crowd. "I haven't seen you for two years, Bill. I thought you'd gone wild up in the scrub!"

He was active in the ring with his whip which he skilfully manipulated as a lasso when he wanted to "mouth" a horse in order to find out its age.

Or he would cry, "I've ridden this horse myself!" and to prove he wasn't talking at random he threw a halter over the neck of a fine-looking mare. A second later he was on his back on the tan. With a smile and a joke he remounted to cheers from the crowd.

"How much for this, gentlemen?" Charlie Coles would bawl as a medium draught gelding entered the ring. "Give me a start somewhere."

"Fourteen pounds," an enthusiastic farmer responded.

"It's yours, sir," Charlie promptly replied.

"Hold hard; now look here," interjected Kidman. "That seems like robbing the man. Make it £12..." The result? A farmer, all smiles, who was an even more enthusiastic buyer for the rest of the day, his ideas of immediate requirements expanding from four to six horses!

"What age did you say that horse was, Mr Kidman?" enquired another who had just purchased.

"Couldn't possibly say," Sid replied from the ring. "Born long before I was."

"Paint on the wither, please," yelled another to ensure identification of his purchase.

"No occasion," Sid replied. "You'd know him anywhere; he's only got one eye!"

"Ah, now, then, you have got a bargain," showman Sid said to another buyer, "but listen! Don't you turn him out or you'll never see him again. There isn't a fence this side of the Gulf that will stop him from making home. It has taken me three years to catch him!"

When Charlie Coles enquired as to the age of another horse, Kidman jested, "If I was buying him I should say twenty-five years but as I am selling, let it be four years."

When Charlie suggested £10 as the opening bid for another horse, Sid said, "You're too extravagant. Make it £8 to start."

When an attractive little horse had been knocked down for £13 and was leaving the ring, Kidman yelled at an attendant, "Hurry up and open the gate or he will jump it! He's disgusted at the price he fetched. I can tell by his looks!"

OPPOSITE:
Charlie Coles and Steve "the Colonel" Margrett, two of the colourful personalities from the annual Kapunda horse sales. (David Ross Coles)

All through the day — and every day — there were jokes at his own expense and jokes at the buyers' expense, sufficient under ordinary circumstances to damn any sale but not when Kidman held the ring.

"Beats a circus!" or "Wouldn't have missed this for anything!" were remarks that came from the crowd.

On one occasion, Archie Bevis, a noted South Australian whose antics contributed greatly to the amusement at the sales, failed to put in an appearance on the first day. A telegram was sent to him by Kidman saying, "Your presence at the drafting gate can alone save the sale from being a frost."

The unsuspecting Bevis made haste for Kapunda to find himself met at the railway station by a brass band. A "decorated chariot" drawn by four mules from a local circus and escorted by outriders and plenty of pomp took him to the sale ring where the whole proceedings stopped to allow for effusive greetings and cheering before Archie was placed formally in charge of the drafting gate. More bombs and crackers than ever seemed to explode in the vicinity of the gate that year — but Archie soldiered on, working both gravely and industriously as he fancied his presence to be imperative!

Amidst all of this annual tomfoolery, the horse sales blazed away, with a familiar phrase, "Knock him down!", frequently yelled by Kidman. Often, when a price had been reached in the bidding that Kidman considered fair, Sid would bring a halt to proceedings.

The three little words cost him money, usually 10 shillings or £1, but if he was a generous seller then he was dealing with generous buyers not disposed to lose a valuable animal for the sake of a sovereign or two. Commenting on this, an *Adelaide Observer* journalist said in 1903, "Kidman practically gave some of the horses away. A man looking at an animal before the sale was approached by Kidman with: 'He's a nice horse. What will you give for him? Go in and bid and I'll knock him down to you.' And he did. I saw such an incident. The gentleman bid £15 and the horse was knocked down to him. Before it left the ring one of the Indian horsebuyers offered £25 for the same animal. There were scores of such cases."

Another feature of the sales were the young boys who often ran to Kidman with a bunch of telegrams. He'd scan the contents quickly and thrust them into his pocket, remarking on some, "Oh. I have fixed up the purchase of Lake Albert Station..." The amount involved was £85,000. For the casual attitude he paraded, he might have just bought a dozen eggs.

Tearing open some telegrams evoked a more dramatic response. He'd interrupt the sale to tell people: "I've just got a wire from Thargomindah Station saying 4 inches of rain has fallen there. What's the good of trying to get another pound or two out of these animals. Knock 'em down! Knock 'em down!"

And Charlie Coles did. He had the arduous job of talking in good voice for a fortnight, and his offsider, Thomas, kept the sheets and tallies.

Selling singly, Coles could move through a horse a minute — which is tantamount to speed selling, a feat emulated by his brother, Ross Coles, in later years when he handled the Kapunda sales. Ross was said to have been even faster than his brother. There were daily newspaper reports. One, in 1910, read, "Mr [Charlie] Coles ran through 101 in 101 minutes. Useful draughts brought £47 each, and 100, mostly carty stamps from Eringa and Annandale, averaged £29.7.0, and 130 light sorts and ponies from Mundowdna ran out at £12 a piece. The mean for the day was £19.10.0. Lots for tomorrow are expected to be heavier and the average price higher."

And the next day: "The crowd was kept in good humour all day by the pleasant sallies between the owners and the buyers and the accepted practice of firing bombs and crackers behind unsuspecting people created much merriment. The highest price of the sale so far was reached with £52 for a draught mare. There were not so many heavy horses as expected but it was evident that anything with weight would fetch high prices. Eringa, Durham Downs and Coongie were the principal stations contributing to the supply and the average for 253 was £18.12.6. A fine lot of 103 from Eringa averaged 1 shilling under £28 and 150 light stamps yielded £12.18.0."

The following day: "A total of 307 was sold for the day making an aggregate for five days of 1,256. The average price reached a round £20, with 110 draughts, medium and light, from Mirramitta and Norley averaging £30.15.0. The balance was mostly light stamps with a number of ponies from Tickalara. The sales continue tomorrow."

Buyers were obliged to move their horses out on sale day so a fresh lot could be brought in for the following day's sale. Townspeople gathered to watch a big mob come into town in a cloud of dust. Sometimes Kidman's chief horse drover, Charlie MacLeod, would bring them in, but more often than not it was Sid's daughter Gertie Kidman. She could both ride and flick a whip most capably.

"Gertie was a bit of a character, a bit wild," said Norman Gurr. "She didn't mind lapping around on wild horses. Edna was the same. At one of the sales old S.K. was actually slinging in a bid himself for a horse. At last the horse was sold and the auctioneer knocked it down to Gertie Kidman. It was S.K.'s turn to be wild. He said, 'Put it back again,' and someone bought it for half the price. S.K. had forced the bidding up and Charlie Coles laughed like billy-oh.

OVERLEAF:
A scene following the horse sales, with Sid mounted on the horse at far right.
(Mrs G. Scheid)

"S.K. did a bit of laughing himself at the end of a sale. He used to get these trick gadgets. With one, you looked through a peephole to see a picture and then turned a screw on the side to see the next picture. Instead, when you turned the screw you were squirted with eau de cologne.

"At one sale a fella came up and asked him for a job. S.K. said, 'Oh, I don't know. Can you catch fowls?' The fella said, 'Yes,' and Kidman said, 'Then come and see me at the end of the day.'

"He did and they went up to the big main house to the grounds where Mrs Kidman had the chooks. 'Catch me one,' said Kidman, and the bloke caught him a chook. 'No, not that one — that other one,' Kidman said, and the bloke caught it, and S.K. said, 'No. No. That one over there.'

"The fella went on catching different chooks for five minutes. Then Kidman called a halt to it and said, 'That'll do. Report to the office on Sunday.'

"The cove left and Kidman remarked to a couple of onlookers, 'He's a willing enough fellow, I'll give him a job.' It was a funny old way to qualify for one though — catching chooks."

Post-sale, laughs and pranks continued. Kidman shouted drinks for the buyers and downed a ginger ale himself. The Indian buyers, in particular, tried hell, west and crooked to return the shout and induce Kidman to have a grog. The reply was always the same: "No, you don't. You coves can drink but I won't. You can't get me to have more than one ginger ale!"

There were parties, dances and a horse sale ball. Alex Robb, son of J. E. Robb, one of the biggest Indian horse exporters, recalled, "Men wore shirts with a spare celluloid collar and we used to take the collars off for a wash-up before dinner. Steve 'the Colonel' Margrett came along one night when six of us were in the bathroom having a wash. Someone complained the chip heater water wasn't hot enough. So the Colonel threw all the collars in and burnt them. He had to replace the lot the next day, of course. It was all good, clean fun and no one was ever hurt or offended.

"We stopped at the pubs. They were always full. We'd put our shoes outside the door to be cleaned for the next day. By 10 o'clock at night there were pairs of shoes up and down passageways.

"The Colonel would mix them all up...men's shoes with ladies' shoes and put ladies' shoes outside men's bedrooms and vice versa. It caused chaos.

"In the latter years of the sales there was a new policeman in town who was very strict about 6 pm closing. Ross Coles used to get him to take a bit of a drive out of town for hours on end, enabling us to stay on in the pub with Ross lining up drinks on the bar and auctioning them off and with the publican nearly having a coronary about being sprung."

Mort Conway, of Alice Springs, a former Kidman drover, recalled, "Charlie and Ross Coles were two of the best salesmen in Australia and both well liked. In 1921, when Ross was selling at Kapunda, he lost his voice. His brother, Charlie, was there — just back from England. They closed the sale up for half an hour while Charlie whipped down to the police station, renewed his licence and came back and carried on in Ross's place."

Kidman knew the horse market as well as he did the cattle markets. His views were often sought. By 1912 he was advising, "Breeders of horses in Australia should devote more attention to the production of good, light animals of the stamp suitable for artillery and cavalry purposes.

"In my opinion, insofar as South Australia is concerned, the supply of draught horses (which has received tremendous impetus owing to the rapid opening up of new agricultural areas) has reached demand and, indeed, a surplus. There are fewer really good light horses in Australia now than there were fifteen years ago."

It was almost as though he had advance knowledge of the Great War which was to follow in two years time, when Australian horses, of the very type he urged, were to play such a major role in desert campaigns, and in no small numbers.

Despite increasing mechanisation, the horse sales continued until 1936, when the Indian trade closed up owing to the mechanisation of the Indian army. They were not always of a fortnight's duration, sometimes lasting a week, sometimes less, depending on drought, feed and the ability to stage the horses down from the north to trucking depots. Towards the end of his days, Kidman saw the sales surge into great prominence again in the Depression times, when men on the land could not afford either cars or expensive machinery and returned to the horse. Not each of the thirty-six years for which they ran gave Kidman £33,000. If they had, the sales would have grossed him nearly £1.2 million. The gross figure probably nestled comfortably under £1 million, which across the space of thirty-six years wasn't bad bickies. Despite all the emphasis given to Kidman cattle, his horses remained a very important and reliable string to his financial bow.

12
Friend of the Omnibus Man

SID KIDMAN turned 50 in 1907. It was a time of assessment, certainly on the part of his wife, Bel, and three daughters, Gertrude, 21, Elma, 20, and Edna, 18. Sid had never stinted where his family was concerned. His wife, his daughters and his young son, Walter, received the best he could give, whatever they wanted. The girls and Bel Kidman gully-jumped him for a trip overseas. Kidman had little say in the matter. His family howled him down. Money wasn't a problem; he needed a good holiday; he had always promised Bel a trip "back home"; the whole family could go — even little Walter, aged 7. The girls yearned to take in the stylish life in England and the Continent. Bel Kidman was adamant. Kidman agreed.

To his wife fell the job of organising an itinerary for a year, as well as educational considerations: finishing schools for his daughters and school in England for his young son. Kidman used the preparatory time to make sure his interests would be left in the right hands at home. There were long debates with bankers and with Bel. Her stepbrother Wally Will was left to run the show from the office at Kapunda. Will already had a senior hand in office dealings. Kidman cemented it further, being a strong believer in family ties in business, something that was to become more apparent in years to come.

In 1908, when Australia's population was hovering at 4 million and the accent was on arrivals rather than departures, the Kidman family took its leave, but not before a gala farewell was organised at Kapunda. Kidman had brought business, money and status to the town. There were ripples of concern. Was he leaving for good? Was the whole family going? Had he made enough money to get out, not only from Kapunda but also from Australia? Bel Kidman allayed any such fears.

On 24 March 1908, the Kapunda Institute was packed to capacity to accord a civic farewell to Mr and Mrs Kidman. The Mayor of Kapunda, Mr Rees Rees, and Mrs Rees received the guests along with the Rev. A. G. Fry and Mrs Fry in a hall that had been "tastefully decorated by the ladies". The night was sparked by a musical program rendered by, among others, Mesdames C. J. Coles and W. G. Thomas (obviously connected to the families of the stock agents and auctioneers Coles and Thomas, who presided at the

Kidman Kapunda horse sales). As the ladies warbled, Kidman's mind was no doubt fixed on the record year at the sales in 1907, when 2,260 horses had been sold.

In his bon voyage speech Mayor Rees said, "Mr Kidman has not taken an active part in municipal or other affairs of the town as his business takes him away from home so much; but we all hope that when he returns from England he will become more prominent in local affairs...(Hear, hear)...and perhaps enter the Town Council and become a councillor and subsequently become the mayor. (Laughter and applause)

"Mr Kidman has been closely and very considerably identified with the business of Kapunda. The large stock sales and the horse sales (believed to be the largest in the world) are due to Mr Kidman. This means business to the town. (Applause) Mr Kidman has been a great advertisement for Kapunda and I feel sure his visit to England will advertise Australia better than anything else could. He has plenty of energy, knows Australia thoroughly and will always speak well of it.

"I would like to say a few words concerning Mrs Kidman. (Loud cheering) She always takes an active part in anything involving the welfare of the town, especially charitable work. (Applause) She is always ready to assist both with her hands and her pocket and is held in high esteem by all in the town and district. (Cheers)"

Taking the dais, the Rev. A. G. Fry said, "Mr Kidman has been known in Kapunda for upwards of thirty years. We all admire his sterling qualities. When croakers are about seeing nothing but sheer disaster, he comes along with an encouraging and cheery note and his words go a long way to establish confidence when people are almost despairing. (Applause)"

Town dignitary Sir Jenkin Coles (well known to the Kidman family) said, "Mr Kidman has the reputation of being an honest and straightforward man, who, when he makes a bargain, can always be depended upon to carry it out faithfully. (Hear, hear)

"I have known Mr Kidman for more than thirty years and he has placed me and my family under a personal obligation that will never be forgotten. He is a wonderful man. (Applause) I do not know a second Sid Kidman in the whole of Australia. I know no man with the far-seeing qualities he possesses and the result of that foresight is that Mr Kidman has been prosperous beyond his own expectations and any money he possesses today he is well worthy of. (Applause)

"He has always been generous and likewise Mrs Kidman, who is always at the front door when there is any good work to be done. (Applause)"

Getting to his feet, Mr H. Jackson, JP, said, "Mr Kidman has displayed both energy and perseverance. He has travelled the bush and endured hardships and discomforts when other men would be wanting to wear kid gloves. (Laughter)"

Rising to respond, Sid Kidman was received with prolonged cheering. He thanked the assembled friends for the hearty reception and kind words. It was gratifying, he said. "I've travelled all over Australia and I am always glad to get back home to Kapunda.

"The 1907 horse sale was the largest in the world for one owner and I am sorry I cannot be present at this year's sale. I think the numbers may be down but next year I will be yarding 3,000.

"My family and I leave for England on Saturday but it is not my wish to leave South Australia. I would rather be out in the bush where I am always happy, whether I have 5 shillings or £5 in my pocket.

"The auctioneers and other institutions have assisted me in my business. If I want £5 or £10,000 I always get it because I keep my promises.

"I am not a platform speaker. I am not used to standing on a platform speaking as the other gentlemen who have said such nice things about me. I am more used to sitting on a stockyard fence and talking. (Laughter)

"I expect to be away for about a year. I may go to America and get a billet there...(Laughter)...so as to get some Yankee experience. (Laughter)

"But I will be pleased to get back to Australia because it is the freest and best country in the world. I doubt that I could go anywhere where wheat crops could be grown to surpass those of South Australia within a radius of 150 miles along the coast from Adelaide to Georgetown.

"In my business dealings with people, if I cannot do them any good I have never intentionally done them any harm. We only have a short time to live and a long time to be dead (Laughter) so we should do what good we can while we live. (Applause)

"I've not taken the interest in the affairs of the town I might have been expected to have done because I can't leave my business to attend to them. But it is my intention when I return from this holiday to take more interest in the affairs of Kapunda. (Applause) I might, perhaps, stand for Parliament...(Laughter)...if I can get my wife's approval. (Laughter)

"Some of my men away up on the Katherine River in the north have sent me a costly dressing case. I thank them very much for it. We have always been on the best of terms. But I'm not used to these sorts of things. I have always carried my clothes rolled in a rug. (Laughter)

"I've received a farewell telegram from one of my stations where the message had to be sent 200 miles to a telegraph office. (Applause) I do appreciate it.

160

"I have great faith in Australia. It is a prosperous country. My advice to young men is to 'go north'. If people had not gone north years ago we would not be where we are tonight. They would never have got further than North Adelaide. (Laughter) There are thousands of miles in the country where a young man of energy and pluck can make a living. (Applause)"

Kidman thanked the gathering again for its kindness. It rose as a body to sing "For he's a jolly good fellow", after which supper was served and a dance struck up.

The Kidman family went home that night in good spirits and with various presents: in addition to the dressing case presented to Sid, Bel received a silver bridge box, Gertrude, a pair of field-glasses, Elma, a smelling salts bottle, and Edna, a silver-backed mirror. These were not gifts given by the Kapunda community but presents from Sid's men on his stations in New South Wales, Queensland and South Australia.

Two official duties were to be undertaken on the trip. Bel Kidman had been appointed a delegate to the International Congregational Council in Edinburgh by the Congregational Church Union of South Australia, and while in England Sid was to manage the New South Wales section of the Franco-British Exhibition (whatever that was).

There were banks in England, as well, that ought to be visited. They held properties in which he had more than a passing interest. It wouldn't hurt to see Bel and the girls off to museums and theatres and get among the action a bit himself. He was armed with bankers' advices, introductions and big names. This jaunt to England might haul jolly well after all.

The *Asturias*, at the time, was the finest floating palace ever to have reached Australia. The family passage money amounted to more than £800, and a suite of salons and boudoirs was especially outfitted to accommodate the Kidmans.

A member of the metropolitan press who interviewed Sid before the ship's departure wrote, "The Kidmans will travel in quite a princely fashion. Yet in ordinary everyday life Sidney Kidman is one of the most unassuming men to be met 'neath the Southern Cross, and I venture to predict midst all the pomp and vanity that will surround him on his European trip he will long for a bit of outback mutton and damper and billy can of tea.

"Shortly before he left he was induced to climb into a small frockcoat and high hat in order to fittingly appear at some social function. Those who beheld Sidney in all his glory say he never looked so uncomfortable before in his life."

Life could not have been all that uncomfortable aboard the *Asturias*. Kidman rebooked on it three years later to take Bel, Gertie and Edna overseas (Elma was married by then and his young son,

Walter, at school at St Peter's College, Adelaide). On board during the second trip was Dr Critchley Hinder, who wrote a letter to Bob Holloway, the manager of Hinder's property about 100 miles south-west of Mitchell, Queensland. The letter read:

Kidman, the Cattle King, is aboard. Very likely you have dropped across him. His wife and two daughters are with him. He is a big man with BUSH written all over him. His wife is a happy sort of woman and the girls not beautiful but apparently good natured and perhaps lacking that degree of refinement that one meets with the outback.

I had a long yarn to the old boy about his properties. He appears to have them all over Australia. The largest is about 7,000 miles. He says that pretty well the best proposition is well-back New South Wales country. He owns two or three well west of Bourke; one very large one near Milparinka. He says his last lambing out there was 100 per cent. He had 30,000 lambs. He says they are not too dear and rents are low and you are not likely to get many cut into you.

He recently got hold of a place — 500 miles, two horses, 11,000 sheep and 300 cattle — for £11,000. It is about 100 miles west of Bourke. He further says that the biggest wethers he ever saw came from out that way. His last clip in that country averaged 10½ pounds and he never saw better saltbush country anywhere. His information ought to be good.

He must be a rather mean old bird, or he has a mania for making cash, for as far as I can see, he buys a fresh patch every time he makes a fresh pile of coin. His income could be £200,000 a year. He says horse-breeding on the plains pays well and he also breeds mules.

He is a bit deaf, otherwise I should talk more with him, but it is hard pumping questions into a man shouting loudly and I have not often got him into a quiet corner. Last time he went overseas he brought out a few men — bus drivers and such like fellows.

Of all Kidman was to do on that first trip overseas — buying and selling on a grand scale and meeting influential businessmen and nobility — it was his dealings with the London bus drivers that caused more than a mild flutter in the English press and a furore back home, where the Australian press huffed and puffed and blew it into an issue that Kidman could never understand.

OPPOSITE:
Bel with Gertie, Elma and Edna, around 1908. (Joan Hopkins)

The family went its different ways in London, with Bel and the girls on shopping sprees, young Walter in the care of a nanny, and Sid out and about the hustings on business and teaming up with the family at night for a dinner party or the theatre, where he often fell asleep within minutes. He was sought after by the English press as soon as he arrived in England. The *Daily Mail* reported, "Accompanied by his wife, son and three daughters, Mr Sidney Kidman one of the most interesting personalities in the Empire arrived in London last evening by the steamer *Asturias* from Australia.

"Known as the Cattle King, Mr Kidman was born in the island continent fifty-one years ago and has never been in this country before. A modest man, he was disinclined to talk about himself but is enthusiastic in his praise of Australia."

The *Daily Mail*, overlooking the national patriotic raves, concentrated on Kidman personally as "working his way up to being the largest horse-breeder and greatest cattle-breeder in Australia. He owns more than 100,000 head of cattle and more than 10,000 horses and is master of more than 20,643 miles of territory in Queensland, more than 7,567 in South Australia and more than 21,000 in New South Wales as well as the Northern Territory. He has thirty-two cattle stations and at his home at Kapunda take place the largest horse sales in the world. He has travelled bullocks as far as from 1,700 to 2,300 miles to markets for sale and has had to pay as much as £500 a month for condensed water for 140 horses. This year he has branded 16,250 calves and expects to brand 18,000 next year."

There were similar reports in other papers. Kidman settled into London with ease, talking frankly around banking tables with peers, knights and business barons and, as the whim took him, hotfooting it around London on his own. His absorbed London through the soles of his feet, going where he wanted to, talking to anyone and everyone and asking questions and expecting to receive answers. He often received stares, less on account of his outgoing manner and more on account of his drawling voice and the manner in which he wore a hat — not square on but decidedly side on, a very strange hat worn at a very definite tilt, which Londoners thought quite odd.

London, to this bushman, was almost a nightmare. It was all bricks and concrete but at least there were horses. The horses hauled the omnibuses with drivers at the reins calling, "Bank! Liverpool Street!" Kidman climbed aboard, preferably up front next to the driver and close to the horses, checking them out and bombarding the driver with questions. Where did they come from? How long did they work? What were the shifts? Where were they housed? How much were drivers paid? The questions went on and on. The drivers were only too willing to yarn, especially when the man with the strange voice and hat tipped them for letting him have a go behind the reins. The horses were in good nick. The drivers were compassionate and capable, and worked long hours, but they were worried about their future. Horse-drawn buses were being phased out and motor-buses were being introduced.

"Yer stranger", as Kidman became known, became "yer regular", tossing around grandiose ideas to London bus drivers about a new life in Australia, for which he was prepared to stake them. Would they like to go to Australia and work on his properties? If they had no other skills than omnibus-driving then their scant livelihood stood threatened by the introduction of motorised vehicles. Kidman asked them to think it over. Some of them thought he was mad.

London papers latched onto the matter, one reporting:

> The efforts of the Cattle King may not yet be inspiring emigrating among London omnibus drivers despite the fact that 250 horses are to be disposed of this week and that daily the number of bus drivers becomes less.
>
> Inquiries today by an *Evening News* representative showed that the conditions of the busman's life (which even in the good old days was hardly an enviable one) are now rendered all the worse by the ever present fear of dismissal.
>
> The driver works seven days a week and fifteen hours a day for £2.9.0. If he takes a day off he sacrifices a day's wages.
>
> Hard though their present lot is, some busmen interrogated have not displayed great enthusiasm to become Australian stockmen.
>
> Several have been offered berths by Mr Kidman. "He got up here alongside me," said one, "and began asking me how long I'd driven and such like. And then I twigged. I'd heard of him and I didn't want to go."
>
> Another expressed his anxiety to stick to the horse bus until the last and with an optimistic smile pointed to a motoring rival. "They'll want plenty of horses here soon," he predicted. "Those things won't last. They'll break all the banks in the world."
>
> A real enthusiast for migration was a veteran of 60. "If Mr Kidman comes and asks me I'll pack up and go tomorrow," he said. "Just my line too. I used to break in young horses and then that went down and I had to do somthing — so I did this. London's whacked!"

Kidman was not offended by any who didn't wish to go, but he was happy for those who said they would. He pledged to pay their berth to Australia, and that of their families, and give them work at his stations.

Bel Kidman, happy with the impact they had made on London,

165

KIDMAN: THE FORGOTTEN KING

if not England, was not happy about the business with the bus drivers. "Why, Sid," she said. "You must be growing foolish. What do you know about these men? You've never seen them before in your life and now you are going to take them in without knowing anything about them?"

With a glimmer of humour, Sid said to his wife with mild reproof, "My dear, I took you without knowing very much about you and I have never had cause to regret my choice." Thereafter Bel Kidman had nothing more to say on the subject.

In touch with his Kapunda office, Kidman gave instructions to buy Mount Poole, 593 square miles of country in the Barrier region of New South Wales where, more than thirty years ago, he had tailed German Charlie's cattle. He paid £24,500 for the station.

He'd also had his eye on Innamincka Station for some time. It was owned by English interests and had been troubled by recurring losses. The trustees of the late Hon. William Campbell jumped at the opportunity to sell the 9,175 square mile holding, which included Merty Merty, on the Cooper. It was one of the best stations in South Australia. Kidman paid £32,000 for it. He advised the Bank of New South Wales in Sydney, and bank manager W. E. Frazer remarked, "It is a fine property and cheap at the price. Kidman has also bought Mount Poole and Diamantina Lakes. All are paid for."

Diamantina Lakes was 2,132 square miles in far western Queensland on the Diamantina River. Kidman wanted the station for his Queensland chain. The Bank of New South Wales records show he bought it for £27,500 from combined English–Australian interests, although elsewhere it has been said that he paid £28,500 for it.

He did a spot of selling as well, unloading Victoria River Downs in the Northern Territory and Carlton Hill on the Ord River. Victoria River Downs is said to have covered 12,500 square miles at the time and Carlton Hill, 1,516 square miles. It was at the time the largest, and still remains one of the largest, land sales ever settled in Australian pastoral history. The sale included stock, which amounted to around 100,000 head.

On 25 March 1909 the *Daily Mail* reported, "The largest land and cattle property in Australia has just been purchased from Mr Sidney Kidman and others by a London group supported by Bovril Limited. The property is of enormous area being one-quarter the size of England and Wales and a company to be known as Bovril Australian Estates Limited is being formed to acquire and float it."

Less than ten years before, the Kidman brothers and their partners had outlaid £27,500 for it. It represented a fantastic capital gain: the sale price was £180,000. By the time of sale, Sid Kidman held a six-sixteenths share of the property. Writing to the Bank of New South Wales in Sydney, Sid advised his share of the sale proceeds as

£59,000. He expected to get £28,000 in cash and the balance in a share interest in the property. Jauntily, he also "promised to secure" the Bovril account for the Bank of New South Wales no doubt causing bank manager Frazer to swoon with delight at the mere thought.

Bovril invited subscriptions for 250,000 preferred ordinary £1 shares and a further 100,000 deferred shilling shares, to give the company a capital backing of £255,000, with Bovril supporting the issue substantially.

The *Daily Express* cited the sale as "the sensation of the moment in financial circles", adding that the board of the new company was particularly strong, consisting of Lord Brassey, the Hon. Cornthwaite H. Rason (Agent-General for Western Australia), Sir Edward Wittenoom (chairman of the Local Board of Advice of Dalgety and Co.), Mr M. C. Thomson (director of the Colonial Consignment and Distributing Co. Limited) and Mr Sidney Kidman, the Cattle King, whose holding of Australian pasture was, at the time, nearly 50,000 square miles in extent.

Christmas 1908 had come and gone and Kidman was homesick. He'd remembered the Christmas cattle markets and cabled J. C. Stanford, well-known Melbourne stock salesman, to present a bullock to each of the principal buyers at Flemington, and twenty prime bullocks were given away. He had instructed his agents to give every man and boy who had worked in the yards at the Adelaide Christmas sales a sovereign. The gesture cost him more than £40. A young boy, while admiring the glittering coin on his dirty palm, remarked, "'Ope 'e goes away next year, too, and the year after that."

Now with the Victoria River Downs business settled, it was about time he wrapped up the trip. He had been away from Australia for a year and he wanted to give big cities the shake and return to the outback.

Pencils and notebooks poised, the London press gathered for a farewell interview with Kidman. And why not? What an odd bod he was — more money than you could poke a stick at, up to the hilt in enormous land transactions, yet chumming up with illiterate, down-at-heel London bus drivers. The headlines appeared the next day: "From omnibus to ranch" and "Great cattle owner's London recruits". A typical report ran, "During his stay in London, Mr Kidman has made himself the friend of the omnibus man. In fact he is sending out four drivers with their families to his stations in Australia, paying their passages and giving them excellent wages. He intends to do this also for another twenty lads, including two pages from his hotel.

"'Your omnibus drivers are fine fellows,' Kidman remarked. 'I've done a powerful lot of omnibus riding in London, up on top talking to the men about their horses. I've said to them, "You write to me if you want to come to Australia." The first four of them are now going.'"

When his ship arrived at Perth, he was still harping on his London bus drivers as a tour highlight. A Western Australian journalist filed a small piece of copy that read, "Mr Sidney Kidman, the Australian cattle owner who has returned after a long sojourn in England, said he was astonished at the wages in London.

"'Just fancy a man with a wife and family earning 12s. 6d. a week. I brought out several omnibus drivers with me who had been working seventeen hours a day, all for 5 shillings. They were all good horsemen and will prove useful on my stations. I am bringing out about twenty-five of these men, as well as some fine thoroughbred stallions and Welsh ponies.'"

The newspapers, particularly in the eastern states, had a field day. In Melbourne it was suggested that "playing fairy godfather to London bus drivers and transplanting them as boundary riders was enough to make the Man from Snowy River turn in his grave". "The insufferable impudence of it!" thundered the *Barrier Daily Truth*, in the Labor stronghold of Broken Hill, adding that if Kidman intended to get cheap labour by his "philanthropy" that he'd do well to remember that there were plenty of men in Australia needing jobs. People wrote letters to newspapers tossing both brickbats and bouquets: "Mr Kidman is an admirable man. He should be congratulated and not condemned on his humane gesture" and "Kidman may well sit back and take umbrage over the outcry he has caused — if he knows what the word 'umbrage' means". Piles of letters reached the Kidman office, enquiring what on earth he was doing and asking how he dare introduce such undesirables. The federal government wrote to Kidman demanding an explanation, and the matter became important enough to draw editorials in newspapers. Sydney's *Evening News* noted:

Mr Kidman has just returned from a trip to the Old Country where he found the people "as thick as flies" and only too anxious to get away from it if they were able to do so. The visitor appears to have been particularly struck with the capabilities of the London 'bus drivers for station work; so much so that it is said he is importing a score or more for the purpose of employing them on his stations. Of course, Mr Kidman's experience should be sufficiently extensive to enable him to decide as to the suitability of men for his work. But unless there has been some extraordinary development in the typical London 'bus driver in the last few years, a more unlikely individual out of whom to make a good horseman could scarcely be conceived. However Mr Kidman says such is the case and that as all-round station hands the erstwhile wielders of the whip through the congested London thoroughfares would be a success. He adds that if Australian pastoralists would only give them work, thousands of such men would be glad to immigrate. But apart from the question of fitness, it is of interest to view the attitude of the federal government when confronted with such an alarming proposition as populating the country by means of any scheme, practical or otherwise. At the very idea of a happening of the kind, we have the Minister for External Affairs up in arms with a disquisition on the federal law bearing on the subject. Mr Batcheler, referring to the regulation dealing with immigrants brought out under contract, remarks that no agreement of the kind has been submitted to him and that if such a document is in existence, it will have to be produced. The Minister reserves the right to approve the terms of engagement and there must be no displacing of men now in employment by the new arrivals otherwise the law will be strictly enforced. And in this statement we have the ruling motive for federal interference with all proposals of a similar nature to Mr Kidman's. Mr Batcheler might just as well have said straight out that the policy of his government was to ear-mark all work for the men at present in this country. If there are not enough to perform it today, then it can wait until tomorrow; but no outsiders, 'bus drivers or others, must be allowed to come and share it. Thus the whole question is simplified into the issue that no immigrant must journey to Australia in search of employment unless it can be proved that he is not interfering with any local occupation he may represent. And presumably the onus of proof is to rest with the new arrival; indeed, it is only reasonable to suppose that the government expects the immigrant to have made himself thoroughly acquainted with all such probabilities before venturing to leave his native land. This is immigration with a vengeance. Yet what other conclusion is to be drawn from Mr Batcheler's declaration? He says he is doubtful as to whether there is any demand for labour on the great stations in the interior. As to this, we may fairly consider Mr Kidman a better authority than the Minister, seeing that he owns many of them himself. And if he did not want men, he would be unlikely to go to the trouble of bringing them to this country. The incident is only one more example of the jealousy which animates the supporters and representatives of Labor when any endeavour, even on the smallest scale, is made to interfere with what it regards as one of its chief prerogatives which is to regulate the peopling of the country to its own will and pleasure. And this, needless to remark, is on the scale of what mathematicians generally refer to as a "minus quantity".

Kidman had put his big foot, unintentionally, into the wider issue of immigration that was worrying the newly formed Commonwealth, still struggling to emerge from the results of the Depression of the 1890s. Australia was becoming selective as to who got a foothold in the country, and there was much talk of new arrivals "undermining the Australian standard of living". The basis of the fear was entirely economic: that hordes of foreigners, with their inexhaustible energy and capacity to work hard for low wages, were dangerous competitors. Cheap, sweatable labour had to be kept out of the country.

In Adelaide, the *Register* said, "Mr Kidman has gained some notoriety because of his twenty-five London 'busmen. It was said he was bringing out cheap labour under contract. The authorities have found out their mistake.

"His position in the matter arose out of a generous desire to give a new start in life to a few men whom his practised eye led him to believe would work their way to better things if they had a chance in Australia and it was simply a generous impulse to give a helping hand to these men who came out under his patronage."

Sid had his own "few" words on the subject: "People complain about hard times! Why, I pay plenty of men £2 a week who don't work half as hard as I did for 10 shillings. Those who cry out about hard times want to go to England and see the heartbreaking poverty there is among the masses. It would make them think how lucky they were to be in such a fine country as this.

"The Labor Party has made a great deal out of very little. The twenty-five 'busmen consisted of four, with their wives and families. The others were all young men from various parts of England. I paid £17 a head for their passage and gave them work on arrival. If anyone else can give them anything better, they are welcome to do so.

"It is my intention if I return to England to assist some more out. There are thousands there who would jump at the chance to emigrate if they only had places to come to.

"I have had 100 letters if I have had one since I returned from men in all parts of England asking if I could give them work. The men I brought out here won't replace any of my other men. I've got plenty of work for another fifty or sixty at any time if I can get them to suit me.

"Wherever I went in Europe I advised anyone who could afford it to come and settle in Australia. But I found in England if one said much about Australia, the first thing people said would be, 'Oh! But the Labor Party!' Nothing has done more harm to the cause of emigration than the experience of the 'six hatters'.*

"What I see of the aims of the Labor Party is to place restrictions on the progress of the country instead of helping us in our greatest need — to get more population.

"I have frequently met with the remark 'If Australia is such a good country, how is it that you only have a handful of people?'. I would tell them of the millions of acres almost going to waste in the coastal districts, especially in Queensland, that could be put to the plough. This was impressed upon me when I saw thousands and thousands of people making a living on small plots in Italy, France and Germany, many of them on mountain sides and among rocks — places, we would say, couldn't feed a bandicoot. Truly, the people here don't know how well off they are."

That Australians ate better than bandicoots was to some extent due to Sidney Kidman. A Melbourne paper pointed this out: "Despite his year-long absence, Mr Kidman has been supplying the Sydney, Adelaide, Broken Hill and Melbourne markets with cattle from his Queensland runs at the rate of 1,000 head per week. Had it not been for this source of supply, it is probable that the price of beef would have almost reached famine rates in Melbourne."

Quite a few people bit the hand that fed them over the bus drivers incident. Kidman didn't have time to waste on its aftermath, but it did provoke him to some thought. At 52 years of age he'd been a Labor man all his life. He'd come up the hard way, supplied the miners with meat, provided employment, his transport and coaching business had helped the outback along, and his big stations created a ripple effect — immediate work for men and spin-off work for supplies, transporting equipment, work in country towns, on the railways, in post offices. He thought he wasn't deserving of such a backhander by the federal Labor government over his busmen. So he did something about it. It is hard to pinpoint just when it occurred, but the busmen business sparked it. Kidman changed politics and became a Conservative.

---

* By 1901 the majority of the population was Australian-born and the Immigration Restriction Act (the White Australia Policy plus dictation test) was a move to screen undesirables. They included Asians and Italians (who were thought to be not quite white), and, although they were white, there was some resentment against British people. Organised unions, determined that their members would suffer no competition, took their stand on the clause in the Act denying entry to "persons under a contract to perform manual labour in the Commonwealth". The arrival of certain boilermakers under contract to the Western Australian Railways caused sufficient alarm for an attempt to be made to exclude six hatters on their arrival from the United Kingdom.

13
A Close Shave

WALLY WILL, Bel's stepbrother, had run the office like clockwork in Sid's absence. And a few good seasons put Kidman in a position to "go shopping" again. That meant a trip to his bankers. Barely home, he set off for Sydney to see the Bank of New South Wales. He'd been one of their regular customers for nearly ten years. He had first realised the value of credit in his butchering days at Cobar, when it had worked in favour of the miners to whom he was selling meat. In his earliest days as a station buyer he'd put cash up front. Those days were gone. He had expanded quickly and assistance from the bank had made it possible.

Banking records at the turn of the century show that a wary and close eye was kept on Kidman. He was required to toe a strict financial line — and he did — to the point that nearly a decade later a "comfortable" position existed between the bank and Kidman. Kidman had not let the bank down. His business was considerable. The bank felt easier about dealing with him, to the point of leniency at times.

In April 1909 he called to see the Sydney manager of the Bank of New South Wales on four occasions. Mr Frazer, in his manager's diary, recorded:

> Kidman called and gave a favourable account of his trip to England. His account of interview with leading Englishmen in his particular line of business was very interesting. Borthwick, for instance, was establishing meat works in Queensland. Sir Thomas Lipton, the tea magnate, had missed joining the Bovril Estates Co. but was joining Kidman or likely to do so. He showed a very complete system of book keeping respecting cattle sales. A total of 20,990 cattle had realised £135,000 odd. Calves branded? 30,000 for the past year. He would, in a few years, have no necessity to buy stock for sale. He owned — paid for — 28,000 head of cattle and 6,000 horses. Debtors? He was owed in respect of sales of stock to partners and interests in partnerships some £40,000. Outstanding liabilities? Kidman said he owed nothing outside the bank. Victoria River Downs? His share of purchase money was £59,000. He expected to get £28,000 in cash and the

A CLOSE SHAVE

balance, interest in the property. I lunched with Kidman and
Cope (solicitor) at the Australia Hotel. Kidman was very
informative on Queensland matters — graziers, meat etc. and the
designs of the Niall clique in creating a monopoly in cattle
purchases. Cope, on the other side, proposed a combination of
pastoralists, by which, under organisation, cattle could be sold
on the station at remunerative prices thus defeating the third
party. Left Kidman and co. discussing the plan. Something
evidently to come of it.

With mutual assurance established, Kidman wrote to the bank a few
months later saying that he had purchased Berawinnia Downs,
Tilberoo and Durham Downs from the London Bank. He could resell
Tilberoo at about £4,000 but thought he could do better by hanging
on to it for another twelve months, when it would fetch £10,000. He
bought the three stations for £100,000 (paying £25,000 down, a
further £25,000 in three months, with the balance to be paid within
the next six months). It got him into a spot of trouble. He couldn't
find the remaining £50,000 in the required time.

He went to the Bank of New South Wales straight away. Bank
manager Frazer's diary on 16 July 1910 read:

Mr Fearon, the Adelaide manager called. Discussed Kidman's
affairs with him. He said that with respect of Kidman's purchases
from the London Bank, £50,000 was still owing and the bank was
requiring him to pay up the money. Mr Fearon recommended us
to take securities on the properties and stock in question and
advance the money. We support the view and consider that
Kidman should be more liberally treated than he is by us. The
general manager is to consult us on the matter. There is no doubt
that the Kidman connection is one of the most valuable in the
books and we should cultivate it as his position is quite sound.

Kidman received the money and repaid the bank within a year.

The three stations were important to his strategic chain, particularly Durham Downs — 3,500 square miles of fattening country
in south-west Queensland nourished by Cooper Creek, with floodplains stretching for 12 miles. It was less reliable than the Diamantina
yet the station had been flooded so many times that its homestead
was built on stilts. Tilberoo was 700 square miles of country on the
Paroo River in south-west Queensland; Berawinnia was a holding
north-west of Wanaaring, New South Wales, adjoining the
Queensland border. Overstocking and rabbits had reduced the
carrying capacity of all three. In 1897 Durham Downs carried 27,500
cattle and 7,500 sheep; Tilberoo carried 33,000 sheep and 14,500

cattle; and Berawinnia, 46,000 sheep and 400 cattle. When Kidman bought them, Durham Downs could muster 7,000 head of cattle, Tilberoo, 3,000 cattle and 12,000 sheep, and Berawinnia, 12,000 sheep.

Satisfied with these acquisitions, Sid turned his attention to Rochdale, 200 square miles in the Boulia area of far-west Queensland. It adjoined Carandotta, which he'd bought in 1903, and he instructed the Carandotta manager, Jack Edge, to check it out. Kidman and Edge bought it in partnership from (a man with a classy handle) Le Vicomte De Satge for £1,600. They mustered the run and in eighteen months had sold sufficient fats to pay for the station, which they then sold for £16,000 on a walk-in-walk-out basis.

Information came Kidman's way that Warenda and Tinapagee were for sale. Warenda, 4,000 square miles and owned by E. Weinholt and Company, was south-east of Carandotta and one of the best places in western Queensland. It would give him access to markets in three states. Tinapagee was a large holding north of Wanaaring in New South Wales, stretching almost to the Queensland border. Before the turn of the century, it had carried 69,000 sheep. Kidman had decided to diversify: cattle and horses would always come first, but he now bolstered those interests with sheep and wool. Berawinnia and Tinapagee were the start of the sheep stations.

Further enquiries showed that Warenda and Tinapagee were for sale at inordinately high prices. It prompted Kidman to do something particularly stupid. He wired an offer on both believing the offers were so low that they would be treated with scorn; still, sending off such offers might enable him to find out the lowest prices the owners would accept on the places. He offered £74,000 for Warenda and £43,000 for Tinapagee, chuckling about how that would put the cat among the pigeons. The smile was wiped from his face quick smart when both offers were accepted. With so much of his money tied up in recent acquisitions, he didn't have a brass razoo to make good his offers.

The smart-Alec tactic caught him out neatly. If he truly believed the offers would be knocked back, then he must have expected to put on his haggling hat and try to beat them down in price, as he had done in the past with other station purchases. If he genuinely thought that his offers were ridiculously low, he must have expected to go up in price. If he didn't have a combined £117,000 at hand for such low offers, where did he expect to get, perhaps, £140,000 if he had to meet their purchase price? He had not even asked any of his senior managers to inspect the places. He could, of course, send a telegram stating that acceptance had come too late. But that wouldn't wash. It would damage a reputation he had carefully built up. With barely a penny in his pocket, he could hardly reapproach the bank. The bank had recently lent him £50,000 and might not have taken too kindly to having the weights dropped on it for £100,000 so soon afterwards. Kidman played this hand very closely.

His eldest and youngest daughters, Gertie and Edna, had been bitten by the travel bug in Europe: they wanted to travel again. He told them to cancel any fancy ideas about overseas jaunts every year. If they wanted to see a few sights, they could accompany him on an inspection of his properties. They wouldn't need too much in the way of fashion fineries, just breeches, shirts and big-brimmed hats. The adventurous nature of it all appealed to the girls, but not to Elma, the second daughter, who preferred to remain at home. Cupid had a hand in her decision: Elma was being courted by Mr Sidney Donald Reid.

Sid had outlined the trip to the girls months before the money crisis and preparations had been going on for it. Kidman now speeded things up. The sooner he was out of town the better. It wouldn't hurt to be incommunicado for a while as he tried to sort things out. Wally Will was filled in on the situation. Every saleable beast — horses and cattle — was to be put on the road. And Will could tell the Bank of Australasia (which was looking after Warenda's sale), and anyone else who enquired, that he would be "hard to find" for a while, with Will, of course, keeping Kidman informed by wire as to how the strategy was working — everything from mob numbers to rainfall on stations and market prices. His chief cattle drover, Pat Kennedy, and horse drover, Charlie MacLeod, were notified by return wire when they next contacted the Kapunda office.

With the air of a man without a care in the world, Kidman set off with his daughters, taking the train to Farina, South Australia, and then switching to horses for a 1,000 mile ride before reboarding the train at Cunnamulla, Queensland, and going on to Brisbane.

Kidman was now 53. He'd ridden in the saddle over much of Australia in earlier days: from South Australia into the Northern Territory, all around New South Wales, almost up to the Gulf Country, across to the Queensland coast at Rockhampton and Townsville and certainly through Victoria, which to him was like a pocket handkerchief. On this occasion, Sid had a stint in the saddle when he felt so inclined, but for the most part took the ribbons behind the buggy.

He informed his most senior managers, Galloping Jack Watts, at Bulloo Downs, and John Brooke, at Mundowdna, of the reason behind the pressure to get every possible head of stock to market. His various stations wired what they would be able to contribute. Where Kidman felt the numbers weren't high enough, managers were asked to reassess their numbers and lift them. If his daughters had knowledge of the dramatic business nature of the journey, they revealed not a trace of it when the party arrived in Brisbane in September 1910. An interview with the Kidman girls appeared in the *Brisbane Courier*:

"My hands are an awful colour," said Miss Gertrude Kidman, when interviewed at Lennon's Hotel, "but what can you expect after five weeks in the sun?"

With their faces and hands burned to the brown of a wood berry they presented a picture of happy good health that spoke volumes for the virtues of the simple strenuous life. I say the strenuous life because it was no "specially conducted" tour replete with comforts across two states, for Mr Kidman is essentially a bushman and travels as such, so that while the girls had the advantage of good mounts, the stages were long — 60 miles on one occasion — and the fare at times decidedly the reverse of luxurious.

"We lived for three weeks on salt beef and damper," said Miss Edna Kidman with a laugh, "for we started from home with very little meat expecting to get a further supply at our first stop. However we were disappointed again and again until finally at one stage they offered to slay a goat on our behalf. We declined, preferring the good old salt beef, and so our daily diet continued to be a little monotonous."

Owing to the heavy rains the rivers and creeks of Central Australia were in many places dangerous and impassable and the journey was much prolonged by the extra distances which had to be travelled. One stage covered about 350 miles without seeing a house or hut of any kind. It is estimated that the party travelled about 1,000 miles counting the necessary detours.

Dressed in breeches, coats and leggings, the girls rode horses and camped at night in a small tent carried by the buggy in which Mr Kidman drove. One remarkable fact is that for most of the distance they were riding through stations either owned by their father or properties in which he has an interest. On account of the rise in the Cooper, they had to face the sandhills in the Lake Hope country, and where it was necessary to cross that and other streams, the water often lapped at their saddles and flooded the body of the buggy. One of the girls had a nasty fall through a horse taking fright and for a few miles had a rest in the buggy. This was not the only mishap, for in driving over a sandhill, a "road" gave way from the wheels and the buggy overturned, Mr

---

OPPOSITE:
Gertie and Edna in riding gear. (Photographer: D. E. Porter; source: Kapunda Historical Society)

Kidman and all the paraphernalia being tumbled out.

"This sort of thing did not make for speed," the girls said, "for father had to get down and simply drive the horses up with the trap and, while going down, he was scarcely able to keep his seat."

Camping out was not the least enjoyable part of the trip, for the girls laugh yet at their quaint makeshifts, and their beds of "bush feathers" — fresh young boughs — which, Miss Edna says, "don't make half a bad nest!"

Following Mundowdna and Clayton a line was taken for the Eathadna Mission Station and the stay there was much enjoyed. The blacks were full of humour and greatly struck with the appearance of their visitors whom they at first took for young men until, on closer inspection, one of the young Aboriginals penetrated the disguise and exclaimed with a triumphant smile: "My word, that fella Kidman piccaninnies."

The travellers then struck out for Kanowinna and hereabouts the great sandhills encountered long ago by Sturt provided some exciting and difficult work. So steep were they that they appeared like walls, the horses floundering through the loose sand one minute and sliding down a moving slope the next.

A stay of three days was made at the Innamincka homestead and the drafting of the many hundreds of horses for the Kapunda horse sales provided plenty of sport. The Queensland border was picked up at Nappa Merrie, where a delightful homestead set in an exquisite garden on the margin of a fine lagoon drew admiring comments from the girls.

"You never saw such stocks. There were huge beds of them and in the orchard, heaps of oranges, peaches and other fruit." In fact it was not the bareness of the desert that struck the girls but its fertility.

"Why," the girls declared, "at almost every place we went the gardens were beautiful with an abundance of fruit."

At Durham Downs the girls were struck by the excellent house keeping of the gins, who had everything beautifully clean and at many places where they could not remember a white woman, the pantry and kitchen shelves were covered with white paper and as neat as the heart of a woman could wish. The great muster at Nockatunga was a sight worth seeing and after several long stages Bulloo Downs was reached and another halt called for a few days.

One of the hardest stretches was a 60 mile stage to Thargomindah Station. From there they went to Norley, north again to Ardoch and down to Dundoo where the family was away from home and the travellers with some misgivings took possession of the premises and passed a somewhat nervous night expecting the rightful owners to appear upon the scene at any moment.

"We had all manner of camp mates," said Miss Edna, "and one of the queerest was at Bob's Tank with a 'dogger', that is, a man who goes out after dingoes. Last we arrived at Moongarrie and then on to Cunnamulla where we struck the line and leaving our horses — very reluctantly it must be admitted — we came on by train."

Asked to say a few words on the trip himself, Sid said, "I have not seen some of the country looking so well for thirty years, especially at Durham Downs and Innamincka. I was surprised to see so few rabbits. They had practically died out in places and I went for probably 100 miles with scarcely a rodent to be seen. The stock roads are in splendid condition and all through south-western Queensland a grand season is being enjoyed."

And, perhaps, by no one more than himself. His quiet application on the five-week trip saw the removal of mob after mob after mob from each station to markets in Adelaide, Brisbane and Sydney, and a larger than usual number of horses dispatched for the Kapunda horse sales. He would be able to muster up enough money to see the Warenda and Tinapagee sales through. No longer incommunicado once he arrived in Brisbane, he wired off acceptance of the offers, and sent Jack Edge, of Carandotta, to inspect Warenda.

Mr W. E. Frazer, the Sydney manager of the Bank of New South Wales, has in his diary notes of 5 September 1910: "Kidman called. Said he had purchased Warenda Station from the Bank of Australasia for £74,000 — £ 4,000 cash, £33,000 15th December and the balance at two years carrying 4 per cent." There is no mention of Tinapagee. Mr Frazer's diary on 13 December that year says, "Kidman called. His Kapunda horse sales that year grossed £38,000."

He had bought Warenda and Tinapagee by the skin of his teeth.

14
An Injection of New Blood

SID AND BEL had been home from their first trip overseas less than two years when the travel bug bit again. It infected Bel and she quickly transferred the symptoms to Sid. She had caught the travel disease in a fairly exotic manner. Not England again. Not the Continent. Not America, where Sid was itching to go to have a look around and see how things were done. But India...

She outlined her plans when she knew she had his undivided attention. He had been going like a bull at a gate at business since they'd returned from their first trip. Certainly they had Elma's impending marriage to consider, but after that, why not India? Why jolly India at all, Sid wanted to know? Bel, ever intent on educating her husband, pointed out that he was quite a distinguished member of the British Empire — did he not own or control more land than England, Ireland and Scotland put together? He was acknowledged as a most patriotic Australian, and it would be a fine expression of loyalty to go to India in 1911. Sid grumbled that he had enough potential business on the books and more than enough travel on the plate to keep him rolling along in Australia until he dropped dead. Bel cautioned him against dropping dead. A holiday break would sustain him, and it would please her. It would add to the social education of their two other daughters, Gertie and Edna.

King George V had recently ascended the throne, and he would be the first Emperor to visit India. There was already some discussion about the decision to move the Indian capital to Delhi and so the 1911 Delhi Durbar was bound to be a grand occasion. The word *durbar*, Bel explained, was really a court held by a sovereign or viceroy...a huge levee in a special sanctum where people, notably the Indian princes, paid homage, and where important people from the Empire gathered to grace the occasion. Sid still wasn't overly impressed. It sounded like a frippery trip with no business to boot — certainly not where cattle were concerned. Now, why hadn't she said America instead?

But Bel was determined to have her way. "What of your Kapunda horses, Sidney. Have they no relevance? Have they not gone from Kapunda to India for ten years?"

"I'd recognise every blooming one that ever left Kapunda," he bawled.

"Then we should see after their welfare and what can be done to improve the trade."

"You're right, Bel," he said. "You are quite right. The horse trade is important to me. If the big plan ever sours, I would still deal in horses. Get me the dish of wheat to feed the fowls while you tell the girls they are going to India. I have seen two faces at the window the whole time we have been talking. They will be anxious to know the outcome."

Kapunda was agog that the Kidmans were off to India (but not little Walter who was left at school at St Peter's College, Adelaide). News travelled further afield, drawing journalists to Eringa. Some travelled no further than from Adelaide, but one, James Cassidy, came from 12,000 miles away. He was in Australia writing articles for the *Scottish Farmer* and repaired immediately to Kapunda to see the Empire's "biggest farmer". Sid was happy to oblige, rolling off the facts and figures of his own particular empire, but journalist Cassidy had a fine eye for minor detail as well. His report, in part, read:

I was impressed by the characteristic freedom from ostentation and the wholesome simplicity that distinguished Eringa, Kapunda. It may be that an episode in their home life represents this atmosphere. Mrs Kidman had put on a very plain, homely and comfortable indoor jacket. Her observant husband noticed it at once. "I like to see you in that, Bel," he said, stroking the sleeve. "I like to see you much better so than in any stupid fal-de-lals." "I never wear them," Mrs Kidman said. "I wear nothing stupid." Nor does she, but the preference evinced by her husband is so typical of the style he preferred and of the style of their home that I have no hesitation to quote this pregnant remark on this occasion.

One of the greatest treasures which he brought into the drawing room, where we were sitting around the fire, was part of two forked branches of a tree which he held up before us.

"There's no hocuspocus about this," he said. "This is part of the very tree under which Burke and Wills died. It was under it they lay down; it was under its branches they expired. I cut this down myself." His voice broke slightly. He was away with those grand pioneers in spirit. He, who had known something of their hardships, riding thousands of miles under a baking, blazing sun, who had suffered hunger and thirst and made his way across trackless deserts, none with him but the dumb beasts he led and drove. He appreciated that historic tree, the tree that witnessed the end of life, of the great tragedy of those noble hearts who heard and obeyed the strange call of wild places. Sidney Kidman's heart also is courageous and British to the core.

It was all stirring stuff for the Scots reporter. (Sid, whose earlier souvenir of the Dig Tree had been burnt in the 1904 Kapunda fire, had helped himself to another souvenir as he was, by rights, entitled to, as he then owned Innamincka Station on which it stood.)

The Australian press, likewise, savoured the details of the forthcoming trip and many columnists, decidedly less in awe than the Scots reporter, hurled themselves into snippets such as this: "I see that King Kidman of the monarchy of cattle runs is going to see King George in the glory of the Indian Durbar — both famous men in their way, one by right the other by might. You want a fat purse to see this Durbar business through. I believe King Kidman has had to send a big cheque over to India for the privilege of having a tent for his wife, daughters and himself. Only a tent, mind you, not even the back room of a second rate pub. The Kidman family doesn't leave until December, so apart from losing his interest on his big outlay, the uncrowned monarch of Kapunda stands the chance of anything happening to make him miss the gorgeous Durbar." Sid didn't mind banter of this sort. It made him laugh; he couldn't have cared less if they'd put him up in a second rate pub in India (Bel's opinion would have differed), and the fact that they were dossing down in a tent sounded fine by him.

He felt more awkward at home when he was forced to climb into best bib 'n' tucker for the marriage of his second daughter, Elma, to Sidney Reid on 28 June 1911. The girls, he guessed, would all be leaving the nest before too long. Elma, his second daughter, aged 23, was the first.

Sid was quite happy about the match. Sidney Reid, at 22 nearly a year younger than Elma, was a fine stamp of a fellow and had a lot of get up and go about him. The Reids were a noted Adelaide family who in were the timber business. They sold timber for the lining of the mines at Broken Hill and later expanded business to Johannesburg, South Africa, where the family had lived for some time. On their return to Adelaide, they continued in the timber business and one of its outlets was a fine furniture shop, in which young Sidney Reid did not seem to be particularly interested. It wouldn't hurt, Kidman thought, to get Sid Reid interested in the pastoral business — the more family involvement, the better, and it would still be ten years before Walter could be expected to take a hand in the business.

Sid and Elma were married at the Congregational Church, Brougham Place, North Adelaide, and Elma was described as wearing "a sweet frock of white souple satin with a ninon overdress and ropes of pearls on the bodice. The bridesmaids, Misses Gertrude and Edna Kidman, wore primrose satin with heliotrope lace ninon tunics. Master Walter Kidman acted as page and wore a black velvet suit with white silk stockings and buckled shoes." There was a grand reception at the South Australian Hotel and, after their honeymoon, Sidney and Elma Reid went to live at a splendid house, Holmfield, at South Terrace, Adelaide, which Sid Kidman had bought for them.

Then it was off to India. What Sid thought of it all is to some extent revealed in a letter he wrote from Delhi to his friend and business colleague, the Hon. John Lewis. "I am just writing you a few lines so you will see where we are. My friend, Major Gregory, asked me to come up with him in his car, so I did — 950 miles. It took us 4½ days. We saw plenty of wild deer, wolves etc. coming up. We came through 200 miles of drought-stricken country, as bad as north of Hawker. We passed through Poona and who should we meet but your son Gilbert. I was pleased to have met him. We got a splendid lunch. We had not had a decent feed for two days. India is a different country from Australia — no hotels. Your son has a nice home. We did 200 miles that day. The roads, or main ones, are splendid in India. I saw 200 of Gove's horses land in Bombay, also the one you sent your son. Well, this Durbar is just wonderful, 75,000 troops and 10,000 horses and 26 miles of tents. Some of the rajahs' camps cost £40,000, tents and gardens. The King arrived yesterday and got a great reception by the rajahs of India. The wealth of these rajahs is beyond anything in Australia — diamonds, jewels etc. I never saw such turnouts in my life. India is a much better country than ever I expected to see."

Back home, newspaper columnists sniped at Sid: "The Cattle King is certainly getting above himself. He failed to turn up for presentation to the King the other day. How jealous of each other these monarchs are!" People were appalled at such discourtesy.

The items were extremely unfair to Sid, and also, where the evidence is concerned, not true. The Durbar was held at noon on 12 December 1911 and its official directory contains the complete list of people to be presented to King George at the Durbar and for the duration of his stay in India. Kidman's name was not on it; virtually only the major princes of India and the high officers of the military and civil services were presented to the King. The King's diary for the length of his stay in India reveals no mention of Kidman or the fact that he was stood up by him. The story is almost certainly apocryphal.

Sid had a bonzer time in India. While Bel and the girls went on shopping sprees for jewellery and enormous Persian carpets, he knocked around with the men — and the horses — excited beyond belief when he could pick out his own horses from a distance. Daily, he drew an increasingly bigger entourage, as men trooped around with him marvelling at his capacity to shout, "That's mine. That's mine. And that. And that!" And a closer inspection would prove him right...the BD1 (Bulloo Downs brand), X70 (Eringa), DL5 (Diamantina Lakes) or the diamond tail ♀ of Innamincka. No one could argue that Sid didn't have a memory like an elephant where his horses were concerned.

There were some things, though, that Sid just didn't get right. Back home again, he couldn't wait to tell all the boys in the outback about the glories of India. Roy Dunk was a young stockman working on Currawinya Station when Kidman stayed the night there, on the way to Bulloo Downs on his first station inspection after his return.

"We sat up half the night listening to him talk," Roy recalled. "He explained the fabulous wealth of the rajahs and princes and the rugs on the elephants in the main procession and the number of diamonds and rubies embedded in them. He was given a tour of inspection through one of the mansions of one of the princes, and was telling us about what he saw. 'Everywhere tiger skins, lion skins but what took my eye was this huge head of an incredible hulk...' 'Oh, no! no! *no!*' chipped in an English chap called Digby Gell, who was staying at Currawinya overnight from Hungerford. 'No, Kidman. You mean *elk.*'"

There were official calls to be made as well on his return; Sid ear-bashed his bankers on the subject of India, according to the 29 April entry of the Bank of New South Wales's Sydney manager in 1912: "Kidman gave a very interesting account of his trip to India and the trade possibilities, especially with horses. Says best season ever his stations experienced as a whole. Kidman looks considerably aged these past six months. Becoming quite white."

Sid may have had white hair at the age of 55, yet he remained exceptionally fit and as candid as ever. He reported to the federal government on the Indian Remount trade, saying that it could be bolstered considerably; he could breed and sell horses from £6 to £7 cheaper than he had been selling them, causing a newspaper to comment, "As he has sold thousands upon thousands of horses, the profit he has been making out of the geegee alone is immense."

And there was another official engagement: for the second year in a row Kidman, as the father of the bride, shouted the couple a sumptuous wedding, this time that of his youngest daughter, Edna Gwendoline, aged 22, to Sidney Hurtle Ayers, of the distinguished South Australian Ayers family.

It made for three Sids in the family, Sid himself, Sidney Donald Reid and now Sidney Ayers, who was the son of Harry Lockett Ayers and a grandson of Sir Henry Ayers. The Ayers family came to South Australia in 1841 from England, and in 1857 Henry Ayers embarked upon a political career that spanned more than thirty-six years. He was successively a private member, Minister of the Crown, Premier and President of the Legislative Council — a powerful man not only in politics but also in business, a member and chairman of many boards, including banks. Although Sir Henry had died in 1897, the name Ayers remained topdrawer. Bel was delighted at the match. Sid could not have cared less one way or the other. If Edna was happy, that was the main thing. Unlike Sid Reid, Sid Ayers did not show much enthusiasm for getting involved in the "family business".

The wedding, on 10 July 1912, was almost a carbon copy of Elma's: everyone down from Kapunda for the ceremony...the same church...the same minister (the Rev. A. G. Fry, of Kapunda) of-ficiating. "The bride was beautifully gowned in deep ecru oriental satin trimmed with pearl trimmings. Miss Gertie Kidman, in attendance, wore a dainty frock of periwinkle blue taffeta shot with silver with an upstanding ostrich plume completing the Grecian bands of her coiffure. Master Walter Kidman acted as trainbearer and was dressed in a page's costume of black velvet."

There was no hotel reception this time: guests repaired to Holmfield, South Terráce, Sid and Elma Reid's home. Later, the bridal couple left for Warenda, Clare, an imposing home bought for them by Sid Kidman and, on 29 July, sailed for a honeymoon tour of Europe and America, also probably shouted by Sid.

After so much socialising, Sid decided it was time to concentrate again on business. He was pleased to report to the bank in August 1912 that he had had a record sale of 1,000 prime to extra-prime bullocks, travelling to Hergott Springs, at £15.15.0 a head and that he had decided to buy Morney Plains, 90 miles out of Windorah in south-west Queensland, with his brother Tom Kidman. It was a 994 square mile holding, for which they paid £25,000 on a half-share basis. It was the first time that Sid had entered into a business part-nership with brother Tom, who had remained independent of Sid's operations until now and prospered in his own right on the land in the Naracoorte area of South Australia.

Tom's son, Sidney Nunn Kidman, was sent to run the place a while later, and in her diary his wife, Anna Beryl de Garis, recorded:

It was a novel experience for me travelling from Naracoorte to Windorah every stage of the journey became progressively rougher. The homestead was a humble weather-board with verandah around three sides and surrounded by other buildings, a pantry and kitchen, a harness shed and meat house and an office and store room with a sandy court yard in the middle.

We had three gins, Penta, Couch and Old Maggie. Donald, a hunchback, was a wonderful rider and breaker-in of wild horses.

They were true, trustworthy servants and devoted to me. At times when Sid had to leave the place, Old Penta slept on my door mat with her kangaroo dog. I really believe she would have killed anyone who tried to get in. I made their dresses and knitted dilly-bags for them to carry their "treasures" in. We were there when war broke out. I had a Red Cross bag and sold butter to all the drovers who went through. They paid dearly — but gladly, as all proceeds were sent to Naracoorte Red Cross.

There was great excitement one day when we received a "mulga wire" that the Germans had been defeated. I quickly tore up some old clothes of red, white and blue and made up a flag. Dear Sid climbed up and put a pole on the chimney and hoisted the flag. The mail came once a week — on Friday at midday — and in the next mail we received the worst possible news. The Germans had advanced almost to Paris. Oh dear. Down with the flag and on with the fight.

In his own buying-up battle Sid Kidman then secured Durrie, to the north-east of Birdsville, for £30,000. It was a 3,498 square mile holding, with a 70 mile frontage to the Diamantina, and much of the property was nourished by its braided channels. Sid then bought Tobermory, directly north of Norley Station and on Gumbo Creek. He went halves in the station with the manager, Galloping Jack Watts, as a thank you gesture for the faithful stewardship he had shown in running and managing several of the south-western Queensland stations. Towards the end of 1912 he was offered £20,000 for Carandotta, but refused to part with it for under £25,000 without stock. And the place had 14,000 head of cattle. He swung his attention away from the Channel Country to his furthest interest, Victoria River Downs, in which he was a principal shareholder as one of the directors of Bovril Australian Estates Ltd. Kidman informed the bank that it now had 120,000 head of cattle on it and was worth, at a low estimate, £230,000 — £50,000 more than when sold to Bovril Australian Estates three years earlier. Victoria River Downs was certainly paying its way. Kidman had another reason for dwelling on his interest in the north; rumour was that the English company Vesteys was about to set up operations there. He wasn't quite sure how extensively. There wasn't much harm they could do him with 80,000 square miles of his own, but, just in case they had any ideas about moving into Queensland, it wouldn't hurt to bolster the chain there, especially towards the Gulf. He was a bit strapped for funds to be buying outright, but he thought the Victorian William Angliss might well be interested in some partnership deals.

The year 1912 was rung out and 1913 ushered in with a flurry of more matrimonial activity. Sid was not in a position to go to see his bankers in Sydney in January, but he wrote to them advising that he had "a bill or two falling due and would have cash to meet them a few days before or after".

The Sydney bank manager noted in his diary of 22 January, "As usual Kidman is very casual. He also advises he has bought 3,000 bullocks from Townsville. They have to be paid for 6–8 weeks before he gets paid and the assumption is that we are expected to pay for them. We need to know how Kidman stands with Adelaide as regards overdraft limits and actual liability. It strikes us, it is not so much a saving of exchange which Kidman alleges, as commitments in excess of his banking arrangements. There's no doubt of the strength of his position, although there may be some temporary pressure on him."

The most immediate pressure was the marriage of his eldest daughter, Gertie, on 25 January 1913 to Lieutenant (later Captain) Nelson Clover, of the Royal Navy. The wedding followed the family pattern: same church in Adelaide and same reception at Sid and Elma's place, Holmfield, as there had been for Edna. Edna and Sid Ayers were not there, as they were still overseas on their honeymoon. This time the bride wore "white Liberty satin with plain pointed skirt in fishtail design. Her bridesmaid, Miss Gove [related to Theo Gove, the horse exporter from Melbourne], wore white satin with touches of pink and a tunic of white Valenciennes lace. Master Walter Kidman acted as a page in white sailor suit and as the bride left the church more boys in sailor suits — this time the genuine article from the Naval Reserve — made an archway of bayonets for the bride to pass under down the steps. A further touch of naval etiquette was given with the unharnessing of horses from the bride's carriage which was dragged by some twenty bluejackets from Lieutenant Clover's ship, HMS *Protector*. It seemed a little odd that the Cattle King's daughter should not be conveyed by horses to her wedding breakfast."

Gertie and Nelson spent their honeymoon at Mount Lofty; there was nothing much Sid could do about buying them a home in Adelaide, since Nelson was bound to return to England for Royal Navy duty. One thing was certain, there was no hope of this fellow either ending up in the family business. Sid pinned all his hopes on Elma's husband, Sid Reid, who was proving an exceptionally bright and eager force in handling the business in Adelaide. It wouldn't hurt, Sid figured, to take young Sid Reid on a major tour of the outback stations so he could get a better feel of things.

In the meantime, Sid put out feelers, wanting to be informed of any move the Vesteys made. He didn't have long to wait. They struck like lightning in the north in 1913, causing much consternation.

The brothers William and Edmund Vestey laid the foundations

of their family empire in Liverpool in 1876, when they started importing and wholesaling foodstuffs from America. It was the Australian technology — the development of refrigeration — that enabled them to go global. It was not meat that put them into the millionaire status, but eggs, eggs imported from China at the turn of the century. Deals for the eggs were made on a barter system with war lords in the Chinese provinces. The peasants were paid in cloth to crack eggs by the thousands, and the yolks were whipped up in a giant whisk and shipped chilled from Shanghai. The lucrative business eventually collapsed in the turmoil of political events. The Vesteys then went out to plunder the world for meat. They were particularly excited by what they found in the Argentine: there, cattle were slaughtered largely for their leather, and vast quantities of offal and low-grade meat were cast aside. So they built their own cold stores, bought ships and ran a vertical operation, from the slaughterhouse to the butchershop.

In Australia, the Labor government's plan for developing the north-west of the continent on the basis of small-scale owner-occupied properties was abandoned when they were ousted in 1913 after three years in power. Vast tracts of land became available for lease. The Vesteys sent out Evelene Brodstone to deal with this interesting project. She had started working for William Vestey in Chicago as a 21-year-old woman in 1895 and in such an impressive capacity that he quickly made her his permanent travelling secretary and, ultimately, his mistress. In a short time, Evelene became not only the confidante of the family but also a Vesteys troubleshooter.

To handle the Australian transaction, she travelled from Britain to New York by liner. Then, as the only passenger on a chartered train, she crossed the country to San Francisco, where a Blue Star (Vestey-owned) ship was waiting to take her to Melbourne. Once in Australia, the 39-year-old woman did not muck about. Within a short amount of time she had signed leases for 36,000 square miles — greater than the area of Tasmania. The largest of the places was Wave Hill.

Much of the land was held with peppercorn rents. That the Vesteys were in Australia at all was largely due to the Administrator of the Northern Territory, J. A. Gilruth, an Aberdeen Scot of extreme conservative views, who privately "invited" the Vesteys (later to be known as the "gilded tax dodgers") in. Their presence in the Top End by 1914 and the speed with which they took up the "invitation" caused a major shock and talk of monopolies and beef trusts. From the moment the absentee landlords gained a toe-hold in Australia, they were regarded with resentment, bitterness and antagonism.

Sid was astounded by the scale of the lightning strike. It had taken him eighteen years of careful planning to negotiate his 80,000 square mile empire; yet, like a couple of scalded cats the Vestey boys had moved in and snapped up 36,000 square miles of country. It always pleased Sid in the years following to see a stockman, whom Sid rated as "not much chop", and, therefore, not worthy of promotion, leave his employ and gain a job as a Vesteys manager or a position with Vesteys that soon became that of manager. It led to the bush tribute to Kidman men that "a Kidman stockman was a Vesteys manager", or in plain-speaking terms, the Vesteys managers were very second-rate chaps.

On 1 July 1913 Sid, with son-in-law Sid Reid and his brother Malcolm Reid, left Adelaide on a 3,000 mile inspection of the eastern stations. They went to Sydney by train, staying for a fortnight, during which they saw yard after yard of Kidman cattle sold at Homebush. Sid caused some amusement to the buyers by insisting on the auctioneer accepting the first bids offered. The result was that about 300 cattle in pens of fifteen to twenty-five were sold in ten minutes, with Sid good-humouredly telling the buyers that the less he got for his cattle the less commission he would have to pay.

When the auctioneer, Charles Wood, reached what the Cattle King considered the value, Sid would clap his hands as a signal to stop and yell, "Knock 'em down. Knock 'em down!" When the auctioneer still kept on, Kidman pulled his arm, gesticulated excitedly and again yelled, "Knock 'em down, I tell you." The buyers encouraged him and needless to say his sales were particularly fast; in some instances the booking clerk had to call a halt. Sid saw that every buyer got a yard at shillings below what they were willing to pay. They wished that "Knock 'em down" Sid would visit Homebush more often.

During the fortnight in Sydney, Sid disposed of about 12,000 head of cattle privately to the Queensland and Sydney Meat Works, exclusive of the mobs sold on the markets every day at Adelaide, Melbourne and Sydney. As many as 6,000 bullocks came from one of his Queensland stations.

The three men left Sydney on 18 July in a Ford motor car, travelling through the Blue Mountains, where it was snowing, and then on to Wellington and Bourke, which they reached on 23 July. Sid pronounced Bourke's trucking yards as the best he had ever seen, with every possible facility for loading and unloading. They then

OVERLEAF:
Galloping Jack Watts (left) of Norley Station, one of Kidman's most trusted managers, shares a bush lunch with the boss. (The Kidman family)

headed for Boorara, a west Darling station of 1,300 square miles, running 30,000 sheep, 200 horses and 1,000 cattle. On 30 July they left Boorara, striking their first puncture after 1,000 miles of travel (caused by a tyre striking a mulga stump). They travelled to Tinapagee, to Wanaaring and Thurlow Downs, where the country was very bad, then on to Berawinnia, which had one of the best woolsheds on the Paroo. On 4 August they crossed into Queensland to inspect Caiwarra, where shearing was under way and the expectation was of 800 bales of wool. There was abundant feed at Caiwarra, as there was from Eulo through to Tilberoo (a 700 square mile holding held by Sid in partnership with his nephew Tony Kidman). It was originally a sheep run, but it had converted to cattle because of the wild dog menace. Both Tilberoo and Caiwarra were experiencing one of the best seasons for twenty years. From Tilberoo the party again headed for Boorara, passing on the way a mob of 500 Kidman cattle travelling from Durham Downs to Bourke.

On 9 August they were about 20 miles out of Boorara and mounted on horses when Sid showed the fine style of his horsemanship (at the age of 56) by setting off through the scrub at full gallop after an emu. He was still a competent, active and strong rider. From Boorara the travellers went on to Kilcowra and on 13 August arrived at Thargomindah and then at Norley. It was managed by Galloping Jack Watts and was 1,628 square miles of the total of 9,000 square miles that he managed for Kidman. By 18 August they were at Durham Downs (approximately 5,000 square miles with 25,000 cattle) where they found feed plentiful and all the cattle fat. Twelve miles out of Durham they watched the men at work bronco branding, a method of branding cattle in the open and one that was favoured by Kidman as both economical and time-saving. On the road to Nappa Merrie the party encountered a lot of sandy country and experienced a mishap in which one of the back wheels of the car was splintered, requiring it to be left at Nappa Merrie.

From Nappa Merrie the party continued in a buggy to Innamincka, inspecting on the way Burke's Depot (the tree under which provisions had been buried for Burke, Wills and King when they were returning from the Gulf). Innamincka, in South Australia, was an area of about 7,000 square miles, including Coongie, which Kidman also owned. It had 40,000 cattle in splendid condition. The journey back was through Branbury, Dingara and Tickalara, but the country was bad between Tickalara and Bulloo Downs and it was difficult to get good feed for the horses. At Bulloo Downs they drafted horses for sale at Wellington; it was a busy stint at the station with thirty-three stockmen, drovers and visitors on deck at the one time.

On 31 August they left Bulloo Downs and continued in the Ford car through Conulpie Downs in New South Wales, where the country was in a frightful state. The manager at Yantara Station reported that the kangaroos were bad (he estimated 20,000 on the run) and so were the rabbits — they were killing rabbits in thousands. At Mount Poole Station, shearing had been completed and Kidman was assured of a good clip. At Salisbury Downs they found the feed better, but at Yancannia, the largest station in New South Wales, the dust and wind were distressing. On the way to Morden, an appalling dust storm was encountered, and Broken Hill was reached on 6 September via Wonnaminta and Nundora. The Ford car had done yeoman service over the 3,000 miles, during which they had visited thirty-three stations, twenty-two of which were either owned by Sid or were places in which he had an interest.

Back in Adelaide, the press was waiting for Sid to pronounce on the back of beyond and a report in the *Register* read:

12.30. Bennett and Fisher's office. Interview with Mr Kidman. That was how the assignment appeared in the reporters' book on Saturday morning and my initials were in front of it. Now I had interviewed Mr Kidman before and knew that however good his intentions might be that the chances were 10 to 1 that he would not be at the chosen place at the appointed time; not through any fault of his own, mind you, but because of the many people who waylay him wherever he goes. Then again, I recognised that even if the Cattle King was on hand when the clock chimed the half-hour, the odds were 50 to 1 he would be besieged by half a dozen men from all over the country anxious to discuss matters of mutual interest. Therefore I decided to get in early and arrived at the office with five minutes to spare.

"No," said Mr Hughie Davis, "Mr Kidman has not yet come along but we're expecting him any minute." A quarter of an hour passed and we walked out on the verandah of Bowman's Arcade and looked down King William Street. A moment later Mr Kidman came into view. While walking 30 yards he nodded to several acquaintances and at last was bailed up by one. Mr Davis tossed a penny down to attract his attention. A sprightly newsboy promptly snapped up the coin and looked for more. Instinctively Mr Kidman put his hand in his pocket and threw the youngster a duplicate. Mr Davis had a second shot and this time the penny fell on Mr Kidman's head. He looked up and appeared to recollect that he had an appointment. At any rate within a couple of minutes he entered the office. "The train was late," he explained, "and I met two or three friends coming along the street but now I'm here, what do you want?"

"You've just returned from a very long trip through New

South Wales and Queensland, Mr Kidman. What country did you traverse and how did it look?"

"Oh, you'd better get hold of my son-in-law Sid Reid and his brother Malcolm. They went with me and made a heap of notes which should be very interesting reading."

I admitted that that was quite likely but explained my immediate task was to interview him.

"Well my memory is not as good as it was," he replied, "and I reckon I've forgotten some of the places we visited."

"Never mind, Mr Kidman, just go ahead and tell me what you do remember." The thought of the Cattle King's prodigious memory letting anything slip made me smile.

"We left Adelaide in July going straight through to Sydney where we bought a Ford and an Overlander and started for the outback by way of the Blue Mountains and Bourke and all along the way the crops and feed were simply splendid. I've decided to send cattle to Dubbo and Wellington for paddocking. From Bourke we went to Boorara, where the shearing has just finished, thence, Tinapagee, Wanaaring, Berawinnia Downs, up the Paroo again to Tilberoo where things are looking lovely and the stock are in beautiful condition...on to Kilcowra, back to Thargomindah, across to Norley and Tobermory, along to Nockatunga on the Wilson, to Durham Downs on the Cooper and then to Nappa Merrie. The Cooper Creek country, especially Durham Downs, looks remarkable well. We broke a wheel of the Overlander at Nappa Merrie and had to ride on horseback to Innamincka. There we got fresh horses and a buckboard, returned up the Cooper, went across to Bransbury, Dingera and Tickalara and then back to Bulloo Downs, a distance of 220 miles. We found Bulloo Downs, Thargomindah and Tickalara in great heart and all the cattle fat. Having picked up the Ford, we started for New South Wales via Conulpie Downs and Yantara, slipped down to Mount Poole, across to Salisbury, then to Yancannia, Morden, Broken Hill and home."

Mr Kidman rattled that itinerary off with scarcely a moment's pause as though he had merely picked out the principal stopping places on a mental cinematographic film of the vast area he had encompassed. No. Advancing years have not weakened his memory or diminished his powers of observation. The outlandish names of the outback stations he pronounced like a native and although I persuaded him to spell two or three,

OPPOSITE:
Aborigines from Coongie Station in front of their wurley. (The Kidman family)

195

he hustled through them so rapidly that it was almost a sheer impossibility to take the letters down. Therefore, if any of the names are misspelt, blame Mr Kidman.

"Well, I suppose that's all you want?" he said. I laughed, "Why we've hardly begun. Tell me something about the country generally and the sheep and cattle?"

"West of the Paroo to the South Australian border from the Queensland boundary down to Broken Hill the country is extremely bad. In fact I've never seen it worse and never known the prospects poorer. Some very heavy losses of stock are inevitable. They can't be avoided. The lambing as far as I can see is certain to be practically an absolute failure and we will be lucky if we can save the bulk of our sheep. On my New South Wales stations the lambing has been almost a complete failure. I had more than 60,000 ewes to lamb but I doubt if we shall save 5 per cent of the lambs and probably 2 per cent will be nearer the mark. Fortunately, as I mentioned, the country further east in New South Wales is splendid. To give some idea of the difference between the conditions, I started two mobs of sheep from Tinapagee about the same time, one lot for Adelaide and the other for Wellington. Of those for Adelaide nearly 1,000 died and I had to rail the remainder from Mingary to save their lives. The mob for Wellington, which included old ewes and wethers, arrived in capital order and we have just sold them at a good 40 per cent more than I will get for those consigned to Adelaide.

"The track followed by the cattle and a large number of the sheep booked for Adelaide is in a terrible state and there is one stage of 50 miles destitute of feed and on which the water has almost entirely failed. Owing in a measure to the better conditions in the eastern parts of New South Wales, the demand for both cattle and sheep is really good and you can sell any number of stock of almost any class. A lot of the cattle I had originally intended to send to Adelaide I have turned to Sydney. The demand for cattle in Queensland, where by the way, the pastoral position is much brighter than in the western portion of New South Wales, is better than it has ever been before. Recently I sold 13,000 bullocks — bullocks, mind you — to be delivered at Charleville, Longreach and Winton for dispatch to the Brisbane and Townsville Meat Works."

"And what are the prospects for the local cattle market, Mr Kidman?" The Cattle King looked a wee bit worried and with a characteristic gesture he pushed his hat on to the back of his head and quietly observed, "I don't think I'd better say anything about that just now. I'll be getting the latest information next week and I'll be able to let you know then."

"But the public, the people who eat the meat, are anxious to know and you are the man best qualified to make them wise. . ."

"Well, to tell the truth, I don't see where, after the next few weeks, they are going to get supplies from and during the following six months or more cattle must be scarcer and prices higher than they have been for a considerable time. Lately more cattle have been coming to the Adelaide market than it can reasonably take but, with the difficulty in reaching Hergott Springs and Farina and the high railway freights on the local railways and the keenness of the Queensland meat companies, it seems to be certain that Adelaide will go short."

"You said something about the high railway freights in South Australia. Are they higher than those in Queensland?" Back went Mr Kidman's hat and leaning forward he vigorously tapped out the following words on the table with his finger — "Do you know that if the South Australian government does not wake up and provide better railway accommodation it will lose the bulk of its present cattle trade for the simple reason that not only does it pay better to sell in large lots to the Queensland meat companies on the stations than send small drafts to Adelaide but on the Queensland railways all consignments of fourteen vans and over carry a freight reduction equal to 25 per cent off ordinary rates. Further, the vans there take from one to two bullocks more than ours and the same remark applies to the New South Wales and Victorian trucks. According to the capacity of the trucks we pay more per mile in South Australia than they do in any of the other states and, in Queensland especially, every facility is afforded for efficient transportation."

Ding, dong, ding, dong, ding, dong, ding, dong, ding, dong, ding, dong. That was the General Post Office clock chiming a quarter to two. Mr Kidman said he was going to the Show as his friends hadn't given him a chance to see anything on the previous day. I slipped my pencil away and said good-bye. As I passed through the outer office, I saw a waiting young man who had entered at the same time as myself and stated that he had an appointment with Mr Kidman at 12.30. His luck was out. I'd beaten him to the post.

That Sid had not seen much at the Show the previous day was obvious from a press report that appeared the same day as the *Register*'s intrepid Special Reporter struck out for the above interview. It ran:

The Show is a hard place to negotiate an interview with Mr Kidman, for the Cattle King was surrounded by many friends.

"Hullo, Mr Kidman."

"Hullo, Jack! Hullo, Bill! Harry! Jim! Charley!" This modest and unique monarch was holding a levee only it was a levee to which everybody seemed to have the right of private entree. This is how my conversation turned out:

"Where have you been Mr —?"

"Hullo, Bill, old chap. (This is Mr Kidman talking, but not to me mind.) You're looking all right. Saw McDonald and Conroy in Queensland. They want to be remembered to you. Yes. I'll see you tomorrow. Right you are."

Well, thank heaven Bill's gone.

"Had a nice trip, Mr Kidman?" I began again.

"Yes, but the country looks jolly bad, worse than I've known it for forty years. I took a motor from Sydney and —! Coooeee. George! I want to see you. Got something to tell you about a mob of horses. I —! Right. I'll see you Sunday at half past twelve. I'm going to run home to Kapunda but I'll be back over the weekend."

"Yes," I suggested, "you took the motor —"

"Oh, yes. (G'Day, Charley. I'll see you later.) I took the motor from Sydney and made a long tour of my stations. (Look, there's Jimmy!) The country wants rain, rain, rain, and rain and plenty of it."

"How are you, Mr Kidman?"

"Oh, good thanks, Bert."

"Been away, Mr Kidman?"

"Oh, yes. Had a little trip up north."

"As I was saying, the country wasn't attractive...too jolly dry. That's the —! Hey! There's Donald Forbes. Hullo, Don. Yes that's the trouble, no rain."

"But you'll hold your big horse sale this year?"

"That's fixed all right. I can't — See you again in a minute, Alf — I can't say the date yet."

I gave up. It was nigh on impossible to talk to Mr Kidman under such circumstances. I left him talking to "Alf" and the best thing I wished "Alf" was that he would have better luck than I had.

The bewildered reporter would have done better to wish Sid luck. His was about to run pretty thin over the next few years. He knew he was in for a tough time by the look of so much of the land. But not Sid, nor the fazed journalist, nor anyone else had a glimmer of the appalling time that Australia would have to confront over the next few years.

15
The Great War

FOR SEVERAL REASONS the First World War was different from any other previous war. In the first place, during the four years that it lasted every great power in the world was involved. On one side were the empires of Germany, Austria–Hungary and Turkey; on the other side, Britain, France, Italy, Russia, Japan and, from April 1917, the United States. Fittingly it earned the title the Great War and it was more destructive than any previous war in history. Not only was war waged for the first time in the air, but in addition both on land and at sea men fought with new weapons such as machine-guns, tanks and submarines.

The outbreak of war took most Australians by surprise. They responded enthusiastically to being a part of the "big skirmish". Patriotic fervour ran high, with Australian Prime Minister Andrew Fisher making his famous promise to help defend the empire "to the last man and the last shilling". After the war, Australian Prime Minister Billy Hughes somewhat savagely reminded the Versailles Peace Conference (and in particular United States President Woodrow Wilson, who dominated it) of the extent of the Australian commitment. "Mr President, I speak for 60,000 dead. How many do you speak for?"

Altogether, 417,000 Australians volunteered for service; 329,000 served overseas; 60,000 were killed or died as a result of war service; and the total casualties were 226,000. The cost in Australians killed or wounded was high indeed. Australia suffered more casualties in proportion to the total number of enlistments — nearly 65 per cent — than the soldiers of any other nation, including France and Germany. In fact Australia lost more men than did the United States, and our total population was equal to that of Greater New York City at the time — one-twentieth of the population of the United States.

Sid Kidman was 57 when the war started, and the man who couldn't tolerate waste in jam tins or station stores was appalled by the waste of human life the war represented. Had he been a younger man it is safe to say that he would have enlisted — no doubt wanting a berth in the First Remount Unit.

For service in the war, 121,000 Australian horses were sent

overseas, chiefly to the Middle East. From 1916 until the armistice there were never less than 100,000 horses and mules serving in Egypt and Palestine as riding, draught and pack animals. The strategic and tactical importance of the mounted arm and the need for prompt replacement of animals unfit for service resulted in the creation of the Remount Units. The function of the units was to take the horses and mules shipped into Egypt and prepare them for issue in the shortest possible time. Riding horses had to be broken in, trained to work in troop formation and to lead. No mount was issued until it was steady enough for a fully equipped trooper to get on and off under any circumstances. The draught horses and mules had to be broken into harness.

One-fifth of each Remount Unit (forty men) were roughriders, horsebreakers and stockmen from the backblocks and also buck-jumping riders from the shows and circuses. Foremost among them was Jack Dempsey, the leading roughrider in Australia at the time, who had travelled with the Skuthorp, Eroni and Martini shows and had his own buckjumping circus shortly before the war. If age had not barred him, action with the Remount boys would have suited Sid Kidman admirably; he may have even outshone Sergeant-Major Jack Dempsey, considering what Lance Skuthorp himself had to say about Kidman's riding prowess in an article in the *Bulletin*:

The "cattle king" was the best buckjump rider I ever saw. When I was showing on the Gawler Showgrounds, near Kapunda, South Australia, where Kidman lived I had 14 of the best buckjumpers in the land. I was offering £5 to any man that could ride one. Through the crowd pushed a fine stamp of a man who said, "My name is Sid Kidman. I will be here for the next session of the show to ride a buckjumper for you. Tell these people — they all know me — and you will get a big house. I suppose things are not too good with you, feed so dear, and that." I told him business was good but he shook his head. He knew it cost me £19 to get £20 back.

When he returned I was saddling a yellow bay which I called Fausho Ballagh. I was going to ride him myself as he could easily throw any of my riders. Kidman walked into the yard and said, "Is this the horse for me to ride?" I told him it wasn't.

"This is a bad one," I explained. "He gets down on his shoulders and spins in the air like a top. I will bring you in a nice easy one." Kidman walked up to the yellow brute, fixed his stirrups to the right length, mounted and gave the word. Then we let the big horse go. The rider held the reins loose and belted Fausho Ballagh with his hat until he stopped bucking. I offered him the £5 forfeit. "Buy a ton of chaff with it," Kidman said. That night the outlaws had a great feed.

If Kidman couldn't go to the war himself, he was determined to do his utmost to help the Australian war effort. He didn't wait years nor even months, but within a matter of weeks of the war erupting, he swung into action. He was aghast at what the Germans had done during the march through Belgium — not only slaughtering people but also cattle and horses, wrecking agricultural machinery and razing farmhouses.

In his book *Memoirs of a Stockman*, Harry H. Peck, the noted Melbourne stock agent, said:

Not many remember that it was Kidman who started the Belgian Fund for which Australia raised over £700,000 by voluntary subscription to help Belgian farmers with implements and seed to make a new start after the Germans had devastated their country.

I happened to be at the Adelaide market in the spring of 1914 at the time news came through that the German armies had occupied Belgium and that the people of the country were practically starving. We talked about what Australia might do to give them at least a good dinner for Christmas. Kidman knew that at the time there happened to be a large quantity of Australian frozen beef in store in London, so I suggested that instead of asking the public for subscriptions to buy as much of this as possible to send across from London to Belgium at Christmas, we ask stock owners to send into the markets of Australia consignments of stock to be sold for "A Stock Owners Belgian Christmas Dinner Fund" and cable the proceeds to London to buy Australian beef there for the purpose.

Kidman jumped up at the proposal and said, "Right. I will start it off with drafts of bullocks to Adelaide, Melbourne, Sydney and Brisbane," and this he promptly did, with the result that many others followed the good lead and we were able to cable some thousands of pounds to London in plenty of time for Australian beef for Belgian Christmas dinners to be distributed through the good offices of the American consul.

That was the beginning of the subsequent general "Belgian Fund".

In September 1914 the Melbourne press noted, "Mr H. Peck, of J. M. Peck and Sons, last night received a telegram from Mr Sidney Kidman, the 'cattle king', to say that he is sending fifty bullocks for sale at Newmarket on 14 October, the object being to initiate, with the proceeds, a fund to send a shipload of meat to the Belgians. Arrangements are being made to have agents appointed in Melbourne, Sydney, Brisbane, Adelaide and Perth, to receive similar gifts of stock and conduct the sales." Kidman became a regular contributor to the sales.

The Commonwealth government contacted him for help before the end of the year. Kidman received a telegram from the Minister for Defence, Mr Millen: "Am appealing to horseowners for donations of horses. Will you give the lead to this movement? Millen." It did not take Sid long to forward his reply: "Only too delighted to do anything I possibly can for my country. Will give you 200 military horses; also 100 frozen bullocks. Understand horses must be broken in. Have 200 animals just arrived at Oaklands (100 miles north of Broken Hill) from Norley Station for Kapunda sales, principally unbroken, all fat. You can pick 50 or 100 from this lot if you wish. Will supply balance from my different stations or, if you prefer it, will give you horses and cattle value in cash. Kidman."

Perhaps he thought he could improve upon this. Remembering that there was a large number of horses in Queensland ready to be shipped to India, and thinking it would facilitate matters and place the Commonwealth government in a better position to secure a class of horses in one line, he forwarded a further telegram: "Am interested in Queensland in a shipment of about 1,000 horses all ready for shipment to India. You can have them at cost price. All good, picked horses. Kidman."

In reply to these messages Defence Minister Millen telegraphed: "Warmly appreciate your prompt and generous offer. If you can supply broken-in horses capable landing either Adelaide, Sydney or Melbourne, prefer horses: failing that, gladly accept cash. Millen."

Newspapers, under the headings "Mr Kidman's generosity" and "A splendid offer", noted that the 200 military horses and 100 frozen bullocks represented a gift to the value of between £4,000 and £5,000, not counting the 1,000 horses at cost price. And one of the batches of horses was to come from Norley Station. Norley had a prestigious reputation: it had produced Bullawarra, the best all-round horse in Australia in the years leading up to the war (both in racing and hurdling).

Four months after war broke out Kidman made an outback tour of his stations. Between Christmas 1914 and April 1915 Kidman made three trips by motor from Kapunda to Sydney and then to the Gulf Country and home. The trips were to check the reorganisation needed because of the large number of young employees who had enlisted, and to find out how the country and stock were coping in steadily worsening drought conditions. At Wentworth, New South

Wales, returning home from the third trip, he spoke to a representative of the *Western Advertiser*, who asked how many of his men had enlisted.

"Every mother's son has volunteered and gone," Kidman said, "with the exception of two whom I retained because they were absolutely necessary to me as managers.

"They asked if their billets would be open to them on return and were told 'yes' and better ones, and a life pension to any man who might be injured or his dependants." [More than likely Kidman is referring here to young, unmarried men who joined up and not his married employees of eligible age for service, many of whom remained home and continued to work for him during the war years. For the most part his chain of properties was run during the war by a reduced number of employees, with a brigade of older, but none the less competent, men predominant among them.]

The war, Kidman added, was a terrible business. A few years ago on his first venture overseas, he'd travelled right through much of the country already devastated.

"When travelling from Brussels to the field of Waterloo, I met on the road a car which contained a very familiar face. I stopped my own car and chatted with the fellow.

"'What on earth brings you here, Mr Kidman?' he said to me. 'Same to you,' I replied. 'Last time I saw you was on the Darling River and it's a long way across.'

"It transpired that the stranger had married a French lady and settled in Belgium. He was doing well and was quite happy. I had a letter from that same fellow not so long ago saying that the Germans had ruined his farm and home and that he was now completely broke.

"That is the kind of incident that brings the war home to us out here. We owe more than we shall ever know to the Belgians and I think that everyone who cannot go to the front should do what he can by way of contribution to the various relief funds. In this connection I have been very much surprised to find that lots of rich men whom I know have given practically nothing. I cannot understand it."

A fortnight later a far worse complexion could be put on things than the case of the Aussie–Belgian farmer who had at least survived the German onslaught to drop Kidman a line. In the early dawn of 25 April thousands of Australians stormed ashore on a narrow beach at Gallipoli attempting to claw their way up almost perpendicular hillsides heavily entrenched with prepared Turks. The valour displayed

by both the Australians and New Zealanders in the face of such predictable slaughter has become legendary.

Kidman dug deeper into his pocket. When men who had left his stations to serve overseas wrote back telling of the wonderful work done by the Red Cross, Kidman gave handsome cheques to that organisation. But he was greatly concerned that others in a position to be able to give freely were not hauling their weight. He had always been a successful dealer and trader, largely because he had such a shrewd understanding of human nature. Early in 1915 Kidman started to angle his donations differently: in future, he would give a certain amount *if* others elsewhere matched his efforts.

National press reports read, "In response to the offer of Mr

Sidney Kidman to contribute to the Belgian Fund £500 in each of the four eastern states of the Commonwealth provided nine other similar subscriptions were raised, the conditions have been fulfilled in Queensland and New South Wales and cheques for £500 each have been sent to these states on Mr Kidman's behalf by J. M. Peck and Sons Pty Ltd. In South Australia a commencement has been made to raise the necessary number of £500 contributions but there has as yet been no response in Victoria to this particular offer."

ABOVE:
Sid yarding horses before the First World War. (John Ayers Jnr)

205

It prompted Miss Marianne Crooks, of Norwood, South Australia, to send the following letter to the editor of the *Register*: "I noticed in the *Register* of March 20 that Mr Kidman with his usual generosity had offered to give £500 in four of the Australian states on condition that nine other citizens in each state will give the same amount. I have looked in the papers each day since and been astonished that so far there has been no response to his appeal for the Belgians. Surely we will not allow this blessed privilege to lapse of lending a helping hand to those who are suffering so severely and who have done so much to save our Empire. They are now bearing their terrible troubles with a patience which draws forth our love and admiration. I will gladly be one of the South Australian nine to give £500."

Another Kidman strategy was under way and working well. Kidman was to use it repeatedly.

At the Adelaide wool sales in 1915 no one begrudged him the distinction of obtaining the highest price for scoured wool for the year. Before the sale he instructed his selling woolbrokers to give to the Belgian Fund the proceeds of ten bales of wool with a breakdown as follows: three bales, Salisbury Downs (Kidman and Angliss); two bales, Yantara (Kidman and Reid); one bale, Willpoorina (Mrs S. Kidman); one bale, Boorara (Master Walter Kidman), one bale, Tinapagee (Mrs S. Ayers); one bale, Mount Poole (Mrs S. Reid), one bale, Berrawinnia (Mrs N. Clover). The last three named were the Kidmans' married daughters. The record price was 25½ pence for scoured back wool selected from his well-known Mount Poole clip, a figure not eclipsed elsewhere in the Australian wool market that year.

Newspapers acknowledged his donation and also attempted to put it in its right perspective, stating that "it may not have been generally known that the 'Cattle King' had an interest directly or indirectly in about 8,000 bales of wool." In that light ten bales did not appear to be all that much. Kidman was to argue, "What about the rest of the boys doing the same thing?"

He was more open about the tactic the following year at the Adelaide wool sales when, to the surprise of spectators in the "strangers' gallery", Kidman stalked into the arena strictly reserved for buyers and brokers and whispered in the ear of Mr Jeffrey, of Bagot, Shakes and Lewis auctioneers. It was a dramatic entrance and subsequent happenings were equally startling. The *Register* noted:

At the first break in business, Mr Jeffrey announced that the "Cattle King" with his customary generosity had decided to give ten bales of Boorara wool (Queensland station) and five bales of Salisbury Downs (New South Wales station) wool, the latter on account of Kidman and Angliss to the YMCA Fund, also ten bales of Tinapagee (New South Wales station) clip to the Wounded Soldiers Fund. Loud and enthusiastic cheers followed and then Mr Kidman jumped to his feet.

His rising was the signal for further appreciative demonstrations. As though the former gifts were altogether too insignificant, he said he was prepared to give another 100 bales for the benefit of funds to be selected by the South Australian Governor provided that ten other woolgrowers would each contribute a like quantity.

"Hear, hear!" cried the brokers and the buyers and for once the commissionaire in the "strangers' gallery" forgot to cry, "Silence!"

Mr Kidman further stated that he would present £2,000 in each of four states of the Commonwealth on condition that ten others would produce a similar sum in any or each of the states.

This brought the enthusiasm to a climax and it was some time before the proceedings assumed their normal aspect.

Perhaps the wool input had not been enough. It was announced at the end of the sale that the Bootra Pastoral Company (Messrs A. S. Kidman — Tony, Sid's nephew — W. Stewart and S. Kidman) would give a further five bales of Bootra wool to the YMCA Fund and that Mrs Kidman would present five bales of the Mount Poole (New South Wales station) clip. It meant a total of thirty-five bales, valued at more than £400.

By December 1915 Kidman had taken up £15,000 of the War Loan and had given almost £14,000 to the various funds, and his bankers reported, "He is now full of an idea to organise help for soldiers who have lost their sight and we recommend him to see the editor of the *Sunday Times* who will give prominence to the idea."

By 1916 he was receiving news of the worst possible type — news of his Kidman men. They were not letters written by the men themselves. The letters reported their deaths. A typical letter told Kidman that Private G. E. Rogers (one of his cattle drovers in the north) had been killed. It mentioned that Mr and Mrs D. Rogers, of Freeling, had been notified that their second son, George E. Rogers, had been killed in action in France on 5 November. He was previously reported missing. He was 19 years of age and had enlisted in December 1915.

Kidman's brothers, like himself, were far too old to enlist. But his nephews — of which there was a tribe — did. Among them was Tom Kidman (George Kidman's son) and Roy Kidman (Tom Kidman's son).

Nephew Tom, a head stockman working in the Queensland Channel Country when war broke out, recorded in his diary, "I decided it was my duty to enlist. George 'Daddy' Hooper, the manager of Diamantina Lakes, drove me in the old Ford to Winton. I travelled from there to Longreach, was medically examined and left by train to Rockhampton, Brisbane, Sydney, Melbourne and Adelaide. I sat up for five nights on succession in the train. I couldn't afford a sleeper. I had to pay my own expenses as I wanted to enlist in South Australia where my people lived. I could have got a pass to enlist in Brisbane." Tom spent four years in Egypt and France, and returned after the armistice in 1919.

Nephew Roy Kidman (son of Sid Kidman's brother Tom) became a Lieutenant with the 3rd Light Horse Regiment in Egypt and Palestine and was awarded the Military Cross. The award was made for "conspicuous gallantry and devotion to duty in command of an outpost which was attacked by hostile forces. Roy Kidman held the enemy in check and inflicted severe casualties at close range compelling them to deploy in the hills in front of the post. He maintained his position until daylight and by telephone was able to give accurate information as to the enemy's strength and position. His coolness and tenacity were highly commendable."

Sid Kidman was as pleased as punch about Roy, was gratified by Tom's safety and became increasingly mindful as the war continued that his own son, Walter (at school in England and excelling in the cricket eleven at Tonbridge), would soon be old enough to enlist. Until the age of 13 Walter had attended school at St Peter's College, Adelaide. Then an educational topping-off in England was decreed for Walter. He was on his way to school at Tonbridge, England, in 1914 when war broke out and was in the care of his eldest sister, Gertie. Her husband, Nelson Clover, reported immediately for duty and remained in service for the duration of the war. Gertie lived in England at Torquay and kept an eye on Walter at Tonbridge. Sid and Isabel Kidman didn't see their son again until 1919, when he returned to Australia from school.

The war that everyone predicted would be over and done with like a shot defied the prediction. It dragged on. News was not good. It had the effect of making Australians increasingly patriotic. This was certainly so in Kapunda. The war effort intensified, matched by an intense bitterness towards Germans in the community, who were for the most part farmers.

Crowds constantly packed the Kapunda Institute for meetings to raise funds. Ambulances were needed. They cost £400 each. Sidney Kidman gave the first two presented by the town. Why stop there, the town newspaper asked? A community appeal was launched for a third. Sid Kidman gave another £50 towards the £400 needed — or £400 for the total cost of the ambulance *if* Kapunda found a similar amount. When Kidman's alternative offer reached the ears of H. H.

Dutton, he telegraphed a promise of £50, only to change his mind soon after and substitute £400 instead. It meant that the Duttons of Anlaby gave ambulance number three and Kidman matched Dutton's £400 for ambulance number four. The township of Kapunda found money among townspeople for ambulance number five.

Newspapers made sure that they didn't let the law of the day interfere with one report concerning further fund raising in Kapunda to help the war effort:

Wagering in a public place is forbidden by the law but as the spot on which the bet of a new hat was made by Mr Sidney Kidman and one of the business men of Kapunda has not been disclosed, the details of the transaction may be published "without prejudice".

The two men were walking to the Kapunda Institute to attend a fund raising meeting and they discussed the probable amount that would be raised from those present on the night. Mr Kidman was of the opinion that more than £500 would be on the lists before the night was out, but his friend was not so sanguine and he expressed his willingness to hand over a new hat if the total was over the amount mentioned.

When Mr Kidman's turn came to speak, he told the audience of the wager and said he was going to win it. A moment later he put down his name for £750 and the announcement was made between ringing cheers. Later in the meeting, the "cattle king" increased his contribution to the even more substantial sum of £1,000.

As he left the hall an enthusiastic admirer rushed up to him and exclaimed, "Mind you make that a double-decker bell-topper!" A total of £1,605 was subscribed on the night for the Wounded Soldiers Fund.

Kidman made a quick trip to the eastern states and a reporter, seeking a last-minute interview with him before he left, happily got it — while perched precariously on the running board of Kidman's fully loaded car, as it made its way to the Adelaide Railway Station. Sid confirmed a statement that at each weekly cattle market in the future he would contribute one or two bullocks to the war effort.

While east, he handed over a cheque for a further £1,000 to Mr Grant C. Hanlon of the Returned Sailors and Soldiers Imperial League of Australia (a fund was set up to initiate projects that would benefit returned men). Again it was a "first", and Mr Hanlon was hopeful "that somebody else will send a similarly handsome donation as that given by Mr Kidman". In recognition, the League made a presentation to Sid at Central Railway Station, Brisbane, before his departure south on the Sydney mail train: a fine stockwhip, handsomely mounted and suitably engraved.

From England, Sir John Thornycroft (connected to the Kidman family by marriage) wrote to Sid, giving him war news and stressing the need for armoured planes and more ships; allied shipping losses were mounting owing to successful strikes from German U-boats. Thornycroft, a distinguished British engineer, was doing his best. King George V, while on a war tour in France, had made a special trip in a CMB coastal motorboat. The CMBs were British-built craft designed by Sir John to harass the U-boats. Earlier, Thornycroft had built the first torpedo-boat for the British navy.

Kidman said he would see what he could do on both fronts, and when Mr C. Alma Baker, the honorary organiser of the Australian Air Squadrons Fund, made an appeal from England for battle planes, Kidman gave the first. Newspaper announcements were to the effect that "In connection with the appeal for funds for the purchase of aircraft for the British forces, Mr Sidney Kidman the well-known pastoralist has made a gift of an armoured battle plane at a cost of £2,700. The money was cabled to the Bank of England, London, to the credit of the Secretary to the War Office on 7 August (1916). The battle plane will bear the name 'South Australia No. 1 — the Sidney Kidman, Kapunda'." Again, Kidman hoped that someone else would match his offer. They did. A few weeks later, on 17 August, the well-known White family of Belltrees, Scone, presented the second plane, the "New South Wales No. 1".

Within several weeks Kidman found out exactly what was happening with his plane. By sheer chance the first pilot to fly it was Lieutenant J. B. Graham, of Yankalilla, South Australia. On 25 September 1916, he sent a letter home: "A few days ago I was sent away to take over a flying machine and by a coincidence found that it was called the 'South Australia No. 1 (Sidney Kidman)' and was one of the overseas presentation aeroplanes. I soon got my first Hun. Two machines went for me at 10,000 feet. The first chap must have stopped some of my bullets soon after the scrap started and he went down. This rather put his friend off and he cleared home to the fatherland hotfoot."

As more planes were needed, Kidman decided to give another. In May 1917 he presented a further £2,703 for a battle plane — or rather gave the cheque to his wife, Bel, for her to present it under her own name. Kidman also subscribed privately to the war loans as they were announced, usually in amounts of £10,000.

On 28 February 1917 Sid and Bel sailed on the *Moeraki* for New Zealand. It was Sid's second trip to New Zealand, and on the way home he made his first trip to Tasmania, as he was considering extending his empire from the Gulf of Carpentaria in the north to King Island in Bass Strait. He had a look around Tasmania first, and wasn't greatly impressed.

A Tasmanian paper reported, "Remarkably enough this is the first time Mr Kidman has been to the island state although there is hardly a foot of the Australian interior he does not know. He is a man who gets off the beaten tracks — and makes money in the process. 'I think the scenery is Tasmania's greatest asset,' Mr Kidman said, 'but the people do not make half as much as they ought to with the cow, the pig and the dairy.' Mr Kidman could not talk anything but shop for half a minute."

Kidman teamed up with his friend Harry Peck, the Melbourne stock agent, for a week in Tasmania before catching the boat across to King Island. In his memoirs Peck said:

He had never been in Tasmania before and was being shown around by the Attorney-General of the day, who was an old chum of his youth at his home town of Kapunda, South Australia. He was like a school boy on a holiday with the zest and interest he showed in everything.

On our visit to King Island to inspect Yambacoona, on which he bought out the late Claude Macarthur's interest in that station, we were shown around by Tom Strickland, the managing partner, who was very deaf in the right ear. Kidman was deaf in the left and if by chance they were on the wrong side of each other when riding around, their conversation was like two auctioneers going at the one time!

I remember that the bullocks were very sleek for that time of the year — just like groomed racehorses — and this puzzled Kidman until in one of the rolling sand dune paddocks he and I took a spell in a hollow while Tom Strickland and the stockmen were mustering the paddock. A bunch of bullocks came over the rise and went on feeding and we saw that they were only eating the dried seed heads of the melilot (which has the biggest seed of all the edible legumes). Kidman was not aware of this but picked up a handful of the heads and, on rubbing the seeds, said, "Why, the jolly beggars are living on corn," and that fact had a good deal to do with clinching his purchase of an interest in the station as Kidman had a great preference for good fattening country in contrast to purely breeding country.

On 19 April 1917 Kidman advised the Bank of New South Wales in Sydney of his trip. A diary account by manager W. E. Frazer records, "Kidman gave a great account of prosperity in New Zealand but value of land and stock too high. He is taking up some 10,000 acres freehold in King Island about 120 miles south from Melbourne on which to fatten stock for that market. He says the venture is a good one."

It may well have been, but he did not hold on to it for long. In 1920 the Tasmanian government asked the company to put a price on the station for soldier settlement. Consulting his partners, Kidman said, "Let them have it for as reasonable a price as possible so that the soldiers may do well." Harry Peck asserts that in that first year they probably did better than any other returned soldiers group in the country. At the clearing sale in the summer of 1920 the soldier settlers bought half-fat bullocks on Yambacoona in hundreds at an average of £7 to £8 and sold them in Melbourne early in the following boom-price winter from £20 to £25 per head. No one was more pleased than Kidman.

Not satisfied with having donated planes to the First World War effort, Kidman organised business partners to go into shipbuilding early in 1918. Messrs Kidman and Mayoh secured a Commonwealth government contract for the building of six 3,000 ton ships, and work on the ships was started in a yard in Sydney Harbour.

In the public mind he was seen as a caring man who'd made great contributions — the man who'd started from scratch and made a pile but who always maintained the common touch and concern for others. People wrote to papers commenting on his generosity. One piece of fulsome praise suggested, "In his own walk of life, Kidman of Kapunda is just as big a man as the K. of K. [thought to refer to Kitchener of Khartoum] on the other side of the world." The press liked the style in which he gave — it was straight, bluff and hearty — and his strategy of being in first and being bold enough to challenge others to match his contributions and to coax others to follow. Wherever he went some cause or another was always on the receiving end of a further fifty or a hundred brick-red tenners. Press men, who sorted out the war and the affairs of the country in the pub closest to their newspapers, were not quite as complimentary. If Kidman was tossing money away in big bundles, what was the old boy worth? Just how wealthy was he?

They fell over themselves to find out and they asked in all manner of ways. In the outback they spoke to his stockmen: "They tell me this Kidman is a millionaire..." "Yeah, he'd have to be," was the surly reply. "He has a million bloody packsaddles and they ought to be worth a quid apiece."

They tried to nail Sid down on stock estimates. Asked by one interviewer if his cattle totalled one million (when the number probably would have been between half to two-thirds of that figure), Kidman didn't answer but asked a question himself: "Man, do you realise what a million cattle would be worth today? I don't know how many; better go and ask my office." And, of course, his office didn't know either. He was asked the question sneakily, officially, directly, casually and constantly. In fact, he started to worry during any interview when he wasn't asked the question, and on more than one occasion when a journalist sought to wrap up a talk with him without having aimed the question, Kidman raised the matter himself. In a typical case, Kidman said, "I suppose you, like most people, would like to know how many cattle I own?"

"Now that you have raised the question, I am saved the trouble and I am sure the public would like to know," the reporter replied solicitously.

"Well, all I can say is that I have never counted them! I could not get to within 25,000. My bankers have never asked me to have a bangtail muster," Mr Kidman said in a jocular vein, "and I am confident they will not ask."

"Perhaps we can get at it roughly in this way, by calculating the number of head to the acre?" was the further suggestion made by the reporter to Mr Kidman, whose laconic reply was, "I have about 80,000 miles of territory in all states except Victoria — and the task is beyond me."

It became impossible for the press to make a comparison of his war donations in relation to his overall wealth. The man in a better position to know was the tax man. Kidman paid state taxes in each state in which he had holdings and, as of 1916 with the introduction of the Income Tax Act, Commonwealth income tax as well. For contributions to war funds, a tax deduction was allowed for any monetary amount in excess of £5. The interest earned from any money put into war loans was exempt from taxation. Gifts in kind that went to the war effort (in Kidman's case, shipments of horses, frozen beef, mutton, wool, and donations of livestock auctioned at regular markets) were not tax deductible.

Just as the Australians who served in the Great War were all volunteers, any effort to help the war was also voluntary. No one was forced to make a contribution. That Sidney Kidman did is to his credit. In any case, the war overseas wasn't the only one he had to fight.

16
Battles at Home

W HILE HE GAVE to the Great War, Kidman faced his own war, and on several fronts. Since 1913 another drought had been hitting him severely. The overseas shipment of meat for the war effort combined with the drought forced a rise in meat prices. Kidman, more than any other pastoralist, was singled out for blame. When prices ran high because of the meat shortages, he was accused of understocking his runs. There were slurs about a "meat trust" that forced prices up and kept them up.

In South Australia delegates on the Trades and Labour Council urged people not to eat meat. That was the "only way to drop the price and put Kidman in the Destitute Asylum". Kidman's conservative politics combined with the meat shortage and high prices were like a red rag to a bull where the unions were concerned. When it was known that he was going on a trip to New Zealand towards the end of the war, some members of the South Australian Parliament suggested it might be "a good thing if the seamen refused to carry him".

When 75,000 head of cattle died in the drought from 1914 to 1916 on Diamantina Lakes, Durham Downs, Sandringham, Glenglye, Annandale, Thargomindah and Innamincka stations alone, Kidman was accused of "breeding them cheap and allowing them to die cheap". In Parliament he was attacked because of the size of his holdings. He appeared before commissions, boards of inquiry and parliamentary hearings. "Curtail Kidman!" was a cry taken up by many.

The curtailing had already started where Kidman least expected it and where it hurt most: with his bank. Extracts from the Bank of New South Wales Board Minutes on 10 December 1912 read:

On perusal of the Adelaide manager's letter of 3rd inst. advising that the account of Mr Sidney Kidman had not been reduced owing to payments on account of purchases of cattle since June last, and payment of £11,000 for a property near Adelaide, and that Mr Kidman promised reduction of at least £35,000 by April next, it was resolved that Mr Kidman be required to pay £45,000 by the end of March and interest at 7 per cent. Failing this, he must make other arrangements.

Four months later the 16 April entry of the Sydney manager's diary stated:

> The general manager is alarmed at the position of this account with the bank. The liability, he says, now exceeds £180,000 and drastic instructions have been issued to Adelaide Branch to restrain him. While this is being done elsewhere, Head Office allows the account to grow largely in excess of arrangements. In fact as a "purchase" account, the debt should have been paid off long ago!
>
> We explained to the general manager that for the last three years the account at HQ had been changed from a property purchase account to an operation c/Ac. We understood our reports conveyed this. Under the circumstances the overdraft is not normally high. In fact under the arrangements undertaken with us, Kidman was within his limit. Had we known of the bank's action respecting his accounts elsewhere, we should, of course, have taken similar action with him and in order to take that action now we should be pleased to be furnished with copy of the recent correspondence with Adelaide. So far as having any misgivings about Sidney Kidman's position we are thoroughly satisfied that he was worth from £4/500,000 clear. He may make promises and fail to observe them, but not intentionally so. We have fifteen years' knowledge of him and a more reliable and cautious man we do not number among our customers. The general manager combats this and says the bank cannot rely on his promises. The bank do not know what his position is and it is very doubtful if he knows himself how he stands. He might be worth £250,000 but that was quite problematical. The interview terminated by the general manager saying he would have Adelaide correspondence supplied to us and we were to similarly act in dealing with HQ account. The general manager declined to fix a limit for HQ account but said generally that the account was to be got down. Kidman in his March letter advises that the whole debt will be covered by July or sooner. Keep him, at any rate, to reduction.

On 18 April 1913 the Sydney manager, W. E. Frazer, noted:

> Kidman's direct indebtedness to the bank stands at £120,000, and £20,000 (with partners) and contingent (under guarantees) £24,000. £164,000.
>
> The security is shadowy beyond some £8,000 freehold Adelaide and say £50,000 (quoted £30,000) Sydney. But Adelaide quoting their securities at £150,000...deposits, leases etc. Kidman will be visiting Sydney in a few weeks' time and we shall

discuss matters with him and have the whole position placed in order. There can be no doubt that he has considerable wealth. The cattle dealing trade is highly speculative and a series of droughty years might sweep half of his wealth (on paper) away and leave us with a narrow margin in the face of depreciated property and low prices; that it is advisable to get down to a solid working basis is in Kidman's interest as well as our own.

The 8 May 1913 entry says:

Sidney Kidman called. Long talk with him in connection with the bank's attitude towards him in putting up his overdraft rate to 7 per cent without notice. If they had intimated to him that that rate would be charged, failing reduction of the liability within three or four months to an amount named, he could have understood it; but he strongly resented their action and being in a position to pay off the whole liability within the year by sales of stock, would do so. And if he did not meet with the consideration he had been accustomed to receive from the bank, he could easily go elsewhere.

At one time in his career it would have been a matter of serious concern to him to be suddenly pulled up as in this case, but it did not matter now. He was quite independent of any bank etc. At present time he owned stock — paid for — 200,000 cattle of which 50,000 were bullocks. He similarly owned 200,000 sheep and 15/16,000 head of horses. He had an offer from the Queensland Meat Company to purchase 20,000 on trucks at £7 per head but he would not accept that price. His profits last year exceeded £140,000. He had purchased other stations and large mobs of cattle in excess of that amount. We pointed out to Kidman that with his large profits, further investing in property and stock without reducing his large liability of £180,000 naturally caused the bank uneasiness especially as the security need was of a fragmentary and incomplete class and also the monetary stringency of the times (of which he must have been aware) made it imperative that speculative business of the kind must be restricted. Furthermore, the bank had no information of a definite kind as to his position. Years ago we had a statement now and again; but of recent years these have not been furnished etc. Kidman replied that we could have had the statements if we asked for them. He would supply a statement within a month and send it to us. He recognised that he should not have put his profits into other investments, from what we said, but we should have been more open with him and not jumped a 7 per cent rate on him as we did. Kidman said our estimate of his worth (net) was a very modest one at half a million. He estimated that stock and properties and interests realised today would give him a worth — after all liabilities paid — of over one million. He felt sure of this and we knew he was not given to enlarging his figures. This is so.

Kidman called again at the bank on 15 May 1913. The diary entry stated, "Nothing important. Kept him off the subject of the bank's recent attitude towards him. He is evidently brooding over it but alright with fair handling."

The bank was a little happier on 15 July 1913, when the manager noted, "Sidney Kidman called. Had to give him an interview. Said he had sold 12,000 cattle at prices ranging from £6.5.0 to £6.12.6 — a total of £77,000 which would reduce his debt to the bank to small figures. The liability at Adelaide has been reduced since he last saw us by £20,000 and the HQ debt by £12,000. To give us full particulars tomorrow."

The bank's Chief Inspector Edwards attended the next meeting in Sydney the following day, in order that "Kidman's affairs could be discussed and clearly understood". Sydney manager Frazer noted:

The result of the interview was satisfactory. Mr Edwards said that what had transpired between the bank and Kidman, arranging for the reductions of the liability at Adelaide, had been misunderstood by Kidman. It was agreed that we should revert to the original position with Kidman as regards o'draft rate and that the accounts should show satisfactory reduction which Kidman now clearly understands. He has just sold 6,300 bullocks to Cooke and 6,000 bullocks to the Queensland Meat Coy, the total price amounting to £79,450, so that within the next three months Kidman's position with us should be an easy one, so much so that he is talking of offering for Hungerford's properties (Vanrook, Sterling, Strathmore and Dunbar). Recommend Mr Edwards to rebate one and a half per cent off the overdraft rate charged in Adelaide and Melbourne and place Kidman on best footing of rates all round. He only charged him five and a half per cent at HQ.

There are no entries at all in the Sydney manager's diary for the year of 1914, but in 1915 Sid was on the doorstep again for an interview on 16 March. Mr Frazer reported:

Sidney Kidman called. Said he was practically free of debt to the bank. The bank could now see, he said, that he was equal to his word in paying them off. He harped on the old 7 per cent rate charge threatened by Adelaide Branch and took a very independent stand as to what he could do. We told him he should feel obliged to the bank for putting pressure on him to place him in the cosy positon he was today. Had it not been for this pressure, he undoubtedly would have purchased further stations and stock which, with the drought and war on us, might have placed him in an awkward position. He recognises this but still would not give us credit for kindly intentions towards him. He is evidently very sore and likely to remain so. The only way to cure him is to invite him to go to another bank. He is better off out of our books than perpetually grumbling.

The worry with the bank was only a warm-up to Sid's private war. The one thing that could be said about it was that at least it was kept private. The rest of the hoo-ha received a great innings in public, as authorities took on Kidman and Kidman took on authorities. For the most part he batted defensively, but when the mood took him, he started slamming sixes.

In the decade after the turn-of-the-century drought had ended, Sid had every reason to be pleased with both the seasons and business progress, but there was one thorn in his side: the railways, particularly those in South Australia. Good seasons meant plentiful cattle, which his capable managers and drovers could get to railheads, and then the rot seemed to set in with the railways. As early as 1910 Kidman had something to say on the subject, after returning to Adelaide from an inspection of meatworks in Queensland: "The Queensland meatworks are calling to owners. They take large mobs — the bigger the better — and the railways carry stock at great reductions on the South Australian rates and provide superior yard accommodation and better facilities for handling stock. To reach the Adelaide market we have to travel our cattle, as a rule, 500 miles by road and 500 miles by rail. Less than 500 miles takes stock from Birdsville to the Ross River or Alligator Creek works. The South Australian bogie cattle trucks hold only eight head each whereas the Victorian and New South Wales trucks hold ten head and the Queensland trucks are built on a much bigger scale still. When, therefore, the railway authorities say that the rates for the carriage of stock are uniform in South Australia, New South Wales and Victoria, they make no allowance for the extra accommodation afforded by the rolling stock in the other states. Some of the South Australian trucks carry only seven head and are too low.

"The Queensland yards are equipped with drawgates for which I have been asking the Railways Commissioner here for two years. At Bourke it is possible to yard 1,000 or 1,200 cattle at once and there are two races. Our own yards were erected many years ago when, at the most, 200 cattle could be trucked at once. Now 800 to 1,200 make up one consignment and the same accommodation has to do duty.

"At the Farina yards last week there was a mob of cattle up to their girths in mud which is a disgrace to the country and the Railways Dept in particular. Last year I trucked 18,000 cattle from Farina, which is a much larger number than goes away from Bourke. When Mr Pendleton was Railways Commissioner I offered to build new yards at my own expense if he would lay a siding to them, but he would not meet me. If the railway authorities are not more alive to the interests of the cattle trade the Queensland stock will surely be diverted to the coastal outlets of the state. Out of 600 cattle yarded in the Adelaide market today, 350 were mine — a common proportion — so that the threatened diversion will be a serious matter for this state. Many thousands of pounds will come off the South Australian railways revenue and there is nothing surer that an immediate and substantial rise in the price of beef in Adelaide will follow. South Australia cannot supply her own beef requirements for six months in the year and the bulk of Adelaide's cattle supplies are drawn from Western Queensland."

It was a blunt message to the railways to sharpen up. Expanding further on his railway worries, Sid said, "We have to load our cattle at a given hour. If we are late a fine is extracted; if the trains are late we have no redress. We are under the thumb of the railways authority, one of whose main sources of revenue is the stock traffic. Plenty of other industries will be affected if the Adelaide cattle trade falls off. When cattle are being trucked, the railway people grant a man a free ride but it has to be taken in the brakevan, which is frequently so full of milk cans and other goods that there is no comfort for him. Often he has to stand out in the passageway. Another sore grievance is the way cattle are trans-shipped at Terowie. I have seen with my own eyes the manner in which they are knocked about there. They receive more rough handling at Terowie than throughout the rest of the journey. The trans-shipment usually takes place between midnight and 4 am and there is practically no supervision. I am sorry that the stock agents do not have a man there to watch their clients' interests."

Kidman wasn't on his own in beefing about railways mismanagement. South Australian stock owners banded together, making ten requests for improvements in various directions on the railways and, seven years later when not one had been granted, criticism reached a crescendo and a South Australian inquiry was held into the unsatisfactory running of stock trains. Matters came to a head with sheep rather than cattle when a number of trains bringing stock to the Adelaide market averaged only six to seven and a half miles an hour on the North Line on a journey of more than 200 miles. There were 240 trucks containing approximately 20,000 sheep and they had to travel up to 260 miles. Once loaded, they had forty-three hours in which to reach their destination — yet much of the stock did not reach the market in time.

Pastoralists were enraged by the fact that because their stock missed the market they were obliged to go to great expense to find feed or pasture for the sheep for a further week, and a week under such conditions depreciated the value of lambs just taken from their mothers by 30 per cent. The general public, the pastoralists pointed out, suffered also: more meat meant cheaper meat and the quality of the meat suffered when the journeys were too long.

Sid dished out some caustic criticism when giving evidence before the Railways Standing Commission inquiry in 1918. He was critical not only of existing rail transport but also of the lack of rail expansion within the state. He said that a line to Innamincka would suit him — but not the country. However, a line from Hergott Springs to Birdsville would capture a great deal of the Queensland trade. Should such a line be constructed, he thought that a lot of cattle would be drawn which now had to be droved. During droughts, such a rail line would be especially advantageous, as it would give facilities to remove cattle to better feeding centres, and, in any event, it would bring more cattle to Adelaide, which would result in a decrease in the price of meat. In South Australia, cattle were handled worse than anywhere else in the world. During the last six years he had paid £159,959 to the department for the carriage of stock which meant an annual average of £26,659. For the last twelve months he had railed cattle from Oodnadatta, and trains had been as much as twenty-seven hours late. The authorities, he thought, should be prosecuted for cruelty to animals as no other railways would permit such a thing. Not one train was up to time, although they had to be loaded punctually. The department would reply to not one complaint. It was driving the cattle trade from the state and he instanced 10,000 bullocks which, had he been fairly treated, he would have sent to Adelaide. Unless some alteration was made, he would send no more cattle across at all. He asked only for a fair deal. He paid tribute to the Victorian and Queensland railways and he did not want to make any threats, but he was at liberty to do what he liked with his own cattle. He thought a railway taken 150 miles from Hergott towards Birdsville would be justified as it would tide owners of stock over the dry country. It would carry a number of his cattle, if not those of everybody else. Stock trains should take precedence over both goods and passenger trains, as was the case in Canada and America.

"Instead of being treated as express trains, they often have to·

stand by while goods trains pass through. You go to the sale ring at Gepps Cross on Monday and see the condition some of the cattle are in when they come direct from the truck. The pain they appear to suffer must be excruciating. Apart from the humanitarian point of view, the loss in meat to the community, let alone the loss to the owner, must run into a large figure annually. Say a beast dead in the truck is worth only £1 — that is all the abattoirs give us and it is not always the poorest beast that is trampled upon — then the average loss amounts to thousands of pounds a year purely on account of official apathy to improve the conditions," Sid said.

Asked whether his drovers, in loading the cattle, were responsible for the trouble, he replied, "Don't labour under that delusion. As a rule they think too much of the stock after having driven them for weeks to do anything that would prejudice their sale. In nearly fifty years' experience with these men I have met few who neglected to properly tend their herds."

"What about sheep?" Kidman was asked. "Well I have not had so much to do with sheep as with cattle," Sid replied, "but provided that the vans are not overloaded and a man travels with them in the train and picks up any animals that are down at stopping places, they are all right. You can easily get in among them in a truck whereas you cannot apply those measures to cattle. I have always instructed my drovers not to unduly crowd bullocks in a truck but that has had no effect in getting them to market in sound condition. It is time the Railways Department adopted some remedy."

Rather than adopt any remedies, the Railways Department attacked Sid. Replying to the complaints, the General Traffic Manager, Mr A. N. Day, said he had heard Mr Kidman's evidence. A lot of it was incorrect and he could not believe much of it. Mr Kidman stated that he was not going to send any more cattle to Adelaide. It was very much a matter of markets where cattle went, he said. The embargo in Queensland had had a big effect on the Adelaide supplies. From 1 May 1917 to 11 May 1918, 182 cattle specials were run and at least one-third arrived on or before time. The trains came from Cockburn or north of Farina. Stock had to be transferred at Terowie and that work occupied time. Sometimes stock did not arrive at the hour specified for loading and that threw the train's running time out all the way to Dry Creek. Stock trains were given preference over everything except passenger trains. It frequently happened that some beasts were footsore and weary and fell down in the trucks. The drover would ask that the trucks should be shunted at the next station so that the animals could be removed. That frequently occupied half an hour. Stock owners crowded as many bullocks as possible into a van regardless of the animals, so long as they were got down to market. When a drover made a mistake he liked to "shoot at" someone and there was nobody better than the railways. Bad loading and tired cattle were the causes of much of the trouble.

In Parliament, the Minister of Railways, Mr W. Hague, said that he believed the trans-shipping arrangements at Terowie were inadequate and that something would have to be done to give greater facilities. Much of the delay was caused at the break-of-gauge stations. Sir Richard Butler said that nearly the whole trouble in handling the stock in South Australia was owing to the break of gauge and the sooner the state faced that question, the better.

Sid's running battle with the railways had intensified during the First World War. The problems he encountered were not resolved then, or later, to any great extent, and to the end of his days his antagonism towards the railways surfaced regularly. He maintained that they were not run within South Australia or elsewhere on a business basis but rather to serve political interests.

While that matter was on his mind during the war, another that stung him deeply was the building of new cattleyards at Gepps Cross, Adelaide, in 1914. He was in Queensland when they opened and, on his return home in September, he wasted no time in directing some flak at the officials responsible for them.

"I was pleased to be at the cattle sales last Monday," he said, "but very disappointed to see how badly the yards work and what a terrible waste of money there has been in erecting them. I was in Queensland at the time they opened and had several paper cuttings sent to me stating how unsatisfactorily the yards had been constructed. It is a pity that Mr Ellery and Mr Ives [sic] who superintended the whole construction of these yards had not taken the advice of the stock agents or got their opinion and also the opinion of the master butchers.

"The yards must have cost an enormous amount. I am referring to the cattle yards and the selling pen. Mr Ellery and Mr Ives [sic] have had a lot of praise for what they have done; but if the government had had some practical person, from Queensland or some other part, who understood the working of cattle and how to erect yards much cheaper and better and more convenient, it would have paid them better.

"Anyone can see they have had to pull all the centre out and I understand they got a practical stockman to point out what alterations to make so that the cattle would work. They have also had to pull down some other divisions and cut away some of the main posts supporting the main ring to make it large enough to let anyone through.

"The ring is about five times too big, and — to give the public some idea of how the money has been spent, and what it will cost to maintain it — in this ring they have three manholes or escapes for three men to stand behind to turn out the bullocks whereas the old yards had only one. The gates are nearly swung all the wrong way and the yard accommodation is not as good as it was in the old yards. The pig-selling pens are put away over the other side of the cattle yards and they have to carry the pigs by trollies a terrible distance around the railway and the cattle yards and across over to the killing place. Pigs in any other part of the world are trucked alongside or killed where they are sold as it is most difficult to remove fat pigs especially in the summer. It is a great pity the government has not taken a more active part in the construction of the abattoirs. Mr Ellery is a capable and worthy Town Clerk but he could hardly be expected to be in his right place as the sole director in connection with the construction of these yards. It is much more difficult to work 1,000 cattle in the present yards than it was at the old yards.

"I have travelled about different parts of the world and visited more saleyards, I think, than any other man in Australia, and I must say this is the worst constructed and most expensive I have ever struck. The best yards I ever saw were in Glasgow, Scotland, where they unload the American cattle and kill and sell them. It is a great pity all this money should have been spent in South Australia to drive the trade out of the country instead of fetching it into it. I understand the small butchers will be driven out of their business by the high charges. One of the leading butchers tells me he would willingly give them £1,000 a year to allow him to leave the abattoirs and kill his own stock.

"I understand it costs 25 shillings to kill a bullock and land it in Adelaide. This is ridiculous and the charges are out of all reason. The yard fees are 1s. 6d. a head. In Melbourne they are 6d., Sydney 5d., and Brisbane 6d., with every facility for watering and (if you like) feeding at the railway. This is a very unfair charge as a man with a calf has to pay the same. I had eighteen calves there last Monday and had to pay 1s. 6d. a head yard fees. Of course it is not going to last and if the government or public don't take some step to make some alterations it will put 2d. a pound on their meat.

"If this charge is not reduced it is my intention to send all my cattle to the Queensland works as I can have them killed there for 5 shillings or 6 shillings and (another thing) reduce my rail costs by 25 per cent and I am paying the South Australian railways something like £30,000 a year. But my rail account won't be £5,000 here next year and it will put the price of cattle up £2 or £3 a head to the consumer and the butcher.

"Remember, I am not only talking. I have the bulk of the cattle and their natural outlet is Adelaide but with the increased facilities I can deliver them to the seaports in Queensland cheaper than I can to abattoirs in Adelaide. I am not dictating to the railways or the government but I am in a position to take half the cattle away from the market, which I have made up my mind to do and they will begin to feel the pinch within another week or two as eight mobs of cattle which would have arrived here about Christmas have been turned to Sydney, Charleville and Winton and there are several mobs to follow. If the government does not take some steps to alter the present conditions it will be a serious thing to the customer and to the country."

The abattoirs attack developed into an instant ruckus. It showed Sid in a fed up, fighting and straight-out threatening mood. People were alarmed. Anti-Kidman letters (usually under a pseudonym) appeared in the papers overnight. The Metropolitan Abattoirs Board got its act together and replied officially to Sid Kidman's criticism. It was difficult, the Board suggested, to take the criticism seriously, and yet the Board found it could only retaliate on two points: in relation to the pig-selling pens and as to whether other advice had been sought in the construction of the new yards. It said:

In his remarks about the pig-selling pens at Gepps Cross, Mr Kidman states that the pigs have to be carried by trollies a terrible distance round the railways. The "terrible distance" is a few hundred yards and Mr Kidman forgets that the pig markets in the old yards were three-quarters of a mile away from the cattle yards and that pigs had to be carted by the purchasers not a few hundred yards but in most cases for miles, in order to get them to their private slaughterhouse.

His statement that Mr Ellery and Mr Ive superintended the whole construction of the yards is not correct and the statement is equally incorrect that no advice from the stock agents was sought. As a matter of fact the plans for the yards were approved by Mr George Bagot, of Bagot, Shakes and Lewis, and Mr T. Yates [sic], of Elder Smith and Co., on behalf of the Stock Agents Association. The following letter from those gentlemen speaks for itself: "We beg to inform your board that we have inspected the plans for the proposed new stock markets in company with your resident superintendent, Mr H. P. Ive, and several slight alterations which we believe will conduce to the better working of the markets, were included in the plans at our suggestion. When complete, we think the markets should be right up to date and we intend to report to the Stock Salesmen's Association that we have inspected the plans and consider them satisfactory."

That wasn't really quite the truth of the matter, George Bagot said as the press debate continued:

> I am sorry to add anything more to this much-debated question, but must correct a wrong impression that exists. When the plan of the lamb and sheep markets was completed Mr Yeates and myself were invited by the superintendent to look at them. We attended in our private capacity. Examining the plan submitted, we pointed out a very necessary alteration — that the plan did not provide for means of moving stock from the ramps to the other parts of the market and that there were not any medium-sized yards in the vicinity of the drafting races. These suggestions were adopted. The above constitutes all the assistance the stock salesmen were given the opportunity of offering in the design of any of the markets, and we never saw the plan of either the cattle or pig markets. The Stock Salesmen's Association was given an opportunity on 17 January of inspecting the saleyards and certain serious shortcomings were pointed out to the superintendent and only one minor alteration was then promised, but not yet undertaken. On 14 June, after receiving notification that the yards would be put in use on 14 July, we wrote that we hoped the stock salesmen would not be asked to attempt to hold sales of sheep and lambs until some hundred crossgates in the races were erected. In August the lanes were gated with about half the number of gates necessary and no further representation has had any response until Wednesday last. We have made repeated representation on the question of fees in the cattle market, pointing out that the flat rate of 1s. 6d. a head, irrespective of value and weight, bears unduly heavily on the owners of small cattle and fees are being lost in consequence.

That Sid Kidman was browned off about the entire matter was obvious. The Metropolitan Abattoirs Board, in the planning of the new yards, displayed discourtesy in not even asking the opinion of the man who supplied most cattle to Adelaide. It was tantamount to a slap in the face to Sid Kidman and he didn't like it, hence his stinging attack. He had worked himself to a fever pitch with this one and, although right may well have been on his side, many people felt it simply would not do for him to keep making such dire threats publicly about withdrawing or withholding his cattle. The ruckus ended up very quickly in the South Australian Parliament, when Mr Anstey placed three questions before the Premier: did the government intend to take any action in reference to Mr Kidman's threat to practically stop the supplies of beef to people of the metropolitan area; did the government consider it wise for any one man to possess such monopolistic power as Mr Kidman had; and would the government consider the advisableness of introducing legislation to deal with the matter? Predictably, the government set up an inquiry — the Metropolitan Abattoirs Commission of Inquiry — to look into the matter in 1915. The matter of the new yards at Gepps Cross and their planning almost slipped into the background as a secondary issue. The Commission was set up chiefly to look into the business affairs of Sid Kidman, and to "curtail" him. Some irate people felt curtailing was too mild for the Cattle King. They wanted to see him crushed.

It was only natural that, with the inquiry pending, talk of a "beef trust" should rear its head again. It had been mentioned a few years earlier when it was feared that big American meat interests had their eye on Australia and were hopeful of setting up business here, aiming to corner the market and create a monopoly that would keep prices high. The first to scoff at the idea was pastoralist Frank Connor of the firm Connor, Doherty and Durack, which had big interests in Western Australia in the Kimberleys region.

> "A 'meat ring'!" he said, "There's nothing of the sort. I am sick and tired of the old cry against the 'beef buccaneers' as they call us. The small man or the big man who grows mutton — you never hear a word about him! People bawl and blatherskite about a meat ring but I could prove to you that the man who ships cattle to Perth does not get very much out of it when the cattle are delivered. We have practically pulled out of that trade now and confine our attention mainly to Manila."
>
> "If there is no local meat ring, is there such a thing as a meat trust — the American trust?"
>
> "I know of no meat trust but I know very well what people are coming at. When American firms come here it simply means that in consequence of the curtailment of the American beef supplies they have to look for fresh sources. America is an importing country now. Look at the shipments that are going from Australia and New Zealand. You need have no fear of a so-called trust taking control of the meat market here, for how could they do it without getting control of the means of transport and the stock routes which is impossible. If the Americans or more English firms came in to the business in Australia, the effect would be beneficial instead of detrimental to every interest concerned."

Kidman agreed with Connor and pooh-poohed the idea as ridiculous. "There are continual increases in butter, chaff and land and nothing is said," he remarked, "but directly there is an increase in the price of meat people start crying out about a meat trust and the most ludicrous stories are circulated.

"I am not frightened of forty beef trusts," he added. "I am pleased to see the Americans come here because they will teach us many things, just as they taught us how to bore for water. We wouldn't have had the fine bores we have now all over New South Wales and Queensland if it had not been for the Americans introducing the system which has been the salvation of the country.

"I have just been over the new works being completed by Swifts (an American firm) on the Brisbane River and when they are finished they will be an asset to the country and of the greatest benefit to Queensland. They will do away with the necessity of cattle being sent by road to Bourke and then by rail to Sydney. There is no railway in any part of the world where cattle get so badly knocked around as on the line from Bourke to Sydney."

But rumour intensified, prices remained high and the activities of visiting officials of American meat companies were watched closely; the matter culminated when Mr Justice Street sat as a Royal Commission of Inquiry into the Meat Export Trade of Australia in 1912. Everyone from inspectors of stock to rural journalists, and the heads of pastoral and meat-canning companies, including Otto G. Malkow (representing the Chicago firm of Swifts Packing Co., and the Australian Meat Export Co., of Brisbane, of which he was managing director), were called to give evidence, as was Sidney Kidman. The press put Kidman's evidence in the entertainment class, largely because of his colloquial speech and casual manner and his frequent use of the phrases "that's a bit hot", and "that's a bit swift". Mr Justice Street found that there was no evidence of the trust, as a trust, operating in Australia, and that there were three companies purchasing, apparently independently of one another, and exporting to America and the United Kingdom. Sid was certainly found to be in the clear. He guessed, however, that the Adelaide mob would put him through the same hoops again.

Sid's evidence before the South Australian Commission of Inquiry, consisting of Mr Moseley (Chairman), the Hon. F. S. Wallis, MLC, and Messrs Hudd, MP, Anstey, MP, and Blundell, MP, was very much along the lines of what he had said earlier and contained no surprises.

Mr Kidman remarked that he disposed of stock all over the Commonwealth. He strongly objected to the system of condemning cattle which prevailed at the abattoirs. Of all the yards he had visited throughout the world he had never seen any so badly erected as at Gepps Cross. Better facilities for dealing with cattle were to be found in Queensland, where the government was constructing railways in all directions. For years cattle had been dispatched to Adelaide at a loss due to higher railway freights and difficult conditions.

In regard to condemning bullocks at the abattoirs, those in charge seemed to do what they liked in the matter and unless some improvement was effected he would keep his cattle away altogether. The Government Produce Depot at Port Adelaide was a fine thing for the country. A poor bullock would realise more in Europe than a good one here. He understood that £300 or £500 had been given for the plans for the new yards. For the money spent there should be something better to show. Questioned regarding his expenditure in his business he remarked that he had spent about £128,087 in four years on the railways. He was agent for no companies whatsoever.

Trade would be driven from the state unless South Australian authorities were not careful. He was arranging not to bring his stock to Adelaide unless there was some improvement and they could not get stock without he came in.

He said he exported stock and up to the present 5,241 bullocks had been shipped by him. In London he received 4½d. a pound for beef that would not be eaten out here.

He said he worked in conjunction with no American or English firms and he was of the opinion that American houses were not trying to secure control of trade in Australia.

Asked what he thought of the future prospects of the beef trade in South Australia, he said, "There is nothing to stop beef from keeping as dear as it is now. The only thing that controls the beef market in Australia is the rain."

Continuing, he said that the government should be more liberal with their railways and should do everything possible to assist the farmers. He suggested some more practical person should be in control of the abattoirs. Mr Ellery was all right as Town Clerk but they wanted men with experience at Gepps Cross.

Regarding the pastoral value of the country — 5,000 miles in South Australia was not as good as 1,000 miles in New South Wales. He emphatically denied that he practically had control of the meat market in South Australia. He gave some interesting particulars of his methods of business. Every shilling he made was put into bores, stations or was spent. He enjoyed his money and that was why he expended £30 a day for meals at the Delhi Durbar. Mr Kidman remarked that the sale ring at the abattoirs was so large that very soon the auctioneers would be losing their voices through having to shout across so big a space. It was hard to tell these things to the authorities in an interview because they were "above getting near".

Asked whether he still intended to keep the Adelaide market high in view of the war, he said, "I do not control the market, but if it suits me to send my cattle elsewhere for better prices, I will do it. I am going to sell in the dearest market. At present this is the highest and when this commission has finished its work, if there is not some great alteration I am going to change my route."

In his evidence, Mr T. G. Ellery, the general manager of the Metropolitan Abattoirs, accused Sid of "weather vane" peculiarities.

Mr Ellery said Mr Kidman was like a weather vane — he blew in one direction today and in another direction tomorrow. It was difficult to take him seriously because most of what he said consisted of vague generalities, exaggerations and distortion of facts and Mr Kidman objected to the abattoirs because they had neglected to send his manager and himself an invitation to the opening ceremony. His whole grievance appears to be about this.

Mr Kidman said that they did not give him a fair deal if animals were condemned here compared with other states. He instanced that an 800 pound bullock if condemned would only return him 2 shillings per 100 pounds weight whereas he got £3 straight out for condemned animals in Queensland and that they were worth that amount for boiling down. The abattoirs were not a commercial concern and could give Mr Kidman nothing more than what other customers got, either large or small.

Mr Kidman in his criticism of the yards said that they had pulled down a lot and altered a lot. They had spent much money on them. The answer is they had not pulled down a lot and altered a lot and that Mr Kidman said the cost of the alterations ran into thousands. Mr Kidman, to put it mildly, did not know what he was talking about. Mr Kidman ran away with the idea that the yards were built by someone who knew nothing about cattle and he asked why the Abattoirs Board did not get someone who understood such things in the first place. Yet expert men in the business had favoured the plans for the yard when they had inspected them. Mr Kidman said the management "could not be approached. You could not get near any of them, especially Mr Ellery." Mr Ellery gave an emphatic and flat denial. He had never refused anyone a hearing when one had been asked for.

And so it went, tit for tat, disappointing everyone who had hoped for a big display of fireworks and for both riveting evidence and revelations.

Mr H. P. Ive, the Resident Superintendent of the abattoirs, in his evidence said that insinuations were not fair criticism, but they were all that could be expected from Mr Kidman at any time. He could, in fact, be proclaimed the champion romancer of Australia. The Cattle King seemed to be as frightened of stating facts as the devil was of holy water. Mr Ive presented the Commission with some interesting facts: from 6 August 1913 to 12 August 1914 the total number of cattle yarded for the fifty-two weeks was 54,014. Of that number Mr Sidney Kidman yarded 12,063 or a percentage of twenty-two and a third. Of the total number yarded by Mr Kidman, 3,885 cattle, according to the geographical position of the stations as published in Elder's Review, would necessarily have to come to Adelaide. This would leave the percentage that could be turned off by Mr Kidman at 15 per cent.

The final report of the Abattoirs Commission, when delivered in May 1915, had very little to do with the abattoirs at all and addressed itself to the wider issue of monopolies in stock-raising and the meat supply generally in South Australia. The commissioners said:

The information we obtained has been considerably added to by the recent and complete report on the Meat Export Trade of Australia by Mr Justice Street on behalf of the Commonwealth government.

Mr Justice Street's findings showed that there was no evidence of a meat trust, as a trust, operating in Australia.

Fortunately for South Australia, as long as the trade is done through the Produce Department, the government will have some control over the export of both cattle and sheep. The danger of a foreign trust cornering the meat supply is not the only one that threatens Australian producers and consumers.

There is the possibility of persons securing the control of the markets through having practically a monopoly of the stock-producing country. The Surveyor-General has informed us that of the 150,597 square miles of country let on pastoral lease in South Australia, 83,000 square miles are probably used for cattle-raising and of this area Mr S. Kidman and his family hold 16,064 square miles or one-fifth of the whole.

These leases are all for forty-two years and most of them have over thirty years to run; in some of the other states the pastoral leases are for much shorter terms. The same pastoral lessee is probably interested in other pastoral properties held by companies and in giving evidence before the Commonwealth Royal Commission on the Meat Export Trade, he [Kidman] admitted that the total area of his pastoral properties in Australia was

49,035 square miles, of which the annual rental is £14,142 per annum and that he owned on his own account from 230,000 to 260,000 cattle and from 150,000 to 190,000 sheep. In addition Mr Kidman is largely interested in twenty other stations in New South Wales, Queensland, South Australia and the Northern Territory. He did not state the area of these when giving evidence but with regard to one of them he said he was the principal shareholder in Victoria River Downs, the largest station in Australia on which there were 110,000 cattle.

It is practically impossible to say how many cattle Mr Kidman is interested in directly and indirectly, but there is no doubt that he owns throughout the Commonwealth far more than the total number of cattle in South Australia.

Seeing that we have to import 45,000 cattle annually, Mr Kidman is in a position to seriously affect the price of meat in the Adelaide market. We have no evidence whatever that he has ever attempted to do so, but witnesses have told us the danger exists and the interests of the general community demand that steps should be taken to avert it.

It is difficult to suggest a means of doing this without possibly injuring the stock-raising industry. Past experience has shown that a large proportion of the pastoral country in the north is subject to drought which renders its occupations in comparatively small holdings precarious, and we hesitate to suggest anything that might result in the surrender of leases.

If it were possible we would like to see a limitation of the area which one lessee might hold as is the case with the land that is held under the Crown Lands Act. This could be achieved by the Commissioner of Crown Lands refusing transfers to persons who already hold land beyond a certain carrying capacity. At present the Minister can only object to a transfer under exceptional circumstances. Having given full consideration to the question and being deeply sensible of the desirability and necessity of developing resources, we have come to the following conclusions:

1. That the government should have power to prevent the transfer or allotment of pastoral leases if such transfer or allotment is in their opinion to be inimical to the interests of the general community.

2. That the Pastoral Board when alloting pastoral leases should be instructed to give precedence to those applicants who hold the least area of land if it is satisfied that such applicants can develop the country.

3. That pastoral lessees should be required to send in returns annually of the number of stock on their leases and the amount

spent on improvements with a view to ascertaining whether or not the stocking and improvement conditions are being observed.

4. That the question of the danger of a monopoly of pastoral country and the consequent effect on the general community should be referred to the next Premiers Conference with the object of taking inter-state action to avert it.

Sid was all smiles when he turned up at the weekly sales after the report had been released. "Boys," he said to a milling group of agents and buyers, "I gave that 'Hellery' and 'Hives' fits..."

"Yes, Mr Kidman," a butcher intervened, "but you should have given the Commissioners a little poem..."

"Which poem is that?" Sid asked.

"Run! Run! Run as fast as you can, You can't catch me I'm the Cattle King man!" Bystanders dissolved into uncontrollable laughter, Sid in particular.

That the Powers That Be had no hope of "curtailing" let alone "crushing" Kidman was as plain as the nose on anyone's face. He had the upper hand and there was little they could do to bring him to heel unless at some time in the future the premiers in other states did decide to gang up against him, and he thought that unlikely. But the matter simply would not rest. The question of the South Australian meat supply and the proper use of pastoral lands leased from the Crown was raised in Parliament by the Minister of Industry, Mr R. P. Blundell, in 1916. So far as the local supply was concerned the state was in a worse position than it had ever been before, he said. It ate more meat than it produced and, unless something was done to restock the country, would be in the positon of being unable to feed itself with meat. Where the American beef trust was concerned, they didn't need to go outside Australia to find a squatter who, he feared, did not stock his land as it ought to be stocked or use it as it should be used and who was keeping other men from doing what should be done with it. That man was Mr Kidman. He acquainted Parliament with the size of the Kidman holdings. The following debate took place:

MR ROBINSON: That's too much for any one man to hold.
MR BLUNDELL: It is too much. It is more than one man can stock. The whole of the conditions of the leases must be carried out or the government will cancel them.

OPPOSITE:
Sidney Kidman in 1916.

MR MOSELEY: There is no harm in asking a man to stock his land.

MR BLUNDELL: Before Mr Kidman came in, there was a greater number of cattle and sheep in South Australia. He must stock the land and use it rightly however or give it up. We cannot afford for one man to hold the greater portion of the country. We shouldn't talk of a meat trust when we have another problem with which to grapple. If we don't, it will grow into as big an octopus as the American meat trust.

MR ANGAS: The conditions are that he must stock so many head to the acre.

MR BLUNDELL: The government is going to look into the matter. If it doesn't have the power to act, it will ask the House to give it the authority.

MR JAMES: Is that how you defend your butcher's shop by attacking Mr Kidman?

THE HON. J. VERRAN: What do you want?

MR JAMES: You shut up!

The newspapers had a field day. Headlines screamed, "When will the politicians understand?" Many reports ran along the lines of this one:

Mr Blundell does not mention that Mr Kidman has many thousands of fat cattle in Queensland that he is prevented from sending to Adelaide by the Labor Government of Queensland and there are lots of other Queensland pastoralists wanting to send fat cattle to Adelaide but were stopped in the same way by the embargo. So the monopolists really are Mr Blundell's political pals, the Queensland Labor men. But Mr Blundell couldn't be expected to see that far — he isn't paid to look that far!

At the present time Mr Kidman has 17,000 cattle on the roads in Queensland that he wishes to put on his drought-depleted runs in South Australia, but the border embargo stops him. So that is how one Labor Government helps another Labor Government to create a meat famine. Labor Governments then blame the man on the land.

Mr Blundell speaks of Mr Kidman preventing others from stocking and using "the greater portions of the pastoral country". The Labor Minister is not aware of the fact, of course, that much of the country Mr Kidman holds in Central Australia was "stocked" and "utilised" by other men before him — and they went broke at it. Mr Kidman got much of the land from the banks, and mighty glad they were to get rid of it.

If Mr Blundell wants it, he can go out there now and travel

over 1,000 miles of unoccupied country pretty well as good as what Mr Kidman holds. The main difference is that Mr Kidman's country is improved while the other is still in a virgin state. But there is nothing to stop Mr Blundell from improving it — if he is big enough of bank balance and stout enough of heart. He ought to be warned, however, that only the "big man" — big in money and heart — can make a do of it out there.

If Mr Blundell wants to, he can get land enough out there to make himself and all his friends squatters — squatters as far as area goes. It is there stretching away for a thousand miles waiting for him. But perhaps Mr Blundell knows it is easier to draw a State Minister's salary in Adelaide!

During the Address in Reply debate in the House of Assembly, Mr Young (Liberal) advised the government to be "very careful how they proceeded with their proposal to curtail the pastoral holdings of Mr Sidney Kidman". If it had not been for him, he added, there would not have been very much meat in South Australia because he had succeeded where others had failed. He might have too much country, but he was not the man they should shut out of the market without giving the matter much consideration. As to the idea of making him stock up, where in the world was he going to get his stock from at present, battling both an embargo and a drought?

In the Legislative Council, the Hon. John Lewis (a friend of Kidman's and a business colleague) said:

If the government offered me some of the land in question, I would not take it.

South Australia is under a great obligation to Mr Kidman. He has done a great deal to feed the people. If it had not been for him, sheep and cattle would many times have been at famine prices here. Only last Monday our market would have been pounds ahead of what it was if Mr Kidman had not bought cattle from Victoria to sell here. Of course he considers his pocket also, but we have much to thank him for. We hear some people talking about Mr Kidman not stocking his country. I would like to meet the man who would go up and stock that country. Mr Kidman bought the land referred to from the banks which had got it because the previous owners had failed. The public do not know what the country is like. Mr Kidman must have lost heavily last year and is to be commended for what he has done for South Australia.

A typical letter to the press was that of John Hogarth, of Smithfield, South Australia:

If there were a dozen such as Mr Kidman meat would not be so dear as it is now by a half. But for such as he, half the country would not be occupied or stocked. Mr Blundell talks of compelling lessees to stock their country. That shows how little he knows about the country. One season the country may not be fully stocked with twenty head of cattle to the mile. There comes a time when it is fully stocked with one head to 20 miles. There should be no stocking clause in a lease — only an improvement clause.

One thing that is preventing country from being taken up are the demands of the AWU [Australian Workers Union]. The rates of wages and the conditions of labour they demand are causing many who are interested in stations to clear out while they have something instead of waiting to be ruined. If the government interfere in the way they talk of doing, meat will be scarcer and dearer. The only way to have cheaper meat is to encourage those who have money to invest it in taking up country — not by putting obstacles in the way.

Sid finally got around to saying something on the matter himself: "When people talk about wanting cheap meat, they forget what has happened in the last two years. We have had a tremendous drought in the north of Australia and the country is very short of not only cattle but sheep also. When cattle are lost in a drought it takes five years to replace them under the most favourable conditions because a bullock does not reach its highest market value until it is four years old. Then we must remember that frozen beef, mutton and lamb have been very freely exported from Australia and large quantities are still being exported. When war broke out there was an increased demand for exports in cold storage and Queensland, the great cattle-producing country, has placed an embargo against the export of meat from the state unless it is intended for the imperial government. So long as beef and mutton are being carried to England to supply the fighting forces, the demand is bound to be keen. Therefore the question is one of supply and demand. In a nutshell, meat is dear on account of the drought in certain parts of Australia and the fact that for years we have been exporting our surplus stock."

Asked about market control and monopoly, Sid shook his head, saying, "The heavens control the markets." And asked about Mr Blundell's remarks, Kidman replied, "I have my own opinion on that matter and I will leave you to guess what it is."

17
New Ventures

ADDING TO THE ANGST of Sidney Kidman's detractors was the fact that, despite the war, the horrendous drought and the succession of hearings, commissions and inquiries, which increasingly sought to contain his expansion, Kidman continued to buy up places just as merrily as before.

In June 1913, at a time when the Bank of New South Wales was hot under the collar with him, Sid outlaid a large sum for Fulham Park Stud, a 700 acre Adelaide establishment owned by W. A. Blackler, who disposed of it because of ill health. It was a nationally renowned horse stud with quarter-acre paddocks for spelling horses. The transaction drew instant shudders of dismay from many people. They were unwarranted. A press report some months after the sale noted:

> When Mr Blackler decided to dispose of the old-established and almost world-renowned Fulham Park Stud, fears were entertained that it meant the passing of the home where so many great racehorses first saw the light. When Mr Kidman came along and purchased the property nearly everyone thought that he had secured it merely as a speculation and intended to cut it up and sell it in blocks.
>
> No one had ever really associated the name of Kidman with anything but stations and cattle but those who knew this remarkable man better than the general public were not at all surprised when he announced that he intended to raise thoroughbreds, and, if possible, uphold the highest traditions of Fulham Park in respect to the breeding of high class racehorses. When Mr Kidman took possession there were only a couple of brood mares and a few foals there but he was not long in having it restocked. He did not follow the policy of some stud masters of attending the public sales and securing worn-out mares but commissioned Mr J. Nestor (who has had experience with horses in England, Australia and India) to pick him up a half a dozen English-bred mares and a couple of English-bred stallions. It remains to be seen how Mr Nestor's choice works out but the guarantee is given that, so far as Mr Kidman is concerned, he is

just as keen on producing a good racehorse as he is first-class cattle. As a further evidence that Mr Kidman is anxious to do all he can to make the proposition a huge success, he has ordered that successful sire, Sir Simon, to be sent down from Norley Station.

Sir Simon had sired Bullawarra, the Kidman-bred horse which went on after great Australian success to compete in the Liverpool Grand National. Sid's immediate plans for Fulham Park were pushed to one side in 1914 when war broke out, and the stud was made available to the military as a remount depot.

Sid had won not a few bush races himself in his youth and he did care about good quality horses, although he never became passionately interested in horse racing as a sport; he also had little interest in gambling. Years earlier he had been at the races at Morphettville with his brother Charlie Kidman and a group of men, when Charlie Kidman said to one of them, "Put £50 on my horse. He will win and win easily. It is a good thing, Sid. You had better back him."

Sid turned to one of the others and remarked, "I don't like backing horses. Shall we try and make up £1 for him?" The men did and Sid's contribution was a modest 5 shillings.

Strongly cautioned by the bank in 1913, Sid gave his bankers a wide berth for a while and in the latter part of 1913 steeped himself in negotiations with his Melbourne friend William Angliss. If it was too hard to expand further on his own, then he would go in for partnership agreements. Angliss was agreeable. Both men got on well together, in fact they were birds of the same feather in many respects with William Angliss's abhorrence of anything smacking of carelessness or waste perhaps even more pronounced than Sid's. If Sid couldn't stand the waste of a nail on his stations, Angliss could not abide the unnecessary use of a postage stamp. There were certain properties in which they had a mutual interest, and when Sid called at Angliss's Melbourne office to talk the matter over, he found that Angliss had company. Angliss had just promised Colonel Arnott a donation to help the Salvation Army. Introducing the two men, Angliss said, "Here is a man who can help," and Sid said, "I will give what Angliss has given." When Colonel Arnott left he had an additional promise of £2,000 — both men could also be exceedingly generous.

Angliss was seven years older than Kidman and a self-made tycoon. He started off in London as a butcher and came to Australia in 1884. In 1898 he bought five three-storeyed shops on the north side of Bourke Street, which he renovated into nine large rooms with a capacity for storing 20,000 carcasses of mutton and lamb. A large refrigerating plant was installed, along with machinery for the manufacture of smallgoods. The premises also contained a large butcher's shop and offices, which remained his headquarters throughout his career. He entered the meat export trade during the Boer War and opened offices in London and Liverpool in 1909. In 1912 he formed the company of William Angliss and Co. Pty Ltd.

In April 1914, Angliss purchased his first cattle property, Miranda Downs, a leasehold on the Gilbert River north of Normanton, Queensland (it's believed that Sid had shares in the station). In partnership, they acquired Salisbury Downs, almost 500,000 acres (it had been more than 1 million acres in 1889) in the Wanaaring district of New South Wales. They paid £44,000 for it through the London Bank at Broken Hill; the purchase price included about £24,000 for stock (28,000 sheep, 1,008 cattle and 176 horses). Advising the Bank of New South Wales of the transaction, Kidman told the Sydney manager that he had told Angliss that he preferred all his business connections to be placed with the New South Wales Bank and that Angliss had agreed. (Perhaps this was a little sweetener for the bank boys after recent sour times?) Salisbury Downs was remote and devastated leasehold country, but it could be used intermittently for staging stock towards markets and railheads, allowing the land some opportunity to regenerate.

The partnership turned its attention back to the Gulf Country and acquired Fiery Downs, a well-grassed and well-watered area, and the adjoining 810 square mile Augustus Downs Station. Augustus Downs was bought for £80,000 with several other shareholders apart from Angliss and Kidman. It carried almost 20,000 cattle and its position on the Leichhardt River meant good, permanent waterholes. In 1915 the Augustus Downs syndicate acquired two properties adjoining Augustus Downs and Fiery Downs: Lorraine and Talawanta. These covered an area of almost 2,000 square miles for which they paid £110,000 (£50,000 down and the balance on mortgage to the Bank of New South Wales). The syndicate then took up Rutland Plains, 650 square miles of wild country on the western coast of Cape York Peninsula and added Vena Park and Iffley Downs (a total of 1,087 square miles) to the growing patch of properties south of the Gulf of Carpentaria (Talawanta, Lorraine, Augustus and Fiery Downs). Sid informed the bank that his interest in Rutland, Iffley and Vena Park amounted to one-quarter of £180,000. Then, acting on his own, Sid bought Undilla, a smaller Queensland property of 566 square miles on Quartpot Creek, north-east of Camooweal. The

OVERLEAF:
The Salisbury Downs meathouse, made from bush timber and cane-grass. (Alan Barton)

purchase price was £25,000 (including the stock of 4,000 cattle and 600 horses).

What the Labor government in South Australia thought of this buying spree is anyone's guess. If the matter had been raised at any Premiers Conference with the aim of uniting to restrain Kidman, it had failed. In South Australia they sat back congratulating themselves that a stern "warning off" had succeeded and Kidman had made no further attempts to buy up in that state (with the exception of Fulham Park). It, perhaps, had everything to do with the fact that Sid was more interested in New South Wales back country at the time than he was fearful of any constraints from South Australia.

Keeping business in the family, Sid entered into a partnership with Sackville's son, Anthony Kidman, to buy Bootra and Monolon sheep stations (326 square miles adjoining Salisbury Downs, which he held with Angliss). Then, in what must have been one of his smallest acquisitions, Forders Station — a mere 15 square miles — fell into his lap. He had been after Forders for years, its strategic position counting for everything and its size for nothing. Forders would be his second major "depot" after Mundowdna — a spelling depot just out of Broken Hill, with rail access to markets at Sydney, Melbourne or Adelaide. It would make the marketing situation more flexible. That being the case, he would strengthen his western New South Wales holdings even further. He added Clyde and Yandama stations to his First World War purchases — a big tract of land amounting to 3,128 square miles. Yandama was in the top corner of New South Wales and, curiously, part of the station spilled over into South Australia. It adjoined Mount Poole, which he already owned and which adjoined Mount Sturt and Mount Arrowsmith, on which he had his eye.

Sid had known the country like the back of his hand since he was a boy working in the region. He'd seen it thick with feed — and sheep. But millions of sharp little mincing hooves, and the rabbit, had taken their toll since those days. Sid saw it as being able to support only cattle.

Confident at that stage that his-son-law Sid Reid was an asset to the business, he had gone into partnership with him in 1913 to buy Boorara, a 1,200,000 acre holding in far western New South Wales, for £30,000. Tom Trader took over the management of the place, but he incurred Sid's annoyance on at least a few occasions. The first was in relation to the sending of telegrams. A telegram that reached Sid saying, "1,000 stock left for Adelaide today. Trader", drew the response from the office that "14 words are allowed for one shilling in telegrams, so full value please". The next time he was obliged to dispatch stock, Trader found himself three words shy of the fourteen — so he signed off the telegram with "love and kisses". Later, in 1917, when Sid had bought Currawinya and Trader was moved across to manage it, Kidman came out for his usual inspection. Trader said to him, "We should get one of those hot air engines to pump water from the river like we got at Boorara." Kidman, then partially deaf, said, "I can't hear you. . ." Trader repeated, his voice at exactly the same level, "I wish you'd buy the bloody engine like they got at Boorara. . ." "That's enough of that, Trader," Sid replied as quick as a flash. "Mind your manners!"

In May 1916, Sid reported to the bank in Sydney that he would be drawing on it for £33,000 to pay back the purchase money on Weinteriga Station, which he held in partnership with Angliss, of Melbourne. The bank noted the price at £65,000. It was a 771 square mile holding in the Wilcannia area of New South Wales, with water supplied by the Darling. Sid also told the bank he was confident that meat prices would "go even higher after the war" and that he was "quite opposed to the bank's view that investors in station properties are now sitting on the top of the wave. Station property, well placed, is the best investment in the market. We are subject to droughts and losses — but the recuperation powers of the country after rain are wonderful. There's no fear of any drop in pastoral products. It's rather the other way about."

Sid did a spot of selling as well, but not much. He'd bought Carandotta, in Queensland, from the bank in 1903 for £20,000. In 1910 he sold off 800 square miles of it for £9,500 and sold off the remainder of the station in 1916 to a New Zealander, Williams, of the Queensland Stock Breeding Co., for cash and adjustment of stock equivalent to a sale price of £86,000: almost five times his money back on the place in thirteen years.

Then, in a complete break with his buying pattern, Sid moved into Western Australia, buying Glenroy, a station in the north-west Kimberleys. He must have been interested in the area for a while, having told the bank earlier that year that he had knocked back an offer on Lissadell Station (in the same area) made to him by the owners, Hill and Durack. "All the stock are on the road and it will take three years to get a return from the place." Neither station would have had any relevance to the Central Australia–South Australia chain or to the north–south chain, but Glenroy must have had stock that suited — certainly the station had plenty of feed and water — but flushing the stock out of the wild King Leopold Ranges and getting them to market would be a problem.

The last two places he bought in 1916 were Yancannia and Lake Elder, which were acquired on 27 and 29 December. Yancannia was a large holding of 1,487 square miles west of the Darling, almost adjoining Mount Poole and Yandama (which he owned) and separated only by Cobham Lake (on which he had his eye). Lake Elder was in the heart of the sandhill country on the South Australian

border, north of Cockburn. It was tough, dry country, but it sprang back well after rains. Kidman gave it to Con White to manage. Not all Kidman managers took their wives to live with them on the outback runs; Con White was one who did — perhaps unwisely. Myrtle Rose White based her first book, *No Roads Go By*, on the life of hardship she faced during the years she spent on the station; it was hardship she faced not happily but with an increasingly resentful heart...the drought, the dust-storms, the ever-encroaching sandhills, the extreme desolation and isolation, and the way the lot combined to mock hard-working efforts and gnaw at the spirit until only bitterness remained. The Whites were to be six years at Lake Elder, and when they left it was to go to Morden, New South Wales, where Con managed for Kidman, and later to Wonnaminta.

Sid had swung a neat little deal for Yancannia. The purchase price was £80,000 for the 1,487 square mile holding, with 45,000 sheep, 16 milking cows, a team of 20 working bullocks, 300 horses, 30 camels, all station plant and machinery, including two motor cars, on a walk-in-walk-out basis for delivery on 31 March 1917. His partner in the deal? The Adelaide manager of the Bank of New South Wales, Mr A. H. (Augustine) Fearon. Naturally, they kept the matter very private, since head branch of the bank in Sydney was demanding reduction, and restraint. A second quick agreement transformed the partnership into the Yancannia Pastoral Company, incorporated in New South Wales with a nominal capital of £100,000 in £1 shares — 90,000 of them paid up in the names of the previous partners, Kidman and Fearon, and the remainder in the name of Sid's son-in-law Sid Reid.

Sid's determination to get the places he wanted knew no bounds. An agreement, dated 29 December 1916, stipulated that the Shaw brothers, Oliphant and Tom, (who had sold Yancannia) would also sell Lake Elder and Tindara to Sidney Kidman and Edward Peter Tapp for £25,000. It briefly designated the properties as being held and worked together as one property with all the cattle and horses running and pasturing thereon. The stock was estimated to be 1,500 head of cattle and 136 horses and the plant was included; the delivery date was 12 April 1917.

Kidman added Currawinya to the pile of properties later that year. It was more than 500,000 acres, just over the Queensland border near Hungerford, and next door to another of his First World War purchases, Boorara. He held it for only a short time and then sold it to the Belalie Pastoral Company. He also advised the bank in

---

OPPOSITE:
A camel carting Yandama wool. (John Ayers Jnr)

May that year that he would be drawing on it for £25,000 for part purchase of Murra Murra Station in the St George area of Queensland. Again, it was not a long-term or vital link in the north–south chain, but just something where he saw possibilities of a healthy turnover.

Yancannia was one of the last of the great west Darling properties left in private hands and Kidman's purchase of it and the rapid buying-up of several others marked the end of the reign of the "shepherd kings" and the final break-up of an established order that had begun to crack twenty years before. He was accused of "muscling" into the area by those who remained and also of "raping the land" that came under his ownership or control. It ought to be mentioned that no one was held at gun point or had their arms twisted behind their backs to sell and also that the pastoral industry there was ravaged by overstocking, by an ill-advised selection system and by the rabbit by the turn of the century. In 1894 the area held nearly 8 million sheep; by 1901 the numbers were down to 2.9 million. Kidman appeared on the scene fifteen years after the damage was acknowledged and at a time when dispirited people shackled by economic fetters to a desolate wasteland wanted out: the century's second major drought was another reason for many people to want to leave the land.

While Sid could not have claimed to have had a non-stop run of brilliant seasons since the end of the 1901 drought, at least he hadn't had a bad trot. He had had ten years to add to his chains, which, it seemed, were now due to take a second hammering, the north–south chain in particular.

The really bad signs were there, Sid told Bel, who, accompanied by her mother, Mrs David Will, gave herself over to steadfast prayer at the Kapunda Congregational Church, hoping that Sidney's worst fears would not be realised. The last decade had been a good one for them minus any significant drought. She was well aware of the abject misery it caused — stock, men, their families, businesses and the country — and now at a time when the country most needed Sidney for the effort he was ploughing into the war, it seemed destined to strike again.

Sid concentrated on the daily pile of telegrams describing stock movements and rainfall conditions on his stations. Thunderstorm activity dictated just where and just how many stock could be staged to feed.

Victoria and parts of Western Australia experienced the driest year on record in 1914, as did portions of South Australia, and the inland areas of New South Wales experienced almost twelve months' drought; 1915 was one of Queensland's worst drought years. The most vulnerable territory was Sid's north–south chain trailing through south-western Queensland, with its subsidiary branches in New South Wales and north-eastern South Australia. His secondary chain, the Central Australian–South Australian chain running hundreds of miles to the west was less threatened.

The system used before was again enforced immediately. All available fat cattle were to be put on the roads. The head office wired drovers as to where to pick them up and their market destinations. This left a "breathing space" for the stations and the store and breeding cattle that remained. There was more water and grass on each station for them. The drought rolled down from the north when the rains failed and the "three rivers" did not come down. The cattle travelled slowly south, held on feed at each station and kept one step ahead of the drought. At the Queensland border, depending on feed, water and markets, some continued south through New South Wales to the railhead at Broken Hill, and others went through into the north-eastern corner of South Australia to Farina. This time, the trucking depots Sid had acquired since the 1901 drought, Mundowdna and Forders, proved their great value as stategic points with water and feed, where the travelling mobs could be spelled briefly before being railed.

Kidman's chief cattle drover, Pat Kennedy, and horse drover, Charlie McLeod, and the drovers they contracted succeeded in getting mob after mob through. It was just as important to Sid to get his horses out where possible because of the prices they were fetching at the Kapunda sales. The job of the managers on the drought-stricken stations was to muster the stores and breeders within easy reach of waterholes, bores and feed. As the lesser waterholes dried up, stock were moved to permanent waterholes. As the feed diminished around the bores, the stock staged south along the chain. Try as they might, Kidman's top-notch men did not always succeed, and as drought tightened its grip, with feed and water severely depleted, store losses were inevitable. In 1914, 1,200 stores perished in the Coonchere sandhills in the north-east corner of South Australia when the drover, anticipating a drink for the cattle at a specific waterhole, found it dry. He attempted to move the distressed mob on, but it was impossible. Every head perished and he was only able to save two horses out of his entire plant.

There were some moments of respite. Tom Kidman, Sid's 26-year-old nephew (George's son), was the head stockman on Monkira Station in 1914. He recalled, "There was practically no rain in 1914. A drover arrived to take 1,000 bullocks to a property further down the Cooper as we were losing a lot of breeders and young cattle. While mustering these cattle we had violent thunder and lightning one night but no rain. The following day the boss (George 'Daddy' Hooper) came out to the camp and said they had had ½ inch at the station. I said I thought it had rained further west of the run where there was feed but no water. I asked him to go and have a look at Gymercky Creek where there were several good waterholes — but dry. After we had mustered and delivered 1,000 bullocks to the drover, I returned to the station and the first thing I asked was 'Did you go out to Gymercky?' The reply was 'No. The rain that fell here didn't extend a half mile so I turned back.' After a couple of days I said to him, 'I'm going out to Gymercky tomorrow. I won't be satisfied until I have a look.' He said, 'You'll perish your horses. It's 30 miles out there.' But I insisted and when he saw I was determined he said he would go with me. There was a dam halfway and when we reached it it was full of water, although there was no sign of rain as we were travelling up the watercourse and the catchment was all the other way. As we went, we could see that the rain had been heavier and green feed starting to show. After travelling several miles we reached the summit and the fall was all the other way. It was less than a fortnight after the storms but as far as the eye could see there was Mitchell grass about a foot high waving like a wheat crop for miles and miles. When we reached the creek we found it had run a banker about half a mile wide. We camped there for the night and were nearly eaten alive by mosquitoes. We returned to the homestead next day and immediately started to muster and shift the starving stock onto the lush pastures."

Keeping the stations going by maintaining supplies became a problem. Horse teams were unable to travel, as the teamsters had to cart feed for the horses as well as stores. Sid had realised the value of camels as beasts of burden and, as he had acquired stations, he had arranged for camels to be introduced and for his managers to become proficient in their breeding and use, so many of his stations could use their own camel teams when drought made the going too tough on horses. Also, in having his own camel teams to move stores, Sid could avoid the crippling freight costs faced by others. The cameleers operated out of Broken Hill to stations as far away as Durham Downs in south-western Queensland.

Writing to a friend about the drought, Anthony Kidman (Sackville's son), who held an interest with Sid in some west-of-the-Darling holdings, said, "I have just returned to Cobar from an inspection of our pastoral interests in Thargomindah and Cunnamulla in Queensland, and Tibooburra, White Cliffs and Wilcannia districts in New South Wales. The country is in a very bad state everywhere and it is the biggest drought known in the Tibooburra district. The country is a moving sandhill for hundreds of miles. The people are experiencing great difficulty in getting meat. They are practically living on tinned meat brought by camels. We have 400 camels carting foodstuffs and horsefeed to our various stations."

When it reached the point of camels being the only animals

capable of travel, it spelt a lingering death for the remaining cattle on stations. Marooned in a sea of arid country, they were shifted where possible within a station to those waterholes that remained. When they, too, were gone, the stench of death soon pervaded the country as thousands of carcasses rotted in the burning sun until only their bleached bones remained.

In December 1915 Sid informed the Bank of New South Wales that he had lost 60,000 cattle and was being offered £12 a head for stores in Queensland. The losses, until that time, would not hurt all that much, he added, because he still had plenty of cattle. Within six months the figure stood at 75,000 with most losses incurred on Diamantina Lakes, Durham Downs, Sandringham, Glengyle, Annandale, Thargomindah and Innamincka. The final 1914–16 drought cattle loss stood at 85,000. Around 50,000 sheep were also lost, mainly from the stations Sid had bought up in western New South Wales in the First World War.

The success of the chain system should be examined in the light of the losses sustained. During the turn-of-the-century drought, Sid held seventeen stations in a fragmentary chain and suffered a loss of 70,000 cattle; in the First World War when the drought struck, he had three times the number of stations in a healthily linked chain and he sustained the marginally higher loss of 85,000. Without knowing the exact numbers of stock held at the time of both droughts, it is impossible to evaluate losses on a percentage basis. Certainly at the turn of the century he would have held fewer stock (even then he would not have known the exact number), and by the First World War, Kidman was not lying to governments, commissions of inquiry and parliamentary hearings when they wanted to know the size of his herds. Sid couldn't tell them because he didn't know himself. "I could not tell you to within 25,000 or 30,000," was the standard answer. It went no further than that. Given that he was receiving £12 a head for store cattle in Queensland, the loss of 85,000 at that price was £1,020,000; at £15 a head for fat cattle, the 85,000 had a market value of £1,275,000. Added to that should be the meat and wool market value of 50,000 sheep.

So what was the total loss financially? the press asked. Sid replied that he was genuine in saying he did not know. The press did its own sums and gravely assessed Sid as the largest loser of cattle in Australia in the drought, but not necessarily of sheep. They calculated the loss at more than £1 million. Nervously, the bank raised the matter. Again, Sid said he did not know, but that cattle estimates were accurate at around 85,000 and the sheep loss was somewhere over the 50,000 mark. The bank accepted the figures, noting that "Kidman is invariably under than over the mark in quoting to us".

By April 1916 telegrams were reaching the office reporting splendid rains on the south-western properties. The three rivers of the north came down, bringing mighty walls of water, soaking, spreading and finally subsiding, and leaving as their legacy a fresh bounty of feed. Once again the chain had received a fairly severe rattling, but, all things considered, it had withstood the shake quite well. The rush was on again for Sid's managers and drovers to stock up, while he attended to buying up more stations and also to the other irons he now had in the fire: shipbuilding, roadbuilding and railway construction.

Despite angry threats by Labor members of Parliament and unionists that seamen should refuse to carry Kidman if he attempted to leave by ship for an overseas trip, there was no such drama as he and Bel left on the *Moeraki* on 28 February 1917 for a visit to New Zealand. Casting his glims over the meat trade was only one reason for going — he gave great accounts of New Zealand's prosperity on his return, but said he found the value of land and stock too high; the other was to look into a roadbuilding proposal.

Sid had entered his "construction" era and was one of the partners in the Australian firm of Smith, Timms and Kidman. He was sounding out the prospect of building a tunnel and modern road between Lyttelton and Christchurch. The length of the proposed tunnel was 1 mile and 50 chains and the width 40 feet. This would allow an 18 foot concrete road for traffic and two tram roads. The cost for excavation, with about a third of the tunnel concreted, would be £400,000. The lining would run to £30,000. The cost of forming an 18 foot traffic road between Christchurch and Lyttelton would be £80,000 and macadamising would require another £10,000. Such a road would have a concrete foundation of 7 inches and a 3 inch asphalt surface. The most direct route would be through Opawa and a tramline could be provided from there to Lyttelton for another £76,000. The whole scheme would run to around £700,000, or about £624,000 with the tramline eliminated. Sid left the New Zealanders to think about the proposal.

Back in Australia, there was increasing concern about the allied shipping losses during the war. Although it was a war in which both aeroplanes and submarines featured for the first time, there was a swing in the United States to revert to timber-built ships for the general cargo trade. Australia thought it a good idea to build some as well, because the shortage of tonnage by 1918 was starting to become acute. The firm of Kidman and Mayoh tendered successfully for a government contract to build six 3,000 ton ships at shipbuilding yards within Sydney Harbour. They were to be sailing ships with auxiliary power, and with hulls constructed of Australian hardwood. Sid was quite happy to take on the role of shipbuilder: it was good business and there was a good bonus offered for completion within the contract time.

Fred Aarons, whose father had been a friend of Sid's in earlier days, bumped into Sid in the foyer of the Australia Hotel, Sydney, in 1918. The chance meeting drew Aarons into the shipbuilding operation. Giving an account of it, Aarons, who had been brought home from the war because of injury and had just been released from hospital, said:

We talked only briefly. I told him it was good to be home and that I'd soon be back in civvies. He looked hard at me for an instant, his active mind seemed to be at work. I told him I'd have to be pushing off as I had an appointment and these words seemed to halt his temporary aberration.

"Just a minute," he said. "Are you going back to the bush right away?"

"Well, not at once, anyhow. I'll have to have a look around for a bit of country."

"I'd like to talk to you," he said. "What about a bite of lunch with me tomorrow?"

I readily assented. We shook hands and parted. I wondered what he wanted of me and was not left long in doubt after we had met as arranged. In his usual direct manner he gave me the reason. "You see," he began with a smile that wrinkled his tanned features, "I'm in the shipbuilding business." It was my turn to grin. "Shipbuilding?" I echoed. "What the devil —"

"All right, I'll explain. . . ." And so I listened while he told me of his entry into this strange field of enterprise as far away from his usual sphere as the North Pole. He spoke of the government's concern about the transport of the country's surplus wheat owing to the heavy loss of freighters during the war and how it had been decided to have a number of large wooden sailing ships to fill the gap. He had joined forces with a businessman to build these ships in the quickest possible time.

He stressed to me how important it was to have the supply of timber kept up to the shipyards from the forests and how this was one of the problems that seemed to be bothering his technical associates.

Then looking across the table at me with that serious, almost stern expression, he said, "And this is where you come in." "How do you mean?" I asked in genuine surprise. "You know the north coast," he said. "You were born there, weren't you?" I nodded. "Well," he continued, "as an army officer you'd know something about organisation and the working of men? You know as well, that for every straight tree there are half a dozen bent ones and it's the bent ones these fellows want and don't seem to be able to get. I think you could do a job like that, eh?"

The following afternoon I met the principals of the company and the engineer and remarked that I might know blackbutt, turpentine and tallow wood but was hardly a timber expert. Mr Kidman's reply was quick. "I'd suggest some advice from the Forestry Department's men. They're sure to have plenty available in the timber country up there." His last words to me were, "You can do this job alright. It's a job worth doing too. It'll widen your experience and you'll be doing something for the country you've already served."

I could not help turning over in my mind this new and unexpected side to the personality of a man who was known far and wide as a bushman and shrewd cattle dealer. I knew that, to many, he had made his way by innate sagacity in the restricted sphere of cattle dealing and that his business was transacted by some sort of rule of thumb; his wealth resulted from these factors boosted from time to time by sheer luck. To some extent I shared this opinion but thinking over recent conversations with him I realised that Kidman, whose way up the ladder of success had been a triumph over both the harshness of nature and difficulties of competition, would have succeeded in almost any walk of life into which the fates had turned him.

I learned later that it was Mayoh and his brother who had constructed the greater part of the north coast railway in New South Wales and had also done a large share of the Sydney Underground construction. As a result of discussions I agreed to undertake the procuring of the heavy timber needed for the construction of four of the ships. The terms of the contract were quite satisfactory to me and, as the job was urgent, I left for the north the following night.

After arriving in Kempsey I was put in contact with a man who was to be invaluable to me throughout my work in the forest belt. He was Charlie Murrill, world champion axeman, 6 feet 3 inches of bone and sinew, whose life was spent felling trees for girders or competing in woodchops along the coastal belt. He and his axeman brother, Amos, brought me into contact with the best timber-getters on the north coast. My task thus made easy, it was no time before I had a few hundred men felling and squaring heavy timber from the headwaters of the nine rivers from the Queensland border to the Hunter Valley.

Within three months, bullock teams were hauling into river loading depots all kinds of squared timber from great ironbark rudder stocks weighing up to 11 tons and measuring 30 feet in length to small ti-tree "knees" of ½ hundredweight, all dressed with the broad axe according to blueprint.

During the following months I made several trips to Sydney to confer with my principals but did not see Kidman again until nearly a year had passed and my job was nearing completion. He was kind enough to make a few appreciative remarks concerning my work: "I knew you'd do the job alright," he said, "and I bet you liked that kind of experience, didn't you?" "I've enjoyed every minute of it," I replied. "I have you to thank for it and, as a matter of fact, I'll be sorry when the work is finished."

He put out his hand. "We mightn't meet again for some time," he said. "I think you're able to fend for yourself, but if you want any help from me at any time..."

The work at the shipyards went on long after I had procured the necessary timber for the construction of the ships. But, of course, they never sailed the seven seas, these Australian wooden ships. After one or two had been launched with much eclat, the government of the day called a halt to all further work.

The war ended late in 1918, and Mr Poynston, the Minister in Charge of Shipbuilding, considered it sound policy not to complete the wooden ships. It would cost the Commonwealth government £179,000 to cancel the contracts for the building of the ships. Kidman and Mayoh's contract for six wooden ships was varied by the cancellation of four of them and the firm was to be paid at the rate of £5 a ton dead weight capacity for the four ships, which amounted to approximately £52,000. Two other companies were to be paid £55,000 and £72,500 for work done on their contracts for the building of six ships.

The matter didn't rest there. Kidman and Mayoh had virtually completed two ships, the *Braeside* and *Burnside*. The government said it was entitled to refuse to accept delivery of them and cancelled their contracts. Kidman and Mayoh instituted an action against the Commonwealth, claiming £88,000 for work and labour done and material supplied, or as damages for breach of contract.

The government insisted that Kidman and Mayoh undertook to construct two wooden ships and were paid approximately £104,000 by the Commonwealth to do so and had failed absolutely to carry out the contract. Sir Mark Sheldon was called in to act as arbiter in the claims between the government and the company. He found that £76,665 was due by Kidman and Mayoh to the Commonwealth and directed that it should be paid, plus their costs and the costs of the Commonwealth. The full court granted an order to enforce the award of the arbiter. Then Kidman and Mayoh obtained leave to appeal to the Privy Council. The Commonwealth then applied to the High Court against the leave to appeal...

It assumed the proportions of a right royal legal battle, its intensity perhaps even surprising Kidman who, years earlier, had expressed his own view about the law: "I never go to the law myself, and as to agreements, I make them as short as possible — the shorter, the less possibility of misunderstanding." There was nothing short about this one. It was long in terms of time being settled and in money, costing Sid more than £100,000. The fate of the *Braeside* was to be sold to the Union Box Co., at Ryde, for breaking up and the remainder of her was towed through Sydney Heads and scuttled. Sid's biggest regret was that the wonderful work of the superb axemen of the north coast forests, their enthusiasm, craftsmanship and loyalty, all went for nought.

In August 1919, while the matter of the ships was raging in the courts, Sid, in partnership with Joseph Timms, put up an £8 million proposal to the Commonwealth government to construct a north–south railway from Oodnadatta to Pine Creek in the Northern Territory, which would make a Darwin–Adelaide rail link complete.

His first job was to talk the matter over with the bank in Sydney. The bank noted, "Re the large rail programme originated by Timms and S.K. Have no fear of S.K.'s position in his embarking on a contracting scheme of this kind — assuming it comes off. S.K. has the rare facility of attaching capable men to his ventures no matter how diverse they might be and we have never known of his failure in any one instance. Timms is a thoroughly experienced railway contractor and S.K. makes no mistake in joining him." Joseph Timms had been engaged on the building of the Darwin to Pine Creek rail line thirty years before and had advanced to other construction and irrigation work. He had joined Sid in putting forward the tunnel–road proposal in New Zealand.

People had been aware of the need — and the benefits — of such a north–south railway line for twenty years. The Transcontinental Railway Act had been passed in 1902, but since then nothing had been done about it, as various alternative routes were put forward and deliberated. Sid, fed up with the railways that did run, was equally concerned about those that didn't run at all because they'd never been built! The country was crying out for them, to which he might have added his own personal cry. Sid was also experiencing a renewed interest in the Northern Territory and hoping to add to his central–south chain of properties there. A railway line from Oodnadatta to Pine Creek would serve him well, particularly as a means of lifting stock in times of drought and getting them to market to avoid appalling losses. Sid had also never quite recovered (despite thirty-five years) from his sale of the one-fourteenth share in BHP. He was happy enough with the quick profit at the time...but in retrospect...and now there was talk of great mineral wealth in the north ...why, a man never knew what he might stumble across. He knew the country and Timms knew railway building. It would be a jolly good thing all way round.

The proposal was treated seriously by the Commonwealth government and received with raptures in Adelaide by many people who'd never given much thought to it before. Men were returning from the war and the new railway would mean jobs — and plenty of them. "Truly, what a Godsend Mr Kidman was" was an expression frequently on everyone's lips. It was Bel Kidman who remarked quite tartly about "people running with the hares and hunting with the hounds". And in more elevated circles, clubs and the establishment there would have been a few ripples of shock, with people posing the question "Good God! Could Kidman really do it?", and not a few responding, "If he won't who will? Not the bloody government." or "Give him his head and let him have a go!"

Smarting, perhaps, from the way the ship-dealing business was proceeding, Sid allowed Joseph Timms to be chief spokesman on the railway as the press clamoured for more details of "two giants in finance undertaking work of more than ordinary dimensions and importance to construct the long debated transcontinental railway from South Australia to the Northern Territory linking Adelaide with Darwin". The press insisted that the north–south railway would mean the development of great mineral and pastoral wealth in the interior that could never be properly exploited until a line or railway was put through. New South Wales and Queensland were moving actively to link up certain of their railway terminals with those of the Northern Territory (or so it seemed at the time). In South Australia, it was generally acknowledged that the state would be greatly handicapped if it were superseded by any scheme that either of the two eastern states might finalise. The other states were all talk, and Kidman had put on the hat that said "do", and the "do" he wanted was straight up through the Centre, the shortest possible link.

The chairman of the Australian Railways and Territory League, Mr Simpson Newland, hoped that the Commonwealth government would accept the offer after making full enquiries. The question of price was for the experts to determine. An offer in London at the turn of the century to build the line had been estimated at £6 million sterling and the £8 million cited by Timms and Kidman did not seem exorbitant; in fact, in comparison with the enormous wealth lying dormant in the country, £8 million was a mere bagatelle. Asked whether, if the line were built in terms of the present offer, there was a reasonable prospect of it paying interest and working expenses, Newland said that it would pay from the outset, for the country would be developed by the line and there were great possibilities in the Territory. He added that if the line had been constructed at the time of the 1914–16 drought, stock in South Australia, where feed was short, could have been moved to the Northern Territory. The freight received might not have paid interest on the cost of the line, but several millions in value of stock could have been saved.

Commenting on the proposal, Mr Joseph Timms said, "We are prepared to lay down a line of railway at a scheduled rate to be fixed by the Commonwealth engineer-in-chief and our firm's chief engineer. We will find the whole of the money and take payment in government bonds and we would undertake to have the rails through in three years. We are not particular where we start. We could begin at both ends within three months and we don't anticipate any engineering difficulties until we start to negotiate the mountainous country in the MacDonnell Ranges and the big waterways and rivers.

"Our offer is for a single line, fully ballasted. Regarding gauge, weight of material, curves, grades, width of cuttings, banks and bridges — these details will be fixed by the Commonwealth government and the work will be done under strict supervision. It will be a first-class line either 4 feet 8½ inches or 5 feet 3 inches, which would permit a speed of 60 miles an hour and with a proper start we could employ 5,000 hands."

The South Australian government pressed the Commonwealth government for an answer on the matter and in Melbourne (the then federal capital), the Acting Prime Minister, Mr Watt, said that the matter was "receiving serious attention". Today the north–south line is still "under consideration", but at anticipated construction costs that make the Timms and Kidman offer look like peanuts.

Not daunted first by the Commonwealth government's dilly-dallying and then by rejection of the proposal, Sid turned his attention to construction work elsewhere: the Tod River Water Scheme, which involved supplying water to Port Lincoln, South Australia, and the peninsula to the west. It was a £1 million plus project, initially let to the Concrete Steel Contracting Co., of South Australia, to create a reservoir on Footlillie Creek, 18 miles north of Port Lincoln. Its holding capacity, when completed, was to be 2,400 million gallons and the building of the embankment was no small job. It was to be 1,153 feet long at the top, 415 feet wide at the base and 81 feet in height, allowing a depth of 75 feet. The water to fill it would be supplied from the Tod River and Pilowarta Creek. The contract was let to the CSC Co. in 1918, but financial difficulties set in and a receiver was appointed. The outcome was that Sid Kidman, with the approval of the South Australian Commissioner of Public Works, took over the contract.

"There is a great cry in this country, and in this state in particular, for water, Sid said. "Any project that will help overcome this problem is a worthy one. This contract is a big one and I am also taking over the whole of the Steel Concreting Company's works and will complete other contracts it has under way."

Asked why he was moving into such areas when his name and reputation were synonymous with stock dealing, Sid replied jocularly, "There is no money in meat — so I am going in for contracting!"

Shipbuilding, roadbuilding, and railway and dam construction represent a side of Sidney Kidman's business life largely unknown or greatly overlooked. These pursuits also give an indication of his personal wealth at the time.

18
Trouble in the Bush

FOR SID, HOWEVER, it was time to put a fresh focus on the bush again. The years 1918–20 were again those of drought, particularly in New South Wales, while in Queensland during 1918–19 there were twenty-two months with less than average rainfall. Sid sent his nephew Anthony Kidman on an inspection tour of the holdings in the western division of New South Wales. The news was grim. "The stations north of a line extending east from Broken Hill to Wilcannia are in a state that history has never known before. Neither black men nor white men can remember a drought with such awful effects. Stations that used to carry 100,000 sheep are at present carrying only 6,000 or so. Other stations that used to carry 80,000 sheep have not a hoof on them. We have had to shift all stock from Mount Stuart and Mount Wood stations or we would have lost them entirely. Morden and several other stations (an area of some 200 square miles) can be used to take stock from the drier areas. These properties will give temporary relief only; the only salvation possible is rain. Artesian bores afford only temporary salvation because they can only give water to limited areas and the whole stock of a station cannot be kept close to them.

"But we have just completed two bores on Yandama Station. Both were successful; one at 2,200 feet struck a flow of 200,000 gallons of water daily and the other at about 1,800 feet struck a flow of 150,000 gallons daily. We have started sinking others at Lake Elder in South Australia, east of Corona, where there is a good flow and have another bore in construction at Clyde in southern Queensland."

Of a further inspection trip undertaken in 1920, Anthony Kidman said, "The drought has nearly wiped out the western portion of New South Wales north of the Darling as far as the sheep industry is concerned and a number of stations have been abandoned. Even if rain fell tomorrow they would be unable to take sheep back onto the properties owing to the presence of wild dogs. I don't think 100,000 sheep would cover our losses in western New South Wales. In the Dubbo district we are now paying £73 a thousand a month for sheep on agistment, which, I think, is a record."

If there had been some initial surprise, then uneasiness, over

258

Kidman's entry west of the Darling, it now intensified. As the fortunes of landholder after landholder plummeted, there was Sid, or his son-in-law Sid Reid, or his nephew Anthony (Tony) Kidman, willing to buy up and add the place to the Kidman interests. In the five years following the First World War, Sid bought up as if there was no settling: Nundora, Corona, Packsaddle, Mount Arrowsmith, Boxhole, Thurlow Downs, Urisino, Morden, Mount Sturt, Cobham Lake, Wonnaminta, Mount Wood, Purnanga, Wyarra and Elsinora were added to his chain in western New South Wales alone. All up, his ownership and interest in western New South Wales amounted to more than 22,000 square miles, and added to the 85,000 square miles held in Queensland, Western Australia, South Australia and the Northern Territory, it brought Sid up to his 100,000 square miles of country. He had lost a slice of mileage when he had unloaded Diamantina Lakes and Monkira in Queensland in 1918, and increasingly his eye was on the Northern Territory hopeful, no doubt, that the railway would proceed.

The general public marvelled; the press marvelled; but in western New South Wales many people would have used one word only to describe Sid...vulture...hovering and cruising only to come in and feast on others' misfortunes and wing away, bloated. How they hated him. He didn't have to live there and put up with things, day in and day out, in the way they did, in their constant struggle to preserve the work of fathers and grandfathers before them. To boot, Kidman was changing the order of things — forsaking sheep for cattle.

If Sid cared about what others felt and thought, he didn't allow it to show. He knew the land west of the Darling well. He'd ridden over it as a young boy when he'd worked for German Charlie, acted as a guide to the overlanders, traded in horses, worked his bullock teams and droved sheep and cattle for Sack to Broken Hill. He could recall the recovery rate of the country fifty years ago after rains and floods. It didn't respond in the same way now. In fact it was in a parlous state. It had suffered from misuse, from greed, overstocking and the infernal rabbit. But it was hard lines to start hammering him for the woes of the area. He was only a bloke — perhaps the only bloke — with a cheque book, who was able to go around picking up the pieces and see what he could make of them. People could like it or lump it. Some places, like Corona, were ideally suited to sheep; they would stay that way. But sheep tore at the land and there were so many parts of it where, if you eased up a bit and ran cattle instead or used the places as feeding stopovers for travelling cattle, the land would have a better chance of coming good again. In any case, the land was his, so he could do with it as he liked.

It was satisfaction to Sid to look at a map and to see his holdings running into each other: Wanaaring ran into Urisino which ran into

Salisbury Downs which ran into Bootra which ran into Monolon. Tinapagee ran into Elsinora, which ran into Thurlow Downs, which hit the Queensland border. Yancannia bordered on Cobham Lake, Packsaddle and Wonnaminta. Yantara bordered on Yancannia, which bled into Mount Wood, Mount Stuart, Wyarra (Waratta) and Mount Sturt, which bordered on Yandama, which overflowed into South Australia. Flowing south from Yandama were Mount Poole, Mount Arrowsmith, Packsaddle and Nundora. And they were all his — along with a large slice of resentment. It was quite bitter in Sid's time, when many of the locals would have welcomed the chance to "get their fingers around his leathery throat". Resentment was never expressed openly in his presence — always behind his back. He was altering the old order of things. Change was being thrust on the area by an "outsider" who didn't even live there. And when he did choose to visit, his behaviour was quite odd (to say the least).

Russell Barton was a young man in his mid-twenties working in the area at the time, and he recalls Sid rolling up unexpectedly at a station soon after he had purchased it. It sent the departing manager's wife into a flap, racing for the dusting cloth and the best silver and floral decor for the impressive dining table. "The dining room is very elegant, Mrs Rankin," Sid said, "but don't put flowers on the table for me. I'm not used to all of this." The manager's wife was crestfallen — denied the right to entertain him as best she could (when the chances to do so were so lean) and gossip about the occasion later. Instead, Sid ate and yarned the night away with the stockmen.

It was not what he did at but what he did with the places he took up that aroused great ire. Bob Routledge, who was in his twenties, was team-driving bullocks and camels west of the Darling at the time. Speaking of the local resentment, he said, "They reckoned Kidman was the ruination of the back country because he turned a lot of sheep stations into cattle stations and sheep fences were no good to him for cattle. With cattle, he didn't need men. He didn't like a high wages bill. He didn't seem to like paying money at all.

"At one stage they were shearing 100,000 sheep at Salisbury. Kidman converted it to cattle. At Momba where they'd shorn 500,000 sheep, it became cattle. Cobham went to cattle. So did Nundora, Mount Arrowsmith and Wonnaminta. When they changed over (at Momba at least), the blackwire was taken from the fences and shipped off on boats and sold down south. When Kidman took the Salisbury wire out of the fences he didn't send it away because there was still such an outcry over the stripping of Momba. As far as I know the Salisbury wire could still be there out on the run where they made the stacks. In relation to Urisino, Kidman instructed the iron from the shearing sheds to be removed and transported to Bourke by camel and, from there, railed to Sydney.

Momba, at the time he took it over, was employing sixty men (it could have been more) and for cattle purposes he only needed a couple of men.

"Three of his main stations in the west he kept in sheep: Yancannia, Corona and Weinteriga. He did improve those, cutting big paddocks to smaller, putting down wells and sinking dams. At Yancannia he had 120 bullocks in the plant putting down dams and cleaning out old ones and he put in some good wells on the other two places. So many of the other places went to the pack out of neglect — neglect of men to work them. There were some bitter thoughts and feelings directed towards him for doing away with employment — not just regular workers but also shearing teams."

Roy Dunk, born in 1892, was a stockman on Currawinya Station, Queensland, in 1913 when Kidman bought the adjoining property, Boorara. Tracing the changes that followed, he said, "Currawinya's southern boundary was the New South Wales – Queensland border fence. All the country from Hungerford to Thargomindah was sheep country and the biggest trouble was dingoes. Stations had to employ professional doggers so they could run sheep economically and boundary riders were put on to set dog traps.

"Boorara was in the centre of this sheep country when Kidman bought it. It was rough country and some of it nothing more than miles of stony hills. One section of them was known as the 'walls of China' and it had caves, plenty of them and they were ideal places for dingoes to breed. When Kidman bought Boorara the first thing he did was sack the doggers and sell the sheep. He didn't like sheep. He called them 'jolly little monkeys'. He stocked the place with cattle. The cattle broke the fences and went straight into neighbours' places. The dingo population increased alarmingly and it got to the stage that neighbouring properties couldn't cope with dingoes and went broke. When they did, Kidman came along and bought their places for a song.

"Much the same type of havoc went on west of the Darling when he converted from sheep to cattle there. Some of the places were well-improved properties with substantial buildings and quarters (in some cases buildings were duplicated because the shearers wouldn't live with the rouseabouts so there were two kitchens and two sets of sleeping quarters). During the war, the price of building materials, particularly galvanised iron, fetched a high price even second-hand. So after selling off the sheep, the buildings had no use and Kidman wrecked most of them. He stripped the shearers' quarters, took the iron off the woolsheds and sold it all at inflated war prices, the galvanised iron especially. I remember an article in one of the papers at the time saying that Kidman 'unimproved more country than any ten to twelve men'. He wasn't the hero most people thought."

Locally expressed anger found its way into a further barrage of anti-Kidman letters in newspapers. Writing in his defence to the *Sydney Stock and Station Journal*, Mr R. M. Pitt, of Pitt, Son and Badgery, said:

Within the last few years Mr Kidman has come into the far western country of New South Wales beyond the Darling with South Australia as the boundary on the west and Queensland on the north and these are the driest and most precarious parts of the whole of this state. Once again he is playing the part of the rescuer. The country out there has been the grave of the hopes of many of our most enterprising pastoralists. They went out there with hopes running high, made a brave fight of it, and failed. Numbers of them have been ruined. It has been will-o'-the-wisp country luring men on to destruction. There have been a few good years but the bad years have been many and the average has been against the pioneers. It is very light-carrying country requiring 10–20 acres to run a sheep. The only chance is to work it in large areas. You may get rain on one part of the run and you can shift your stock to it. You must always keep a reserve of unstocked country to minimise disaster.

As showing what the men out there have to face, may I mention that Yancannia, north of Broken Hill, was bought less than two years ago by Mr Kidman with 70,000–80,000 sheep on it at a high figure. Yancannia has always been looked upon as one of the best improved properties out there. TODAY, WHAT SHEEP HAVE NOT BEEN SHIFTED OFF IT ARE DEAD. This, unfortunately, partly holds good of a number of other properties bought by him west of the Darling. Fortunately, for the good of New South Wales, Mr Kidman has the means, the courage and confidence to restock these properties, and which no doubt he will do as soon as the seasons permit.

What the general public should realise is that Mr Kidman goes right outside the settled and safe areas, takes the risk of going where the small man cannot and should not go and few big men dare go and there improves the country and adds generally to the meat and wool production of the Commonwealth. He is thereby a benefactor to his country and, as the venture is a pure speculation, if he does have good fortune, he is entitled to it as if he loses no one would want to share the loss.

The sad experience of my company in financing men in the vicinity of Bourke during the 1890s was such as to everlastingly convince me it is no place for the small man. The whole if the country west of the Darling and a big portion of it for a considerable distance this side from Bourke to Menindee can be worked successfully only in large holdings by wealthy men or companies and they often have disastrous losses. For closer settlement it is absolutely unfitted and to send small men on it is simply sending them to ruin. To the small holder, it is a cruel death-trap. Those who think differently, let them try and they will soon be wiser but poorer men.

The Sydney *Argus* took up the matter in an editorial:

Many a Melbourne or Adelaide man in business shudders when he hears of the west in New South Wales, for inside of ten years it was first a Golconda, an el dorado and next a land of giant Despair. Money was poured out from Melbourne and Adelaide to improve that country lavishly and money and labour abounded in that far country until a dreary succession of natural and legislative misfortunes swept all away and left the owners stranded and their leases, stock and homesteads to be taken over as small assets against an immense debt.

Men are now agitating for opening up the west to small settlement. There are claims that the west is the worst monopoly in the country. We hear it asserted that monopoly is gaining ground. There is a great outcry against Mr Sidney Kidman. The Western Land Board was bad enough but Mr Kidman threatens to be worse by far. Labour is to disappear. For twenty men needed to run sheep, two or three are needed to run cattle. And the western towns, threatened with still further depletion of their limited population and trade, fear that extinction is upon them. All these various influences have led the Legislative Council of New South Wales to appoint its select committee to take evidence, make an interim report urging that it be converted into a Royal Commission to continue its inquiries. In New South Wales, we are tired of Royal Commissions. They cost much money and seldom do anything.

In Sydney, in clubs where pastoral men meet, you can hear the great change discussed and practically all the authorities agree that it is inevitable. It is not final and that is why they consent to it ad interim. Why sheep go out and why cattle come in and why the station men sell out to Mr Kidman... It is because the wild dog is being driven out of South Australia by vigorous destructive measures and the dingo with its usual cunning has moved up along the border fences, found weak places and poured in in a flood upon country where the drought has almost wiped out the rabbits and left it what remains of the sheep to prey upon.

With no help from the government to maintain and strengthen the heavy, high fences necessary to keep out the dogs, with their own resources for boundary and interior fencing impaired by drought, the station holders find the dog pest worse than all the others. Local attempts to keep down the pest by bonus have been exhausted. Therefore those who are tired of the fight sell.

Meantime, all the outcry against Mr Kidman is in vain. If, for the present and until we manage to get a hold upon the wild-dog pest, sheep are not a paying proposition in the west and cattle are — then it must be cattle and not sheep. And we ought to be thankful that some means are to hand for ensuring the occupation, reasonable improvement and the revenue-yielding possibilities of the country. It is no use to rail at Mr Kidman as a monopolist. Put in bald terms — Mr Kidman or nobody, cattle or nothing, the north-west in anyone's hands or no one's hands, there is only one answer. If Mr Kidman is willing to risk his money in a long speculation against drought, dogs and perhaps uncertain markets, surely it is far better for the West that he should have the country than that it should year by year go out of occupation, the improvements vanish, employment stop, rent cease and all have to be done over again when the time comes. To argue against Mr Kidman is simply to argue the plain facts of the case and to batter one's head against a wall. The West is a land of big areas, big banking accounts or credits and big hearts. It will not be in our time a land for "small" men.

Sid could detect another fight looming over his western New South Wales holdings, but for the moment two other things claimed priority. One meant yet another appearance before a commission: this time the Federal Commission on Taxation of Leasehold Estates over which the Commonwealth Statistician, Mr G. H. Knibbs, CMG, presided. Sid remarked to Bel that the only thing different about all these commissions was the person asking the questions. The same old questions were trotted out, to which Sid gave the same old answers in his frank and casual style, and whatever Sid had to say on such occasions was always considered good mileage by the press.

The press noted that when "the two giants met" (both dealt with figures in a big way) it seemed amusingly anomalous that the famous pastoralist could not tell the notable statistician the numbers of stock he held:

Giving evidence, the "Cattle King" remarked, "People think they know, but they don't. I don't even know myself."

The "Cattle King" was an interesting as well as useful witness to the commission and he continually interpolated little reminiscences concerning himself in between answers to questions put by Mr Knibbs.

One which amused the commission greatly concerned his early days in western New South Wales. "I was all over that country in 1871," observed Mr Kidman. "I was horse hunting on a station around the time at 10 bob a week and because I asked for a rise I got the sack." Those present enjoyed the joke, especially when Mr Kidman said, "and nowadays drovers get their £1 a day!"

Sid also told the Commission that he had paid £4,000 out of £9,000 taxation on Crown leases. He regarded the estimated freehold value of the leases as unsatisfactory, and although he didn't consider the valuation satisfactory, he had accepted it and had paid, subject to objections, a portion of it. He expressed the opinion that if the government insisted on the payment he would prefer to abandon his leases. It was desirable for the commission to see the land he held: among it was some of the lightest-carrying country in the world. He said that as soon as he saw the plant and stock on any station he made up his mind what he would give for it. He did not value his leases at more than 5 shillings. He never included the value of his leases in that of his stock and improvements. He attributed a large element of his success not merely to the stations themselves but to the purchase and then fattening of store bullocks. Some of the country was not even taxable, and, to undertake to use it for pastoral purposes, people must have money or persons to back them up. In New South Wales and north of Adelaide they were passing through one of the worst droughts ever known and the whole success of the pastoral industry depended on rainfall. He didn't mind paying a fair tax, but tomorrow the state or federal government could have every acre he held in South Australia on any terms if they paid him the value of the improvements. He would be glad to get out of the pastoral industry if he could on account of labour conditions, droughts and taxation. He only maintained his interest in South Australian properties because he could not get out of them. It would, in his judgement, pay the government to let the people on the land for nothing if they would put stock on and improve it, and where he was concerned himself, if the government continued with the tax, he wanted out.

The headlines screamed, "Kidman 'Glad to get out'" and "Another weary king", with some commentators sniping, "We should all be glad to get out of any industry providing we'd done as well out of it as Mr Kidman. It's a hard world for kings now, anyway. But some of the others did pretty well before they abdicated."

His early retirement was foreshadowed. But was he bluffing or serious? Serious, it seemed, as within a matter of days after the announcement a plan for a lengthy visit overseas was announced. It was a trip that had everything to do with the other major thought that preoccupied him — his only son, Walter. He had finished his schooling in England and returned home after the war, but with a disability that alarmed both Sid and Bel, particularly because no medical help in Australia seemed to be able to cure it.

19
Walter's Difficult Apprenticeship

WALTER KIDMAN was not quite 8 years old when he set out with his parents and sisters on the first family visit to England and the Continent in 1908. He was the youngest in the family by ten years, and his big sisters, Gertie, 22, Elma, 21, and Edna, 18, had fixed notions of what they wanted to do and see on the trip — parties, dances, dinners, the theatre — with which Bel Kidman heartily agreed, glad for her girls to have opportunities that she had missed. She wanted the best for them and for her only son, Walter.

Taking Walter everywhere with them posed something of a problem on account of his age, especially on evenings out, when something more suitable was organised for Walter. Usually a page boy at Langham's Hotel, London, minded him in the Kidmans' suite at the hotel at night and in the daytime often took him to visit the waxworks, the zoo, or to various museums and attractions. (Almost fifty years later when Walter Kidman was in London collecting theatre tickets from the booking manager at Grosvenor House, the booking manager remarked, "I was the page boy detailed to look after you on your first trip here with your parents.")

While the girls trekked the Continent with their parents, Walter remained in England, where he was put into a preparatory school, Caldicott, at Hitchen, 50 miles north of London...an unsmiling young boarding boy in long pants and a bowler hat.

Gertrude Kidman, the most boisterous of the girls, wanted no part of any further educational and refining processes in Europe (which no doubt amused Sid), but Elma and Edna were not averse to continuing their schooling with the daughters of nobility, at Dieudonne in France, where everything from shcoolwork to etiquette was undertaken in French. (Whatever they learnt in a year "lapsed pretty quickly once they returned home", according to Elma's daughter, Joan Hopkins.)

Only Walter and Gertie returned with their parents to South Australia in 1909. Walter went to school as a boarder at St Peter's College, Adelaide, interspersed with holidays with his father visiting Mundowdna, Kidman's cattle depot not far from Hergott Springs. For three years in a row he had a social role as page boy when his sisters married, Elma in 1911, Edna in 1912, and Gertie in 1913. He looked somewhat sullen in all official photographs.

A Royal Navy man, Gertie's husband Nelson Clover was committed to return to England in 1914, and she begged her parents that Walter be allowed to go with her and her husband for further schooling in England. Whatever Bel said was all right with Sid, and Bel was never overly fond of rearing children although, at the age of 13, Walter Kidman could hardly be termed a child. He was the same age as his father had been when he had set out on a one-eyed horse with 5 shillings in his pocket. Walter, a more protected, dependent and less robust youth than Sid, would travel in much finer style. From an educational point of view, Bel thought a few years in England desirable for her son, and Walter made no protest, although any clamouring or appeal on his part to stay at home and finish school and move into the business would have reversed the decision instantly.

In July 1914 Walter left with Gertie and Nelson Clover for England. War was declared when the ship reached the Suez Canal. Nelson reported to the British Consulate at Port Said and was told to proceed to Malta by first available ship (which happened to be the one in which they were travelling). At Malta, Nelson boarded a destroyer and Gertie and Walter continued to England, first staying with Nelson's mother at Cheshire and then buying a house at Torquay. Walter went to school as a boarder at Tonbridge, Kent.

He enjoyed life in England with his outgoing sister. Despite the war there were house parties, tennis and boating parties, hunting and shooting parties, and Walter Kidman notched up a reputation as a fine shot. He also had the potential of being a fine catch (the only son of the wealthy Cattle King), which meant no shortage of attractive young women on the scene. Being in England during the war years wasn't at all bad for Walter Kidman, and it was out of the question that he should return home until hostilities ceased.

One week after the end of the war, in November 1918, Walter was on his way back. He'd hurried to get a berth in the *Balmoral Castle* sailing from Liverpool on 17 November, and that's where Walter's hurry ended. He came home in leisurely style, via the United States, New York nightclubs and Niagara Falls, holidaying, sightseeing and prolonging the good time for as long as possible before sailing from Vancouver for Sydney.

At home, Sid and Bel hurried from Adelaide to meet him — only to find flu raging on board the ship when it reached Sydney. It was under quarantine for a week in Sydney Harbour. Walter recalled how anxious his parents were to see him, even if it was only for a

---

OPPOSITE:
Walter Kidman at St Peter's College in Adelaide. (The Kidman family)

glimpse. "They came out to the ship in the afternoon in Sir Owen Cox's yacht but could not get all that close. The best we could do was to wave to one another. I sent a message to dad for £70 to square up my debts on the ship."

The joy of having their son home was intermingled with shock. Walter Kidman was afflicted with some disability that caused his right hand and arm to shake. It was dismissed, at first, as something that had resulted from "playing rugger at school" and as something that would disappear in time. If anything, it became worse, and while Sid had a fair numbers of things to worry over — drought, pastoral taxation, evidence at commissions, his western New South Wales holdings, railway building prospects — Walter's impaired health shot to the top of the pile. Various specialists in Australia were consulted, but, according to the Kidman family, remained mystified.

There was no doubt that there was an element of truth in Sid's pronouncement that he would be "glad to get out of the pastoral industry" after the almost non-stop run of problems during the war years. He'd just about had a gutful. And there was every reason to believe he had opted for an early retirement when he announced grand plans for a big extended trip overseas. Journalists pitter-pattered up to his home again, pencils poised, for what may well have been grand finale interviews. His impending retirement was treated seriously and quite sympathetically and sadly by many press people, who took the view that a large and colourful Australian was about to disappear from the scene. The question "Why go, Mr Kidman?" was put frequently. The answer, as assessed by the press itself, seemed to be "insurmountable pressures". Some press people would have been delighted to have seen Kidman make an exit — and preferably on the seat of his pants. Elsewhere, a long-term view of his life was recorded: the early struggles to the stupendous financial efforts in the First World War to assist the Empire in a war that the right side had won. There were those who'd made the ultimate sacrifice in that war, but hands up those at home who'd done as much as Mr Kidman to ensure such a correct conclusion? Hand flapping was practically nil and a sudden rush of public sympathy emerged in Sid's favour.

A typical interview, with generous sentiments, was headed "Cattle King off to America", in which the unnamed reporter said:

> It is difficult to pin Mr Sidney Kidman down to one subject. You want a whole packet of pins! He can travel faster over acres of talk than any man I have interviewed — much of it irrelevant, some of it thrilling and all of it interesting. I think he gets that habit from his strenuous wanderings across the scattered dominions of his cattle country, which must give him a wonderful sense of the continuity of things. There are no fences out there, only

the blue mists that are drawn along the horizon and are never reached.

There might have been easier ways of making money, but Mr Kidman saw a fortune for the fellow who was willing to put up the journey over the rough tracks and did not mind the heat and the loneliness and the long, patient years to victory. Half a century ago, this great Australian could have been bought for sixpence. Today, I know, I would have to write out a cheque for seven figures.

Mr Kidman now owns more of the British Empire than any other man. He is the largest horse dealer and cattle owner in Australia and has taken up shipbuilding as a sideline. When he gets to America and goes talking with a Yankee journalist, there will, I am certain, be an elaborate illustration of how far Mr Kidman's bullocks would reach with the horns of one touching the tails of another or just how near the sun they will get if tipped skywards. Personally, I don't know and don't care but you do a bit of record travelling on the map in following Mr Kidman's lead pencil as he traverses his big chain of holdings. On the wall of his office there is a detailed geographical plan running from the tip of Queensland to South Australia and with intimate lightning touches he skips along for hundreds of miles calling every station and river by name and simplifying the process by interpolating the details of the number of hoofs there, how many have been sent away, and the why, wherefore and whatnot of the whole business; also, to make the problem easier still, the rainfall records for each centre. When the journey is over, you have the impression you have been tied to the tail of a comet.

I spent an hour with Mr Kidman one day last week and what I really wanted him to say for publication took five minutes. The rest was delightful irrelevancy, such as the Delhi Durbar, the fine art of dough banging, the mutton-birds of King's Island and the way to cook a bullock's head — all very interesting, of course, but it wasn't business. What I wanted Mr Kidman to discuss was his forthcoming trip to America. The Cattle King has never been to America and I have been wondering what splendid material O. Henry might have got for a chapter in his *Heart of the West* if Mr Kidman had gone over there some years ago and met that lamented genius. He could have written of him as he wrote of "King" McAllister — of his resolution, his gay courage, his contumacious self-reliance, his pride as a reigning monarch of hoofs and horns. It is remarkable that Mr Kidman has not gone to see that spacious country before and compared it with Australia's familiar distances and our bullock with his Yankee brother. But he is going in July! Mrs Kidman and his son, Mr

Walter S. Kidman, are to accompany him. As a matter of fact, Mr Kidman does not intend to stay in the cattle business for much longer.

Next month he will be 62 and he wants the privilege of a longer afternoon than most rich men allow themselves after the strenuous day in the sun. He is turning philosopher now that he has amassed wealth and sees the glamour fading. "Health," he preaches, "is better than money. We can only eat three meals a day and what's the use of making ourselves miserable?" Of course it is an easy dictum to observe when you've made the money. Mr Kidman said the same thing years ago and he went on adding to his already large fortune. But today, there is a more serious note. He has just come through a painful operation and the old bushman who had never known what illness was through all the tough campaigning in the big spaces is going to sit down on what his pluck and luck have brought him. Mr Kidman's retirement was definitely foreshadowed during our chat and the necessary arrangements for carrying on the business are being put in the hands of Messrs W. Will, Anthony Kidman and Sidney Reid. The Cattle King is taking off his crown.

"How long will you be away?" I asked. He did not know and did not seem to care. "I'm going all over America," he told me, "and then on to England. It will be my first trip to the Yankees' country. I've got a little business there I want to have a look at. I want to see the cattle stations and what's best to be done. I'm retiring from business altogether."

"Had enough of it?" I suggested. "I'll see," he contemplated. "I want to go over there and live a bit. I'll be back in any case in a year or eighteen months. I'm turning a number of my stations into companies. We intend to put a few men there and they'll run themselves much easier. The properties are too big to conduct satisfactorily as they are, I think. Of course the cattle proposition is quite a different one from what it used to be. We can sell our beasts every year from 100 to 10,000 or 20,000 to the meatworks in Queensland. The bulk of the cattle that used to come to South Australia will go there. The South Australian railways handle them too badly. I told them what I would have to do if they did not treat the cattle better but they took no notice. Only yesterday I instructed my manager at Norley, Queensland, to start 1,500 bullocks in three mobs to southern markets but they will not come as they usually do to Adelaide. Only my South Australian cattle will arrive in Adelaide. I said I would pull out of that market and it will be a very hard thing to replace the cattle I used to fetch along. I have paid the government £30,000-odd a year for railage but can't stand the way they handle the beasts. I am not blaming the men but the authorities. In any other part of the world they would be prosecuted. But I am not going into that story any further..."

Then we got on the long trail again. Mr Kidman picked up his pencil and ran it over the big map which set forth in sweeping curves and long straight lines the wide dominions over which he reigns. And I saw the dust clouds of cattle moving from a hundred points in the lonely stations to the busy market places. Mr Kidman loves his monarchy of hoofs and horns and he will hate to get off the throne that he has established by his dauntless enterprise and personality.

Fuel was added to the "impending retirement" fire in Kapunda, not by Sid, but by Bel when she mentioned that on their return from the long overseas trip they would possibly be leaving the town and living elsewhere.

In August 1919, the Kapunda Institute was again jam-packed as the community turned out to give Sid, Bel and Walter a bon voyage party, with Kapunda truly hoping that that was all it would amount to, not a permanent farewell.

The chairman of the Kapunda Council, Mr March, said Mr and Mrs Kidman had taken a great deal of interest in the town and district in almost every sphere, and Mr Kidman had done much at different times to beautify the town, always being willing to spend money in improving it. Mrs Kidman had told him (the speaker) that when they returned they might be leaving Kapunda, but he sincerely hoped that that would not be the case. In all patriotic movements Mr and Mrs Kidman had taken a leading part. Mr Kidman was always "jealous" for Kapunda and had helped the local war loans effort by putting in amounts to Kapunda's credit. Some people might say that war loans were an investment, but Mr Kidman had not looked at it in that light but rather as providing the sinews of war. When he (the speaker) had heard that Kapunda's quota in the war was £30,000, he had said immediately that the town had been set an impossible task, but Mr Kidman had mentioned to him that they would get the quota and instead of £30,000 they had raised £47,000. (Applause) On a sporting note, Mr Kidman had been a member of the bowling club since its foundation and had always taken a keen interest in it, although he might not have been topnotch as a player. He was president for three years, which was a record for the club. When they had wanted a clubhouse, Mr Kidman had paid for the timber. Every sporting and community organisation had something to thank Mr Kidman for, as well as the local hospital, where he had put in some time recently as such an ideal patient that the staff were sorry to lose him. (No member of the family was able to shed any light on the

operation Sid underwent at the time.) Some people said Mr Kidman was a wealthy man but he had not attained that wealth by sitting down and taking things easy but by grit and hard work. (Applause) He (the speaker) hoped the sea voyage would give Mr Kidman the rest he needed, as he could not knock about much on board ship.

The Mayor of Kapunda, Mr T. Jeffs, highlighted the business Mr Kidman had drawn to the town, apart from the annual horse sales. Mr Kidman had also assisted the Kapunda Foundry, the town's leading industry, and had had an interest in it for some time; the big contracts taken out lately were due to the fact that Mr Kidman was behind them. They had prospects of a contract amounting to £30,000, and there were other contracts for over £25,000 in view and a contract from Sydney worth £50,000, if they would take it. But it depended on Mr Kidman as to whether they took the contract and, if he sanctioned it, the town would be grateful to him for doing so.

Several other speakers praised Sid and Bel sky-high, after which an illuminated address was presented to them.

Sid was given thunderous applause when he arose to respond, but before he could do so people leapt to their feet singing, "For he's a jolly good fellow". Sid thanked them for their address and good wishes. He said he had always admired the town where he and Bel had lived for thirty-four years and where their children had been born and raised. He'd come to Kapunda first on a horse and was now leaving in a train. He would have preferred not to be going but it was all on account of his health. He hoped to return and if they didn't live in Kapunda he would always keep up his connection with the town and have a representative there.

Kapunda was despondent at the thought of the Kidmans leaving for good. In Sydney, before they sailed for the United States on 21 August 1919, Sid coped with a non-stop round of interviews from reporters. He lacked his characteristic good humour; in fact it was said that the "old boy" seemed so serious that the retirement announcements were for real. It amounted to nothing of the sort. Sid had thrown the "retirement" rock into the pond and was sitting back, watching the ripples with enjoyment. It was true that a good break away from it all wouldn't hurt him a bit and he *did* want to see how the beef industry operated in the Yankees' country. Bel wanted to see Gertie and Nelson in England, but the main reason for the trip, regardless of what was said publicly and to the press, as immediate

OPPOSITE:
The illuminated address presented to Sid and Bel by the Kapunda townspeople in 1919. (Photographer: D. E. Porter; source: Kapunda Historical Society)

members of the family and closest friends knew, was to seek the best possible medical treatment to cure the affliction of his son, Walter.

If Walter Kidman saw the reason for the overseas trip in that light, he made no mention of it. In the brief account of his life he later wrote for family members, he listed the 1919 departure as "a business visit to America as the guests of Swift and Co. with whom Dad did a considerable amount of business in Australia at the time. Often he had £60,000 or £70,000 lying idle with their firm in Brisbane and they would eventually wire him asking what they would do with the money? Dad would reply: 'Just leave it there and I will find a use for it later on.' Swifts sent a special man from Winnipeg to look after us during our trip through America."

And look after the Kidmans he did, shepherding them around to visit Swift and Co.'s operations throughout the country, notable ranches and the cattle sales at Denver and Kansas, and also to a list of specialist doctors in New York and Boston who might have been able to cure Walter's ailment. Specialist after specialist was consulted and tests carried out. They are not once alluded to by Walter in his memoirs; in fact, he seemed to regard the trip more in "playboy" than medical terms. "Whilst in Chicago," he wrote, "I persuaded Dad to buy a Cadillac for use in England as I knew there would be no new cars to be bought there post-war and that second-hand cars had reached a fantastic price. Swifts arranged this and we took delivery of the car when we reached England."

But for Sid there was the business element as well. In the United States he was hailed as the greatest cattle rancher in the world and, for that very reason, was hounded by the press. Journalists found him amazingly frank.

"You Americans are paying the highest prices on record for shoes and leather goods and submitting to substantial increase in the prices of woollen goods while Australian markets are glutted with hides, beef products and wool," he said while visiting Denver, Colorado.

"I have been astounded by the prices that prevail in this country. I see boots in store windows for $20 and $25 a pair. In Australia the meatworks are glutted with cattle and hides and we can buy shoes for a song compared with the prices in this country. I recently bought many thousands of boots for men on my stations for 11 shillings a pair, about $2 of your money.

"I have determined not to buy anything here unless I have to. I paid £5 [not quite $25] for the suit that I am wearing and they tell me I would pay $75 for it here. We can still buy a good suit of clothes for $25 in Australia. Our price of living is about half of yours in America."

Asked why Australia did not release its huge stocks to the United States, Sid said, "The Imperial government has commandeered all our staples and is regulating the export. I believe they do not yet permit shipment to your country but are directing our goods to England."

Kidman confessed to being "greatly amused" by the Americans' idea of a large cattle ranch. "When you speak of ranches of 5,000 acres and 10,000 sheep it causes an Australian some mirth. On some of my own ranches I can ride 250 miles, if I do it on horseback, without getting off my own ranges. Last year we sheared 250,000 sheep. But I do not wonder at an American being satisfied with 10,000 sheep when I learn of the high prices they are fetching in this country. When I left Australia there were 1 million bales of wool (each bale containing 350 pounds) stored and waiting for ships to carry it to different parts of the world. If it could be shipped to your country it would lower your prices considerably."

The family stayed in England for some time. Walter was glad to catch up with friends, Bel was glad to see her daughter and son-in-law, and Sid was poking about in meat and business circles, but again the paramount reason was medical help for Walter.

Walter was attempting to come to grips with the problem, which was embarrassing rather than anything else. Impeded by a dithering, shaking right hand and arm, he switched to his left hand for writing, tennis and shooting, and with a shotgun, with a great degree of success. Years later when he visited England and stayed with the Vesteys and Lord Saville he always managed the biggest bag at the hunt.

Soon after they'd arrived in England in the summer of 1920 the press was hounding Sid. "There's Kidman, the Australian millionaire," someone pointed out to London journalist H. N. Southwell, who immediately sought to interview him.

Mr Kidman was pointed out to me in the premises of the Bank of New South Wales. He was leaning against the well-barred counter that shuts off the gold and silver and notes from the wealthy and impecunious alike. His hands were in his pockets and his soft, felt hat tilted back from his forehead round which clustered much iron-grey curly hair. He proved to be a most agreeable, friendly man and though I asked him a few questions, he certainly did the lion's share of the conversation. We made an appointment for a more settled interview and just before parting I said, "Well, Mr Kidman, you've made a big pile out in Australia according to public opinion and I suppose some of it came to you pretty easily?" He laughed, pulled out a fistful of shining new sixpences and said, "Well that's all I ever carry about of it."

In a few days we met at the Langham Hotel, one of the old-time, swell places in the West End that shrinks from publicity but never has a room to spare except for its regular patrons. It is a comfortable, luxurious hotel in a perfectly calm locality fronting to Great Portland Place and has none of the slap-bang style of modern hotels with showy entrance and shouting page boys; but is as dignified as a dowager duchess whose dress is not quite up to date. But it is a much-sought abode and one finds it difficult to be selected as an eligible.

Mr Kidman took me to a handsome old lounge room and talked for a full hour though it was dinner time and his daughter, Mrs Clover, a charming young woman who lives at Torquay, and his only son, Walter, came in several times to know if "father was coming in to dinner". But the warrior had settled down to what seemed to be his favourite topic — life in outback Australia.

He is an entertaining talker; no brilliant language, no wonderful originality of expression, no special flavour of humour but full of reminiscence and description delivered in a quiet, leisurely way that made me enjoy listening...[Southwell then recounted Sid's life story, which Kidman didn't seem to mind repeating over and over and over again to anyone who enquired.]

He didn't appear to worry over the loss of what most people would call fortunes...He said, "I've had my share of great ups and downs, I can promise you. But I'm right with plenty to eat and a bit of clothes and I'm not extravagant about that." He was wearing a blue serge that I have heard called "millionaire's cloth".

I asked him did he drink or smoke? "Drink? Of course I do; but if you mean liquor, well I'm not a teetotaller but I don't drink except now and then a drop of porter and lemonade. As for smoking, yes, but I've never finished the smoke of a pipe, cigar or cigarette in my life."

Asked how he liked the Old Country, he said, "Too wet and too cold. Ever since we've been here it has been raining and the winter both in Canada and here is altogether too cold for me. I like the sun — even if it does dry up the ground."

He has been active in the city and last night went to the military tournament and saw some wonderful horsemanship. He goes occasionally to variety entertainments but has never heard Melba.

His observant eyes soon found fault with London's handling of butchers' meat. "Handling, conveying and protection of carcasses is absolutely wrong and against public interest. Your butcher shops cannot compare in neatness, order and cleanliness with those of Australia." But all the same, he agreed that the Smithfield Meat Market is one of the world's wonders. "The reception and distribution of 1,500 tons of meat daily is a huge work and well done."

Though some of what I tell you sounds like question and answer, it was only like that at brief intervals because the "Cattle King" spent over fifty out of the sixty minutes in yarning, just yarning as if we two were in a solitary humpy hundreds of miles from a town, with a big billy on a wood fire, a damper baking in a camp oven and a bit of cold corned beef waiting to join the other two later on.

And it was all on the same subject. Crossing the continent from Port Darwin to Adelaide, or driving with his wife in a buggy from Townsville to Adelaide and all they saw and did on these game attacks on the trials of travel in lonely outback Australia. "Lonely, did you say? No. I'm never lonely in the bush and it has no trials for me. There's more excitement, of a sort, more to see, more to occupy your mind crossing Australia from north to south than all your flash Piccadillies and Strands, Why, the scenery in the MacDonnell Ranges is remarkable, not like any other place I've ever heard of and if you crack a whip among the hills you can hear the echo for miles. When the railway runs from Oodnadatta to Port Darwin it will open up a deal of very passable pastoral land that is now wasting. Just think of those two chaps that tried to cross the country in 1861 and had the hard luck to be done before they could finish it. Burke and Wills died near the dried-up waterhole, Mulcaboro (neither of us could spell it), which is on my present station, Innamincka."

When he was in Bristol attending a company meeting in which he has an interest, the chairman told him of a monument to Wills within 7 miles of Totnes, Devon, where the explorer was born. So he took a train to Totnes and secured some good photographs of the memorial to the adventurous man who lost his life crossing Australia nearly sixty years ago.

His experience with the blacks is extensive; he knows their language and employs a good many of whom he speaks favourably. But his real affection is for the bushman, the man who lives in the saddle. "My men," he said, "are terrible good fellows, good to work and good chaps to each other, only too pleased to find an excuse for helping someone else. Not softies, you know. By thunder, no; but if trouble comes to anyone of them, it soon finds a soft spot in his mates."

It is an old story how Mr Kidman some years back chummed up with some of the London drivers of horse buses and used to sit in the centre on the perch in front and pass humorous remarks on the traffic. He would take a penny ride and get talking to them with the result that a number went to Australia to work for him. Their fares were paid for them and they were soon attending to real healthy horses instead of city mokes. Two of them are now managers for the big owners and splendid fellows, so he says.

To be candid, I much enjoyed yarning with Mr Kidman, or rather listening, because I could not get a word in edgeways. He has made a lot of money by the help of shrewdness, luck and thrift — three very good friends for any man to have. And he sticks to his simple way of living, his love of country life and his aversion to conventionality.

He said to me, "You know, I can't stand all that fuss about dressing for dinner." But he had to go to dinner and on the way we passed a small, cosy bar where two chaps were testing cocktails. Mr Kidman said, "Will you have a drink?" I said, "Yes," without a second of delay and that it would be whisky and soda. "Well," he said, "I think I'll have a drop of sherry," and a beautiful lady radiating the bar with smiles produced the refreshment. We drank to Australia and I could see that he was no expert at the game because he drank his wine with the quick sups of a schoolboy and with none of the tricks of the connoisseur.

The toast to Australia may have been a reminder to Sid as to just how long he'd been out of the place. It was really time to think about pushing on home again. He knew that Sid Reid, Wally Will and Tony Kidman had everything under control; the purchase of a few properties in the north of Western Australia had been handled while he was away, and Sid was keen to see operations expand into the Northern Territory as well. However there was no question of leaving until every medical possibility had been investigated where Walter was concerned. Walter, on the other hand, seemed more concerned about remaining in England to trip around. Sid made an abrupt decision to return home with Bel, leaving Walter to persevere with doctors, a little perturbed about the life of ease his son was intent on pursuing.

Sid returned to Sydney towards the end of 1920 with, the press suggested, "the conceit knocked out of him for he has had it demonstrated before his eyes that, as far as the cattle raising industry in Australia, of which he is the monarch, is concerned, it is practically nothing compared to the wonderful capabilities of the United States in this regard".

Commenting, Sid said, "It was my first trip to America. I should have gone there years ago." It should also be said that he showed no trace of conceit.

"America is a great cattle country and what has helped to make it so is the packers. In Chicago they put through 50,000 every day and up to 10,000 on Saturday. They handle and distribute meat to all parts of the world. In Kansas City 25,000 to 30,000 a day are dealt with and at Denver City, 12,000 to 15,000 a day. The numbers yarded and sold are remarkable. They sell nothing by the animal. It is all sold by weight at so many cents a pound.

"We think we have a pretty good number of cattle in Australia. Last year in America they had 63 million and in Canada, about 10 million. What have we got in Australia? About 13 million. That will give people an idea that they do things in a much larger way than we in Australia.

"I travelled a great deal about America and Canada to different ranches. You know, they are small compared to Australian stations. A large ranch would have 7,000 to 8,000 [of stock] and on that ranch they would grow 20,000 tons of alfalfa (lucerne we call it). It would carry them over the fall of the year.

"I do not think their sheep are anything to be compared to Australian either for mutton or for wool. As far as I saw, they were a sort of crossbreed. They have very few good merinos. Americans shear their sheep in the open. They have no wool sheds.

"But for their cattle! It's the way they handle them. I went over Armours, Swifts Cuddys and Nelsons huge establishments and was amazed at the efficiency with which they were carried on. I'm sorry I didn't go there years ago. I would have got a lot of good information.

"I had thought of buying a ranch over there but after seeing the land and conditions I have come to the conclusion that I would sooner stick to Australia. America cannot fatten cattle as quickly as we can and our animals are out in the open all the year round. We haven't to grow turnips for our stock. The grazing is all that they need and that is where cheapness comes in.

"Australia can hardly help going ahead if we can get the right type of immigrant. We want men ready to lead a rough but healthy and well-paid life, who will stick to the open and not hanker after the towns. One difficulty we have at present is that men have a tendency to stay in towns instead of going out on to the land. Millions of acres of splendid country are awaiting development and if a man has a little money, he can hardly go wrong. It is unfortunate at present that the Labor government in Queensland is not doing much to encourage immigration. We must increase our present population."

Sid reaffirmed that he wanted to see a railway constructed from South Australia through the Northern Territory to link up with Port Darwin. "My partner and I have offered to continue the line which now ends 680 miles north of Adelaide. We are prepared to find the whole of the money and take payment in government bonds. The work would be completed in three years and open up great tracts of virgin country."

Asked about his drought losses in the years 1918–20, Sid replied,

"I am sorry about the great losses caused. Sheep and cattle in New South Wales suffered more than in any other state. My losses stand at around 140,000 sheep and 40,000 cattle but I am hopeful of good seasons so everything will come along finely."

No one asked him about his retirement, but back in Kapunda, moves were set afoot to leave the town and to live in Adelaide. A large, fine house was secured at Unley Park (the suburb was sometimes referred to as Millswood). It had vast grounds (plenty of room for Bel to garden to her heart's content and run a few chooks). The office at Kapunda had been a secondary one for years, with Sid Reid, Sid's son-in-law, conducting the bulk of the business from offices at the Richards building in Currie Street, Adelaide. The move would bring him close to his major office, but what to do with the vast place at Kapunda? He had an idea in mind that he thought would be appropriate.

Early in 1921 Walter Kidman returned from England. Sid nipped in the bud very neatly any plans Walter may have had for continuing the fancy-free life. When his ship docked at Fremantle, Western Australia, Ted Pratt, the Kidman pastoral inspector, was there to meet it with instructions to take Walter north on an inspection of the newly acquired holdings.

In his slim journal, Walter recalled, "Dad had just bought Lissadell and Yeeda (almost 2,000 square miles) from Mr Game, an English tea merchant. We went by ship to Derby and then 25 miles to Yeeda (1,230 square miles) on the Fitzroy. A man by the name of English was manager and he took us in a T-Model Ford to Fairfield, about 90 miles from Derby, where Ted and I got horses and set off to ride over the King Leopold Ranges to Glenroy where the meatworks were. The night we reached Glenroy I made my first damper. I don't think it would have won a prize in a cookery contest!

"The Kimberley country was wild with any number of hostile blacks about. We visited Glenroy, Mount House and Lissadell stations (all of which Dad had interest in at the time) and then rode back over the King Leopold Ranges to Fossil Downs, in which Dad had bought a half-interest for £75,000. Bert Keuhn, the Glenroy manager, sent a black boy to show us over the range; he wore no clothes, carried a spear and leapt from rock to rock.

"Dad had the half-interest in Fossil Downs with William Mac-Donald. A man called Leahy was manager. We spent a week looking over the place and then set off for Fitzroy Crossing in a T-Model Ford. It had to be pulled across the Fitzroy by about twenty black boys. We went back to Yeeda, then Derby and on to Fremantle by boat."

Walter Kidman had gone from one extreme to the other. After twenty-one years of gracious living, he was pitched into his father's business for the first time at its roughest and furthest flung extremities — damper instead of pheasant, a T-Model Ford hauled by blacks across a river as opposed to a Cadillac purring through green and shaded English counties, a night campfire instead of nightclubs, and no doubt Ted Pratt, one of Kidman's most trusted men, was expected to give a full and confidential report to Sid as to how Walter had coped.

Sid was coping on a different front at the time. It seemed to require him to be in legal offices constantly. The wrangle with the Commonwealth government over the wooden ships contract had yet to reach a conclusion and, privately, great changes were being wrought within the Kidman business.

Not only was Sid obliged to pay pastoral tax on his leases, but also state income tax (and he had interests in every state and the Northern Territory, with the exception of Victoria and Tasmania), as well as federal income tax, which had been introduced during the First World War. His entire business was being restructured into companies with he and Bel, their daughters and their husbands, and Walter as the major shareholders. Much of the organisation was left in the hands of his son-in-law Sid Reid; the aim was tax minimisation and Reid was a capable and hard-headed business fellow. Just when other friends and business colleagues seemed to be slowing down, Sid Kidman seemed to be busier than ever and constantly on the hop between Adelaide and Kapunda, where the mail piled up and sometimes went unanswered.

Early in 1921 Kidman received a sharp vice-regal rap on the knuckles for failing to attend to his mail and was requested, crisply, to telephone the private secretary of the Governor of South Australia, Lieutenant-Colonel Sir William Weigall, in Adelaide. The private secretary curtly reminded him that two earlier letters had been sent to him to which he had not replied, hence the request for urgent telephone communication.

"What about?" Sid bawled.

"The recommendation for your knighthood and your reply," was the answer.

"First I've heard of it," Sid told him. "Oh, I just don't know. I'll have to ask the wife and see how she feels about it."

Bel was duly consulted and puffed like a pouter pigeon with pride. Of course Sidney should accept it. It was his duty. Due recognition was being paid to him for the great effort he had made for

---

OVERLEAF:
The large, imposing home Eringa at Unley Park, showing a small section of the extensive grounds surrounding it. (The Kidman family)

his country in both business and war assistance. In fact Bel was pleased to the point of ecstasy. She was happy for her husband and not averse to the Lady Kidman tag which would accrue to her. But she saw the honour mainly as a vindication of all that Sid stood for and a direct poke in the eye for his hard-working detractors of the last several years. It would be a nice slice of come-uppance for the lot of them — accusing members of Parliament, jealous business colleagues, disagreeable unionists and the nit-picking press.

Deep down, Sid felt honoured, yet the more exposed side of his nature genuinely could not have cared less. It was a great token of respect, but Sid figured he had that anyhow, certainly from those who counted the most — his men in the bush. He knew several knights and didn't bother with this "Sir" business when talking to them — they were just Bill, David or John and to them he'd still be just Sid. No, this honour business would mean more to his offsider and companion of thirty-six years, his wife, Bel. He had always thought of her as a grand lady, and now she would have the title "Lady" officially. Sid wrote to the Governor saying he would accept the recommendation, not quite as casual in his letter as he had been in his telephone response.

In the months before the honour was made public, the mere thought of it no doubt remained paramount in Bel's mind, yet it was quickly shunted to the back of Sid's. He went ahead with the plans he had for the big estate, Eringa, at Kapunda. Kapunda had been their home for all their married life — first at Bald Hill, although those days seemed so far back, and then Eringa. Eringa remained special to him. It was the place where he had climbed to success, and nearly to his death when he went hot-footing it across the roof trying to put out the fire. He had been away from it more than he had lived in it, but he didn't want the place sold to anyone else. He didn't need the money and he wanted to see it remain intact and yet useful, so he gave it to the people of Kapunda as a present if and only as long as it was used as a high school to assist in the education of children. The South Australian Department of Education did not need its arm twisted behind its back to take him up on the offer and fall in with the requirements. When one of its officials, marvelling at Sid's generosity, asked "Why?", he received a very direct answer. "I did not have too much in the way of schooling or learning," Sid said. "Much of it came from my wife who was a school teacher. It will please the two of us for our home to be used as a school."

In June 1921, Sid got his gong and became Sir Sidney. The Governor-General, Lord Forster, released the details of the King's Birthday Honours and the list appeared in the press on 3 June (the day on which the dominions celebrated the birthday of King George V). Sid was one of only three Australians to receive a knighthood, showing how thinly the top honours were spread over the enormous slice of the world that counted for pink on any atlas and represented the British Empire.

If initially Sid did not fully appreciate the honour being accorded him, it now became most apparent. The other two knights, both from Sydney, were Hugh Dixson and Benjamin Fuller. Dixson, aged 80, was a businessman of substance who had sought to lend support to the British Navy by means of a battleship as a gift from Australia. He had inaugurated a fund with a £5,000 donation, but when the fund failed to fill, the money was redirected to the education of English boys at Australian agricultural colleges. Benjamin Fuller was a well-known theatrical proprietor with large interests in every Australian city. In the year before his knighthood he made substantial public donations in the interests of education. He said he was "tickled to death" about receiving the knighthood. He had recently given £1,000 to a New South Wales Rhodes Scholar to enable the completion of a brilliant scholastic career and later on gave two sums of £5,000 each for educational purposes. And then there was Sid, knighted for "services rendered to the Commonwealth". He happened to be in Sydney at the time the honours were announced (less by design than accident) and didn't have much to say on the matter at all. Others did. In some circles he was laughed at: the raw bush bloke — barely literate to boot — who'd swung out of the saddle and into top status. Jealousy drew no shortage of snide and petty remarks. Yet if they reached Sid, they appeared not to sting or wound him.

News of his knighthood was plastered throughout the press, not just here but in the United States and in England, where *The Times* said, "Sir Sidney Kidman is not only a public benefactor but the largest landholder in the Empire. He owns over 32,000,000 acres which carry some quarter of a million cattle and many thousand horses. He neither smokes, drinks or swears. Such an exemplar amongst the Order of Knights might confound Falstaff at the first blush — literally — and convert him at the second." *The Times'* estimate of his holdings and cattle was half accurate. It referred to the holdings owned outright by Kidman. If his interests and partnerships in stations were taken into account, then the figure would have stood at double the amount: 100,000 square miles or 64,000,000 acres. Cattle numbers were well over 500,000.

The average Australian, to whom Sid was far better known than Hugh Dixson or Benjamin Fuller, took the view that "Mr Kidman's knighthood was richly deserved", especially when the press trotted out the full meaning of "services rendered to the Empire" and tallied up the not inconsiderable assistance he had thrown behind the war effort. People were genuinely surprised that one man had given so much. There were a few armoured battleplanes, ambulances, shipments of horses, beef and wool (or funds from the sale thereof), plus the fund for the Belgians, the almost give-away sale of Yambacoona for soldiers' resettlement, and vast donations to the Red Cross Society and the Salvation Army (Kidman cared deeply about the work the Salvos did during the First World War and donated huge amounts, to the point that he accorded the organisation a half-share interest in one of his stations; when research was being done for this book the Salvation Army could not produce one single record of his benevolence towards it). There were shipments of beef, mutton and horses, plus shipbuilding (something of which he knew nothing), in a bid to assist Australia's war effort when others of comparable wealth were loath to do so. Men from his stations and from his own family had gone to serve overseas. Some had come back. Some had not. He was not obliged to look after them in any particular way (the various governments had said they would do that), yet he was paying pensions to men who'd returned disabled and to the widows of his men who had not returned; he had kept jobs open for those who did return, with increased payment, proud of the stint that they had done overseas but that age had denied him. He had been astonished by the meanness of many wealthy fellow Australians when the war called for their donations, and, too simple and sincere, he'd lunged head-on into commitments when he could least afford to during the 1914–16 drought.

So there Sid was, a knight of the King's Empire. Where his own "empire" was concerned, his men on the stations, managers, drovers and stockmen (who already walked tall under the Kidman "brand"), were pleased for the boss. Norman Gurr, a contract drover for Kidman at the time (who later managed Clifton Hills, South Australia, and then Nareen, Victoria, for Malcolm Fraser's father), said, "I never heard anyone in the bush go crook about it." But perhaps Norman was wrong: there was one important Kidman employee who couldn't come to grips with his boss's new name and was forever going "crook" about it.

Telling the story himself, Gurr said, "Messages of congratulations came in from his men everywhere. They were short and simple...things like 'we are proud of the fine honour you have received'. They were sent off under the names of station managers with the names of many men attached. We paid for the wires ourselves.

"A few months later Kidman was beating around the bush again and was staying at his Mundowdna depot in South Australia. A number of his drovers had delivered cattle there and were camped, as was his chief horse drover, Charlie MacLeod. Sid hauled Charlie in for a yarn and Charlie was known as 'the Rager'. He was a bad-tempered old fellow and known to kick his quart pot off the fire if it didn't boil before anyone else's. Sir Sidney sent Charlie from the station to the Frome River where Pat Kennedy, his chief cattle drover, was camped. 'Tell Pat to come up to the station. I want to see him,' he told Charlie.

"Charlie delivered the message to Pat and Pat said, 'What's he want to see me for?' 'I bloody dunno. Perhaps he wants to make you Sir Patrick Bloody Kennedy!' was the spat-out reply."

That poor Charlie was having trouble coming to grips with Sid's new title was obvious a few years later when, once again in the bush, Sid, after a yarn with Charlie, asked him to take a message to Wally Will, his wife's stepbrother, and to tell him to cut short a bore inspection and return to the station to see him. Alex Robb, the son of J. E. Robb, one of the Indian horse exporters, who was in the camp at the time, said, "Charlie rode in and taciturn as ever said to Wally Will, 'Mr Kidman wants to see you up at the homestead.' Wally said, 'Charlie, I've told you before, he's not Mr Kidman any longer. He's *Sir* Sidney. Anyhow, what's he want to see me about?'

" 'How the bloody hell do I know what it's about. He might want to make you the Honourable Bloody Wally Will for all I know.' "

After that everyone gave up on Charlie, who continued to refer to Sir Sidney as Mr Kidman for as long as he remained in his employ. It is unlikely that Sid ever corrected his old horse drover; perhaps he even respected his dogged determination to refer to him as Mr Kidman. In fact Charlie was something of a favoured employee. Mort Conway, a Mundowdna stockman, was assisting Charlie MacLeod with a big mob of horses on the way to Adelaide for the Kapunda horse sales in 1921 when Sir Sidney pulled up unexpectedly in a car. His initial greeting, Mort Conway remembers, was "You're travelling, Charlie," and Charlie's response was "I'm not travellin', Mr Kidman, I'm bloody flyin'."

With the exception, perhaps, of Charlie MacLeod, most employees allowed the tongue to roll easily around the "Sir Sidney" title, although if pounced on unawares, some merely said, "Sir", some addressed him as "Sir Kidman" and some fumbled in speech between Mister and Sir. It should be said from the outset that it didn't matter to Sid how his men addressed him. This knighthood business was not of his doing. He wanted only the goodwill, hard work and respect of his men, and if they stumbled a bit over the tag that went with the title, well, it was nothing to worry about.

Equally, his rogue mates who attended the annual Kapunda horse sales wondered whether or not the fame and glory heaped upon Sid had altered him. The pranksters were determined to find out and Sid, who hadn't come down in the last shower, anticipated the extra crackers and stink bombs that would be let off in closer-than-ever-before proximity to him at the sales that year. The fun and games was led for the main part by Steve "the Colonel" Margrett, and when it was said that Sir Sid was having a shave or beard trim in "Bomber"

Thomas's barber shop as a prelude to the sales, a string of lit crackers was tossed into the shop around the barber's feet as he went about his work. A throat was nearly slit. But it was not that of Sir Sid, but of John Horsley, who somewhat resembled Sid and who was the manager of his Fulham Park horse stud in Adelaide.

Sid proved at the sales that year that he could take it all, whatever pranks and ratbaggery anyone dished out to him. "But could he be taken for a fall in money?" the Colonel wanted to know. The new knight still had a reputation for watching every sixpence and shilling. The boys up north had relayed how he'd lost a bob out of his pocket one night around the campfire and been a bit unsettled about it — and quite jubilant when he'd found it the following morning. On another occasion Sid had produced a handsome quart pot during smoko at a camp. One of his men admired it, prompting Sid to say, "It's new. I'll sell it to you for 1s. 6d." The deal was struck and Sid later remarked that he'd made sixpence on it.

Steve "the Colonel" Margrett wondered how Sid would like to be taken for a few bob and paid Mickey Woods to put into effect the bit of skylarking that he and the other horse exporters had in mind. It happened when the sales were finished, and Sid was leaving by train for Adelaide along with the Colonel and several other men. Sid had never lost his childish fascination for occupying the window seat. As the train was preparing to shunt out, Sid was hailed at the window by a yelling Mickey Woods, a general handyman around Eringa, Kapunda. Thumping on the side of the train, Mickey said, "Ya got change of 10 bob, Mr Kid — aaah, Sir Sidney? I need change of 10 bob quick."

"Well, now, Mickey," Sid replied, hitting his pocket as the train slowly started to move, "we'll see what we can do."

A swift look revealed that the most change Sid could come up with was 8 shillings.

"That's all I've got, Mick. That'll have to do you," said Sid thrusting the coins at him.

"Ta, Mr Kidman — aaah, Sir Sidney. Thanks so much," Mickey replied, pacing the train along the station and handing a folded note to Sid through the window. The train gathered pace, and Sid opened the folded note, which proved to be a jam tin label! The Indian horse exporters fell about the carriage hooting with laughter.

One of Mickey Woods's duties as a Kidman employee was to follow Sid around with a few spare horses when he was making sulky trips in the Kapunda area. The next time Sid saw Mickey after the "jam tin label" incident was one such occasion, when he and Bel were taking an out-of-town trip at Kapunda. It was a stinking hot day and Sid drew the sulky up under a tree, motioning to Mickey Woods to pull up as well. "It's a hot day, Mickey," Sid said. "We're stopping for a drink. I suppose you would like one too."

"Oh, my word," Mickey replied, unable to believe his good fortune as the boss produced a brown soft-drink bottle from Bel's hamper and handed it to him. Not only had Sid not ticked him off about the jam label, but he hadn't even mentioned it, and now here he was offering him a nice cold drink on a hot day.

Mickey's opinion changed quickly after a healthy swig or two, which sent him dancing on the spot and spitting and spluttering. The bottle had kerosene in it. Bel Kidman was appalled and ticked Sid off instantly. "Sidney!" she said. "You *must* not do things like that ! Especially now that you are a knight." Sid didn't say a word — just gave her a slow smile.

Bel took the knighthood very seriously. Their eldest grandchild, Joan Hopkins (née Reid), an 8-year-old girl at the time, recalled, "After the knighthood, Grannie opened a fete every Saturday for a year and laid foundation stones. She always went in a car with a chauffeur and we went trooping along with her. It was no bother to Gran. But she didn't spoil us. We always said we were lucky to get a face washer and cake of soap she'd bought at a fete for a Christmas present."

June 1921 saw another big occasion for the Kidman family. Walter turned 21 on 26 June. A large and lavish party was held in Adelaide, at which Sid made his only son a gift of his Fulham Park racing stud, something Walter treasured and would hang onto for just on fifty years.

Leading up to the festivity was a long and serious father–son talk about Walter taking an expanded role in the business; it was not without elements of "pull your socks up, son". Walter was his only son and he and Bel loved him dearly. But a bit more grit and application wouldn't go astray, and less emphasis on this flash and frivolous lifestyle — fast cars, fast friends, fancy parties, and smoking and drinking. Sid certainly hadn't built the business up that way. It came first — above and beyond and before anything else — and that's where Walter should be putting it and with more effort and energy. Why, look at Sid Reid, Walter's brother-in-law. He'd been with the show nearly ten years and had done wonders. Sid Reid worked hard and was a top hand, as good in the office as he was in the bush. The family had done well out of the business and always would, as long as

---

OVERLEAF:
The Kidman daughters and their babies (from left): Edna Ayers with Henry, Gertie Clover with Pattie, and Elma Reid with Joan. (Joan Hopkins)

the family pulled its weight within the business. Sid impressed on his son that he was 64 and would keep the seat warm for a while longer in order to give Walter more time to acquaint himself with the business, not just acquaint himself, but pitch in in earnest. Walter had had the benefit of a good education, something Sid had lacked, but education in high places wasn't everything. What Walter lacked was an education of the bush; that was equally important. In fact, an understanding of the bush was essential, and not just the bush but also the men who toiled in it for the company. They were good men; they were hard working and they were loyal. Walter ought to get to know them and understand them because they were an integral part of the "empire". If Walter protested about a preference for the office side of things in Adelaide, Sid dismissed it quickly. The office side was well under control. Sid Reid was a whiz, and new bright finance brains had been brought in when the business had been restructured into companies: H. J. Bird was the secretary and Norman Ford, the accountant. Walter needed his apprenticeship in the bush, and Sid was determined to see that he served it.

That matter sorted out, Sir Sidney gave himself over to thoughts of a new shopping spree. With the recent acquisitions of Yeeda and Lissadell and a half-share in Fossil Downs in Western Australia, he figured he had about 105,000 to 107,000 square miles all up, and after twenty-six years and his first venture with Owen Springs, he was keen to get into the Northern Territory again. It still remained the last outpost, with a lot of possibilities. And if the railway went through, giving a total link from Adelaide to Darwin, then there were good business advantages for a fellow with large slices of country close to it.

Sid's bank records show he was in a position to buy up again. The Bank of New South Wales half-yearly report for 1920 contains the inspector's remarks: "Mr Kidman is a wealthy man said to be worth £750,000. Of the war bonds held last year amounting to £86,700, £45,000 worth have been withdrawn as Mr Kidman required them to be lodged as security for payment of balance owing on a station property in Western Australia recently purchased by him. He deposited bonds to the value of £23,000 recently. He paid £53,000 Federal Income Tax for the year ending 30/6/1918 and has been assessed at £60,000 for 30/6/19. The high prices of stock are going a long way towards making good his drought losses."

The bank also noted in the report that "Mr Kidman is guarantor for all below to the extent of £85,000." The list read, "Edna Ayers, Diamantina Lakes Station, G. S., Thos and A. S. N. Kidman, Yancannia Pastoral Co., Hawke and Co., [the foundry at Kapunda], the Kapunda Institute Incorp., Alexander Denholm, A. E. Lille-crapp, Bootra Pastoral Co., Corona Pastoral Co., Weinteriga Pastoral

Co., Yandama Pastoral Co., Mount Poole Station, Yancannia Pastoral Co. Pty Ltd, Kidman and Angliss, Salisbury Downs A/C, F. N. Kidman, Kidman Bros No 2 A/C, W. A. Gordon Belalie A/C, (Blake) Miller and (Jack) Edge, Norley Station, Kidman, Curr Bros and Angliss, Hain Rowley and Co., Julius Gove No 2 A/C, McDonald and Kidman and Gertrude Clover."

But an interlude *not* recorded in the official Bank of New South Wales files and diaries suggests Sid may have been somewhat strapped early in 1920. In a private letter in 1984 Owen Francis said:

> I was one of the ledgerkeepers in the Bank of New South Wales in Adelaide at the time and the Kidman account was in one of my two books.
>
> One day the accountant told me that Sidney Kidman was being interviewed by our manager, Mr A. H. Fearon, and that Mr Fearon required the account figures for reference so I wrote on a piece of paper the authorised Kidman advance limit, the existing debit balance and the security value held. I took this paper into the manager's room where the two gentlemen were sitting facing each other across a table and placed it in front of Mr Fearon.
>
> He looked at it and without waiting for me to leave the room said to Mr Kidman, "We have protected your paper (i.e. cheques) to well over your limit but it can't go on. What are you going to do about it?"
>
> To my amazement, Kidman boomed back, "Nothing! The question is, what can *you* do about it? Sell me up with the land and stock markets so low and we will both be at the bottom of the well; advance me a further £50,000 and we will both be on top in six months' time."
>
> I had reached the door as this interchange took place and, of course, could not eavesdrop and therefore do not know to what height the argument reached but about fifteen minutes later Mr Fearon came around to my ledger and marked up Kidman advance limit an additional £50,000 and initialled it!
>
> I would have loved to have been there for the ten minutes or so of argument that followed. I was only getting £100 a year to Mr Fearon's £1,000 as manager but was still shocked to hear him spoken to in that way. I realised the force that Mr Sidney Kidman was.
>
> I should add that the Kidman forecast was correct and that his account was back in order in the six months he had mentioned.

What Mr Francis did not know as the young ledgerkeeper and what was kept something of a secret from the rest of the hierarchy of the Bank of New South Wales was the fact that the dispute took place between Sid and a manager who had divided interests: on the one hand he was the manager of the Bank of New South Wales in Adelaide, a bank that had severely cautioned Kidman a few years earlier about any further pastoral expansion, and on the other hand he was the fellow who, at that very time, Sid had talked into an £80,000 partnership in the purchase of Yancannia Station in the west Darling area. As recorded by Mr Francis, it was another win for Kidman. (Mr Francis's salary estimates were fairly accurate: the Bank of New South Wales Archives shows Mr Fearon as receiving £1,140 a year in salary and allowance and Mr O. C. Francis as £145 in salary and allowance at that time.)

In any event, what Sir Sidney wanted for his son, Walter, took place, and in 1922 he was sent on another rigorous trip outback, again under the umbrella of the Kidman travelling manager and trusted servant, Ted Pratt, Sid believed that if anyone could teach Walter the ropes, Ted could.

Walter's brief account of his life recalls, "In 1922 Ted Pratt and I left Adelaide in a T-Model Ford to visit all the Queensland properties. We got to Marree and then set off for Mungerannie on the Birdsville Track but there had been quite a lot of rain on the lower end of the track and we were bogged many times and ran out of cigarettes...

"We rode out to Cowarie, managed by Walter Neil, and spent a week looking over the property and then set off on horseback to south-west Queensland. We had two riding horses apiece and one packhorse each. Twelve miles north of Cowarie we had to swim the Diamantina and got most of our flour and sugar wet. It dried out after a few days. We used the same six horses all the trip and when we arrived back at Cowarie they were just as good as when we left with them.

"From then on we were in No Man's Land right up to the Herbert Gate and didn't see a single soul and could have camped anywhere for the night as there was plenty of feed and water for the horses.

"West of the Georgina I noticed hundreds and hundreds of dead trees, which proved in years gone by floods went right out there and kept the trees alive but by then they were all dead.

"We went through the Herbert Gate and set off 90 miles to Annandale and spent several days there. Wilfred Steele was manager at the time. While there Jimmy Davey arrived with a plant to lift 1,000 cows to Tingatinganinna on the lower Strzelecki. We mustered these cows mostly on Dubbo Downs and Glengyle. The nights were terribly cold with black frosts nearly every night and when we made camp each evening Ted Pratt used to cut a huge green log and put it on the fire and it would burn through until morning so we were able to keep quite warm.

"Mr Edwards was managing Glengyle at the time and the previous year had branded 10,000 calves there. He had a lot of Port Adelaide boys working in the camp and said to me if we ever felt like giving them a bonus we couldn't do better than to give them a case of jam as they were great jam eaters.

"We spent a month or so at Glengyle and Sandringham then went across to Monkira, which Dad owned at the time and subsequently sold to Foster and Fraser, and then on to Morney which was managed by Mick Cusack. From there we rode down the Diamantina via Farrar's Creek and on to Durrie. The season was wonderfully good there and we had to cross the Minnie Plain, a big, flooded area on which wild ducks were nesting in profusion. We did not have much tucker and Ted discovered a nest with nice fresh duck eggs in it. Ted knocked the top off one and swallowed it whole. He did this with five or six. I tried a couple but couldn't face any more.

"We had a look over Durrie and then set off for Birdsville and down the Birdsville Track to Cowarie again. We had to cross Goyder's Lagoon plain which was in flood and swim all the channels, about seven in all. After arriving back at Cowarie we went to Mungerannie and picked up our T-Model Ford and set off for Adelaide. We'd not gone more than 50 miles when we broke an axle and Ted discovered he'd left the wheel puller at Mungerannie. However Billy Stewart was close handy with a mob of Innamincka fats so Ted borrowed one of his horses and rode back to Mungerannie returning that evening with the wheel puller. We pulled off the wheel, put in a new axle and set off the next day but going over some rough sandhills broke a front spring. Ted cut a mulga stick and put this under the spring which saw us to Adelaide.

"I went away with him again soon after to Macumba where Ernie Kempe was manager. We went to Oodnadatta by train where Ernie met us and drove us 30 miles east to Macumba. It was a very hot summer and we were there in February. We set out on horseback for a ten day look over the property but our meat went bad after a few days and we had to live on Johnny cakes and jam. Arriving back at the homestead we set off for Eringa, the northern portion of the property, in a T-Model Ford, and after a day's battling in the heat we reached Bloods Creek where we relished some cold beer and went on to Eringa 30 miles west. We had a look over the run and I well remember one day pulling up for lunch and having a bit of a rest afterwards and when we went to make a move and put the bridles on the horses the bits were red hot and we had to pour water over them before they could be put into the horses' mouths.

"Camels were used a lot then and Ernie Kempe told me on one occasion he'd been riding one from Eringa to Macumba in very hot weather when it pulled up and lay down and refused to budge. He even lit a fire under it but it still would not shift so he had to walk 40 miles to the Macumba homestead, which was a long walk in that kind of weather.

"Ernie and I went riding around the Macumba run with two black boys. One night we camped at a place called the Gypsy Hole. After dinner we rolled into our swags and about midnight it began to drizzle with rain. Ernie woke me up and said, 'I've been bitten by a snake.' So I put on a quart pot to get some hot water. When the fire brightened up I could see lots of centipedes about 9 inches to a foot long running everywhere so I hurriedly got into my boots. It turned out that one of these had bitten Ernie on one of his fingers and it had swollen to about three times the normal size. We bathed it in hot water for an hour or so and the swelling went down. We discovered that I had settled down for the night over a centipedes' nest so I lost no time in shifting about 100 yards to be well free of them.

"Going away on these trips with Ted Pratt was a grand experience for me and I consider him to be one of the most able bushmen I have ever known. He knew almost every inch of that country and could find his way anywhere."

Another report to the boss went, no doubt, from Ted Pratt to Sir Sidney on how Walter had coped — or not coped. There was further travel in store for Walter, but not within Australia. On 18 September 1922 he left with his father for another trip to the United States, specifically to go to Boston for further medical treatment for Walter. The visit naturally included business but they were not away for long. Norman Ford, the company accountant, notified the Bank of New South Wales on 13 November that he had had a cable from Sir Sidney in Boston saying that an operation for Walter was not necessary and they were leaving on 20 December to return home.

For Sid there remained the depressing fact that, despite his wealth and influence, he could not help his son with his worsening affliction. Where Walter was concerned, anxiety crept in. Why on earth should he be stricken so? What was the nature of this damned ailment? Specialists said it had nothing to do with rugger or being hit on the hip with a cricket ball; some had mentioned polio and paralysis. He didn't know. No one seemed to know. But it was getting worse. He jammed his shaking right hand in his coat or trouser pocket as often as he could. His father met everyone with a warm and firm handclasp, something he could never do, so even the business of day-to-day introductions became something of a nightmare to him. He took to "hiding" in the background of official photographs or else held his right hand down with his left. In group conversations he opted for crossed arms and hands under his armpits to put a clamp on the perpetual twitch.

He was doing his best to fit into the business niche as his father wanted, and travelling around under Ted Pratt's umbrella had been a new and interesting experience. Managers and stockmen, informed that he was "S.K.'s son being introduced to the business" were courteous, but, behind his back, many shook their heads. It didn't do to talk too much but the comparison was inevitably drawn: "The young bloke isn't a patch on the old man."

And there was the old man, still blazing away at 65, in good physical shape apart from being hard of hearing. It still wasn't beyond him to perch on the rails at a stock sale, musing over prices and anxious for the ring to be cleared for the next lot to be admitted. Sometimes, wary animals, despite hissing and hat flogging, refused to leave the arena. "Oh! Learn the man. Learn the man!" Sid would mutter, then yell to anyone close by.

"It's all right for you, Sir Sidney, sitting up on them rails" was a frequent reply from the saleyard hand trying to cope with the problem.

"Don't give me that! Don't give me that!" he'd roar vaulting from the rails and producing a vast handkerchief from his pocket. Any reluctant cattle would be taunted towards him, often at full bore, while with split-second timing he executed a handsome half-turn and cattle charged through the open gate. He'd whack a hat on their backsides in annoyance and return his vast handkerchief (always big jobs in paisley prints) to his pocket.

Walter Kidman was aware of his father's toughness and bravado. But Sid wouldn't last forever and his death worried Walter Sidney Palethorpe Kidman, certainly over the matter of the control of the business. While Walter had been boating on the Thames, shooting grouse in Scotland and away overseas for health reasons, the business had been built up considerably by his brother-in-law Sid Reid, who was now making many of the major decisions. He was an older, dominant fellow and Walter felt consumed by him. When his father died, it would be Reid he would have to deal with. He was the boss's son, yet Sid Reid was further entrenched in the business and was acknowledged for his capacity. He could visualise the run-in there'd be if he attempted to assert himself over Sid Reid. Perhaps it wouldn't happen. If it did it would spell trouble.

In the short term there was more trouble brewing for Sid himself in relation to tax. On 25 August 1924 a High Court writ for £156,066.14.3 was issued against Sir Sidney Kidman, grazier, for land tax alleged to be due to the Commonwealth for the financial years 1915–16 to 1922–23 inclusive. The writ was issued by Cyril W.

Crowley of the Commonwealth Crown Solicitor's Office on behalf of the Commissioner of Land Tax and served on John Jolly, 121 William Street, Melbourne, as Sir Sidney's representative. Sir Sidney was given twenty-one days in which to enter an appearance to the action. Sid described it from the outset as a "load of sheer piffle".

The matter had a fine airing in federal Parliament in Melbourne, with allegations from the Labor opposition that big landholders had been allowed to escape payment of large sums due on leaseholds and that Kidman, as the largest landholder in the British Empire, was a major offender. As a result, yet another Royal Commission was set up, with Mr Justice Edwards of the District Court of New South Wales appointed as Commissioner to inquire into the allegations made by John Scullin.

Mr Scullin said it was curious that "all the large pastoralists had found difficulties associated with land tax as soon as the Labor government had gone out of office in 1915" and that "preferential treatment was being given to wealthy men. For the years 1914–1921 the department had had to submit default assessments to Sir Sidney Kidman and there was no record of his having been fined once in those years; however a large number of small holders had been prosecuted and fined. In March 1923 an instruction had been issued, 'Compel Kidman to furnish his returns', and he had been granted an extension of time to September. In November he had been threatened." (Loud Labor laughter)

The federal Treasurer, Dr Earle Page, said:

> I strongly hold that this is not the place to disclose the private affairs of taxpayers, still because Sir Sidney Kidman has been definitely named I have secured information from the Commissioner of Taxation as to Sir Sidney Kidman's position. When members see how much Sir Sidney Kidman has paid and how his properties have been assessed they will realise that the Commissioner and the Deputy Commissioner have been most assiduous.
>
> In July 1922 the Commissioner became aware for the first time that Sir Sidney Kidman had not complied with law as to forwarding returns. He immediately called for a report and also consulted the Crown Law officers. He found that a prosecution for failure to supply the returns would not lie but he took immediate steps to have returns made out. A prosecution which was ordered in South Australia failed on a technical point.
>
> The information I have shows that Sir Sidney Kidman submitted returns for 1914–15, 1915–16 and 1916–17 and he paid the taxation assessed on those returns. Subsequently, largely on account of difficulties regarding Crown leaseholds, he found

difficulty in supplying returns. The department thereupon issued default assessments and collected all money owing up until 1921. All that Sir Sidney owes at present is one year's assessment made early this year of £20,000.

Dr Page proceeded to read the correspondence that had passed between the Commissioner and Sir Sidney's agent, John Jolly. "The House will see," he said, "that the facts in regard to Sir Sidney's land taxes were that the taxes on freehold had been paid for practically the whole time, the exception being this year, and in regard to Sir Sidney's Crown leaseholds, nothing had been paid since the beginning. There was nothing new in that position. It was the same when the Labor Ministry was in office."

Dr Page added that the Budget papers revealed that considerable sums for land assessments were outstanding from 1912–13 up to the present time, and he maintained that the Act relating to them had been passed without due deliberation and that the Commissioners had been set an impossible task. Already two Royal Commissions had conducted investigations into such taxation and now a third was sitting and securing conflicting evidence as to what would be a just and equitable basis upon which to levy the tax.

The deputy leader of the Opposition, Mr Anstey, said that Dr Page's statements failed to answer the definite charge that Sir Sidney owed some £100,000 for land tax and did nothing to answer the charge of the partiality shown by the Treasurer in shielding from public gaze large pastoralists with several years' land tax in arrears, while the names of the smaller men were freely published.

Summing up the position, the Prime Minister, Mr Bruce, said that the Ministry took full responsibility for its actions in respect to taxing Crown leaseholds. Despite all the Opposition's attempts to make political capital of that issue, the facts were simple. The tax had been suspended after a certain time because it had been found that it was impossible to collect it under the system authorised.

Two Royal Commissions had been appointed to discover an equitable system. Both had failed to do so. They had reported that there was no just basis on which the tax could be collected. Acting on that report, the Ministry had asked the House to authorise the wiping out of the arrears of tax. Immediately the Opposition had seen an opportunity to make political capital, irrespective of justice or right, and had bitterly opposed the proposal. The House had declined to accede to the proposal and had instructed the Ministry to proceed to collect the arrears. The Commissioner had again attempted to do so, and finally he had come to the Ministry and said he found it impossible. Dr Page had made a full statement to the House, and the Ministry had appointed another Royal Commission to devise how the decision of Parliament, that the tax must be collected, could be put into effect. That was the whole position, nothing more and nothing less.

During the third Royal Commission, the file relating to Sir Sidney Kidman's land taxation was examined by Mr Justice Edwards. The officer in charge of the file, John Ryan, said that the taxpayer did not make a return for land tax for 1916–17 until about 30 September 1924, when returns for all the years were lodged. Sir Sidney now owed land tax amounting to £156,000, including £20,000 on freehold. Repeated attempts were made to obtain the returns from Mr John Jolly, Sir Sidney's representative, and frequent extensions of time were granted. In December 1918 a demand was issued for the payment of outstanding taxes amounting to £4,679. In the 1914–15 return the taxpayer showed that the total unimproved value of land held by him amounted to £64,503. Another departmental minute, dated 30 July 1919, stated that a comparison with the income returns showed that Sir Sidney had interests in a number of joint ownerships that were not disclosed in his land tax return on 30 January 1920. Mr Jolly wrote asking for a further extension of time for sending in Sir Sidney's returns and indicated that a further extension might be necessary. No returns had been received to date by the taxation officer in regard to Sidney Kidman; Kidman and Castine; Kidman and Gunther; Kidman, Haney and Kidman; Kidman, Durham and MacLeod; Kidman and McLean; Kidman, Miller and Edge; Kidman and Oats; Kidman and Mooney; Kidman and Reid; Kidman and Robertson; and some other Kidman interests.

Releasing his findings in 1925, Mr Justice Edwards said, "It is not correct to say that the present government relentlessly pursued persons who owed small amounts of land tax and were less strict in collecting land tax from those who are assessed large sums. The big pastoralists have no advantage in this regard as compared with the struggling farmer and the small landholder. I can see nothing in the figures I have examined or in any facts put before me to warrant any suggestion that discrimination was made between large and small taxpayers and I emphasise the fact that the government in no way interfered with the Commissioner of Taxation in any respect of these matters."

Dealing with the charge that the amounts of land tax outstanding as shown in the Budget were owed exclusively by large taxpayers, the Commissioner stated that the Budget showed the outstanding land tax on 30 June 1924 was £2,114,914. The correct amount as shown in the ledgers of the Commissioner of Taxation was £2,057,882. The differences between the valuations of the Commissioner of Taxation and some of the Crown lessees was illustrated in the case of Sir Sidney Kidman. The Commissioner of Taxation claimed from Sir Sidney Kidman, for the eight years up to 30 June 1922, a sum of £136,065. Sir Sidney Kidman valued his Crown leases at nil, or a sum that did not render him liable to tax. In fact, although Sir Sidney Kidman had not paid any tax on Crown leasehold for eight years, he had paid to the Commissioner so much in the past that, if his valuations were sustained, the Commissioner would be in debt to him to the extent of a few thousand pounds.

The debtors to the Commissioner of Taxation at 30 June 1924 numbered 4,746, of whom 3,767 each owed less than £100. More than three-quarters of the debtors were persons who owed less than £100 each. Nothing, said Mr Justice Edwards, was put before him to show that any big landowner was or had been defying the department. He did not think that the facts showed that Sir Sidney Kidman defied the department. Crown lessees were not paying tax because they had not been asked to pay, the same concession being extended to all such lessees, whether large or small, until such time as a satisfactory basis of assessment was reached.

The number of persons who did not send in returns for the years 1922–23 and 1923–24 to the central office (which dealt with returns from persons who held land in more than one state) were 2,062. Very few prosecutions were instituted. In fact, considering the large number of persons who did not send in returns, the prosecutions were practically negligible. The reasons stated for non-prosecution were various and in one case, that of Sir Sidney Kidman, no reason for non-prosecution was given, Dealing with the circumstances of the Kidman case, Commissioner Edwards said, "I am fully satisfied that the Commissioner of Taxation was not guilty of any impropriety in failing to prosecute that gentleman. I may, perhaps, add that Sir Sidney has now sent in all returns for which he is liable and has been prosecuted for those omissions for which he was not protected by the twelve months' limitation contained in the Commonwealth Crimes Act, 1914."

Afterwards, Sid appeared before the City Court in Melbourne and was fined £10 with 4 guineas in costs on a charge of having failed to furnish a land tax return. Mr Knight, in opposing the nominal fine, remarked that a heavier penalty would serve no purpose to a man in Sir Sidney Kidman's position.

No sooner was that matter dealt with than Sid was again attacked in Parliament, this time in South Australia, when the Attorney-General, the Hon. W. J. Denny, said that a cause of regret where the proposed Oodnadatta–Alice Springs railway was concerned was that so much of the area to be served by the railway was landlocked by one man, Sir Sidney Kidman, with a "very approximate" estimate of 39,043 square miles.

In answering the criticisms levelled at him, Sid said that the

Minister had drawn attention to areas held by him either personally or by companies in which he was interested and then quoted a mass of figures that were quite misleading and unfair. The areas in which he was interested and which would be served by the proposed new railway were Macumba, Eringa, Hamilton, Crown Point and Bond Springs, totalling 11,780 square miles. The last two stations were in the Northern Territory and were held by the Crown Pastoral Co., in which he was a shareholder. Sid added that he had taken over Macumba after it had been thrown up three or four times. He had paid for the improvements on it and spent £15,000 in boring for water. If the government was prepared to give him what he had spent on that run he would hand it back to it. There were millions of acres north and north-east of Macumba that nobody had yet taken up.

"In case the Minister does not know, I would like to tell him that Innamincka and Coongie stations (which he mentioned as part of the 40,000 square miles) adjoin the Queensland border fence. The nearest point on the proposed new railway is distant 300 miles or more. For many years Innamincka cattle have been trucked at Farina and will continue to be trucked from there for reasons that should be quite obvious. The railway passed through Farina forty years ago. With regard to Lake Elder and Quinyambie, two companies in which I am a shareholder, these properties adjoin the New South Wales border fence and are at least 350 to 400 miles south-east of Oodnadatta. Stock from these properties is always trucked from Cockburn on the Broken Hill line where the railway was opened up thirty years before.

"Annandale Station (2,574 square miles) close to Oodnadatta belongs to the Crown Pastoral Co. [Sid and his family] and I'm sure it would be prepared to let the government have it in payment for the improvements.

"Mr Denny also referred to 2 square miles of land I hold at Morgan but surely it is stretching the meaning of the word 'contiguous' to use it as suggesting that land on the River Murray distant, say, 100 miles east by north from Adelaide, and already served by railway can possibly be near that or adjoining Oodnadatta.

"All the other country referred to by the Minister has been served by railway for more than thirty years. East and west of the land through which the new railway should pass there are thousands of square miles of country unoccupied at present. Some of it has been taken up in the past and abandoned. Any country I hold I have bought and paid for and am quite willing to sell out — lock, stock and barrel — at any time for what I have put into the place. Only twelve months ago when things were looking much better than they are at present, I was asked whether I would be prepared to sell out to an English company. I immediately asked the government whether it would consent to a transfer. The answer was 'no'."

Sir Sidney reflected for a while and then in his quiet way added, "I do not know why public men and other people should continually use my name in these matters. I am accused of not paying my tax. Recently I was alleged to be owing £156,000 which, after investigation, was shown to be without foundation. But no apology is forthcoming.

"It looks as if some people appear to be obsessed with the idea that a man should not work hard while he is able and enjoy the fruits of his labours in his declining years. This I have done and am doing. And I am quite unable to see why, in a great country like this, the man who goes out and occupies the waste spaces should be subjected to all sorts of unfair criticism. During the greater part of my life I have lived and worked in the back country. The land I occupy is totally unfit for any other use, subjected as it is to droughts more often than good seasons."

At the time that he lined up for the Denny criticisms, Sid was 68 with his sixty-ninth birthday just around the corner. He protested to Bel that he really had had enough and wanted out — no more bluff and beating around the bush. Bel asked him to hang on for a while longer until he was 70; it would give Walter some more time up his sleeve before taking over. "No reason he can't do it now with Sid Reid there as well. He knows the whole show inside out." But once again he deferred to his wife's wishes. That was exactly what worried her. Sid Reid, twelve years senior to Walter, did know everything and Walter didn't know enough.

20

A Retirement of Sorts

T HE PASSING OF TIME — a quarter of a century — had led to considerable changes within the Kidman empire. It was by now both mammoth and complex, and the days when Sid and his brother Sackville had operated as a two-man show, with Sack calling the shots from Broken Hill and Sid doing the leg-work in the bush, were well and truly over.

Sack's death in 1899 had flung Sid on his own. To keep the business rolling, Bel's stepbrother, Wally Will, was brought in as office manager to handle the paperwork, while Sid continued to do the outback inspections, with Wally accompanying him from time to time. Wally gave the business his faithful attention: this was one reason for Sid wanting to bring more family members with the same type of mettle into the business.

The show expanded rapidly towards the First World War, and son-in-law Sidney Donald Reid's decision to pitch in had been an absolute blessing. The Kidman company then had two offices: one at Kapunda run by Wally Will and one in Adelaide run by Sid Reid. Sid Reid had an equal flair for office administration and periodic station inspections with Sid, when his clinical business eye detected cost-cutting measures time and time again.

With increasing commitments, Sid needed a full-time travelling manager to relieve him, and in 1914 Ted Pratt was appointed. In selecting Pratt, Sid had chosen a man in his own mould who knew the bush, knew men and knew cattle. Pratt was competent, but not universally liked.

Mort Conway, a 16-year-old part-Aboriginal stockman, was working at Macumba Station, South Australia, in 1919 when he first encountered Pratt. Of Pratt, he said, "He'd had the job for a few years...inspecting the holdings and the travelling cattle and any improvements done (which from where I worked seemed to be little although they had made and opened up a stock route from Innamincka into New South Wales and were putting down bores and tanks on dry stages). Pratt was Kidman's top man. What he said, went. He even travelled to Western Australia where they had several properties — Mount House, Yeeda, Glenroy, Fossil Downs. He was liked by some and others called him a bit of a bloody pig. He didn't like me because I was a poor bugger picked out of the scrub. I wasn't too keen on him either. He wouldn't speak to me at times. I don't suppose I was on my own there. He was a sneaky man who would arrive unannounced and catch you by surprise. He was a short man, an eagle-eyed fellow and if he didn't like you he wouldn't say anything until he got home to Adelaide and then he'd give you the sack. He sacked quite a number. Old hands called him a crawler. He'd started off as a cook on Innamincka Station. He was a hard man. He was hard with Charlie MacLeod, Kidman's top horse drover and the best judge of horses in Australia. Charlie MacLeod hated Pratt. Pratt had a big salary and even shares in some of the stations. He was manager at Cowarie, South Australia, and had shares in that place and others with Kidman before he took up the job of travelling manager. When he finally retired as travelling manager in the 1940s he was kept on as an 'adviser' in the office and the job went to Ernie Spencer."

Despite Pratt's competence, the job was too big for him or, rather, the number of stations increased so rapidly during and immediately after the First World War that it was impossible for him to cope.

One main growth area was the region west of the Darling, and Kidman's nephew Tony (Sackville's son, who was a partner with Sid in a few stations) was elected to work that area as travelling manager. Much of it was sheep country, although there was some conversion back to cattle. Washington Irvine Foulis, the manager of the show-place station, Corona, had a supervisory role over all other sheep property managers in the western Darling Division of New South Wales. Foulis was a tough, dour man; his brother Stan Foulis managed Gnalta Station for Sid.

Being supported by tough and competent men did not mean Sid Kidman was taking a back seat in his own business. He continued to make his own inspection trips wherever and whenever he felt like it, but the "seat" he took on them changed from a saddle to a buggy and then a motor car. Sid Reid was usually the chauffeur. Sid applauded new technology and harnessed it to work for him. Returning from his first trip overseas in 1909, he'd brought a Mercedes and a chain-driven Nagant Hobson cream sports model. Cars became important to him, but it is incorrect to say he could not drive them. The answer, according to his grand-daughter Joan Hopkins, was that "he was a hopeless driver. He was so used to a horse and to looking about him as to not enjoy driving for the concentration it required. He'd driven himself in the bush but in the process become so excited by what he was looking at as to run the car off the track and into a ditch. After that he always had a driver, but he didn't like to be closed in and never allowed the car hood to be up. He always wanted it down so he could see all around him.

"When Dad [Sid Reid] was taking him outback in a car, if they got lost Grandpa would say, 'We're a bit bushed, Sid. Those sandhills should be over there.' No matter where he was in the outback he knew exactly where he was. In 1913 when Dad and Grandpa went on the 3,000 mile inspection trip they were the first to take a T-Model Ford into the remote areas of Queensland. Nobody had seen a motor car out there then."

Before the First World War Sid's Kapunda horse sales were handled by the firm of Coles and Thomas, a business started in Kapunda in 1861 by Jenkin Coles (later Sir Jenkin Coles) and carried on by members of the Coles family. In 1922 it was reorganised as Coles Bros, in which four Coles brothers were involved, Harold, Norman, Charles and Ross. The Coles and Kidman families had always been close, and they owned the stock and station agency between them. Sid Kidman was largely responsible for financing the reorganised business to the point that his son-in-law Sid Reid was initially appointed to the board and later became a prominent and dominant chairman.

Where cattle were concerned, the company of Bagot, Shakes and Lewis had captured much of the Kidman business. Walter Kidman described in his memoirs how they lost the trade: "In 1920, my father, the Hon. John Lewis, and a third partner, Mr Pearce of 'The Gums', bought Witchelina Station between them as a third interest each. After a few years they were not too satisfied so Sir Sidney bought out Mr Pearce for £10,000. When John Lewis heard of this he also wanted to sell out on the same basis, to which Dad agreed.

"He sent my uncle Wally Will around to Bagot, Shakes and Lewis in King William Street, Adelaide, to get the leases of Witchelina and Uncle came back and told Dad that John Lewis would not hand them over until he paid three or four thousand pounds to Bagot, Shakes and Lewis in spite of the fact that Witchelina had 2/300 bales of wool about to be sold on the market. Dad was most annoyed and went around and had a terrific row with the Hon. John and whilst walking back to our office in Currie Street he came through Bowman's Arcade and was just passing Bennett and Fisher's office when Hugh Davis happened to see him go by and spoke to him. He could see that Dad was in a pretty bad rage and asked him inside for a talk. The outcome of this was that Bennett and Fisher got most of our business, which was certainly lucky for them as Dad was on his way to Dalgety's at the time to give it to them. Had Hugh Davis not seen my father passing by Bennett's office, it might have been a different story altogether."

It was a lovely plum for Bennett and Fisher, and Kidman argued that if his son-in-law Sid Reid was a director of Coles Bros, that his son, Walter, should be accorded the same treatment with Bennett and Fisher. It would even things up nicely. The company was happy to oblige.

The expanding chain of stations was constantly in need of supplies and the contract to supply many went to the South Australian firm of G. Wood Son and Co., a large firm of wholesale and manufacturing grocers. At Broken Hill it had, in addition, a large hardware section that sold windmills, troughing, bore casing, pumping engines and pumpjacks, woolpacks, shearing machinery, sheep dips, shearing combs and cutters, and the rest of the goods used on sheep and cattle stations. The company manufactured groceries under Anchor, Woodsons and other proprietary brands, traded with hundreds of store keepers in Broken Hill and surrounding townships, and supplied the majority of rations, hardware and station equipment to the sheep and cattle stations in the west Darling area, the north-east area of South Australian and the Channel Country in the south-west of Queensland.

Freight cost money and the Kidman company went to extraordinary lengths to save costs wherever possible, to the point that a pint-sized Broken Hill employee, Jimmy Cann (a noted bush jockey in his twenties in the 1920s), would be told from time to time: "Get into your short pants. You're making a half-fare train trip." Jim would oblige and as a paying passenger was entitled to take luggage, usually a crate of jam or 56 pounds of horseshoes or anything else that could be taken free of charge.

Until 1923 Wood Son and Co. carried goods from Broken Hill to outback places mainly by camel teams, although there was still one donkey team and a couple of bullock teams in operation. But on 12 December 1923, Robert Bessell and his partner, Pfeffer, took the first loading ever to leave the Wood and Son warehouse by motor lorry and from then on motor transport quickly eliminated all forms of animal transport.

Wood Son and Co. supplied Kidman stations in the west Darling region, in south-western Queensland and north-east South Australia. Some properties in northern South Australia were best served from Adelaide and not Broken Hill. Kidman stations that were served by Wood Son and Co. and that owned their own camel teams would allow camels to carry goods from Broken Hill to any one of the Kidman properties or to back-load bales of wool or bundles of sheep skins from any Kidman place to the railheads of Broken Hill or Tarrawingee. The Kidman interests had set carriage rates applicable for each of their properties and, from time to time, Washington Foulis, manager of Corona, would advise Wood and Son the rates per ton applicable. One such advice stated:

Kidman Carriage Rates
as per Mr Foulis letter of 25.8.1922

To	From Broken Hill £	From Tarrawingee £
Yancannia	7. 0.0	6. 5.0
Bootra	7.10.0	6.15.0
Urisino	11. 5.0	10.10.0
Wonnaminta	5.15.0	5.. 0.0
Morden	6. 0.0	5. 5.0
Salisbury Downs	7.15.0	7. 0.0
Nundora	5.15.0	5. 0.0
Mt Poole	8. 5.0	7.10.0
Weinteriga	5. 0.0	—
Yantara	7. 0.0	6. 5.0
Yandama	8.15.0	8. 0.0
Durham Downs	14.15.0	14. 0.0
Naryilco	9.15.0	9. 0.0

Jim Fiddaman, the Wood Son and Co. accountant at Broken Hill, said, "Mr W. I. Foulis seemed to have full control over the Kidman camel teams, although they carried goods to and from all properties including faraway Durham Downs in south-west Queensland. The cameleers under some form of contract to Kidman interests were Harold Herdy, Thomas Davidson and Albert Dingle, and Saidal, Hadje Ameer, Sultan Aziz, Jumna Khan, Mirage Gool and Mudgee (who were either Indians or Afghans).

"Harold Herdy and Davidson and Dingle (who were white men) never owned their teams of camels and worked them solely in the Kidman interest for wages. After motor transport, the need for camels lessened and it would seem that the six Indians or Afghans purchased the camel teams from Kidman. I do know that Kidman interests had Jumna Khan in employment as a cameleer until June 1929 and that Sultan Aziz on 19 September 1929 took the last loading ever to leave Broken Hill by camel team to Naryilco and Durham Downs in Queensland. That load weighed over 9½ tons.

"I doubt if Kidman ever had much to do directly with his camelmen. However if he ran against a team of camels he would question the teamster thoroughly. He was, by nature, a real stickybeak."

The constant accusations of "too much land for one man to hold", coupled with state and federal income taxes and the prospect of death taxes being levied in a similar way, prompted Sid to restructure the business, or the bulk of it, into a series of companies in which Sid, Bel, their son, Walter, and their daughters and sons-in-law, Gertie and Nelson Clover, Edna and Sidney Ayers, and Elma and Sidney Reid, were all shareholders. Other shareholders included managers such as Jack Edge and Galloping Jack Watts, Ted Pratt, Kidman's brother Tom, and their nephew Tony, as well as Malcolm Reid, Sid Reid's brother.

Two financial whizes were drawn into the business to help effect the changes. They were Norman Ford, the accountant, and H. J. Bird, who became the company secretary. They held the reins over a long string of companies in the 1920s: Yandama Pastoral Co. Ltd, Yancannia Pastoral Co. Pty Ltd, Durham Downs Ltd, Glenroy Pastoral Co., Morden Proprietors Ltd, Weinteriga Pastoral Co. Ltd, Lake Elder Pastoral Co. Ltd, Yeeda Pastoral Co. Ltd, Quinyambie Pastoral Co. Ltd, Peake Pastoral Co. Ltd, Naryilco Pastoral Co. Ltd, Bootra Pastoral Co. Ltd and Witchelina Pastoral Co. Ltd, on all of which Sid Kidman was the chairman of directors. He was also a director of Gnalta Pastoral Co. Ltd, Crown Pastoral Co. Ltd, Corona Pastoral Co. Ltd, John Lewis and Co. Ltd, Olive Downs Pastoral Co. Ltd, Lorraine and Talawanta Pastoral Co. Ltd, Augustus Downs Pastoral Co. Ltd and Pastoral Investments Ltd. As well, Kidman was a part-owner of Myrtle Springs, Copley, Mundowdna, Farina, Macumba, Oodnadatta, Eringa, Charlotte, Innamincka, Marree (Hergott Springs), Iffley, Vena Park, Rutland Plains and Fossil Downs. He was also a shareholder in Kidman Estates Ltd.

Any trace of the activities of these companies had been obliterated by 1984–85, when research was being done for this book. Members of the Kidman family either could not, or preferred not to, make them available. There is evidence to suggest that some records were still held until the early 1960s (when Walter Kidman and Sid Reid were still alive), but they have since disappeared.

Two fires have taken their toll on the Kidman records: the first fire gutted Eringa, Kapunda, (the Kidman home which also housed the office) in 1904, and twenty years later on 10 November 1924 the Richards building in Currie Street, Adelaide, a four-storey building in which the Kidman company had its offices, was partially destroyed in a fire. Records that had been held at Kapunda until 1921, when the family moved to Adelaide, had been transferred to the offices in the Richards building, and these may have been destroyed in the fire. But that does not explain the complete lack of records from that time until Sir Sidney Kidman's death and for the years after his death when the business continued, albeit along different lines. A few scant records that have surfaced from sources other than the family, relate to the Bootra Pastoral Co. of which Sid Reid was chairman.

It was first set up as the Bootra Pastoral Co. around 1922 and included Salisbury Downs, 434,306 acres (Kidman and Angliss), Yantara, 202,437 acres (Sidney Kidman and Malcolm Reid), and Bootra, 154,148 acres (Sidney Kidman). In 1924 the partnership was converted into a limited company, registered under the Companies Act of New South Wales as the Bootra Pastoral Co. Ltd. In the minutes of a general meeting in 1927, chairman Reid reported, "I would call your attention to the fact that we have experienced the driest consecutive twelve months in this country since records have been taken from 1880. This year we shore 17,745 for 534 bales. Profit for the year only £505. No dividend. Expenses for Salisbury Downs, Yantara and Bootra, July '27 to February '28: horsefeed, £498, maintenance, £1,266, motor expenses, £469, rations, £894, general expenses, £82, and wages, £2,487. The country is very dry and water is being carted to keep trees alive in the gardens. The Shearers Accommodation Act requires additions to quarters. We have asked for an extension because of the bad year. A big block of Yantara has been resumed and allotted to [Dick] Barlow (the Yantara manager). Mob of fats in charge of drover [Charlie] Bowman going to Adelaide market. Not prime but nice forward condition. Sheep and cattle generally in good condition. Fencing off of resumed portion of Yantara completed. It is now completely 'ring fenced'. Decided to dispense with Mr [Russell] Barton's services and put Mr [Jack] Rogers in charge of both properties [Bootra and Salisbury Downs]."

The other official appointments that were made in the reorganisation of the business included that of Sid Reid as the general manager of the business in Adelaide and Walter Kidman as the assistant pastoral inspector (or travelling manager) to Ted Pratt. These decisions were rounded off in 1926.

In 1927 Sir Sidney could look back on almost fifty-seven years in business — all of the time spent working for himself, apart from the short stint as a young boy working for German Charlie and Harry Raines, and then as a junior stockman on Mount Gipps Station. He'd talked about retirement, hinted at it and threatened it. He now wished to make it a reality.

His retirement, as Sid said to Bel, would please a number of people and in particular the postmen who struggled into Eringa, Unley Park, daily with a mountain of mail and also into his city offices. Leather satchels of correspondence poured into both places. As his empire grew, so did the paperwork attached to it, and as Sid's fame grew, he attracted some amazing — even outlandish — letters from all parts of the world.

It was out of the question for him to reply personally to it all. Sid was no great shakes with the pen, and there are not a great number of letters in existence that were written by him. He didn't write a lot, except personal letters to members of the family and personal letters to his favourite managers both within Australia and when overseas. His business mail was attended to by the company secretary, lawyers and stenographers — letters that he invariably signed with a bold and flourishing signature that extended across three-quarters of a page. He did not have a small, insignificant or wimpish signature.

Editors of major metropolitan newspapers were on the receiving end of such letters whenever Sid felt the need to write. Sometimes it was with a dash of humour — more often than not a stern and direct reply to newspapers, journalists or anyone else who had been "bawling and blatherskiting" in print about him or his business. Whenever criticism arose, he fired back a salvo himself "to set the record straight". Although he could speak his mind most clearly, he was less competent with the written word. In fact he was a notoriously bad letter writer and an appalling speller, which probably didn't worry him at all. His earliest letter on record is his BHP short note of 1884 in which he "sold M James Poole 10 stears... for value receved in considration of 1/14 in Broking Hill mine on Mt Gipps".

Thirty years later things hadn't improved much. Writing a personal letter to his son-in-law Sidney Ayers on 19 September 1917, he says, "I have your 16 September note all you say first all it good you but under cirstance not the proper thing... first all you not strong you have a young wife and dear little boys you get such bad turns it would maddness you enlist. Take my advise and do not enlist. [A portion of the letter here could not be deciphered.] Take my advise change your mind again first your wife and children will always be well cared for if anything happened and Edna and the boys would get £150,000 one hundred and fifty thousands and from 1917 will get £1,500 or more per year I think if not I will [indecipherable] make it up some day The war looking better The man power is strong let America send a [indecipherable] or two Thousands young men who should go The Empire do not ask for married men.

"Sid I would be very sorry to see you change your mind and let those go who should I was suprised to get your letter and you had decided remember on [indecipherable] lake the bad turn you took with kindnest regards to you and Edna and boys Yours Sincerely Sidney Kidman."

The letter is interesting. Sidney Kidman had been in favour of conscription in the First World War and was surprised when the national vote went against it. He said so publicly in the press yet

OVERLEAF:
Sir Sidney, who had fallen into the water during a speedboat ride, sits barefoot with Lady Kidman and friends at a picnic. (Joan Hopkins)

privately entreated his son-in-law not to join up. Some may argue that it represents a double standard; on the other hand Kidman may have felt that the enormous support he had given to the war effort financially squared the account for the entire Kidman family. In any event, his son-in-law did not enlist.

Another letter from Sir Sidney, in a more light-hearted frame of mind, was sent on 10 May 1922 to his grandson Burns Reid: "Oh my dear little grandson I am writing you a letter just to wish you a happy birthday and I hope I will live to see you grow up to a young man so I want you to grow up quick and you and I will go up to Norley and Yandama you will have to drive the car Will you

"I am sending you a small present which please accept See look after Spot will you and the cat How old are you tomorrow or what age are you ask your mother to put you in long trousers

"Burns whatever you do look after Redge and will you always be good to your mother and sisters and dady will you and grow to be a good man you must go into partenies with your Uncle Walter With good luck and good wishes for tomorrow Yours Sincerely Sidney Kidman."

The letter was sent to Burns Reid on his fourth birthday. His brother Reg was síx months old.

Personal outgoing mail from Kidman was kept to a minimum, but incoming mail arrived in bucketloads, not just from within Australia but from around the world. Little office boys were frequently dispatched on messages to take letters to interpreters. Some mail was complimentary; much of it from people wanting money and assistance and quite a few who wrote were either shysters or ratbags. A typical — and frank — request letter came from Charles Howard, Post Office, Boulia, Western Queensland, on 4 June 1927. It read, "Dear Sir Sidney, I took the liberty of asking you to give me five hundred pounds as I see a chance of starting a bit of a Motor Business and have not sufficient money to go on with it.

"Should you decide to give me this little start in a small way and I am successful, will return money, and if not well you will lose money so you know exactly how I am placed. Thanking you in anticipation. Yours sincerely, Charles Howard. PS. Private between you and me should you say yes or no."

It is fairly safe to assume (despite a lack of office records to confirm same) that the answer was "No".

In writing to Kidman's eldest daughter, Gertrude Clover, in England on 18 March 1926, Hugh Gooch, a close family friend and confidant, said, "Your father is always receiving curious letters from people in England and on the Continent some of them claiming close relationship and others begging. The other day he received a letter written in German from the Mother Superior of a Convent in Austria asking for a subscription. He also received, recently, a most illiterate letter from a man by the name of Kidman who claimed to be a nephew. He commenced the letter 'My dear Huncle' and finished up with 'Your loving Nevee'. He's also received a letter from a man who claimed to be his son. He stated that your father deserted his mother and came to Australia many years ago — but as your father went to England for the first time in 1908, he will be able to prove an alibi!

"The enclosed type-written copy of a letter from a lady in Poland is the best thing I have read for a long time."

The letter from Poland is dated 17.11.1925 and reads, "Dear Sir, The papers tell that you are the richest man in the all World over, if you do so, and when you are not yet married, than I would like marry you. I am not more young, but very lady-like and cheerful, and elegant. I have lost my husband and my only son, and in time I was very rich and happy but now I have only 45 hectare of beautiful land and two old ruined houses and nothing for beginning the house-keeping.

"My dream is to marry the richest man in the great world over to help my daughters to be happy and rich. I have three daughters. I like high society life near an English Court and Royal Personage, comfort and richness, diamonds, pearls, rich furs, balls, stately palaces, autos, nice saloon life, sports in Switzerland, Ostend and Biaritz, the nights in Italy and Nice. The Monte Carlo parties and all good things in the world over. They tell the life is so beautiful in Rio de Janeiro and Buenos Aires. If I would be rich I would like make all my country happy, now our country is poor, no industry, no commerce, to sell is cheap to buy is dear, the life is quite impossible.

"Write me all about yourself and your life and give me a good counsel for that I can be happy and very rich. Perhaps you will send me matrimonial papers. I am a Polish Lady, then pardon me my bad English style, it is not very often that I am speaking English. I know french, german, polish, russian and others. I received a good education, am good housekeeper and a high society lady. Write me please. I heard that in New Zealand is nice to live, the life is cheap and the Maori people nice and beautiful ones. Yours truthfully, Vera de la Lys."

Continuing his letter to Gertrude Clover, Hugh Gooch said, "Your father said to your mother, 'Bel, another two words from you and I am off to Poland!' He also said, 'How would you like me to bring her over here and we will all stay under the one roof!' He also asked me if I would like to take her on. I replied that I would rather interview one of the daughters first! We settled down then to a good game of mah jong. Your father — as usual — won as often as your mother did."

Lady Kidman's response was, unfortunately, not noted. At that time Sir Sidney was 68 years old and he and Bel had not long before celebrated their fortieth wedding anniversary. It was all too much for Sid. He contacted his son-in-law Sid Reid and suggested a little inspection of his "estates". The country was drying up here and there and he felt an urge to mix in the "high society" circles he enjoyed most, yarning with stockmen, drovers and station managers, in their "stately palaces". He didn't know about the nights in Italy and Nice, but you couldn't beat a night around a campfire. With the rabbit infestation, he could supply the lady from Poland with any amount of furs. He doubted that they'd be the type she expected. As for "nice saloon life", he wondered how she'd go in 115 degree heat, dining on a hunk of damper and a billy of tea. The saltbush, sand and spinifex was probably not the "empire" she had in mind.

The men had been notified of the boss's retirement and the thought must have crossed Sid's mind on a few occasions that there had been no great response to the announcement apart from a few letters that had trickled in. It didn't particularly worry him. There were only a handful of days left before he and Bel left for Africa and then Europe. There'd be no great Kapunda-style farewells this time. That didn't worry him either. He was keen to push off on his retirement holiday and especially to see the continent of Africa for the first time and tour the arid areas such as Egypt. He wanted to see the Aswan Dam and any other water conservation projects they could show him. That would be something to tell the boys about when he returned home.

He was prevailed upon to have dinner with a few Adelaide friends at the Cathedral Hotel on 19 March 1927 — and was met with a reception that brought tears to his eyes and had his lips quivering under his white moustache and beard. It was only a momentary reaction then the showman in him responded to the style and grandeur of the occasion and he sparkled with bluff and hearty good humour. His old employees and good friends had sprung a surprise party!

Those present were Sir David Gordon (chairman of the evening), Walter Kidman, Ross Coles (of Coles Bros), Monty Winton (manager of Yandama), Archie McLean (manager of The Peake), Ernie Kempe (manager of Macumba), Norman Ford (accountant, Adelaide office), Harry McCullagh (manager of Durham Downs), Harry Peck (of the Melbourne stock and station agency), R. W. Bennett (presumably from Bennett and Fisher), John Horsley (manager of Fulham Park Stud), H. J. Bird (secretary to Sir Sidney), Washington I. Foulis (manager of Corona), Con White (manager of Morden), Duncan Rogers (manager of Yancannia), Sid Reid (manager, Adelaide), Jim Wright (manager of the Kapunda office), John Brooke (manager of Mundowdna), George Lee (in charge of cattle trains), Ted Pratt (pastoral inspector/travelling manager), H. Warner (Adelaide office), Jim Cahalan (one of the oldest employees), Pat Kennedy (the oldest drover), Doug Gordon (son of Sir David Gordon and manager of Myrtle Springs), Hugh Gooch (an accountant and secretary), Jack Edge (formerly manager of Carandotta), Harry Wyatt (head stockman, Adelaide) and Hugh Davis (managing director of Bennett and Fisher).

Sir David Gordon said it was a unique gathering. Some of the men had travelled 700 or 800 miles to be there and there were managers present from five states including the Northern Territory. Sir Sidney, he said, had made a success of his business because he had the Australian characteristic of sticking to a good thing. He had stuck to a number of good things but to nothing that he valued more than his old employees. (Applause)

Each of those men realised what a splendid employer he had. All sorts of stories were told about Sir Sidney, especially by politicians (Laughter) but most of them were untrue. If there was one man who was doing a great deal to develop country that no other was game to tackle and occupy, that man was Sir Sidney Kidman. It was because he had been successful at it that so many were envious of him. Sir David said that if others wanted some of the outback country there was plenty of it left to go around. He doubted if there was any pastoralist spending more than Sir Sidney in the development of the country, and there were certainly few who were more generous and public spirited. Not only had he helped hundreds individually, but in time of war no man had done more for the Commonwealth and Empire. (Applause)

John Brooke proposed the toast to Sir Sidney of whom he said, "He has been more than a good employer; he has been a good friend and made himself 'one of us' in the bush and although his interests might have been at stake, he has made us happy by sitting around the campfire and telling us instructive stories of his earlier days. He is a true man, a man of cleanly habits and thrift and I wish him — and his equal partner in his trials and triumphs, Lady Kidman — a pleasant trip and safe return."

Washington I. Foulis said he had the utmost respect for his employer, whom he regarded as master and friend. (Applause) They would extend the same loyalty to those left in charge while Sir Sidney and Lady Kidman were away.

Archie McLean remarked that he (McLean) was a better speaker at the campfire than a banquet, but he'd been with Sir Sidney for twenty-six years and never regretted a day of it, and there were hundreds who could say the same.

Ernie Kempe declared that Sir Sidney was one of Nature's Gentlemen and the old employees appreciated the many kindnesses he had shown towards them. (Applause)

Pat Kennedy read a brief speech to the effect that he bore the deepest goodwill towards his old friends Sir Sidney and Lady Kidman.

A more polished speaker, R. W. Bennett, said that after comparing his own few years of association with Sir Sidney with the long periods worked by others, in some cases forty and fifty years, he felt like an embryo employee only. Little as that experience was, it was sufficient to give the lie direct to the stories told about Sir Sidney. It was said that he destroyed the value of all the leases he owned. That was not true. The fact was Sir Sidney spent too much on improvements, as the speaker knew to his cost in his failure to reap dividends owing to the policy of improvements that was insisted on. He had first met Sir Sidney at Kapunda about thirty years ago. He was known then as the King of Kapunda but now it was a case of the Cattle King. Any man who could build up such a kingdom himself was certainly greater than one who won a kingdom by inheritance. What struck him (Bennett) was the genius of a man who could keep track of all the doings in his great cattle kingdom. He always knew exactly where the cattle were moving and how soon they would reach the rails. It was like a man directing a small universe. They had been told that Sir Sidney did not pay his taxes but it turned out that, instead of owing money to the Commonwealth, a proper accounting would show the Commonwealth owed money to him. "If he did not pay I do not know that I would blame him," concluded Mr Bennett amid laughter, "for there is no more iniquitous imposition than the federal land tax."

Ted Pratt, on behalf of those present (and others unable to attend), said he had been deputised by employees to make a presentation as a mark of their appreciation. Their difficulty was to find a suitable gift. They were pleased to know Sir Sidney had everything, but thought they had hit upon the right article — a spirit cabinet! In case of severe drought, all of them would be able to call upon Sir Sidney. (Laughter) When he returned he would see a pad to his house just like the bullocks made to the outback soaks. Unfortunately they were not able to hand him the gift, as it could not be procured in Australia, and in the meantime the small token of a flask would be handed to him. (Applause and laughter) It was something he could pop into his hip-pocket when he went to call on the Wesleyan Conference in England (Much laughter) and it might be handy on his return when they joined him again on the far-off northern runs. They were all proud of the service they had rendered to a gentleman and a "white man". (Applause)

Ted Pratt wasn't being cheeky offering grog cabinets and hipflasks to the esteemed boss, around whom a myth had grown up about non-drinking. Sid Kidman did drink — and only of the best. In the bush he drank tea, tea and more tea, until he said he was "up to pussy's bow" or "it was coming out of my ears". And he enjoyed it. He also drank ginger ale. He liked it. He was partial to a cordial that Sid Reid introduced him to and Sid drank by the gallons. It was called 50–50. His grand-daughter Joan Hopkins said, "He also favoured a Bickford's lime juice. But later in life he was ordered to take a whisky every night (by doctors for health reasons) and he did. In fact he had over-proof barrels imported from Scotland." It ought to be said that they weren't for Sid alone and stocked the cellars at Eringa, Unley Park. But he tossed one down whenever he felt like it. Arthur Rymill can recall him announcing, "If Bel can have her wine, and Gert can have her lick-ers, I can have lick-ers," putting one away in one bolt.

What he drank the night of the dinner is not recorded, or whether he savoured a bit of "baccy" as well. For it's another myth that he did not smoke. Sir Sidney, in fact, was quite comfortable later in life proffering cigarettes to press men and having a puff himself. But for the most part he smoked at home, where he ought to have been confined to the "dangerous" bracket. "He had the capacity," said Joan Hopkins, "to go to sleep at the drop of a hat. It was another reason that made him an unsafe driver in a car.

"I can well recall him going to sleep, almost mid-sentence, with a smoke in his lips. He'd wake up suddenly and finding it missing, hunt feverishly among his clothes and the lounge cushions and the carpet. It was more than likely that someone had removed it as soon as he dozed off. He didn't roll his own; he smoked tailor-made and just puffed away."

In any event, it was more likely the menu which captivated him on the night. Someone had gone to a great deal of trouble where the tucker was concerned. There wasn't so much as a hunk of corned beef or damper in sight. The names of many favourite stations were saluted in the festive feast. Always a good trencherman, Sid did justice to the lot.

At the appropriate moment he was "called upon". He made no reference to the menu. Dry Quinyambie sounded believable, along with Corona cutlets, but Bootra ice cream and Kaliduwarry oysters...still, it was the thought that counted. He displayed a homely charm upon rising to respond (the press noted) and he spoke with

Menu

Cocktails
Dry Quinyambie   Sweet Yandama

Soup
Kaliduwarry Oyster

Fish
Fillet of Innamincka Bream
Arboola Lobster Mayonnaise

Entree
Corona Cutlets and Mushrooms a la Weinteriga

Poultry
Norley Turkey and Durham Ham

Vegetables
Crown Peas   Peake Tomatoes
Durrie Potatoes, baked or boiled

Sweets
Macumba Pudding and Eringa Sauce
Bootra Ice Cream

Savory
Mundowdna Cheese
Fruit   Coffee   Gibbers and Raisins

quiet and refreshing directness to his men, addressing them individually and by their Christian names. "I have treated my men in all my time as I have treated myself," he observed.

"I see men who have been with me forty years or more and it delights me. I have lived a hard life..." and out, in abridged form, emerged the Kidman life again. He wrapped up a brief résumé of his life with: "It has been long and interesting and I have been asked by dozens if I would let them write it up."

The Cattle King then gave interesting reminiscences about each of his worthy "henchmen". He started with Pat Kennedy, "a special friend and my oldest employee. He has travelled from end to end of Australia and I count him the country's best drover. I met him first in Kapunda many years ago when we picked up a small mob of cattle and travelled them into New South Wales.

"Jim Wright. I met him in Glasgow. He was not doing much good there. 'You come out to Australia,' I said to Jim, and I must say he has proved himself to be a wonderfully fine man.

"John Brooke knew Jimmy Tyson and worked for him. I doubt if there is another man in this room or in Adelaide who could say that. Brooke and I mustered together for many years and he has been a great man with horses.

"Ted Pratt, our head inspector, started with us at 10 shillings a week. Ten shillings, wasn't it, Ted?"

"No. Seven shillings and sixpence," Pratt replied.

"Oh, well, Ted. I would not like to tell them how much you are getting now! Ted has stuck to me and I thank him, especially for all he has done to help my son in the stock business.

"I see Jim Cahalan present. Jim and I bought sheep together almost from the start and held them for two or three years and then lost money. Jim always had bad luck; but things are better lately.

"Doug Gordon [the son of the dinner chairman, Sir David Gordon] is one of the new school. Foulis took him in hand and today he is manager of Myrtle Springs, with an interest in it, too. Good luck to you, my lad.

"Hugh Gooch has been with us a number of years and has done grand work in looking after the accounts. [Mr Gooch's father and Sid Kidman were cousins.]

"John [also known as Jack] Edge came in from England and was working in a bank. When I first went into western Queensland and bought some stations, he sent away 200,000 sheep, 130,000 head of cattle and 4,000 horses. He removed 38,256 cattle in thirty-four mobs off Warenda in 1910 and 1911 and Pat Kennedy is the man who took the first mob away. This is easily a record for the number of cattle to leave one station in Australia, if not the world.

"When Warenda was formed into a £250,000 company [before

323

Kidman's time], they sent down for an order of 5 tons of long-handled shovels and a ton of Eno's fruit salts.

"When we arrived, we used both to make Johnnie cakes and all sorts with it. It had been there for twenty years. (Intense laughter) John Edge went to the place after I had sold it and did remarkably well.

"I picked up Harry Wyatt when he was driving a bus in London. He is now one of our head men in cattle at Dry Creek and has gained more in Australia already than he would have driving in London for 100 years.

"Hugh Davis is the man who sells our cattle and I must compliment him and his firm on the excellent way in which the business is handled.

"I am very proud of Sid Reid. I have never gone away with a greater feeling of confidence that things will be in good hands. (Loud applause) I consider Sid to be one of the best men in Adelaide for companies.

"Duncan Rogers of Yancannia is the man who can produce the best wool in the world. One pound of it [in weight terms] has spun 50 miles.

"Con White, of Morden, has been with us for twelve years. I think we bought him with the station and that's how we got John Horsley, of Fulham Park, too. (Laughter)

"Seeing Mr Foulis [old Washington Irvine was so dour and sour that even the boss never referred to him as 'Wash' or 'Washington'], the head boss in the western division, reminds me that if you ever want to see improvements, go to Corona.

"Mr Bird, my secretary, is another good friend and I am pleased to see a further one in Harry Peck, of Melbourne, who has come all the way to say au revoir. He remembers Tyson well.

"Harry McCullagh, of Durham Downs, has been with us for twenty years and Norman Ford, our Adelaide accountant, I knew before we even had an Adelaide office.

"Ernie Kempe is a good example of the sort they produce in the bush. He has lived on a station for thirty-four years and everyone who visits Macumba speaks glowingly of the place. Sir Edgeworth David told me he never saw blacks happier or better cared for than at Macumba. It is a dry place and one of the stations which the government has said we have not improved but we are getting something like 3,000 cattle from it this year. It has five bores on it . . ."

An interruption from Mr Kempe: "You have spent £26,000 on it in the last few years . . ."

Sir Sidney, continuing, "Everyone knows Archie McLean of The Peake. It is a difficult place to handle but he does it well.

"Monty Winton is one of our best employees. He is never without a smile. He is a hard chap, a good chap and a partner in the station, too.

"I would like to say a word or two of appreciation where Ross Coles and the Coles Bros are concerned...

"Most of the men I have mentioned I have camped with, galloped with for many years...Good riders all — and a finer set of employees, I never knew. (Loud applause)"

Before the dinner broke up, Sid Reid (who was mainly responsible for organising the dinner) read a list of congratulatory telegrams to Sir Sidney from Galloping Jack Watts (in ill health); Albert Edwards (alias "Spear Grass" or "Tie Wire") who was the manager of Glengyle; Allan Stone, the manager of Mount Poole; Frank Wastell, the manager of Forders Selection; Jack Rogers, the manager of Bootra; Arthur West, drover (wire sent from Innamincka Station); Russell Barton, manager of Salisbury Downs; Artie Rowland, manager of Annandale; Bert Carr, manager of Nundora; Mick Mitselberg, manager of Quinyambie; and last but not least, a message from a bloke who had no truck with fancy knights but knew a good boss when he had one. The message was very short and very blunt, and it came from Charlie MacLeod while passing through Clayton Bore. The few words were read out in entirety by Sid Reid and the message was addressed to "Mr Sid Kidman". Sir Sidney treated it as seriously as he had all the rest, and no one dared to raise so much as a snicker.

Dear old Charlie. His top horse-drover. His hand swept across his eyes as the message was read. Not tiredness, just a few tears in the manner in which he'd started the evening. What a shame Charlie hadn't been on deck. He knew, instinctively, he wouldn't put in an appearance at a turnout like this, especially as he couldn't stand Ted Pratt. The whole business had never been all love and lemonade, but to have had Charlie in their midst on the night would have wrapped up the occasion completely.

Everyone had been so kind and respectful. If anything, the party was a little quiet. He didn't mean that unkindly. But where were the rogue horse exporters? "The Colonel" and Co. were not present. And where was that little flea, Mickey Woods, of "jam tin label" fame? His absence had denied Sid one good laugh on the night.

"The men filed from the dining room to adjourn for port (or an extra grog for the night) in an adjacent room and flapping in their midst was some oily type of waiter. "What an oil painting," jeered Monty Winton. "What an Effeminate King of Waiters," remarked the more loquacious Mr Bennett, of Bennett and Fisher.

"Never a flicker of a smile crossed his face," a guest reported. "He was quite taciturn. He certainly looked smart in his white Eton coat, but his hair suggested the necessity for an urgent visit to the barber and his moustache was a bit 'walrussy'. However, it was his earnest desire that he should officiate at such a reunion of outback men.

"After dinner the members of this memorable party adjourned to another room to autograph the menu cards. Before dispersing, several of Sir Sidney's friends uttered a few words of farewell. Here came the opportunity for the waiter — who was standing by like a sphinx — just to butt in. Pushing his way through, he stood before Sir Sidney and in broken accents exclaimed, 'Can I say one word? I worked for you twenty years ago — on Corona...I was the cook!'

"The Cattle King nonchalantly received the unexpected and impassioned outburst and eyed the waiter, fairly and squarely, remarking, 'I never owned it then; Mr Foulis, here, had it.'

"The cook felt rather nonplussed at the cool reception accorded him by the company and sheepishly ran his fingers through his tousled hair — pulling off a wig and revealing an entirely bald head. *Great Scott!* What a transformation! There before us was George Dempster, otherwise popularly known throughout Australia as 'Curly'. We rocked and roared with laughter and George had scored the trick of the night." The night kicked on a bit after that, with the Cattle King belting down a tot or two.

He was not too well the following morning when Bel lined him up for Sunday morning church. He was glad of the recovery party she'd had the foresight to ask all the boys to on the Sunday afternoon while they were still in town. They rolled up in suits and hats, everyone laughing and carrying on about the night before, the unity, friendship and long years. Sid never stopped looking at the front gate hoping that Charlie MacLeod and Mickey Woods would roll in. It was out of the question for Mickey Woods to attend. He had been detained elsewhere on a charge of swearing in public. When the police asked him to state his occupation, he replied, "Roman Catholic."

Shortly before he retired Sid made two trips to Melbourne. One was at the invitation of his friend William Angliss, who hosted a dinner in his honour and who also wanted to discuss further pastoral partnerships with him in Queensland's Gulf Country. The two were interested in numerous stations, mainly in Queensland, and the latest purchase had been Westmoreland, a 1,672 square mile holding about 150 miles west of Burketown.

William saw Sid off on the express at Spencer Street Railway Station. As the train was moving away Sid leaned out of the carriage window and said, "Angliss, here's two notes I owe you. Will tell you more about it when I return." William pocketed the notes and bid Sid farewell.

Sid was back in Melbourne a short time later for a dinner put on by his friend Harry Peck, and during his stay he called to see William Angliss.

"Angliss," he said, "will you give me the receipt for the dividend on Salisbury? This will save a letter and postage." He knew William Angliss avoided the waste of a postage stamp wherever possible.

"What dividend?" Angliss replied. Sid referred to the two notes he had given him a while back at the railway station. They were of £1,000 each to save exchange. Angliss scrambled to a telephone to ring his wife, who found them still in the trouser pocket of his best suit!

Late in 1926 Kidman and Angliss had sent Walter Kidman on an inspection of the Gulf properties. Walter recalled, "I went to Sydney by rail and then by boat to Cairns, where I caught the train to Forsayth. It was a two-day journey and I stayed the night at a small township named Almaden where children with goat carts met the train and took the luggage across to the hotel. Duncan Campbell of Miranda met me at Forsayth and that night we arrived at Strathmore, one of the Queensland government's stations.

"We spent the night there and the manager, Don McGillip, in conversation after dinner, remarked, 'I think I wear the best kind of trousers to keep the burrs and grass seeds out.' The bookkeeper immediately replied, 'But you never go further on the run than Tuckers Dip which is only 2 miles away!'

"Next morning we left to drive to Miranda and I noticed no less than twenty-four mounted horsemen. 'Are you putting on a general muster?' I asked the manager. 'No,' he replied. 'The head stockman saw three unbranded calves up the creek and they are going up there to brand them.' This will give some idea how the Queensland government ran its stations.

"That trip I visited Rutland, Iffley and Augustus and West-moreland. Duncan Campbell did the driving in a T-Model Ford. I spent a week at Westmoreland. It was some of the most heavily timbered country I have ever seen, with ti-tree, gutta-percha and quinine growing very thickly and often we had to divert 3 or 4 miles to cover a distance of 100 yards. During our travel we struck a lot of blacks fishing and Jimmy Murphy, the manager of Westmoreland, collared a nice 8 pound barramundi from them and put it in a pack bag and that night cooked it in the ashes. It was magnificent."

What, Sid thought, would be magnificent was if the Kid-man–Angliss partnership could get its hands on some of the sloppily run Queensland government stations and, with efficient managing, turn them into money-making propositions. William Angliss was of the same mind, but with Sid Kidman going overseas, the matter of their purchase was left to him.

Sid and Bel disembarked at Southampton on 9 May 1927, the day Sid turned 70. The pencil-toting press noted that he was on a "retirement and health trip" and would stay with his daughter Gertie Clover at Torquay "when not travelling around".

The *Daily Mail* said, " 'The Cattle King' controls or holds more than 60,000 square miles of country (which exceeds the area of England) and is interested in a further 40,000 square miles. It is now said you can almost travel from the Gulf of Carpentaria to the southern coast of Australia and never leave Sir Sidney Kidman's land."

In Sid, some of the English press found a great favourite. There were those who had interviewed him three times over the last seven years, on each occasion that he had visited England. They thought he had timed his retirement nicely, or that he wouldn't have wanted to leave it much later. The old boy seemed to have gone downhill in the last five years and was now so deaf that they had to bark their questions loudly at him. Was he serious about retirement, they wanted to know. "Yes, boys, I am," he replied.

"No more buying up, then?" another asked.

"I didn't say that," Sid replied. "Others will be handling those matters from now on."

There is no record at all of what Sid did during the first six months of his retirement in England, unless in letters sent home to the family from Bel, letters that have been destroyed or lost over the years. It may be presumed that he and Bel visited friends and family and submitted to a travel tour of England and the Continent devised by Gertie and Nelson Clover, revisiting favourite spots or taking in those never seen before. In any event, at the end of October 1927 the Kidmans were in Scotland, with Bel wanting to have a look around Dundee and the area where she had lived before leaving with her mother, fifty-seven years earlier, to sail for Australia. So great had been the changes that she was unable to locate her old home.

On 1 November a press man at Lawton, Coupar Angus, caught up with Sid for a talk, extracting from him his feelings about Scotland. "I've been here once or twice before and to me, as an Australian-bred man, the large number of cultivated fields on the farms is wonderful. I have never seen such fields of potatoes and turnips as you grow in Scotland. The best agricultural land I have seen is between Edinburgh and Berwick. Unlike your farmers here, we do not keep our livestock like human beings. We grow nothing for our stock and in dry times the cattle feed on the limbs of trees."

Asked what had impressed him most during his recent tour, Sid replied, "I think you have two things in Britain that are the best in the world — the roads and the policemen. I have just motored up from Torquay and did not see a bit of bad road and I reckon your people ought to think more appreciatively of their policemen than they do. They are a wonderfully efficient body of men and always very courteous. This is my experience of them." Just what experience that was, Sid failed to expound further. "I have never seen any country like Britain but think Scotland is the best end of the island. The only other country that is so fresh and green is New Zealand.

"Australia is a dry country. We have plenty of water there — drill for it, like the Americans drill for oil, in fact we use regulation oil-well casings in our artesian water wells."

Showing how well prepared he was for an interview at any time, Sid produced a handful of snapshots showing camels carrying huge sections of metal pipe casing. "When they reach my stations, we give them loads of wool to bring back. And Australia produces a lot of wool.

"We, in Australia, are the greatest exporters in the world and cannot use a fourth of what we produce. We need better irrigation systems and once they are developed our 'island continent' is going to be the most fertile spot in the world.

"This year already, because of drought, I have lost 70,000 head of cattle and the figure will go higher. Not one of them was insured. Last year I had to shoot 5,000 horses because of the drought and there being no market for them. Some of my neighbours have been terribly hard hit by the want of rain, but you must remember that I am speaking of 900 miles into the interior and around the coastal areas the seasons are normally good.

"But Australia on the whole is a good country, with great opportunities for men who do not want to stay in the cities."

Questioned about the phrase "on the whole", Sid went on, "We have a few 'red raggers' just as you have some in this country.

"Russia delivered them out there somehow and to some extent I think the recent labour troubles in Australia have been due to the 'red raggers'. This Bolshevik business has been started by Russia.

"I have seen the activities of 'red' propaganda in other countries and believe Russia has done more damage in this way than any other ten countries. We want more people on the land in Australia and they will vote for a Liberal government and a fair deal. While I say this, I must admit there have been some sound men among Labor politicians in Australia." Sid went on to say that in the course of the present tour he had visited many places on the shores of the Mediterranean; he had made a special point of visiting the shores of Gallipoli where the Anzacs had performed such great deeds of valour. He was so overcome by emotion as to prefer not to continue to talk further along those lines and to switch the conversation to Italy, which he said he had visited a "few times before". He also had a word of commendation for Mussolini.

"Naples and many other towns are not half so dirty as they were before the advent of Mussolini, who has put Italy on her feet. I noticed there had been a great clean-up in Italy and I reckon they ought to send Mussolini over to Russia to clean 'the reds' up a bit," he added with a chuckle.

In one respect he missed home. He always did when he went away. In fact he'd cut trips short before just to hurry home because he was the boss cocky and things needed his attention. This slice of travel was different. The show was running well at home without him. He was forced to accept the reality of his own retirement, his day-to-day severance from his own business. News from home was good where business administration was concerned, with Bird and Ford coping well and Sid Reid deputising for him at banking conferences and meetings with managers. Jobs that he could handle seem to have been found for Walter. And Sid's managers, plunged into yet another drought, were operating according to the system and using the chain — by now one of great magnitude — to best advantage.

As the first Tuesday in November rolled around in 1927, the thought must have crossed Kidman's mind that he had a handy and invaluable son-in-law in Sid Reid. Kidman hadn't been the only member of his family travelling over the last few years, and in 1925 Sid Reid had gone overseas and had done quite a bit of good for "the firm". Kidman had mentioned to Sid Reid that he wanted a suitable stallion that would fit the bill for Fulham Park. Reid didn't see it as a casual remark, but rather as a mission to be undertaken with top-level success. Sid Kidman told his son-in-law he could go to 5,000 guineas. Sid Reid went to the Newmarket yearling sales where his eyes were focused on a colt by Bachelor's Double, which appeared the right type, but when bidding started at 5,000 guineas, his hopes were quashed. He was further staggered to see bidding advance to 13,000 guineas.

In London, Reid contacted Captain "Jock" Crawford and told him what he wanted. He had in mind a horse that could first race and then develop into a sire. Crawford advised Reid to visit the Dublin sales, where there were scores of good-looking and well-bred horses available, some of which might not command fancy prices. One that appealed was a colt by Silvern from Addenda with Carbine blood through Spearmint. His bidding price quickly soared to the 2,000 guinea mark, and Reid considered his hopes dashed yet again. But then there was a sudden lull and the auctioneer knocked him down to the persistent bidder from down under for 2,175 guineas.

On his arrival in South Australia, the horse, Silvius, had an easy life in the Fulham Park paddocks and later showed every suggestion of fine galloping ability. Silvius was first introduced to a racecourse in October 1926, stepping out in such workman-like style at Morphettville that the touts seldom let him escape a gallop without clocking him. Silvius quickly proved that he was in the staying class and that he could make light of a dead track. After third and second places, he notched up a run of wins in South Australia. His trainer, Harry Butler, saw possibilities with the 5-year-old and did not forget to nominate him freely for the spring events in Melbourne in 1927, which proved a wise decision. Silvius won the Moonee Valley Cup. The gold trophy attached to the £1,300 prize was valued at £200. It later became a prized possession in the Kidman home at Unley Park until a burglar thought he was more entitled to the trophy. It disappeared and was never recovered. Silvius notched up a second win in the weight-for-age Melbourne Stakes and not surprisingly became a great favourite for the Melbourne Cup.

Cup Day 1927 was bright and sunny, with Sir Sidney Kidman's blue racing colours standing out in bold relief as jockey Ashley Reed got the horse away to a good start. But whatever tactics Reed adopted, Bob Lewis on Trivalve maintained close proximity. The battle of wits continued until the home stretch, with Silvius travelling so well that Reed decided to slip him to the front a couple of furlongs from home. It put South Australian spectators on their feet screaming encouragement. Silvius seemed to have the race won; it was just a matter of his holding the position. In a twinkling the outlook changed, with Lewis riding Trivalve hell-for-leather. Trivalve beat Silvius by a length.

David R. Coles, the son of Ross Coles (of Coles Bros auctioneers) and currently the chairman of the South Australian Jockey Club, was of the opinion that "Sir Sidney had listened in to the race on a crystal set in Adelaide with my family", but as Sid was in Scotland at the time, it may well have been another of Silvius's races. Silvius made amends for his Cup defeat by winning the C. B. Fisher Plate (named after Charles Brown Fisher, an initial owner of Victoria River Downs) on the last day of the Victorian Racing Club's Cup meeting.

It was Silvius's last race. When John Horsley, the Fulham Park manager, discovered a bowed tendon, Silvius was retired to stud after two seasons in which he won about £7,000 in prize money. The stallion was on lease for a while to the Thompsons at the well-known Widden stud at Kerrabee, New South Wales, but later returned to Fulham Park. Some of his progeny reached great heights, among them Sylvandale, which won the Australian Cup and the VRC St Leger, and was placed in the VRC Derby and the Melbourne and Sydney Cups. The horse that beat Silvius in the 1927 Melbourne

Cup had a less rosy future. A few years after his success Trivalve had slid so far down the ladder of fame as to be sold for £7.10.0 and finally ended his life in obscurity in Central Australia.

Sid had been happy in earlier years to see the Norley Station-bred horse, Bullawarra, make it to the Grand National at Aintree; now in Australia's greatest horse race, his horse Silvius had been pipped at the post for a win. It was thanks to Sid Reid's clever eye in the first place that the horse had come his way. In later life, horse racing was an interest Sir Sidney could follow — and he did. But it was never with a consuming passion. However, his son-in-law and son did: Sid Reid became chairman of the South Australian Jockey Club, and Walter Kidman, the chairman of the Port Adelaide Racing Club.

21
Touring the Outback

IT'S HARD TO SAY how long Sid and Bel had envisaged stay-ing overseas, but it was news of the best type that put an end to their traipsing around and had them packing in a hurry to return home. Walter had decided to marry. His intended? A 25-year-old girl of great beauty from the noted pastoral family the Moses of New South Wales. Her name was Muriel.

In an interview in 1984, Muriel said, "My father, Herbert Charles Moses, was a barrister and my parents separated when I was aged 8. Mum couldn't get a divorce. She got a legal separation. He was the naughty party. We lived at Warrawee and I was the youngest girl at school when Miss Marion Clarke started Abbotsleigh. Miss Clarke said, 'Muriel is the baby of the school and the only one allowed to put her bread in the gravy at the hot midday meal.'

"I was at school there until the end of the First World War and, by then, quite used to staying at country properties for holidays and visits.

"I was rung one day at Double Bay [at her home] by Mrs (Barbara) Henry Hill Osborne saying, 'Are you free to have dinner tomorrow night? Walter Kidman is here for a few days on his way to Queensland.'

"I went. Walter took a liking to me straight away. He went off. Came back. Looked me up again. He was a great shot, especially with live pigeons. Later, he often brought a bag of pigeons home offering them to Mum and her friends. I thought him a character. He always wore a hat with a coloured feather in the side.

"I was shy and had no confidence and, after his second visit, he proposed to me. I was flabbergasted. I said, 'I don't know.' He asked me to think it over for a few days. I went upstairs and told mother and she said, 'Oh, I do hope you will consider, Mu.'

"Walter asked my mother on his next visit to our home if I could go and stay in Adelaide for a while and, if I felt that I should like to accept his proposal, the engagement could be announced in Adelaide.

"We were greeted by ever so many members of the family and the office staff at the railway station. Sir Sidney and Lady Kidman were in England but their daughter Edna Ayers and Mrs Violet Crozier, a stepsister of Lady Kidman's, were there as chaperones.

"Walter begged me to make up my mind. I couldn't help but say 'yes', and the moment I did we opened a case of French champagne. Walter didn't like long engagements so we were married six months later in March 1928 at St John's Church, Darlinghurst, in Sydney.

"Sir Sidney and Lady Kidman came back from England for the wedding. All their friends and family flocked to meet them when they got off the boat. They were awfully nice to me from the word go. The week after she was home, Lady Kidman gave an afternoon tea for ninety people for me. Sir Sidney had pernicious anaemia by that stage and wasn't going to the office, but they were delighted about the wedding — both families were — and Lady Kidman gave me a canteen of sterling silver, which I still have, and a magnificent ring, and Sir Sidney, who loved Walter, his only son, gave us our home, our furniture and anything we asked for. Anything Walter wanted, his father made sure he had.

"Sir Sidney bought us a house in Adelaide facing Avenue Street, Unley Park; our two back gates faced each other. It was so we could be close to his parents. Walter went to see them every day."

Sid and Bel arrived home shortly before the impending wedding. Bel and her daughters Elma and Edna were soon caught up in a long round of pre-wedding parties for Muriel and Walter. The nuptials over, Sid left his wife and daughters in Sydney, waved off the honeymooners and returned to Adelaide, where he did put in quite a few appearances at the office, much to the joy of the staff, who were delighted to see him. Just before his retirement he had distributed £20,000, returning seven and a half per cent interest among his old employees and office staff, and those who had been longest associated with him received £1,000 each.

Sid was not keen to immerse himself in day-to-day business affairs any longer, but he quickly teed up a major inspection tour of his western New South Wales and Queensland holdings. They had been battling dry times since 1926, times that now assumed the proportion of a full-scale drought. It was bad in western New South Wales, severe in Queensland, where some places were worse affected than in 1902, and in South Australia in 1927 some areas had their driest year on record. Again, Sid wanted to see how the chain, the managers and the men were coping. His son-in-law Sid Reid was appointed the motor driver for the one month, 2,160 mile tour and they took with them the South Australian writer "Murracurra", whose daily diary was jammed with details of the trip.

OPPOSITE:
Miss Muriel Moses, of the noted New South Wales pastoral family, married Walter Kidman in 1928. (Muriel Kidman)

Sir Sidney, Mr Reid and I boarded the Broken Hill express at Adelaide on 16 May. Lady Kidman, members of the family and other friends gave us a hearty farewell at 5.55 pm and we were soon heading north in the dark, a fact which Sir Sidney regretted as he said he liked to see the countryside. He snugly seated himself in the corner of the compartment beneath a big, warm foxskin rug which he bought at Darjeeling while in India in 1911 and had "40 winks". When he awoke he espied a fellow traveller in the compartment and conversation turned to conditions in the Barrier district. The latter had a selection out from Broken Hill and with blunt candour remarked to the "cattle king", "Some people say you are a necessary evil but if it had not been for you a lot of men about 'the corner' [of New South Wales] would have gone away with nothing in their pockets." Sir Sidney took little notice of this compliment but retorted with a twinkle in his eye, "I have met some fellows who have told me some awful things about myself. Lots of them say, 'Oh, Kidman never improves a place.' Why, we have some of the best improved stations in that country." After we had transferred to the sleeper at Terowie Sir Sidney was very wide awake and when the express pulled up at Peterborough at midnight he looked out to see if there was anyone about he knew. Mr Ken Sawers of Canowie, who was looking for agistment for some of his sheep, joined the train at this station for Broken Hill and it was 1 o'clock before Sir Sidney retired to his bunk. Five hours later he was up fresh and early to have a chat at Cockburn with one of his men in charge of Forder's selection, a depot for the thousands of his stock which travel down the tracks from New South Wales and Queensland.

At Broken Hill we were met by Roy Calder, the manager for Bennett and Fisher Ltd, and after a freezing night in the train we appreciated the warmth of a fire at his home, where Mrs Calder had prepared breakfast for us. Sir Sidney and Mr Reid fixed up whatever business was necessary and then Mr Calder motored us 20 miles out on the Wilcannia road to see a mob of 300 cattle from Mr Reid's Momba Station on their way to market in charge

---

OPPOSITE:
Walter and Sir Sidney Kidman, around the time of Sid's retirement. (The Kidman family)

OVERLEAF:
Sir Sidney (right) chats with drover Charlie Bowman during the 1928 tour of his properties. (The Kidman family)

of Drover [Charlie] Bowman. Momba has lost about 5,000 cattle during the drought with about 2,000 surviving.

Broken Hill! What memories it held for Sid. He marvelled at the changes that had taken place over nearly fifty years, and the wealth it had produced. More than £50,000,000 had poured out of Broken Hill by 1928, and Sid could never resist telling the story of his one-fourteenth share in the original company, which he had sold for £150. He could recall the raw, rough days of German Charlie's grog shanty, where once, when a bushman died, his companions sat the body bolt upright in the bar and, when it came to the deceased's turn to shout a drink, extracted the money from his pockets. Oh, the progress since then! Sid was able to glimpse more of it when the party reached his Corona Station. Murracurra's diary recorded:

Corona embraces nearly 1,400 square miles of country and is highly improved. It has forty-seven tanks, the biggest of which is 24,500 cubic yards and 22 feet deep, fourteen wells and three bores. The deepest of the bores is 500 feet and the shallowest, 16 feet. Only the week before, good stock water had been struck at 498 feet. Comet windmills ranging from 20 foot diameter to 8 foot diameter are installed on thirteen wells and bores and on eight tanks. Corona woolshed, which was built many years ago by William Lake, is of stone and would cost several thousand pounds to build today. It has stands for thirty-six shearers but only twenty are used now. The shed can hold 3,000 sheep under cover. An expenditure of £1,000 has been incurred in improving the shearers' quarters, which are as comfortable as could be wished for. Corona carries almost 47,000 sheep and so far the season has been satisfactory. Three inches of rain fell in a week this year. It was too heavy and ran away too quickly, otherwise there would have been tons of feed about. However, where the creeks flowed over feed is plentiful. Last year a total of only 315 points was registered and what rain did fall was in the nature of irritation showers. It was the driest year since 1882. The highest rainfall on Corona was 20.62 inches in 1911.

Mr W. I. Foulis has been in charge of Corona for nine years. He also has the oversight of Weinteriga, Gnalta and Olive Downs and ranks as one of Sir Sidney's most able sheep managers. When Mr and Mrs Foulis came across from Salisbury Downs they set to work to lay out a garden, and today Corona can boast of some fine orange and mandarine trees, grapevines (which are netted to keep off the voracious parrots) and in the flower garden are good specimens of jacarandas and roses. Everything about the station denotes orderliness and tidiness.

While we were seated around the fire after dinner Sir Sidney recalled the time when a stranger couldn't get a feed at Corona and we laughed when he told us of an amusing incident of the early days. "When this house was being built by Mr Lake, whose position was not too safe, he bought a bullock from me for £6. I did not like the look of things and while on the way from German Charlie's down the other side of Mount Gipps I came in here and collared my bullock. I was getting 10 or 15 shillings a week then and never dreamt that the time would come when I would own the place. In those days dingoes were so thick they used to kill half the sheep." Here Mr Foulis joined in saying that Corona was clear of wild dogs now. They had recently killed the last pair, which had been troubling them for months.

The party left Corona on 20 May, with Sid Reid at the wheel of the Dodge, which was laden with luggage, swags and provisions in case Sid felt like camping out. The provisions included Kidman's number 2 blend tea.

Many hundredweights of this tea are consumed annually on Sir Sidney's stations for which it is exclusively supplied. As a matter of fact the same blend is used at the cattle king's home at Eringa, Unley Park. Station hands fare much better now than they did in the old days of "eight, two and a quarter" — 8 pounds of flour, 2 pounds of sugar as black as your hat and a ¼ pound of rubbishy, willow-leaf tea.

Things were very dry until we reached Sir Sidney's Quinyambie Station. There was a tinge of green on the sandy country following a downpour on 1 April, but another shower is necessary to bring it on, otherwise it will be scorched off.

We met the manager, Mr Mick Mitselburg, and immediately went out to see a mob of 500 mixed cattle on the Quinyambie bore stream. (The bore is 1,496 feet deep and flows 600,000 gallons a day.) Quinyambie has had a gruelling time. The total rain for the last year was only 186 points and the country and the condition of the stock show it. No fresh water was available at the homestead for two years until 1 April, when a big tank caught about 17 feet of water. What a contrast to 1916, when Sir Sidney's Quinyambie Pastoral Company took over the huge run which, with Lake Elder on the South Australian side, embraces about 5,000 square miles. Sid Reid told me in that year all the swamps were filled and it was a waving field of grass and the station hands were six months mustering the cattle. A different tale is told today. Many dead animals are seen and Sir Sidney is sceptical of the manager's estimate of 14,000 head on the place. A bang tail muster will reveal the true state of affairs and it is more than probable that it will be necessary to close the station up for a time.

At Quinyambie we met Jim Davey who told us the pitiful story of conditions on Murnpeowie on which little feed was left for 20,000 and how 900 donkeys were shot there in two days. Jim said, "In one paddock where there had been an isolated thunderstorm, these donkeys were eating up the feed as fast as they could. We were given the use of the paddock provided we got rid of them, so five of us went out early one morning, rounded up about 400 and shot them as fast as we could pull the trigger. The next day we rounded up 500 more and polished them off. The barrel of the rifle got so hot that it bulged away from the stock. We must have used 1,000 rounds to kill that lot and they were beautiful fat donkeys. Still, it had to be done."

The next day we made a run out to Lake Elder, which is run in conjunction with Quinyambie. We motored over a chain of claypans of varying dimensions surrounded by bare sandhills, some bare and hungry looking but perfectly moulded; others sparsely clothed with graceful mulga. We negotiated a steep sandhill to reveal the Lake Elder homestead in the midst of treeless sands. Imagine how it must get the full benefit of a vigorous dust storm! A few yards away an artesian bore flows continuously and the white-bordered waters spread out in a big sheet for several hundred yards downstream where the ground is pock-marked by cattle hoofs. We went on to the site where Nugent, a contractor, is completing a 15,000 yards tank that is ready for the erection of the fluming — and the rain. On the way back to Quinyambie, we halted at McIntyre's bore which is some 900 feet deep and yields a daily water supply of 230,000 gallons. Water, water everywhere but very little feed.

By the time we returned to Quinyambie we'd done 119 miles ride-about that day. After a good dinner and around a warm fire we spent the evening listening in on a fine wireless set. We would switch on at intervals to all the Australian capitals, including Wellington [presumably meaning New Zealand]. And such a medley of harmony and noise there was — dance music galore, a machine-gun-voiced orator waxing volubly on the wonders of democracy and men cooing bedtime stories to the youngsters in velvety tones. A big turn of the evening was the broadcasting from Melbourne's Theatre Royal of the second act of *The Girl Friend*, a rollicking comedy. Continuous roars of laughter floated out from the loudspeaker for more than an hour. When all the Australian stations had closed down, we tried to listen further afield. A Brisbane station was having a little testing conversation

with Rockhampton and so audible was it that one might have
been sitting in the same room. At midnight, as a finale, we heard
a foreign voice speaking and presumed we had picked up Japan —
it might have been China. Then we went to bed.

The next morning the party set off for Sid's Yandama Station, which
was 90 miles north, and a noticeable absence of rabbits was noted on
the way. Murracurra reported:

> Sir Sidney expressed the view that the drought had settled the
> pest and that it would not catch up for a long time, especially as
> so many people were after its skins. We were near a depression
> curiously known as Lake Muck when the cattle king remarked, "I
> passed this tank once when Quinyambie was a sheep station and
> they had poisoned 18,000 rabbits here in one night."
>
> Monty Winton, the manager, motored out to McClure's
> tank to meet us and Sir Sidney gave him a hearty welcome. He is
> a sturdy son of the bush and first met the cattle king at Clayton
> bore years ago when he was with Archie McLean (now manager
> of The Peake Station) who was bringing across 1,200 bullocks
> from Warenda Station in Queensland. On that occasion, Sir
> Sidney, accompanied by Lady Kidman, had come from
> Townsville in a buggy. Since then Winton has done very well
> and is a very reliable man in Sir Sidney's service. It was from
> Warenda that Sir Sidney's ex-manager, Mr J. G. (Jack) Edge,
> started away the record number of cattle ever removed from one
> station in Australia, if not the world — 38,256 head in thirty-four
> mobs over eighteen months in 1910–11.
>
> Swooping down from a high sandhill we opened a gate on
> Yandama boundary and soon got into country smothered in
> good feed, rat tail, rib and other useful grasses. This was the
> result of splendid falls of 220 points on 16 February and 105
> points on 1 April.
>
> Along the track we stopped at Merabie bore which Mr
> Dawes started to sink ten years ago. He ceased operations at
> between 800 and 900 feet and a contractor carried on from that
> depth. In May 1918 when the bore was down 2,033 feet, the
> contractor considered it was on rock and plugged it. He reckoned
> there was a good pumping supply and water was pumped for
> eight days. Three weeks later a blackboy came up to the station
> in a great state of excitement and said to the manager, "That
> bore 'im been bust 'em up." They went back to the site and found
> water gushing out at the rate of 250,000 gallons a day. We saw a
> seagull at this bore. Wherever would this marine bird have come
> from? Sidney Reid said he recalled having seen gulls on Salisbury

and Yantara also. Cattle came under our notice later on and Sir Sidney was agreeably surprised to find them in such good condition.

After the depressing condition at Quinyambie we were relieved to find Yandama in such good heart on the New South Wales side. At one time this station carried nearly 50,000 sheep, but it is now devoted to cattle, of which there are about 7,000 or 8,000 head with an additional 2,000 head on the South Australian side, which also embraces Tilcha. The latter will have to be removed. Yandama and Tilcha are worked conjointly under Mr Winton's management and the area is about 120 miles by about 124 miles so it is therefore a big station. The homestead is built on the banks of Yandama Creek. In front of it is a fine large dam about 11 feet deep, the water in which will last for nine months and keep going 1,000 sheep and 500 cattle if necessary.

Mr Winton told us they would never have lived through the drought in that country but for the bores. Tilcha bore is wonderful. Completed in May 1919 at a depth of 2,345 feet, it yields up to a million gallons every twenty-four hours and the bore stream flows for 30 miles, a long distance for water to run in that country.

Over dinner that night Mr Winton recalled a wild white cockatoo that used to follow him about. The bird became most tame and would even bully the cats in the men's kitchen. When Mr Winton drove away in his car, he would hold out his arm and cockie would alight on it and scramble up on to the hood. It once went out to Lake Wallace and back with him in the car — a distance of 54 miles — the dear old thing.

Later it flew down and stayed a fortnight with Billy Stewart, a half-caste drover, 6 miles from Yandama, and when Billy moved on, poor old cockie died. Reference to Stewart led Sir Sidney to remark: "When I bought Wilpena Pound years ago Billy was manager there. He has been droving for us for years. He was fetching cattle from Innamincka last year. I think he is on the Cooper now."

Despite their distinctive beauty, the cockies are troublesome, especially when large flocks of them foul the waters in the troughs and wells. Mr Winton has supplied guns to his men to shoot them out. One must not get too sentimental over this drastic procedure. The birds are responsible for damage which is too serious to tolerate in country where water is so valuable it cannot be wasted. Gone are the hundreds of Aborigines who, by raiding their haunts in the breeding season, maintained the balance of Nature and other means of keeping them in check have been necessary.

Pottering about the Yandama garden, which boasted a pumpkin that tipped the scales at 45 pounds, was Frank Dahlberg, more widely known as "Tilcha Frank". An octogenarian, he is a real old character. Sir Sidney remarked to him in a playful sort of way, "How is it that you have not made money like I have, Frank?" "Some of us has got to keep a roof over the pubs, sir," was the ready rejoinder. Frank was in the American Civil War and served under President Lincoln. When the war was over he went to sea and in 1867 came to Port Adelaide in the ship *Hugemont*. He subsequently left the sea and with several mates humped his bluey from Newcastle to the Mount Browne diggings. There were thousands of people there and also at Milparinka. Frank has been in the area ever since. "I am now 83 years of age and through Sir Sidney Kidman's kindness I have been here for years and am able to stop here for the rest of my days."

On the morning after our second night at Yandama we heard the noise of a motor lorry approaching the homestead well before daylight. Driving it was a Serb who had come in from 24 miles away to catch the Milparinka mail car which left the station at 6 am. This Serb and three of his fellow countrymen are erecting 30 miles of telephone poles out to Tilcha. They are great workers and in order to get the poles over the soft sandhills carry them in slings from the shoulder. This tidy young fellow had a good, honest face, clear eyes and spoke well. We had an interesting chat with him and he told us he had been in America for several years engaged in labouring work before he came out here. He certainly did not loaf about the city. Another of his companions went to night school at Broken Hill to learn English. These chaps do not seem to require any sort of spoon-feeding and if they work hard and earn good money we cannot begrudge them their success, Sir Sidney says, whether they be foreigners or not. They set an excellent example to the grumbling loungers of the city.

We moved on the next day to Mount Sturt where Mr and Mrs Cecil Bartlett received us at the fine, new stone homestead. A nice front garden is in progress with Fred Blore, another veteran of 82, producing vegetables there. Mr Bartlett's father, Arthur Bartlett, and Sir Sidney are old friends and have roughed it together in days gone by. Once when they were camped on the Paroo, a snake made its hole under their bullock-hide rug but you may rest assured that it did not stay there too long.

From Mount Sturt we went to Mount Poole and came to the site of the deserted gold diggings in the quartz hills. At the homestead we were welcomed by Allan Stone, who manages the run for Sir Sidney, and Mrs Stone. Everything about the place was neat and tidy and we could not resist the temptation to sample the sweet navel oranges growing in the front garden. The homestead is a few miles north of Milparinka near the banks of Evelyn Creek which runs down to Cobham Lake, another Kidman station. There is picturesque scenery a couple of hundred yards from the homestead on this creek, a huge waterhole bordered by precipitous crags known as the Cathedral Rocks. It was here that Sturt and his exploring party experienced such trouble through sickness on their journey to the Great Stony Desert in 1845. The grave of John Poole is under a beefwood tree on the creek and a headstone has the following inscription: "To the memory of John Poole, second in command of Sturt's exploring party; died here July 16, 1845". The station is named after Poole and was one of the first in the district and many years ago carried up to 25,000 with but few watering places. Today there are only 4,500 and Mr Stone told us they had lost about 1,000 so far during the drought. The rainfall there varies considerably; last year's tally was only 5 inches while the total for 1924 was but 270 points in eleven falls and in 1905 it was a mere 179 points — the driest year recorded since 1888 — yet in 1922 5.27 inches fell in December and as a result nearly all the fences between Mount Poole and Cobham Lake were washed away.

After dinner we settled down in front of the fire and spent an interesting evening listening to Sir Sidney and Harry Wheeler (formerly manager of Naryilco and now on a selection of his own) talk about old times. Mr Wheeler asked the cattle king if he remembered the rat plague of 1885 and of course, in his usual entertaining way, Sir Sidney immediately recalled the incident. "Yes," he said. "They came in millions. Everyone said they came from the Cooper. I asked the blacks on the Cooper, 'Where you get 'em that one pfella that all day jump up?' and they said, 'That pfella first time rat, white pfella next time.' I was at Banderoola on Naryilco and they jumped down a tank and filled it up. You could not see the road from here (Mount Poole) to Cobham they had walked over it so much. It was only rat tracks. They would eat anything they could get hold of even pack saddles — anything with grease on. One got Billy Kenny while he was asleep and bit him on the nose. So soon as you lit a fire they would come up and look at you. The blacks would knock them over with sticks and eat them wholesale until they could not eat any more and look (smacking his hands together) they went like that. They disappeared as quickly as they came."

After visiting Olive Downs (96 miles north), the inspection team went on a further 74 miles to Naryilco, a recently acquired Kidman property, a "meagre place" in comparison with most of the other station homesteads. Murracurra's diary continued:

The manager, Mr Flemming, made us as comfortable as he could. We had plenty of good wholesome food and a good fire at night so that these compensated for any other inconveniences which, in the circumstances, were trifling. It is proposed to restore the nice old homestead with its thick walls and furnish it throughout, thus bringing it up to the high standard of the other stations we visited.

I gathered from Sir Sidney that Bates and Caldwell were the first to take this country up when it was all open to Durham Downs. The remains of the old pise walls of the old head station are still standing at Banderoola. Subsequently the run was sold to C. B. Fisher and Amos who fenced it and shore 95,000 sheep in Naryilco's palmy days. They built the present homestead and the latter, who lost his money, intended to convert it to a public house. Sir Sidney says that he bought 10,000 wethers from Fisher and Amos once and lost a lot of money on them. They, however, made an allowance for some of the loss and C. B. Fisher remarked to him, "It is the best thing that can happen to you to make a loss now and then as it acts as a steadier." In more recent years owners were the Morphett Bros and Mr A. C. Macdonald who sold it to Sir Sidney. Carl Anderson, who is 80, looks after the vegetable garden and has been on Naryilco for more than thirty years. He worked for seven years on Milo when that run carried 700,000 sheep. The year after he left he said the numbers went down to 300,000.

Sir Sidney was keen to get out on the run as soon as we had had breakfast the next morning. We went to a site where the Gater Bros of Tibooburra are excavating a 21,000 yards tank. The contractors were doing the job well. The cattle king had a long chat with them. At the next camp we met George Munro, a seasoned old stockman who has been on Naryilco for many years. He could recall the big flood there the year before Mr Macdonald took over, when the place received 16 inches of rain in two days. "Ned Pender and I had to swim 200 yards to get to the homestead. Goodness knows what would have happened to it if it did not have an earth bank around it. That saved it," Mr Munro told us. "Ned Pender," he went on, "was a great horseman on Naryilco. He would ride a horse in from 60 miles away and jump the homestead gate. Those were the days when stockmen wore white moleskin trousers and silk sashes of all sorts of colours. After washing them, they used to iron them with a stirrup iron." Ned, who was contract droving for Sir Sidney for years, is now pensioned off at Mundowdna Station.

That night Sir Sidney was in great form and spent some time with Mr Reid poring over plans and discussing improvements. During the evening two tanksinkers came across from Olive Downs and, after a long interview with the cattle king and his general manager, finalised a contract to make a dam — so much a yard and free meat. Out in the kitchen a couple of Olive Downs station hands who had accompanied them were entertaining their Naryilco colleagues with banjo music. Apparently the terms of the contract were most satisfactory to the tanksinkers for after their departure we heard the party singing lustily as it went on its homeward way in the moonlight aboard a motor truck. Never before has the back country of New South Wales and Queensland seen so many contractors at work. It is a costly business but nevertheless it is a sign of development and progress. It is money well spent. Another visitor to Naryilco during our stay was a plump, well-preserved half-caste with a formidable moustache. He was accompanied by his wife and both were tidy and well-nourished despite the fact that the man said, in a submissive sort of voice, that he had done no work for eighteen months. He ended up getting a contract to do some fencing and kept on addressing the cattle king as "Sir Sid". He was very grateful and said, "Thank you, Sir Sid."

While on the run the next day, having inspected several tanks, we unpacked our tucker box and it seemed that all the flies in the country had turned up to give us a reception. They were so persistently friendly that Sir Sidney took refuge in the smoke from the fire and ate his lunch there.

A large number of cattle loomed up and we soon found it was a mob of 1,050 head from Innamincka in charge of Drover Jim Northeast for delivery on Ashby. Recalling that Drover (Arthur) West had taken a mob through a few days previously, I meant to enquire whether Drover South was anywhere on the road so that the four points of the compass could be completed. Anyhow, the mob from Innamincka was rounded up and, seated in his car, the cattle king was provided with a sort of march past. It was remarkable how quickly both he and Mr Reid could identify their origin by their brands and ear marks. The cattle were in poor condition but, as Sir Sidney remarked naively, "Poverty is no sin."

Mr Harry McCullagh, the manager of Durham Downs, met us at Naryilco that night. He reported that conditions were not too good there and that they had shot a good many horses there during the drought. "There has not been a flood on the Cooper since 1922," he said, "but there must have been a storm up north. About a week ago it started to rise but is falling again. It was red water and possibly came from Kyabra." How life in the bush develops a sense of quick detection of significant detail.

The two-car party pressed on, stopping at Nockatunga Station, owned by the estate of the late H. B. Hughes. It once carried 40,000 head of cattle. In the big droughts of the earlier days the number had been reduced to 1,000. Commenting on the short stay there, Murracurra said:

> Mr Doug McFarlane the bookkeeper acted as host in the absence of Mr Lucas Hughes. He is a wireless enthusiast and we enjoyed a splendid programme in the evening hearing Dame Nellie Melba's voice from a concert at Lilydale, Victoria, and the rapturous applause that followed each of her items. Some day, I suppose, in that far, isolated outback, they will not only be able to hear but also to see what is going on.

The next port of call was Norley Station via Thargomindah, a distance of more than 100 miles. It was a particularly distressing call for Sid Kidman: one of his managers — and great mates — who was responsible for Norley's success, Galloping Jack Watts, would not be there to see him. Galloping Jack's health had been too poor for him to attend Sid's retirement dinner in Adelaide the year before. He and Sid had been half-shares in Tobermory Station and when Sid retired he signed the entire station over to Galloping Jack, who had previously managed both it and Norley. Galloping Jack didn't live long to enjoy the fruits of his retirement, dying at the age of 56 at Tobermory on 1 May, just a fortnight before Sid Kidman set out on this inspection trip. The death of John Levi Watts shook Kidman, who had written to him constantly — not only letters from Kapunda or Adelaide but also from any part of the world where he happened to be travelling. He posted letters to him on board ships, from the Australia Hotel, Sydney, from the United States (intimate letters revealing the extent of his worry over Walter Kidman's deteriorating health). Watts and Kidman had a special friendship — a trusting one to the point that Sid had given Galloping Jack power of attorney to act on his behalf while he was overseas to buy any leases or runs he deemed suitable. Most of his employees seemed to be able to bat on to considerable ages, despite years of hard work, and Watts's premature death was a sad blow to Sid.

Outlining the journey to Norley, Murracurra recorded:

> We ventured via Thargomindah; an interesting feature of this

place is that it was the first town in Queensland, including Brisbane, to have electric lighting installation. The dynamos are worked by a bore about a mile out of town. A run of 18 miles north brought us in view of the numerous buildings surrounding Norley head station, known all over Australia as the place where the famous steeplechaser Bullawarra was bred. It is a veritable botanic garden and a monument to the artistic taste of the late Mr Jack Watts and his good wife and family. I had no idea that we were coming to such a beautiful home around which are fine speciments of poinciana, bauhinia, jacaranda, white cedar and mulberry and huge orange trees heavily laden with fruit, bananas, grapevines and choice roses. The smooth top of a well-trimmed old man saltbush hedge looks as if it has been cut by the aid of a spirit level. A Chinese gardener produces excellent vegetables. All these results are obtained because of a plentiful supply of water. Norley homestead is on the banks of an immense billabong off the Bulloo River. It is 3 miles long and 20 feet deep and has never dried up.

When the late Mr Watts retired and acquired Tobermory last year he was succeeded as manager by Mr P. D. Edwards. Mr Watts had been in the area for thirty-eight years and had managed Tickalara, Bulloo Downs, the Orient, Durham Downs, Clyde, Tobermory and Norley for Sir Sidney with his headquarters at Norley. One of the main reasons why the cattle king went so far north was to extend his sympathy to Mrs Watts and her large family of eight sons and three daughters. "Jack Watts was the most honest man in Queensland," Sir Sidney told me, "and he took as much interest in the stations as if they were his own."

We spent a delightful night with Mr and Mrs Edwards at the restful Norley homestead. Sir Sidney first met Mr Edwards when the latter was bringing down 7,000 from the Gulf for Diamantina Lakes Station. Before coming to Norley Mr Edwards managed Monkira Station for Sir Sidney and Mrs Edwards told us that, while there, she did not see a white woman for four years.

We had a good look around the homestead and Tooma, a black boy, bought out the station sire, a nice stocky-looking colt by Aides out of Compact's Daughter. The horse is very quiet and one day was discovered in a bedroom where he had ensconced himself to get away from the flies.

While pottering around the sheds we saw a lot of old vehicles and these reminded Sir Sidney of an amusing incident that had occurred on a previous visit. He once told Tinder, a Norley Aboriginal King (now dead), that if he could make it rain he would give him a buggy. Sure enough rain did come and Tinder came up for his prize. Sir Sidney picked out the best there, one with red wheels, but Tinder would not have it because he said the red wheels brought up too much thunder and lightning. He was, however, satisfied to accept a buggy with green wheels. A curious superstition among blacks is that motor cars frighten the rain away. King Davey offered to make rain for us while we were at Norley. He came up to us wearing a red corded blazer and holding out his big paw in great excitement said, "Big pfella boss, King of Adelaide, shake 'em hand alonga me." Davey asked me to get him some gibber stones from Tobermory from another blackfellow so he could make rain with them but the latter was out on the run when we got there and, of course, the rain could not be made without them.

Tobermory is barely more than 40 miles north of Norley and we headed in that direction along the Eromanga mail route. Fourteen years had passed since Sir Sidney's last visit to Tobermory and both Mr and Mrs Watts had long looked forward to his visit. Unfortunately he did not live to see his wish consummated. He had only been there eleven months prior to his death and had begun to fashion his new surroundings like those of Norley. The homestead stands in front of a big water-hole on the banks of Jumbo Jumbo Creek upon which a number of overshot dams have been constructed.

A fine garden is in the process of becoming as beautiful as the Watts's former home. Mrs Watts is carrying on the station and has the great consolation of a family of eight good sons and three daughters, the eldest of whom have completed their education in Brisbane. We were greatly appreciative of Mrs Watts's hospitality and greatly admired her for her courage in her hour of trial. Sir Sidney did not leave Tobermory without trying to be of some service to the family. He bought all the horses available and a number of cattle.

We returned to Norley the following evening under a beclouded sky, and right on the spot to tell us he had started to make rain was King Davey. He might have been sincere in his efforts but it was hard to fathom out what was in the back of his mind. He wanted a quid pro quo. "Tell big pfella boss I wantem one pfella tent, two pfella shirt, two pfella trouser, one pfella wheelbarrow [sulky] for horse and cartridge for gun." Sir Sidney generously met most of the demands and instructed the store keeper to hand out the goods. Davey even brought his lubra along in the hope of getting a new dress for her also. He is full of boyish spirit notwithstanding his age and spends his time in sweeping up the leaves in the garden. Mrs Edwards chided him once for carelessness and he thereupon threatened to send up a big dust storm to annoy her. It appears that there is a difference of opinion among the blacks at Norley as to whether Davey should wear the royal robes. Some favour the younger Tooma and when the coronation does take place is should be as exciting as the pre-election activities for the American presidency.

The next day we made a trip to Clyde Station which is carried on in conjunction with Norley under Mr P. D. Edwards's management. Sullen, heavy clouds gave every appearance of a good downpour but the storm moved away to the north of us. We went to the outskirts of Thargomindah town, entered the station known by that name and soon came to the boundary of Clyde. Drover Cavenagh and his wife and two sturdy children were there and the woman was busily preparing the Sunday meal. After a chat we pressed on to the Clyde bore which gives a plentiful supply watering 2,200 cattle during the dry times. The company intends to sink another good bore on this station which was looking in better heart than some of the other runs higher up in north Australia in the Northern Territory.

On our way back to Norley at dusk lightning in the eastern horizon was very vivid. Mr Edwards calculated that there must have been a storm 200 miles away towards Cunnamulla. We arrived back at Norley after a day's tour of 170 miles. Not bad travelling for the cattle king who recently passed the seventy-first milestone of life.

We were seated around the fire discussing the misfortunes of some of the Queensland pastoralists as a result of the drought when Sir Sidney reflected, "I have had some ups and downs too. When my mother died I inherited about £400 and got the interest on it for a few years. The trustee of her estate was a well-known Adelaide lawyer and on one occasion I wanted £200 or £300 to pay George Miller for some horses I bought from him. I got the money but had to pay 8 or 10 per cent for it. In later years I was going across to Melbourne on the express with my wife and I introduced her to the lawyer. He said to me, 'I have always taken a great interest in you, Kidman,' and I replied, 'Yes, and you have always taken a lot of interest out of me, too!'"

The following day we started on our return journey south with King Davey telling us to hotfoot it to Adelaide before the rain came. I am afraid our confidence in Davey was rudely shattered. Some of his rivals must have blown the rain away but he was well recompensed for his effort. That night we made it to Bulloo Downs and were welcomed by the manager, Charlie Easton, and his wife. At one time this was the show station of Queensland. In 1894 it carried 43,000 head of cattle. A year later relentless drought reduced the herd to 14,000. After a couple of good seasons they bred up to 18,000. King Drought returned in 1900 with his terrible sickle, and cut the tally down to a bare 2,700 head. Those were the days when this run was owned by Messrs Jones, Green and Sullivan, who, Sir Sidney calculates, must have made £40,000 a year out of their cattle in good times. A. F. Sullivan, who was manager, was a great horseman, the Cattle King told us. "He used to go and ride in Melbourne. Once when he was coming up to Wilcannia from Deniliquin in a buggy, I followed him for 25 miles to sell him a horse for £12.10.0. I was here before they sunk any tanks — thirty-five years ago, perhaps more. A man sunk them with a lot of horses. They had a fine herd of cattle here then. They kept the studs at Parabeena; it is no good now because there is no water there except a well, and that has fallen in. It was a wonderful country before the rabbits came, but they seem to have left the district now. They came in millions, got into the sandhills, and the people could never get them out. There was a rabbitproof fence, but they got through and thrived. They rung the mulga, butter bush, apple bush, and all varieties that cattle were so found of. They were responsible for reducing the carrying capacity to below 10,000, and in a bad season Bulloo Downs will not carry 5,000." Sir Sidney bought Bulloo Downs with 3,000 cattle for £20,000 about a quarter of a century ago, not long after he was badly shaken through the disaster at Carcoory. Lady Kidman accompanied him up to take delivery of the place.

Few people have done what Lady Kidman has in the way of long overland travel under old-time conditions. Thrice has she journeyed from sea to sea with her remarkable husband, and nobly shared in the many hardships encountered. For weeks and weeks their sole fare was grilled steak and damper for breakfast, lunch and tea. When they went up to take over Bulloo Downs, the Cattle King and his good wife started from Broken Hill in a buggy, called at Tickalara, and after having left Bulloo Downs went to Nockatunga, up the Wilson River to Mount Margaret, Kyabra and Morney, out through other stations to Cloncurry, down to Winton, across to Townsville, and thence home to Kapunda. "When we arrived at Cloncurry it rained very heavily," Sir Sidney said. "People had malaria very badly, and were left to die in tents. One fellow borrowed a cart and was taking sufferers into Cloncurry. On another occasion Lady Kidman and I drove from Sydney to Norley in a buggy. We went to Kyabra, Morney, Monkira, up to Diamantina Lakes, across to Warenda, up the Wills and Burke to Mount Merlin, Noranside, Toolebuck, crossed a lot of open country to Lanrheidol, Woodstock and Winton, down to Townsville, and from there by steamer to Sydney. Another time my wife and I went to Townsville by the steamer *Flinders* and nearly got wrecked. We went out to Hughenden, down the Flinders to Black Sands, and on to Taldora, where I bought 5,000 bullocks. We stayed with Don McIntyre at Dalgonally, and from there we went to another station — I won't tell you the name of it — where I wanted to buy a buggy horse or two. The owner said he would have to ask Maggie, a black gin, if she would agree to sell them. She agreed, and I bought them. We went on to Fort Constantine, Cloncurry, Roxborough, across to Rochedale, and down to Carandotta. We came back by Urandangie, Birdsville, and over the sandhills to Marree." Look at the map of Queensland and see for yourself the extent of country covered by these intrepid travellers.

It was a bracing sunny morning when we left Bulloo Downs homestead after breakfast. Sir Sidney and Easton rode in Edwards's car, and Sidney Reid and I were in the other — both Dodge cars, which are very reliable for that class of country, especially in the sand. We negotiated the watery ford of the Bulloo River, and crossed miles of the same old claypans and sandhills, and mulga and saltbush country. Our luncheon that day consisted of cold wild turkey, scones and billy tea, and we did eat it with relish. When he arrived at the Adelaide gate on the border fence we said goodbye to Edwards and Easton. This is the finest dogproof fence in Australia. It is 8 feet high, and through the eternal vigilance of inspectors, is kept in good order. "It is the greatest asset New South Wales ever had in this country," Sir Sidney described it. "It has kept the dogs out, otherwise we would be eaten out." We carefully shut the gate, and on we went over more miles of sandhills and claypans and plain country. When the Bulloo River comes down it floods these flats for miles, and they grow wonderful, fattening feed. We made our way across Connulpie Downs, passed the ruins of an old galvanized iron hotel, and entered Mount Wood, which bore evidences of a long dry spell. Flat, stony country that used to grow beautiful Mitchell grass was as bare as the boards of a floor. Mr Frank Little (the manager), who had expected us, gave us a warm welcome at the homestead.

We were full of sympathy for Mr Little, who was greatly concerned over the fact that the station had had no effective rain for twenty-six months. The total for 1927 was only 234 points, and but a paltry 42 points for the first six months of 1928. They experienced a tremendous drought for three years from 1918. Mr Little worked out the average annual rainfall from 1904 until the drought broke in 1921: it amounted to 7.09 inches. Since 1921 to 1927 it has decreased to 6.61 inches. No wonder that Mount

Wood cannot carry the sheep it did at one time. They shore 90,000 there once. At the time of our visit the tally was 12,000, and Mr Little feared that it would be necessary to sell them all, and close the place down. As a matter of fact, he has since been compelled to sell half the flock at least.

Having wished Mr Little good luck we headed across the stony plains to Yantara Station. On the way we pulled up at Tineroo bore on the government stock route. The bore is 1,858 feet deep and flows at the rate of 250,000 gallons a day. We read the following quaint notice — certainly illiterate but intelligible — "All travlin sock to pay for warter at Tinrue bore". Somewhat phonetic, eh! A few miles further we came to the white buildings of Yantara. This place, together with Salisbury Downs, is carried on by the Bootra Pastoral Co. The homestead has been closed for some time but is being restored and the new manager will live there instead of at Salisbury. The former station carried 30,000 sheep but after a long dry spell it was closed down and utilised for cattle.

We pressed on to Salisbury Downs, one of the best-watered places in the back country of New South Wales. It has some wonderful tanks and bores. Near the homestead are a big rainwater lake and a dam filled from the bore. The bore is 1,900 feet deep and a stream of scalding hot water has been pouring out of a 6 inch casing continuously for sixteen years. "We had a great sell here once," Sir Sidney remarked. "We put the bore down, built a tank and intended to keep the lake filled. The bore water ran into the tanks and we had to pump them out as the shearers would not drink it. Bore and rain water will not mix. There is something in the bore water that turns it bad." Now the bore stream has been diverted. Dust storms played havoc with this country six months ago and there is not much feed at present. Messrs Kidman and Angliss purchased the run with 40,000 sheep and a fine herd of 1,000 cattle. They shore 30,000 sheep there for several years but the seasons got worse and the run is now stocked with cattle.

We were at Bootra Station by nightfall. The substantial old homestead is of stone and Sir Sidney and I studied the masonry around the doorways and the cattle king paid tribute to the workmanship. We spent the night with the manager Mr (Duncan) Rogers and his wife. Mr Rogers reported the station had not had good rain for nineteen months. There was uncertainty as to whether the flock of 16,660 sheep could be shorn at Bootra owing to the bad seasonal conditions and it was decided to send them across to the Yancannia shed.

Yancannia is 26 miles from Bootra and next morning we

crossed the plains in that direction. The new homestead is beautiful — of stone and with wide verandahs — and sheltered on four sides by a forest of coolabah trees. It must have appealed to the Governor of New South Wales, Sir Dudley de Chair, when he visited the station a few years ago. Everything about the station looks substantial and permanent. A huge, deep waterhole in front of the homestead is 3 miles long and affords great opportunities for boating. The gardens are magnificent and the electric light has been installed, and when the furnishings to the new homestead arrive, Mr Rogers and his prepossessing young wife will have a home equal to any in that country. Thoroughness is apparently the keynote of the company's activities. Some distance down the creek is the big woolshed and scouring plant and painters were just putting the finishing touches to the new quarters to accommodate up to thirty-six shearers. The iron building is more like a first-class outback hotel and ranks with the best on any other station. In good seasons from 30,000 to 50,000 sheep are shorn at Yancannia; this season Mr Rogers reports that 32,000 will be put through the shed.

Of course before some of the Yancannia country was resumed the station carried an enormous flock. Sir Sidney told me he once received a sale note from Melbourne to show that when the run was sold by Reid and Shaw to Shaw Bros, 196,000 sheep were delivered. Many water improvements have been effected on the station and one tank of 27,000 yards has just been completed.

We spent a pleasant evening around the fire at Yancannia. A young Anglican missioner, Mr Judd, was a visitor there for the night. Sir Sidney entertained us with graphic reminiscences of his travels overseas both in India and in America, where in California he met the world-famed movie hero Charlie Chaplin. "I know Charlie well," he said. "He used to come and dance at the hotel where Lady Kidman and I were staying. He is a modest chap. Good Americans are the kindest people to Australians that you could ever meet."

Sir Sidney decided to have a rest at Yancannia the following day, not before he had said goodbye to the young missioner, given him a gift of £5 and seen that the tank of his car was filled with petrol. This was a characteristic act of generosity on his part.

Sid Reid and myself arranged to go across to Momba Station.

OPPOSITE:
Sir Sidney inspects a bore at Salisbury Downs Station. (The Kidman family)

It was a pretty bush ride through scrub and plain country. After we had gone 50 miles, the famous opal fields of White Cliffs came into view. We arrived at Momba to find it in great heart. Unfortunately there is plenty of feed there (after rain in February) but not the stock to eat it. During the drought so far, 5,000 cattle have died. One beneficial effect of the present stock shortage is that the feed will seed well and grow prolifically after the next big rain and it will be as good as it has ever been. Momba is now a cattle station but years ago, before it was subdivided, it carried nearly half a million sheep. The large woolshed at Mount Jack has sixty-three stands. Accompanied by the manager, Mr W. H. (Bill) Ferber, we took a spin around the run and saw a large number of cattle in good condition. Fencing improvements were in progress and a telephone line to White Cliffs, 30 miles away, has been completed. We stayed the night with Mr and Mrs Ferber and returned to Yancannia the next morning.

We met Sir Sidney's nephew Sackville, who is a jackeroo on Yancannia. He is a sterling young fellow and should make good. Chatting before the fire that evening, Sir Sidney referred to the year when the flies were very troublesome to the horses at Yancannia. "The policeman flies came along and gave them what for and chased them away." Reflecting on our experiences with flies on the trip he facetiously remarked, "I have not seen a policeman fly for a long while. They cannot be doing their duty."

The following day we moved on to Morden. Mr Con White, the manager, has used Morden as his headquarters for running Morden, Wonnaminta and Nundora but, owing to difficulty in getting permanent water there, he has transferred to Wonnaminta where the buildings are being restored and renovated and converted into first-class premises.

We stayed the night with Mr and Mrs White at Wonnaminta which was, in bush parlance, a "swell" place when the Kennedy family held it. They shore 80,000 sheep at one time but bad droughts reduced the numbers considerably. Con White (now manager for Sir Sidney's Morden Pastoral Co.) spent a good part of his youth there under the original lessee, R. H. Kennedy. It was a popular visiting place for English people and R. H. Kennedy used to drive eight grey horses in a drag about the station. It is said that overstocking killed this part of the country which used to grow a lot of spear and other grasses. When the present company took it over in 1919, they spelled it for five years. The feed in a good season is now better than it ever was. It has all come back again through the rest and, after rain three months ago, stony paddocks carried quite a lot of grass. The return from one sheep now is as good as that from half a dozen thirty years ago. Wool was then at a low price and a fat wether could be bought for 6 shillings as against 25 shillings to 30 shillings today. Wonnaminta was restocked with 11,000 in 1923 and this year 25,000 will be shorn. The average annual rainfall is between 8 and 9 inches and the lowest total ever recorded was 3.04 inches in 1913. Sir Sidney told us when he first saw the country there was only a wheelmark track to Cobham. There was no Wonnaminta then, no Packsaddle, no Fowler's Gap. Sir Sidney could recall the year before the Kennedys left in 1894, they had the last of a series of amateur turf club race meetings, a two-day fixture combining athletics and racing. "On the second day £120 was given away in stakes and one event was the 14 stone Bracelet. In order to make up the weight, Neil McLean who rode a Cobham-bred mare had a trace chain rolled up in a potato bag strapped across the saddle. When he was finishing, the end of the chain was hanging down flogging along the ground. Mr R. H. Kennedy was a strict disciplinarian. A dozen bookmakers and pugs from Broken Hill were present at the meeting and congregated around a sweat table. They were told to get off the ground as it was private property. Mr Kennedy went down and smashed up a spinning wheel with his walking-stick to clear them off."

It was a cloudless, sparkling morning when we left Wonnaminta for Corona again. Twenty-one miles south of Wonnaminta we halted at Nundora which is now used as a depot. This was originally an off-shoot of Wonnaminta and its fine homestead was built by R. H. Kennedy for his son, Robert. The bricks were brought up from Wilcannia and today it is in good order. Everything about the place was clean and tidy.

At lunch time that day we saw a lot of cattle and pulled up at a waterhole to find Arthur West camped there. He was in charge of a mob of 400 head from Durham Downs in Queensland on their way to Cockburn for trucking to the Adelaide market. Now that Pat Kennedy has retired, West is the oldest drover in Sir Sidney's service. He has been associated with him for twenty-six years and has been all over the well-known cattle tracks of the great outback. The biggest job West has ever undertaken was to bring a mob of 2,800 store cattle from Innamincka to Bulloo Downs with eight men. Arthur West is a tall, lean man with silky-grey hair and a kindly countenance. He was wearing a long coat which was somewhat the worse for wear. The cattle king thought it was time he had a new one and gave an order for one to be sent to him.

We wished West good luck and went to Oakland Downs

selection — part of Nundora — which has the finest stockyards that side of the border apart from being the largest in New South Wales. Their construction represents an example of thorough workmanship. Close by contractors were cleaning out a 16,000 yard tank with the aid of bullock teams attached to a 2 yard scoop. Eleven pairs of bullocks, working outside the dam and attached to a long wire rope, drew the filled scoop out of the tank and seven pairs pulled it back into the dam again after the scoop had been emptied. It was a beautiful sight to behold the slow, dignified gait of these majestic beasts at work.

We were at Corona at nightfall and Mr Reid spoke to Adelaide by telephone that night. What a great convenience the telephone is in the back country. It plays an important part in the stations we visited in New South Wales and Queensland. Just on 1,600 miles of private lines enable various runs to communicate with one another.

That night Sidney Reid, P. K. Martin and myself took turns at the fine piano and were quite harmonious. The next day Mr Foulis took us for a short run to see 4,000 sheep that were on their way from Macumba on the other side of Oodnadatta to Morden. We left Corona the following day for Broken Hill. We had lunch at the Grand Hotel and then set out in welcome rain along the Silverton road for Forder's selection near Thackaringa. On the track we saw a mob of cattle from Bulloo Downs in charge of Drover Davis, a stocky, well-preserved man of over 60 who first met Sir Sidney at Wilcannia forty years ago. The big, open plains at the depot, Forder's selection, were in excellent heart. We had dinner with Forder's manager, Frank Wastell, and his wife and the following day went by car to the Thackaringa siding to join the Broken Hill express for Adelaide.

The final entry in Murracurra's account of the trip reads:

As is the case with all big men Sir Sidney Kidman has often been subjected to adverse criticism. The allegations that he neglects his holdings are quite untrue. He has a better head for business than to allow that sort of thing to happen. Lady Oxford, whose late brilliant husband was a target for rumour mongers, aptly wrote recently, "The most valuable and hardest to learn of life's lessons is never to form a conclusion on hearsay; little that has been written or said of the people and events I have known has been true."

This account of Sid's 1928 inspection tour is the only record to have survived of any such inspection. It is also the only record that can be traced that was made by someone other than Kidman himself, whose accounts were always verbal and only given to press people when they requested interviews. Various people did accompany Sid on inspection trips over the years; many did not bother with diaries but relied on a series of photographs to record the tour. Some photo albums are still in existence, but they have little value when they lack names, dates and places.

22
More Tough Times

DROUGHT TIGHTENED its grip increasingly in 1928, especially in Queensland, and in the heady stench of it all, there was Kidman — to the amazement of some and the dismay of others — buying up again. It added to his reputation as a vulture — feasting on the misfortunes of others — but Sid took the straightforward view that if there were those who wanted out, then he was ready to accommodate them. In this case the owner in strife was the Queensland state government.

Sid had off-loaded Diamantina Lakes Station in 1918. He now sought to buy it back. Initially, when he had bought the station during his first trip to England in 1908, it had been 2,132 square miles. It was now reduced to 1,800 square miles and the going price was £10,000, almost one-third of what it had cost him twenty years ago. It was bought from the government by the Davenport Downs Company (Sid Kidman, George "Daddy" Hooper, a Mr Trenerry and Sam Percival; Sid was the largest shareholder). The syndicate paid £5,000 cash and the balance at the rate of £1,000 a year. Diamantina Lakes again became another fighting link in the pastoral chain.

Walter Kidman had not been sent on some foolish errand when William Angliss and Sid Kidman agreed that he should inspect several Gulf Country properties in 1926. They were all Queensland state government stations, and Walter found inept men and management. He had presented his findings to his father on his return, and Sid chewed the matter over with Angliss and is alleged to have said, "The blooming government up there couldn't run a penny lavatory let alone a string of stations." The remark has been put about widely, but it is doubtful whether lavatories were a penny a pop at that time.

The stations concerned were Vanrook and Strathmore, in the Gulf, and Dotswood and Wando Vale, in the Charters Towers area. Kidman and Angliss agreed to pounce when the time was right, and in 1929 an offer was made to the Queensland government.

Citing the mismanagement, Walter Kidman, in his memoirs, said, "The Queensland government decided it would like to become a beef baron and so purchased Vanrook, Strathmore, Dotswood and

Wando Vale. The government mismanaged these properties so badly that after eight years it had lost £6 million. The government decided to write this off and give itself a fresh start. In another two years it had lost another £2 million. Negotiations took place between Talbot Sanderson and the Minister for Lands in Queensland for the purchase of these stations.

"A syndicate including Sir Sidney, myself, William Angliss and Mr J. A. McPherson and a few others bought the properties for £250,000. The purchase price included the stock on a walk-in-walk-out basis, no muster and no guarantee of numbers being required. We paid £50,000 deposit and £50,000 a year for four years and under the new management the properties flourished and we paid off the Queensland government long before payment was due."

All up, the properties represented an area of 9,000 square miles, and with the 1,800 of Diamantina Lakes tossed back into kitty again, it brought the Kidman empire and interests in 1929 to more than 130,000 square miles of country.

Sid's bankers had nothing to say to him about the matter. The reality was that he no longer spoke directly with them. All banking business was left in the hands of his son-in-law and general manager, Sid Reid, and Reid advised the bank that "Sir Sidney was at present worth £500,000 and that his son, Walter Kidman, was almost equally wealthy." He further stated that "Sir Sidney, up to date, had distributed £1 million amongst his family and employees."

Sid Reid coyly declined to state his own wealth, which, it would appear, surpassed that of Walter Kidman. Reid also told the bank that "Sir Sidney had divided up in the way of companies over £1 million worth of property. This would effect a saving of £227,000 in probate duty. Drought losses could not, as yet, be estimated."

No one could say that Sid Kidman hadn't had enough practice in fighting drought; nor his men for that matter. It had caught him unprepared in earlier years, but now his north–south chain and his Central Australian–South Australian chain were composed of big links rather than big gaps. The reverse had been true when he'd come out fighting first time round in the turn-of-the-century drought. The effective plugging up of the gaps represented twenty-five years of his life. It remained to see how the strengthened chain would hold. The plus factor this time was the big increase in the availability of water as a result of improvements at the stations and also on stock routes, which broke down the big dry stages and staved off the big losses that had occurred in the past. But water wasn't everything — feed came into it too, or, in drought times, the lack of it. The managers and drovers didn't need to have the priority gong belted in their ears. Again, it was "all fats off first" and then "all stores able to travel nudged, nudged and nudged ever towards a market". The stock that could not be staged off were left to their pitiful deaths at the hand of drought. But not all. Some met more humane ends by stopping a bullet. And then there were various measures in between to eradicate horses, which were big consumers of feed and had a lesser priority than cattle. Big, fat donkeys (for which Sid had teed up a handsome export market to Fiji for work at sugar mills and plantations) were shot out; horses, too, as mechanisation usurped their role increasingly. Some met their deaths in more gruesome ways. Priority was given to the stock that would fetch the best market price: cattle.

Sid had an extra "escape route" this time around. He had put down bores from his Innamincka Station into Queensland in the 1920s and in doing so opened up another stock route, which became known as the Bore Track.

Loss reports began filtering in. In 1927 at Yancannia, New South Wales, they'd shorn 45,000. In 1928 they could only muster up 6,000 and the shearers couldn't start on those, because it blew for two days and the sheep were so full of sand that when shearing did start two cutters were needed for each sheep. With the stock routes closing up as feed diminished, nothing could be done to save the rest of the sheep.

Jack Watt, who worked on Cowarie, South Australia, at the time (Jack Watt should not be confused with Galloping Jack Watts), said, "I worked at Cowarie for old S.K. during the big drought of 1926–30. For all of those years the station had a total rainfall of 97 points — and they talk of droughts now." (Jack Watt mentioned this in an interview at Broken Hill in 1984. He died in December 1985.)

"Old S.K. came up to pay us a visit at that time and said to me and Dusty, a half-caste bloke from Alice Springs, 'We're not paying you as we should but we are not earning in the drought.' The award for a stockman was 12s. 4d. and they kept paying it for those who were kept on. Jack Lily, George Crombie, Syd Stewart, Wally Nicholls and Mrs Levine, the cook, were all put off.

"Me and Dusty dug soaks. We made three week trips down the Diamantina with camels, keeping the soaks clean and pulling dead cattle out for the remaining stock. We had 6,000 cattle on the Cowarie books before the drought got too bad and we mustered 106 at the end of the drought. They were tough times. Christ, they were. But old S.K. suffered along with everyone else. In his case it was the old, old problem of the penalty of success. People yapped. They yapped dislike and jealousy and hatred. Some idiots even blamed him for the drought — and the depression — because he owned so much country. Fair suck of the sauce bottle, I tell you.

"Everyone who worked for him tried harder in a drought because that's what it was all about, including his own family. He had a nephew called Claude Kidman [the son of Charlie Kidman, Sid's youngest brother] — oh, Jeez, he was a dag. We saw him once at a station one time and he came to breakfast with his trousers back to front. 'Oh, well, boys,' I said, 'at least we know he changed them last night.' Claude used to get so drunk he didn't know whether he was coming or going. He was a drover and used to deliver most of the cattle to Cockburn. He'd send the plant back but not his little black mare. The reason he kept her was because she wouldn't let him fall off when he was full and he was full half the time — well, some of the time, well much of the time he was droving. But she missed out in a creek one time with Claude and fell into a patch of goatsheads [nasty burrs]. Claude caught our camp up leading the black mare and when he got to camp he yanked something out of his pack and went down to the creek and we went up and spied on him with a mirror stuffed up between his legs looking at his backside so he could pull out the burrs. Well, he could hardly ask anyone else to pull 'em out.

"Christ, he was a good drover though. He got those cattle down the Birdsville Track time and time again. There was a 110 mile rough stage on the border fence without water and Claude Kidman always handled it well — putting 'em over mountains of sandhills, one after the other. My oath he was good. Most drovers had a saddlebag. Claude just had a sugar bag with a big lump of damper and beef in it. When he wanted a feed, he'd just tear off a bit of something and have a chew. He carried no tea.

"God, he was a dag but, Jeez, he was good. Years later, when old S.K. died, he left Claude a poultry farm. Claude said, 'Fancy leaving me a bloody chook farm. Me back's bad enough without picking up bloody eggs!' "

If Claude Kidman was one drover who could achieve miraculous results, then Arthur West was another. He had started off with Sid in early times around Broken Hill but then there had been a falling out — which had nothing to do with Kidman.

Charles Smith, who worked for Kidman from 1930 to 1934 doing several jobs, including investigating duffed (stolen) Kidman cattle, said in 1983, "Arthur West was Kidman's top drover for many years, certainly after Pat Kennedy retired. He had been associated with Kidman from the early days when Kidman had forty head of cattle on the Broken Hill common. Arthur and Sidney were good friends, but when Kidman came back from a round trip which took several months, he found the cattle missing and Arthur as well. It appeared that the cattle had been sold and Arthur had absconded with the money. But Arthur West was footloose and he and the money didn't last long. It always reached Kidman's ear exactly where Arthur was and years later, when Kidman was in south-west Queensland inspecting a mob of cattle, he was told that West was one of the stockmen. Kidman, as was his wont, pulled his buggy up at the camp for tea, but there was no sign of Arthur West at sundown. Kidman gave him a few hours and then remarked to someone, 'I think you'd better go out and get Arthur West. He'll be pretty hungry out there now.' West came in looking fairly sheepish and Kidman said, 'Well, Arthur, it's a long time since I've seen you. You have come down in the world — just working as an ordinary stockman. I'm surprised at you. Wouldn't it be better if you had your own plant and did your own droving? What about your own plant?'

"Arthur West said, 'Where would I get the money to set it up?' and Kidman said, 'Don't worry. Come and drove for me. I'll set you up. You can pay me off. Let's forget what's happened in the past.'

"Arthur duly went to Kapunda and was received with open arms to choose his horses and plant. He only had to name it and he had it. Sid Kidman sent him off then, saying, 'I'll keep you busy. At least you're your own boss now.' Arthur said, 'Thank you. Thank you so much.'

"In every year to come, whenever the matter was mentioned, he always said, 'That old rogue. Did I pay for that plant. Year after year after year they deducted that money. It never reduced. It never seemed to be paid off. I paid for it time and time again and I don't begrudge it. He gave me back my self-respect.' There was no bitterness. Arthur knew he'd done wrong and he was paying interest all right, and paying it at a high rate, but more appreciative than ever of S.K. putting him back on his feet again and gaining his self-respect. S.K. didn't regret it either. Arthur got cattle through time and time again in times of bad drought when lesser men would have failed. Kidman had the uncanny knack of knowing the right man for the right job — and how to get them and keep them."

Mort Conway, a part-Aborigine, was another who contributed to the late twenties fight against drought. In 1984, at the age of 81, he said, "I grew up in Alice Springs. Mrs Stanley was my teacher. Stanley Chasm was named after her. I went to the Ida Stanley kindergarten in Stanley Street. She was a grand lady. I left school in 1916 and got into cattle at Oodnadatta with Ernie Kempe, who was the manager of Macumba Station at the time. He was a tough bugger, too, a man of about 30 or more. He might have been older. He was a cheeky bugger. He'd give you a hiding for nothing...knock you over with anything from a whip to a kick in the backside or a grapple by the scruff of the neck. He'd even hit you with a rock. He was not a nice man. Boys who'd worked with their fathers never got that treatment but I did. He was nice to some and not to others and regarded as one of S.K.'s leading men, managing (at the time) Hamilton, Eringa, and Macumba (his headquarters). But he was a first-class cattle man and horseman. He was strict with the black boys and later had a team that stuck with him through thick and thin. He was kinder to them later when he found that roughness was no use because they'd run away.

"I was at Macumba until 1919. I never saw any money for wages. I know I got 2s. 6d. a week that was paid to government officials at Central Australia until I was 21. Then I got £100-odd.

"In 1919 I went to Mundowdna. Others were paid by Kidman cheque. It had 'S. Kidman and Co., pastoralists' sketched on the top. It was mostly blue in colour with a horseshoe on one corner and a bull's head on the other and his favourite brands as well which were the X70 (of Eringa, Macumba and Hamilton) and the diamond tail of Innamincka and Mundowdna Station. The cheque was such a lovely thing to look at that many men were reluctant to cash it. I was at Mundowdna until 1928. The boss was a kind man and everyone liked him. He never swore. His name was John Brooke. Ernie Spencer, who later became Kidman's pastoral inspector, was there at the time as a cowboy. It was at this depot that we took delivery of all his cattle on his Queensland stations. The following year I was made a Kidman drover. Arthur West was also droving at the time and 'Tom Tiddler' Reid. We were paid £3.10.0 a week and always delivered the exact number, except for a couple that might have been dropped from lameness or pleuro. They were wild cattle. Straight out of the lignum scrub. Sir Sidney always spoke to me whenever he saw me at Farina or at the abattoirs or saleyards at Dry Creek, but he always called me 'Jim' and never 'Mort' or 'Conway'.

"In the late twenties drought he used the motor to try to solve some of the problems. I was issued with a truck from Kapunda. It was to be used for the cattle that were travelling south. I picked up hay at Marree and went north to meet the cattle that were travelling south to Marree to be trucked. They'd been walked from the Channel Country and we gave them a feed of hay every three days. Everything that could be done to save stock and to get them through was done."

Such was the manner of men who offsided Sid in his campaign against the drought. The late 1920s saw Sid call a halt to his buying spree in the eastern states — on a note of exasperation. Things didn't always go his way and the one place he really wanted in western New South Wales was denied him. And all because of a woman, Mrs Edith Dempster. Recalling the rebuff in 1984, Bob Napier, 89, of Broken Hill, who had been a horse breaker on several Kidman stations in western New South Wales, said, "Kidman wanted Tindara [Mrs Dempster's place] right or wrong. But Mrs Dempster was too much for him. She went to the lawyers. It was a real dog fight.

"Kidman had wanted Tindara for years and kept urging his Quinyambie manager, Mick Mitselburg, to see what he could do about it. It was 34,000 acres freehold with full grazing rights to S.K.'s unfenced surrounding country. He wanted it because it was the crossroads between Lake Elder, The Selection, Quinyambie and Corona and because of its permanent water, including Sturt's Yellow waterhole. Getting Tindara would enable Mitselburg to go from Quinyambie to Corona without moving off Kidman country. But Mrs Dempster refused and she didn't take it lying down either: she took the matter to the state Parliament and Jack Lang. S.K. didn't get the place. It's probably the only time in his life he lost out on a property deal because of a woman."

Despite the "dog fight" tag, one suspects Kidman had a grudging admiration for Mrs Dempster. He and his party called on her whenever an inspection was taking place in the area. She always had a splendid meal on the table for the travelling party — and the same old answer for Sid if he raised the matter of her selling Tindara. She was also an excellent horsewoman, not only on the show circuit but in any sphere of station life, and Sid thrilled at one stage to hear of her account of running down a wild dog single-handed. Her story had a nice punch line, which pleased Sid even further. The feat was achieved on a Passing By mare — and Sid just happened to own the mare Passing By.

Sid had further cause to dwell on women as the 1920s drew to a close. The whisper from his wife was that dear Muriel, Walter's wife, was expecting an infant in the new year. Now there was something to look forward to, and as Walter was his only son he naturally hoped the baby would be a boy — and another Kidman who could carry on the family business. Sid was by then the grandfather of eight children: four boys and four girls. They bore the names Clover (Gertie's three children who lived in England), Ayers (Edna's child; her other child, Henry Ayers, died aged 14 in 1927), and Reid (Elma's four children). So it would be nice to have a Kidman in the grandchild stakes. He would sit back and await the happy outcome and leave Bel to cope with the advance side of the baby business, which Bel certainly did.

Muriel, their daughter-in-law, recalled, "The first time I was pregnant Lady Kidman wouldn't let me stay in the house on my own although I only lived 50 yards across a lane from her home. She insisted I move in with her. She was so wanting me to have that baby. I wasn't even allowed to go to the bathroom at night. She put a chamberpot under my bed."

OPPOSITE:
Mrs Edith Dempster (in riding gear), who refused to sell Tindara Station to Sir Sidney. (Rob Dempster)

Most thoughts about his impending grandchild were shoved to the back of Sid's mind as of November 1929, when the stock market collapsed in the United States. All hell broke loose there on 29 October, and the disturbing reports that reached Australia prompted three reactions: some people did not know or understand what was going on; others insisted that something happening in the world of finance so far away could hardly have any relevance or repercussion in Australia; and others knew that the finance boat had been rocked so badly that the ripples would be far-reaching. Sid subscribed to the last line of thought.

The question for him became, how to dodge the ripples? Some measure of scorn was directed at him for taking the issue so seriously, by those who thought it would blow over as quickly as it had blown up; there were sniggers in some high circles that the old bush boy knew a lot about stock and not too much about stock markets.

Sid knew one thing: that some people had short memories if they failed to recall the economic misery of the 1890s and the utter ruin it had caused, certainly in the eastern states. He and Sack were just starting to launch themselves at the time, and they'd been able to sidestep much of the trouble by snappy thinking that took them into Western Australia and its gold rush days. Catering to the boom with both meat and transport had put them on their feet. Forty years later, though, how did he sidestep again? Even another gold rush wouldn't provide a solution this time around. He had an annual wages and rations bill of more than £120,000 for men who worked for him and their families. In the 1890s there'd really only been he and Sack, and perhaps a few dozen others, slogging along together in coaching and on the early stations they acquired. But things were certainly different now. So much more responsibility. As if drought wasn't bad enough, to have this other business, which at its best could be a bad recession and at its worst a good depression, was like a double backhander with a shovel. What to do? Others disposed to his line of thinking would have to "grin and bear it". In a letter to Hugh Gooch, a distant member of the family, Sid wrote, "I know I'll have to bear it but why should I grin there is nothing to laugh at in this matter at all."

Sid was appalled to hear of business people in the United States jumping from windows to suicide or taking their lives in other fashions as a result of the financial crash. Such stories sometimes appeared in the press; they also came to Sid through business contacts in the United States. "Oh, what a crook show all way round," he said to Bel. In an attempt to inject a little levity into the discussion, Bel is alleged to have said, "Entertain no thoughts of jumping from tall buildings yourself, Sidney. I have no desire to be a widow and your death would be a useless waste and I know how you feel about the waste of anything. If the worst is to happen, we still have each other. We have been most fortunate in life so far."

As the Depression bit deeper and stringent economies were the order of the day, much of the rural sector found it could abandon mechanisation in favour of suitable, solid horse flesh. It was a case of machinery costing more and horses costing less and it saw the Kidman horse sales at Kapunda experience an amazing boom. They had tapered off towards the end of the 1920s, but with a renewed market for them, every suitable stamp of a horse was directed to Kapunda. Farmers, trying to stave off financial hardship, responded in a big buying spree.

In other stock areas, Sid was less fortunate. Les Gardiner, of Yunta, South Australia, was a horsebreaker and drover in the drought–Depression. He recalled, "We took almost 1,000 cattle from Iffley in the Gulf to Durham Downs and then any fats from Durham Downs on to Forders near Broken Hill. It was in New South Wales that we lost stock; it was badly drought-stricken at the time. There were five of us on the drove. We were paid twopence a head per 100 miles."

Charlie Flavell, aged 90 in 1984, was a shearing contractor in the Depression. He shore at all the Kidman west Darling stations at the time and for many years afterwards. He recalled, "The drought hadn't broken at the time, and I was at Tibooburra travelling out to Waka to work. We drove up on an empty tank. There was only mud and no water for miles. It was the last tank to go dry in the area and there were 300 or more dead cattle and a large number of kangaroos. They were all bogged; all dead for a month. One of the men travelling with me remarked, 'And they tell me there is a God in Heaven.'"

The hundreds of cattle that died in such circumstances snowballed into many thousands. Frank Kelly, of Broken Hill, remembered the Kidman policy in tough times. "When things were not so good S.K. fired people. It had happened before in tough times so it didn't come as a shock. People took it calmly. Because of the drought and low market there was no use in employing men when there was no money coming in. I was at Salisbury Downs waiting to get my final cheque when the old man approached me and said, 'Hello, boy. How long have you been working for me?' 'About a month in the camp at Yantara,' I said. 'Well,' he said, 'I'm sorry I had to pay you off but things are such that we can't afford to keep you on.

OVERLEAF:
Lunch at Yancannia: Sir Sidney and Sid Reid, with the postman in the background. (The Kidman family)

Things must improve and I suppose you'll get another job on one of my stations later on.'" Kelly did, at Bulloo Downs soon after. "Only," he recalled, "to be sacked the second time around when the old boy made a visit there. The Depression was on and it was almost impossible to get a job anywhere."

Hughie Gilby remembered his good fortune in having — and keeping — a job at Yancannia Station, where he was the gardener, groom and cook and also cut wood for the scour. "I was paid 6 bob a cord (and a cord was 4 feet long, 4 feet wide and 4 feet high with no 'crow's nest' because they wanted wood and not air) and 60 cord of timber was sufficient for all the scouring. I was grateful I had a job."

"Within a few months the bottom fell out of our world as the Depression started with an onrush frightening in its velocity," said R. M. Williams. "Nobody seemed to know who or what had caused such a calamity. Like the beetle that is crushed by the boot, we couldn't guess who wore the boot or why it had been used. We had been through a series of boom years, a condition that most of the population believed would last forever. They ended almost overnight."

Williams had a job carrying bricks in Adelaide at the time. As soon as the building trades were hit, he lost his job and struck out for the bush to take on any sort of work he could. His swag was his home and, despite the fact that he was a skilled bush worker, he was disappointed in his quest for work. "Station owners and others who normally looked to employ workers were in the same position as everyone else. They just didn't have any money. Many of them couldn't even offer food to those of us on the road." Williams was simply one of untold thousands of men — many of them from cities — who humped their blueys around the outback believing prospects would be better and in search of work of any kind.

On one occasion, Williams returned to Adelaide in the hope that things had improved and, not wanting to lug his swag around with him, stowed it away at the back of the Roman Catholic Cathedral in Wakefield Street. On his return soon after, he found the swag gone. It was all he had in the world.

"Being in a desperate position and not having any money I walked from Wakefield Street to Sir Sidney Kidman's house at Unley Park. I knocked at the door and the old lady answered it and I told her my story. She left me standing there while she went away and returned with a fairly new swag complete with good straps and at least one blanket. I remember the swag being neatly wrapped and wrapped in the manner of a packhorse man. I not only appreciated the swag but the fact that she knew how to roll one. It left a big impression on my mind."

Williams was but one of many people helped by the Kidmans in the Depression era. Muriel Kidman, Walter's wife, recalled, "I became used to the sight of queues of people in the driveway at Unley Park. Sometimes the queues stretched down the street. When they first started, I said to Walter, 'What are they doing?' 'Dad's giving them food or orders for boots,' he told me. I was amazed at their generosity. If they knew people wanted something, they gave it."

As in the First World War, Sid's hand was constantly in his pocket. He had been a great admirer of the work done by the Salvation Army both in Australia and overseas during the war, and when he saw the Salvation Army officers riding by bicycle to further their work in the outback, Sid shouted them a car, at a time when cars were few and far between. He was the first to do so. Barbara Bolton, in her book *Booth's Drum* said, "The new vehicles were too expensive for the Army [until] Sir Charles [sic] Kidman the cattle king presented one for the use of Commissioner James Hay and others were gradually acquired." In his book *Aggressive Christianity*, Commissioner James Hay said, "My good friend Kidman gave me a motor car saying, 'You have it and save yourself a bit. You have a great work to do.'"

Sid also gave the Army a half-share in one of his stations, and in 1926–27 the rebuilding of the Melbourne People's Palace was financed largely by donations from Sir Sidney Kidman and William Angliss. In the Depression years Sid continued to make large, generous donations to the Army for relief work, but the Army has kept no record of them; it is a shame also that Barbara Bolton could not even name correctly the benefactor who gave the Army its first car.

It has been asserted that during the Depression Kidman helped out "the woman at the well". This has been cited as another instance of his generosity. Recounting the incident, Frank Kelly said, "Kidman came through a place out from Broken Hill and wanted to water his horses. There was a woman there pulling water from a well with a bucket and a rope. Water was scarce but she allowed him to water his horses. Her name was Mrs Cranston. He wanted to know where her husband was and she told him she was a widow. Her husband, Jim, who had been one of Cobb & Co.'s main horse drivers, was dead. She was carrying on at the place on her own. A while later a crew of men arrived with a windmill for her. It was a gift from Kidman. Mrs Cranston spoke so highly of him for that."

The truth of this story is not disputed, only the timing of it. It is more likely to have happened a decade earlier or during the First World War, when Sid was still known to have travelled about in a buggy from time to time, although even then most of his outback travels were by motor car, and only ever by motor car in the 1920s onwards. Certainly in the Depression era and at the age of 75, Kidman wasn't doing any riding on horseback, although, as Jack

Watt said, "He was still riding at 70 in 1927, when he had a fall chasing camels at Mundowdna after a chestnut mare put a foot in a rabbit burrow. It shook him up bad. He didn't break — or bend either — and he didn't get over the fall."

At its worst, the Depression saw nearly 30 per cent of the country's breadwinners unemployed and in anger and bewilderment people did one thing by way of retaliation. Blaming the politicians, they kicked out every government in Australia. The federal Bruce–Page government was the first to go and, thereafter, every state government; electors were reduced to the hope of "giving the other mob a go — they couldn't be worse!".

For Kidman, the drought and the Depression overlapped by almost a year. Towards the end of 1930, Sidney Reid reported to the Kidman bankers that there had been generous rainfall and floods on some Kidman stations, so 20,000 head of cattle would be finding their way to markets in the near future. By the middle of 1931, good rains and floods had been received almost everywhere, but not before the drought losses of 1926–30 tallied at 100,000 head of cattle, 120,000 head of sheep, 6,000 horses and hundreds of camels. All up, it represented a financial loss of more than £1.5 million.

The stock loss was spread over five years from 1926 to 1931, with more than 130,000 square miles of Kidman country proving that big droughts cost big money, and some people thought Kidman a big fool for allowing himself to be prey to its clutches time and time again. A more realistic view is that if he had not been out in the far back country working it with stock whenever he could, dozens of different individual owners would have been there in his place making the chain strategy impossible. Individual station owners were obliged to move their stock to market along recognised stock routes; the benefit of the chain was that Kidman could generally avoid them and stage stock to market along good patches of feed on his own places. How many stock can a much-travelled stock route accommodate in dry or drought times when feed is either scarce or non-existent? The increased traffic, had the chain stations been held by numerous individuals, would have meant stock losses double those suffered by Kidman. Drought, once again, would have broken individual landholders. The national loss for both the domestic and export market would have been considerably greater.

It was the last drought that Sid was required to fight. He had the satisfaction of knowing that he'd pulled through and the chain had survived, despite enormous losses. It was a victory over drought but could hardly be called a clear-cut one when finances were examined, because the drought ran slap-bang into the Depression. Crowning rains on all his stations did not automatically represent a return to good times as they had in the past.

And as regards the birth of an heir, a grandson by the name of Kidman, things didn't work out quite so well either. On 22 March 1930 Walter's wife, Muriel, gave birth to a daughter, named Isabel Margaret. Sid was happy that mother and daughter were well, sorry it was not a boy, and drank a large glass of champagne on the occasion.

Sid Kidman continued to buy up during the 1926–30 drought. In June 1930 his Oakden Hills Ltd company bought an enlarged Owen Springs — the station in the Northern Territory he and Sack had bought in 1896 (largely to draw on the enormous horse numbers to satisfy the demands of the coaching business) and disposed of five years later. It was 42 miles from Alice Springs and this time covered 990 square miles (sometimes given as 1,399 square miles), as opposed to 600 square miles in 1896. He acquired it from the Hayes family who'd taken it up in 1907 along with Undoolya Station. The rent was 2 shillings a square mile.

Sid's losses as a result of the drought and depressed markets were widely known, and people were staggered that he was in a position to continue to build up. Rumour intensified that he was up to his "vulture tricks" again, but talk fizzled out quickly when it appeared that Owen Springs was the only new acquisition.

In 1930 he also disposed of Hamilton Downs, 716 square miles of country adjoining Owen Springs. It had been bought from the original lessee, Hayes and Son, in 1920 by Robert H. Harris and sold to Kidman interests in 1927. Sid had held onto this station for only three years. It had taken a hammering in the drought and it is likely that Harris got it back again fairly cheaply. Charlie Wright, the Hamilton Downs manager, was transferred to Stirling Station, a 1,614 square mile holding 150 miles north of Alice Springs, which Kidman had bought in 1928 from Harris, Turner and Spencer on a walk-in-walk-out basis, with an estimated 3,000 head of cattle on the place.

Also in 1928, he bought Huckitta, a 2,850 square mile station on the eastern end of the MacDonnell Ranges, from Charlie Dubois. The Huckitta syndicate consisted of Sid, Bel and their four children. It had 5,750 cattle, 400 horses and a complete working plant; the price was £20,000. The transaction was held up for some time with urgent telegrams between Canberra and the North Australia Commission, Darwin. The Commission was seeking advice as to whether it was legally justified in refusing consent to the transfer on the grounds that Kidman interests already held "sufficient area of country" and that the transfer wasn't in the best interests of the development of the Territory. In Canberra, the Home Territories Department allowed the transfer to go ahead.

At the time, Sid's all-up interests in the Northern Territory amounted to 12,900 square miles. He had abandoned some Northern Territory interests years earlier, when his almost equally large aggregation was the Victoria River Downs/Newcastle Waters/Austral Downs group of 12,230 square miles between 1900 and 1910. When Victoria River Downs was sold to Bovril in 1909, Sid remained on the board of directors and was also a substantial shareholder in the station. He retired from the Bovril Australian Estates board in 1922.

Between 1910 and 1926, Sid's holdings in the Northern Territory had stood at 6,300 square miles. In 1910 his Crown Pastoral Co. acquired Bond Springs, a 1,805 square mile run 12 miles from Alice Springs, and Crown Point, a 4,524 square mile station on the Northern Territory–South Australia border. Bond Springs was used for cattle breeding and Crown Point as a fattening depot; they were important links in his Central Australian–South Australia chain. To Crown Point and Bond Springs he later added Hamilton Downs, Huckitta, Stirling and Owen Springs, giving him almost 13,000 square miles by 1930. By contrast, the Vestey outfit, between 1914 and 1916 had moved in and its troubleshooter, Evelyn Brodstone, had snapped up 36,000 square miles of land in the Northern Territory and the east Kimberley area of Western Australia. Wave Hill Station alone was more than 6,000 square miles!

If there was one word that Sid could apply to the Northern Territory, it would have been "frustrating". He'd kept an eye on it for fifty years — not to mention his fingers in some rewarding pastoral pies — believing at first that it was a great place of opportunity and possibility, for him, at any rate. But it hadn't quite worked out that way. In 1885 the total non-Aboriginal population of the Northern Territory was at 3,500, the bulk of them Chinese and Malays who didn't eat meat in the same quantities as Europeans. The population of the Territory increased from 1886 to 1889, while the Palmerston to Pine Creek railway was under construction, but the increased market for meat was still far too small to support the Territory's cattle industry. In 1885, stock from Victoria River Downs alone was sufficient for the local market. In 1888 the market needed only 1,344 beasts, and even this fell away rapidly when the railway was finished the following year. Occupation of new country and demands for foundation herds ceased. Gold around Hall's Creek and Pine Creek petered out. The gloom intensified with the financial collapse of the 1890s. An attempt was made to open up Asian markets with shipments of live cattle, but the trade was never secure because of high costs, losses on the voyage, exchange fluctuations, embargoes against redwater fever and, the final straw, the withdrawal of the export subsidy. In the Top End and the Kimberley area, turn-offs were limited for some years to small, live shipments via Wyndham to

Fremantle or overland trips to boiling-down works at Burketown and Normanton. There was an improvement when the 1902 drought broke and Territory cattle were sought to restock Queensland stations. Characteristically, Kidman seized this lucrative market for Victoria River Downs cattle and in 1904 his drover Blake Miller reopened the Murranji Track to take cattle the shortest way east. But from 1890 to 1909 the annual average turn-off from the whole of the Northern Territory was only 15,000 head, reflecting the small scale of the industry and the great difficulty of finding profitable markets.

Stating his opinion of the Territory during the First World War, Sid said, "It is a rare thing to see any herd of cattle there in good condition excepting a few months in the year. I have been lifting a large number of cattle from the Territory but more from the Barkly Tableland, where the cattle get in much better condition than they do further out; but I never saw a mob of prime bullocks come out of the Territory and if they are fat at starting, they never carry it. One hundred miles of Queensland country will fatten more cattle than 800 miles in the Northern Territory. The same thing applies with horses. It takes three horses to do the work that one will do in Queensland. I am not referring to the Gulf but central Queensland or the north of Adelaide so long as you don't go past the MacDonnell Ranges. The country is too fresh and there is no salt in it.

"It is something similar to a lot of the Rockhampton country and up the Gulf — grass from 1 foot to 6 feet high and stock as poor or poorer than they are in a drought in Queensland. People have spoken of the number of fat cattle that the Transcontinental Railway would fetch out of the Territory but there are very seldom any fat cattle there to fetch out. To give you an instance of the fat cattle that do come out of that country, I was in Adelaide a few days ago and there were eighty bullocks which had come from away up near the MacDonnell Ranges and railed from Oodnadatta to Adelaide, which cost 35 shillings a head railed. These bullocks averaged a little over £4. At the same market there were cattle from Queensland that had travelled 500 miles and were railed from Hergott and they made £9.16.0, so you can compare the two. I have been and still am interested in country in the Northern Territory and if it had been such an attractive place it is not likely I would have bought so much in Queensland and left the Territory alone. I know a number of holders in the Territory who stand in the same position pretty well today as they did twenty years ago. It has been over-rated and over-estimated. It is a very difficult place to get water in and then again, as I have said before, the country is too fresh. One of the best features I see in it is that the cattle live to a great age, especially the cows. The prospects of it as a cattle or fattening country don't compare at all favourably with Queensland or the north of Adelaide. The rents are much cheaper but it pays people to pay five times as much for Queensland country as for the Territory, as 1,000 miles in Queensland would maintain more cattle than an average of 5,000 miles in the Territory. Once they get fat in Queensland, their condition is solid and they carry it. I meet people frequently who ask me about the Territory and if they should go there and my advice to them is to go and look and be very careful; but if they want to get on, to make into Queensland. The whole thing is to do with the sourness of the country and a good deal of poisoned bush which people don't seem to hear about."

The decade from 1910 opened with signs of positive change in the Northern Territory, when the Commonwealth government took control of the Territory and began to install dips and bores on long-neglected stock routes, but Sid remained unimpressed with its prospects. The lack of water concerned him. His stations in western Queensland were only about 10 miles from the border of the Territory, but once over the border the artesian basin ceased and one could ride hundreds of miles without seeing a waterhole or creek. "These lands have been opened for thirty years and they are likely to remain open for another half a century. The federal government has a difficult problem to solve in the Northern Territory," Sid said, "and while I have my own opinion on the subject, I will leave you to guess what it is."

Less than two years later Sid had a somewhat brighter outlook about the Territory, when a proposed rail line was contemplated to link Sydney to Port Darwin. It was suggested that the line would run from Bourke to Hungerford, then Tobermory, Windorah, Boulia, Urandangie, Camooweal and on to Pine Creek in the Territory.

"This would place the settlers in the Northern Territory in the position of having a railway direct to the greatest market in Australia — Sydney. Instead of taking many months to get stock to market, they could be sent in a few days. It would be the greatest way to encourage settlement in the Territory.

"There is no use in Labor or Liberal governments thinking of making the Territory an agricultural country; nature has not designed it for agriculture but it could be the great cattle land of Australia and if settlement is given a chance by having a railway to market, the Territory could supply Sydney and Melbourne and other big cities with all the beef they wanted and millions of fat sheep. The railway would pay for itself and be a permanent asset and any other attempts to settle the Territory would only mean great waste of money. The federal government should also let the land in large areas (it requires much capital) on long, secure tenure, at reasonable rents and with the provision in each lease that the lessee must fence the land and conserve water and stock it within a reasonable period. It is a mistake to let men hold it who will not improve it. With plenty of water and the railway, stock losses would be enormously reduced, especially in drought, when owners had no get-out through drought and often lost half or more of their stock."

When nothing came of the railway, Sid started to agitate himself about one that would link Oodnadatta and Pine Creek, thereby making the Adelaide–Darwin link complete. In 1919 he and his partner Joseph Timms, an experienced rail contractor, had put forward to the Commonwealth government an £8 million proposal to construct the line. Nothing came of that either.

At the time, Sid was still a director of Bovril Australian Estates, which owned Victoria River Downs. He was concerned at the manner in which the Vestey organisation was gumming up the works. During the First World War, Vesteys undertook to build a packing plant at Darwin, one that the Labor government had originally proposed to build itself. It was started in 1914, but the war and scarcity of materials forced the cost from £250,000 to just on £1 million. The plant killed 19,000 the year it opened in 1917, 29,000 in 1918 and 22,000 in 1919 (mostly its own stock) and closed in 1920. It re-opened in 1921 for a short kill only. The effect was profound. It resulted in a crushing loss of confidence in the eyes of potential investors in the Northern Territory, impeding further large-scale capital development in the north.

When Vesteys closed the packing plant, the company blamed "labour indiscipline" and the poor quality of the local cattle, but there was a strong theory that Vesteys became concerned that Australian beef would prove a powerful competitor in Britain for Vesteys' much more profitable South American operations, especially as the Vesteys were far-sighted enough to realise that some form of Empire preference was inevitable. Had they turned down the offer from the Commonwealth government to build the plant at Darwin, there could have been the risk that someone else would have accepted or that a future Labor government may have resurrected the idea of a state-owned plant. So, by being prepared to invest £1 million to build a packing plant and then not run it, the Vesteys stopped Australian beef from competing with South American and at the same time ensured that no one else would compete with them in Australia.

The matter assumed the proportion of a full-scale scandal when the Northern Territory Workers Union suspected, and then proved, that the Northern Territory Administrator, Dr Gilruth, and one of his good friends, John Carey, were working in cahoots with Vesteys. Carey was a government official who held several top posts and had also managed to wangle the job of chief clerk at the Vestey packing plant. The Union complained to Gilruth that this involved a conflict of interests. Gilruth refused to accept the complaint or to forward it to Canberra. Proof came in a letter from John Carey in the Vesteys' office to the London Vesteys' office, stating that the lease of a large pastoral holding with hundreds of thousands of head of cattle on it would expire shortly and that the Administrator (Dr Gilruth) could refuse renewal and grant it to the Vesteys, but it would be necessary to pay him £20,000 to use as graft for officials and Parliament for this purpose.

When the letter found its way into the hands of the Union, all hell broke loose. It called a meeting of the Darwin Council (whose chairman, by coincidence, was John Carey). At a stormy and almost violent meeting, the Council carried a vote of no confidence in Carey, demanding that he be deposed as Government Secretary, the Territory's judge and the official accountant, and hurled out of Council to boot. It also called for Gilruth to be thrown out as Administrator and proposed that until a new person was appointed, the Territory would be run by the Council. Local rage dictated that these two men be compelled to leave Darwin by the next steamer.

The entire grievance was telegraphed to the Prime Minister, W. M. Hughes; a general strike was declared; and the meatworkers marched angrily on the Vestey packing plant. The Commonwealth government ordered HMAS *Melbourne* at full speed to Darwin to maintain order. Gilruth was smuggled on board in an atmosphere of hostility (the navy crew was sympathetic with the Darwin workers) and a Burns Philp steamer carted off Carey. A Royal Commission was ordered, and it found that the Darwin workers had behaved unconstitutionally but that, under the circumstances, it was difficult to blame them.

While there were those who disliked, could not tolerate or even hated Sid, there were many who hated the Vesteys more. If Kidman stank, the Vesteys stank more. Even Sid's detractors conceded two points: at least he was an Australian and the others were conniving Poms; and at least he'd got his knighthood fair and square, and not bought it for £20,000, as William Vestey had in 1919 when Lloyd George was disposed to selling peerages.

From 1922 to 1930 Sid noted that the Vesteys concentrated on live exports to Singapore and Manila and disposed of 46,000 head in this way. But it was a shaky market, which closed off yet again in 1930 when the Philippines invoked the redwater fever excuse to impose another embargo. In the meantime, Sid concentrated on the Alice Springs area, with Bond Springs, Hamilton Downs, Stirling and Huckitta, Crown Point and Owen Springs working as part of his Central Australia–South Australia chain, which was only ever an auxiliary chain to his main north–south chain.

By the early 1930s there was much concern about the undeveloped state of the Northern Territory's pastoral lands. The response of the Lyons government was to establish a review committee. Outlining its aim, the Minister for the Interior, Archdale Parkhill, said in 1932, "Efforts at present being made to develop the cattle industry are not as great as they should be. It is extremely important that there should be an immediate investigation into the terms under which the leases are held, the number of cattle on the properties and in respect to improvements generally. It seems imperative that energetic steps be taken to stimulate activity on the part of those who are at present doing nothing and to give assistance to those who are striving to make a success of the land."

The Northern Territory Pastoral Leases Investigation Committee was set up in 1933 and headed by the Northern Territory Surveyor-General. It inspected virtually every pastoral holding and was painstaking in its approach. Its report to the Commonwealth government in 1935 (known as the Payne–Fletcher Report) saw almost every landholder — big and small — take a fair amount of flak. It stated that the entire north-western section of the Territory was in large holdings controlled by three companies: Northern Agency Ltd (the Vesteys), Bovril Australian Estates Ltd, and Connor, Doherty and Durack Ltd. All held long leases at low rents without improvement or development conditions and enjoyed generous concessions by way of cheap freight and subsidies for structural improvements. The report suggested that these companies held properties too large to be developed to their full capacity under one control and management. It advocated breaking them up into more moderate-sized holdings.

The Kidman interests also came under attack. Where Crown Point was concerned, the Committee found, "At the time of the committee's visit the buildings were in the charge of an old-aged pensioner, the overseer being with the cattle on one of the outstations. The run has been unstocked since the 1928–30 drought. The holding appears to be used as a depot. When the Committee visited in September 1933, the conditions of ten of the eleven leases were not being complied with. Structural improvements away from the homestead were generally out of repair. A number of wells have been provided but not sufficient to cover the whole run. Many of the existing wells at the time of the Committee's visit were out of commission. A letter to the committee from the Crown Pastoral Co. states that 'owing to severe drought conditions Crown Point has carried no stock for about seven years and that it is only in the last year that the company has been able to carry any stock there'."

In relation to Bond Springs, the Committee found, "No fencing has been erected, not even a horse paddock. The position is that the lessee is required to carry on horse breeding over 1,393 square miles of the 1,805 square mile holding and we draw attention to the fact that the horses on the run are just the working plant and barely sufficient at that. There is neither fencing nor horse breeding. Wells, buildings, overshot dam and camp yard built by previous owner. Three white men, eight abos, four lubras. The boys are paid 14 shillings a week and rations, the lubras supplied with rations and clothing and one half-caste boy is employed at £1 a week and rations. Manager's opinion that the run will carry 5,000 head cattle in a normal year."

Of Huckitta, the Committee said, "The outbuildings are of primitive construction and just about habitable. Practically no improvements have been carried out until recently when a few yards were erected and not even a horse paddock has been supplied, the working horses today being hobbled in the same manner as followed by the pioneer settlers in the 1880s. Goods are carted from Alice Springs 180 miles away at a cost of £7.10.0 by camel team and £9.10.0 by motor lorry and we express the opinion that every assistance should be given to lessees in this connection and liberal freight conditions granted, particularly in relation to material required for the carrying out of improvements required and transporting of bulls and horses needed for improvements of herds. It is a poor effort for an area of this size and while the drought years have had a retarding influence, lack of development and a more or less 'don't care' kind of management have been contributing factors."

On Stirling, the Committee reported, "The run is badly watered naturally and there are only three stock wells not including a government well known as Merino which, though provided originally for the use of travelling stock, has been taken possession of by the lessee for station purposes as it is the best source of water on the place. In addition to illegal use, the lessee makes a charge to drovers of travelling stock of one penny per head per drink. During occupation since 1928 there is no evidence of expenditure on improvements and conditions are as primitive as the day that the first lessee arrived."

The Committee cited Owen Springs as being "another example of a fair-sized holding being run without fencing. Not even a horse paddock. There is still a large area unstocked as a result of insufficient water. An indifferent attempt has been made to augment the supply and the few wells that exist are of practically no value for stock purposes. While the lessees have not been in possession for long and the cattle market has not been buoyant they have done nothing by way of improvements. The trouble with the larger holdings in this country, and this is a case in point, is that the lessees appear to be satisfied with making what they can out of the country served by natural water instead of taking the risk of developing the holding and stocking the greater part of it. The run has been occupied by Hayes and Son for a great number of years and little progress made by way of improvements over that period."

384

The most damning remarks against Sid and his management are those concerning Crown Point and Bond Springs, which he had held for twenty-three years by the time the investigation took place. Sid had owned Owen Springs for only three years and Huckitta and Stirling for only five years, so much of the criticism directed at Sid should have been directed equally at the former owners, who either couldn't or wouldn't improve them.

In any event, the report showed Vesteys as the biggest overall defaulters in the Territory, and Sid holding that title in the Alice Springs area. Every holding, from those owned by the big to the battlers, was given some amount of stick, with a greater emphasis, perhaps, on Kidman because of his non-battler status and presumed capacity to pay for improvements. The investigation couldn't have taken place at a worse time — so soon after the 1928–30 drought in the Territory and coincidental with the Depression. At the time of the inquiry, 194,614 square miles of the Territory (523,620 square miles in total) were held under pastoral lease by 130 leaseholders, of whom Sid was but one. (The area held under Aboriginal reserve was 67,124 square miles.)

The picture painted by the report would suggest almost total inactivity on Sid's part in the Territory in those years, but Walter Kidman's memoirs give some indication of how the Kidmans were operating and, to some extent, at least where Huckitta Station is concerned, show that the Investigation Committee's assessment of a "don't care" management attitude was incorrect — or else that Walter continually wore rose-coloured glasses. He said, "In 1929, cattle were selling cheaply in the Kimberleys so we decided to overland 1,000 bullocks from Yeeda, 25 miles out from Derby, to Alice Springs where the railway line had just been completed. Sam Coussens was the drover and he was eight months on the road with them, travelling via Victoria River Downs, Newcastle Waters to Alice Springs. They were railed down to Oodnadatta and sent out to Macumba where the season was good and they were all fattened the following year.

"After Dad bought Huckitta from Charlie Dubois, I visited the property many times. Bill Madrill was the manager. He was there before Dad took over the place and had come from Tanbar in southwest Queensland. He was a splendid manager; had no white men on the place — only blacks — and he had an excellent team.

"I considered the Huckitta horse plant to be one of the best I had ever seen; all the stock horses were mostly thoroughbred and everyone was beautifully mounted. Bill got on well with all the blacks; one old fellow known as Witchetty Jack found twenty big witchetty grubs for me at one time. I'd never had them before. We cooked them over the coals. They were delicious — just like tasting toasted cheese.

Another blackfellow by the name of Jacky lived with his gin on one of the sand wells of the Plenty. They had a piccaninny every year. He said to me and Madrill, 'I make 'em, you work 'em.'

"The first time I went to Huckitta, Alf Draper drove me out. We went via Loves Creek over the Haartz Range and down to the Plenty which was a wide, sandy creek and we had trouble crossing it. There had only been one vehicle over it before and that was Wallis Fogarty's lorry with a load of rations. We had to turn off to the Huckitta homestead at Mount Saintall — Madrill had marked trees about 30 miles from there to the homestead. It was rough travelling but eventually we made it.

"When the railway line to Alice Springs was completed, I bought eighty draught mares from the Commonwealth government and sent them to Huckitta. I also sent two Percheron stallions there with the result that most of the progeny were greys. They made splendid pack horses and bronco horses. Every two years I used to send eighty to a hundred across to Dajarrah and then rail them to Hughenden where they were sold by Winchcombe Carson. The Italians were keen buyers and used to attend the sales and would give almost twice as much for a grey horse compared with a bay or brown.

"The Picton Range runs right through Huckitta. There are many springs emanating from it and a strange thing was that all the springs on the north side of the range had fish in them but those on the south side had none at all. Also the Plenty River ran right through Huckitta and when we were first there, they put down scoop holes in the Plenty for the cattle to water. It was a bad process as it meant they had to keep scooping them out every day or so, so I suggested to Madrill to sink about eight or ten sand wells along the Plenty that were equipped with a windmill; the water was then pumped out to a supply tank and troughs on the bank. This proved to be much more satisfactory."

As to how the local Territorians in the Alice Springs area assessed Sid, Ted Hayes of Undoolya Station said in 1984, when the Hayes family celebrated its centenary in the area, "My grandparents, William and Mary Hayes, came here from northern South Australia in 1884, and soon after that took up country at Deepwell (100 square miles), and after that, Mount Burrell (which is now Mary Vale and was then 2,000 square miles). It was bought from Sir Thomas Elder. They bought Owen Springs and Undoolya in the same year — 1907. Owen Springs was attached to Undoolya and they were run as one area. It was in excess of 2,000 square miles.

"My grandmother, Mary, and Kidman's wife, Isabel, were good friends. They'd grown up as young girls together at Kapunda. In 1930 Owen Springs was resold to Kidman, who had held it many years earlier.

"With the exception of Bond Springs and Crown Point, Kidman never held properties for any great length of time in the Territory. He was not considered a man who considered his land. His policy seemed to be to breed cattle cheap, and let them die cheap on properties in drought times, instead of putting down extra water or moving them to agistment. He didn't go in for any big expense programs here to keep them alive in drought.

"Generally speaking, from the early stages here about the turn of the century, when families bought up holdings that big pastoral companies weren't able to run as a viable proposition (e.g. Sir Thomas Elder), they were successful because they worked as a family unit, were not extravagant, and maintained improvements and added to them. Kidman stood out as a man who was not part of that pattern in this area and I do emphasise that I am talking about the Alice Springs area.

"When he bought properties in the Alice Springs area he allowed the existing improvements to deteriorate, mainly yards.

"But he knew where every drover of his was camped every night, he knew the stock routes, he knew his men, he knew how long it would take to get from A to B, he knew his trucking points at Farina and Marree and he'd truck one mob after another, feeding fat cattle into the Adelaide market every week. I'd give him full marks for organisation. To be able to do that today — more than fifty years later — a mob of cattle into Adelaide every week is something you'd have a job to do even with more modern technology and transport. Generally speaking, people did admire him and at his peak he was certainly a multimillionaire. He may not have had a lot of spending money, as so much was tied up in properties. His empire was at its peak around the drought times of the late 1920s."

What Ted Hayes had to say about family ownership in the area has been shown to be true, certainly in his own family's case. When the pioneering Hayes family clocked up a century in 1984, Owen Springs was once again under its wing and was one of the better places in the district, with many modern improvements. It should also be noted that, when Sid bought it from them in 1930, the family had held it for twenty-three years doing little or nothing in the way of improvements, and it was Sid, in 1933 when the pastoral investigation was taking place, who took the flak that otherwise would have been directed at the Hayes family had it still been in their hands.

For all of its in-depth investigations and long list of recommendations, nothing ever came of the Payne–Fletcher Report. In 1937, when it was published, the then Minister for the Interior, John "Black Jack" McEwen, said he was committed to the Report's proposals and promised to draw up a five-year plan for road and rail development and review all leases with a view to resuming those where the occupier's performance had not been in the best interest of the area. But the Second World War broke out before this could be done. It meant a new order of priorities, McEwen's transfer to the Defence Department, and the total abandonment of the Payne–Fletcher proposals.

Overall, Sid's late entry into the Territory again in 1927, 1928 and 1930 brought him little joy and certainly not the money or excitement that his first purchase there, Owen Springs in 1896, had. It brought him severe criticism and, later, legal worries, as he was pressed for both late payment or non-payment of rents on Stirling and Huckitta. For as long as he lived, the Territory frustrated Sid, and he continually played the game of "iffies" about it. What *if* Vesteys had kept the meatworks open, which would have drawn associated industry to Darwin? What *if* the rail from Bourke to Pine Creek had gone through? What *if* they'd allowed him and Timms to run up the line through the centre? The Territory to him was as a bare wall to Gulley Jimson — suitably geared for a magnificent picture. It frustrated Kidman that he couldn't paint the picture. And he did not live long enough to see anyone else do it either.

23
The Final Muster

I N JULY 1932 Sid's daughter-in-law, Muriel, produced a second daughter, Barbara, and Sid celebrated with a half-glass of champagne. No boy to bear the name Kidman this time around either; still, he and Bel had had to wait fifteen years before Walter was born. Muriel was a likeable young woman and, by then confident of her position in the family, spoke at length to Lady Kidman about the treatment that was being dished out within the company by Sid Reid to Walter. "He treats Walter just as an office boy," she said. Bel, who doted on her only son, raised the matter with her husband, who dismissed it as a storm in a teacup. Their son-in-law Sid Reid was twelve years senior to Walter, and a tough, able businessman. Walter, on the other hand, had served some sort of bush apprenticeship, but he still had a fair bit to learn in the office. He sought to allay Bel's worries, yet Muriel persisted with reports to Bel of Walter's unhappiness because of Sid Reid's attitude.

Sid Reid had his hands full at the time, not only as the company's general manager but also as the organiser of the big rodeo party being put on in Adelaide in September to mark Sid's seventy-fifth birthday. Reid spared no effort to turn on a big party for a big man. It moved Sid to tears — certainly the march past, or ride past, of his managers and stockmen, with Archie McLean dipping the flag in salute. And it moved Adelaide to astonishment — the crowds, the chaos and the casualties. It made headlines not only in Australian papers but also in papers overseas — in England, Canada and the United States, where Kidman was known as either the Cattle King or the King of the Bushmen.

As the year drew to a close, there were signs of ructions in western New South Wales to make more land available to more people by lopping off areas from big holdings and throwing them open for closer settlement. This didn't please Sid at all. By the mid-thirties he owned or partly owned Yandama, Mount Poole, and his western New South Wales showplace, Corona, (all adjoining the South Australian border) and Forder's Selection, strategically placed near the Cockburn railyards for his trucking operations. North of Broken Hill he controlled 15,000 square miles of country in Wonnaminta, Sturt's Meadows, Bootra, Morden, Caryapundy, Olive

Downs, Gnalta, Salisbury Downs, Yantara and Purnanga. On the Darling, Weinteriga and Netley were also his. Sid didn't worry about the proposed land divisions immediately. He was by then well tuned in to the working of bureaucrats. In Canberra, they were investigating all the pastoral leases in the Northern Territory; all these things took time, and often nothing came of them. A similar inquiry could well be held into western New South Wales. Well, Sid thought, such an inquiry would only be a waste of time and money. Blind Freddie could see that carving up the derelict country of western New South Wales wasn't going to solve any problems and would only create new ones.

Sid and Bel removed themselves from the various pressures in 1933 by taking another trip overseas. It was Sid's ninth trip. Bel would have liked to have gone to South America but Sid found no appeal in the idea, and it was back to Mother England, see their daughter Gertie and catch up with family and friends. They had travelled the British Isles, seen most other European and Mediterranean countries, visited Africa and Egypt, India, the United States and Canada, New Zealand, and in 1926 the East, when they went to Java and the Malay States. The latter had been something of a business trip for Sid, as he had looked into the possibilities of expanding cattle exports to the East, but he came home disappointed. There was not a particularly big market, he thought. The natives were not big meat-eaters and the difficulties of shipping outweighed any gain. He had been shipping 200 or 300 cattle a month from Derby to Batavia and Singapore, but it cost £1 a head to have them killed in Singapore. Bigger shipments of 500 would have made it a better proposition. Things in the far north of Australia hadn't improved since, Sid reflected. Selling cattle from the north on favourable terms was a tough proposition: the enormous distances that had to be covered, the costs of handling big herds and the great difficulties of transporting them to market ate up a good deal of money. Even when cattle were killed at Wyndham they yielded only £2 to £4. It was all very well for people to talk about increased settlement of our great open spaces, but those great open spaces demanded that men who went there should have capital, and plenty of it. No settlers without means, or even with moderate means, could hope to handle cattle in the far north and north-west or to open up those vast spaces, as it was so glibly put.

Sid and Bel put the home-based worries behind them and headed

OPPOSITE:
A quiet moment in the garden at Eringa, Unley Park. (Stockman's Hall of Fame)

for England. Sid put his foot down this time where gadding about to theatres was concerned. Bel could go with others but, for him, it was just a waste. Not even expensive tickets in a prominent box could help him much at this stage; he was so deaf he couldn't hear what was going on, and there was no point in paying money just to go to sleep, which he could do with consummate ease. There was more pleasure in yarning with friends — or yelling at them and having them yell at him — in the comfort of their homes or his daughter Gertie's.

They returned in 1934, with what Sid decribed as their "usual load of junk". It was becoming hard to know what to buy the children: Sid and Bel had set them up in their own homes and bought them cars, and also refrigerators and washing machines at a time when they were extremely rare in Australia. Bel bought increasingly for the grandchildren. And another joined their ranks in June 1934, when Muriel's third child, another daughter, Anne, was born. Sid was so disappointed on this occasion that he drank no champagne at all. According to family sources, he sat in a corner and brooded.

Sid was, by then, worried about how things stood in western New South Wales. The Minister for Lands in the Stevens government, Mr E. A. Buttenshaw, had come up with a compromise solution to try to please the divergent interests of both large and small landholders. The new Act of 1934 gave the large holders the option of complying with its terms or continuing in full occupation until the expiry of their leases, most of which were due to terminate about 1946. This date would be put forward by twenty-five years if they chose to surrender a quarter of their areas immediately, a further one-eighth in 1943, and a final eighth in 1948. In this way, considerable areas would be made available for additions to uneconomic small holdings and the accommodation of some new lessees on home maintenance areas. The Act also replaced the Western Lands Board with a Western Lands Commission under a single commissioner, and local land boards were set up under the Commission to decide allocations on the merits of applicants.

The new concept of a home maintenance area was one that would run a minimum of 5,000 sheep in accessible locations, and up to a maximum of 10,000 in remote parts of the division. About 78 per cent of the large holders of the western division accepted the terms, but west of the Darling the average was lower, as Sid baulked at the entire business and steadfastly refused to have a thing to do with it. It did not enhance his reputation west of the Darling, and the writing was on the wall where his empire there was concerned. By refusing the terms, Sid could control his undiminished areas for a limited period; hacked-up holdings were of no use to the chain system enterprise that he had so carefully built up. A chain with big gaps in it would no longer work for him.

Sid Reid and company secretary H. J. Bird made no attempt to get him to change his mind. He was adamant about the matter, claiming that the land carve-up would be disaster, one that would probably have to be reversed in due time. So the Kidman decision stood firm. Oh, the absolute stupidity of it all — impossible decisions made by politicians and public servants with their backsides parked at desks in Sydney, who did not understand the nature of the land and how that marginal country could be best used. In 1934, at the age of 77, Sid contented himself by going to the races and by regularly attending the Adelaide cattle sales.

Charles Smith, who worked for him at the time, said, "He'd slowed up a lot, which was consistent with his age, but he was not prematurely senile. I'd sit with him at the cattle sales at Dry Creek, Adelaide, and he was alert to everything about him and he used to enjoy long discussions with 'Butch' Bone, the Elder Smith auctioneer."

Jenkin Propsting, who joined the firm of Coles Bros in 1924, said, "We sold half of his cattle consignment in Adelaide with Bennett and Fisher selling the other half. S.K. had cattle on the market every week, between 400 and 600, and it would be most unusual for him to pass the cattle [that is, not sell them] should the market be depressed, and sell them the following week when the numbers yarded may have been considerably less. Occasionally it did happen and instead of getting a lower price he would wait a week and get a higher price and he was able to do this because he owned country alongside the trucking yards at Dry Creek. There were haystacks in the paddock so if he wanted to keep a few hundred for a week he could do so. But if Vesteys or Angliss wanted more bullocks and were short they could approach him privately and buy. It didn't happen often. He was a good seller. He didn't um and ah for a price. He'd take the going values. On a good market he was well known for yelling out, 'Knock 'em down,' when he was satisfied at the prices cattle had fetched and had no intention of hanging out for higher prices."

When he wasn't yarning at the cattle sales, Sid, the inveterate talker, was yarning at home, where the boys were always made welcome for a feed — the Coles boys, Ross and Charlie, Hugh Davis of Bennett and Fisher, the horse exporters, Harry Peck of Melbourne, and members of the Angliss family. Any station manager was always asked "up home", especially the younger ones taking over from his senior men, who were gradually retiring. Sid wanted to be sure that they knew the pastoral ropes and asked incessant questions of them, doling out advice or guidance if needed. Whether they were there for

---

OVERLEAF:
Hats off to Sir Sidney after a race win in Adelaide. (The Kidman family)

lunch or dinner, Sid sat at his customary place around the grand dining table — with a couple of big patches worn out of it where he had used a fly swatter with relentless energy. Afterwards, he would always feel the need of a good doze. "In that respect," he would tell people, "I am like a blackfella. They always have a camp straight away after a big feed."

Those closest to him were able to chide him about his love of sleep and his ability to nap at the drop of a hat. Senior managers reminded him he'd never been keen to remove himself from between the blankets or the swag before dawn as they had in the bush. His rejoinder had always been: "You set out well before sunrise and I'll make my own time later and still beat you to where we are going." Fellows such as Harry Peck mischievously tested his post-prandial dozes with comments such as: "What a record price for fat bullocks in Melbourne the other day..." Instantly Sid shook himself awake wanting to know the details, as laughter abounded. If a group of men was there for lunch, Bel insisted he be allowed to have his afternoon sleep in peace while she invited them to a game of croquet. It was more of a challenge. She was an excellent player. If a group was there in the evening, they'd yarn among themselves until Sid awoke, refreshed, often as late as 11 pm, and felt like yarning on into the wee small hours. He was not averse to a whisky or two to liven him up, or an occasional cigarette, and "the boys" were allowed a most liberal hand at the grog cabinet, yet no one abused the hospitality. A frequent visitor at the time was Ion Idriess who was writing up Kidman's life story. Muriel Kidman recalled, "Because of deafness he found it hard to hear what Idriess said. Walter sat on the chair and prompted his father. It was an awful book and everyone said later, 'What a pity someone else didn't do a book while Walter was still alive.'"

The year 1935 rolled around; Joan Hopkins (née Reid), Sid and Bel's oldest grandchild, thinks that they did make yet another overseas trip. If so, there are no details of it, and it would have taken place early in the year. If Sid and Bel did go away again it would have been their tenth trip overseas. Certainly there was not much point in going to England again to see Gertie and her husband, Captain Nelson Clover, who had made plans to take extended leave in Australia. They returned to Australia with their two younger children, Robin and Pamela, in time for Sid's seventy-eighth birthday on May 9. Indeed, there was a larger occasion to celebrate as well.

On 30 June 1935, Sid and Bel notched up fifty years in double harness. The day in question was a Sunday and it called for a big family reunion. Their eldest daughter, Gertie, was there with her husband, Nelson, and two of their three children; their eldest daughter, Patricia, had been married in England in April and, either still honeymooning or house-hunting, did not come to Adelaide for the occasion. Sid and Bel's second daughter, Elma, was there with her husband, Sid Reid, and their children, Joan, Esme, Burns and Reg. Their youngest daughter, Edna, was there with her husband, Sid Ayers, and their younger son, John. Their elder son, Henry, had died in 1927. And Walter was there with Muriel and their three little girls, Isabel, Barbara and Anne. It was a grand family occasion with everyone putting their best foot forward to make it as happy as possible for the old couple. But there were family undercurrents — one of the reasons for Elma urging Gertie to make a trip back to Australia and for Gertie coming.

Sid and Bel were mindful mainly of each other on the day and the road they had travelled together from the times of the late 1870s, when Sid had first passed through Kapunda and made her acquaintance. There had been so much change since then. There had been sadness with the deaths of their two infant children Norman and Edith. There had been jubilation when Walter finally arrived. There had been drought, the Great War, more drought and drought again. There had been personal anxiety over Walter's illness. Yet there had been good times as well. The girls had married well and happily (perhaps not quite so happily in Edna's case). And, despite the great criticisms often directed at Sid, he had endured them, survived them, and his generous loyalty in the First World War had been rewarded with a knighthood. Bel was full of admiration that Sid had achieved so much from such a humble, hard-working start, and Sid believed that much of the good result was owed to Bel's support and encouragement. Bel was certainly a genuine enough person, not interested in taking all he had to offer and sitting back with a life of luxury in the city — she'd made buggy trip after buggy trip in the outback, knocking up her blooming vast crocheted lace bedspreads. She'd roughed it with him, taking the bad with the good. She knew his business and the manner of men who worked for him, and their strengths and weaknesses; she knew how to roll a swag for the boys and get a meal together at a moment's notice, work a garden or vege patch with the best of them, and stand her dig on a street corner selling buttons to aid returned soldiers. She worked for hospitals, churches and many other causes. There was nothing faint hearted about the girl he had married.

When they clocked up their golden wedding anniversary, Sid and Bel Kidman had every reason to praise God as they sat in the

---

OVERLEAF:
Walter and Muriel Kidman's daughters, Barbara, Anne and Isabel. (Anne Abel Smith)

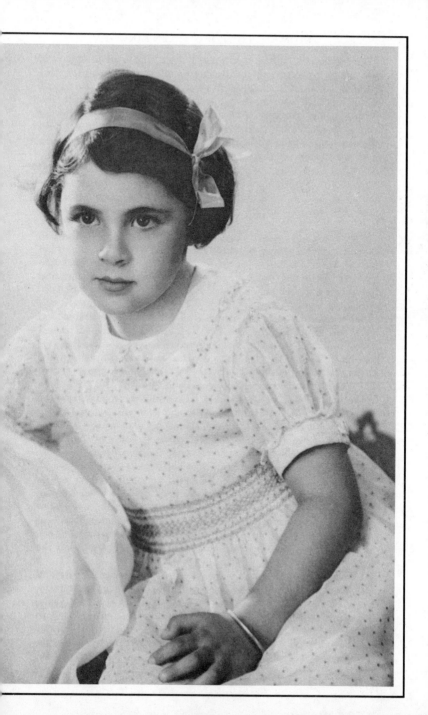

Congregational Church on Sunday, 30 June. The full complement of the family gathered later in the day to celebrate at Eringa, Unley Park, and Sid and Bel indulged in quiet, firm hand clasps as kind and warm speeches were made in their honour. Formalities over, the Kidmans, just like any other family, fell to discussing the growing young grandchildren, the news of the day, both in Australia and on the other side of the world where King George V and Queen Mary had just celebrated their silver jubilee on the throne. While the women replenished their tea cups and gathered around to talk, Sid retreated into the garden with the men to discuss things that really mattered, such as stock dealing, and to size up his young grandsons and assess their capability.

At the cattle sales late in August Sid didn't wait to finish a talk to members of the Master Butchers Association who'd bailed him up. His car was not at hand, nor his driver, who was to call and pick him up at an appointed time. He had one of the boys run him home and he reported to Bel that he "was crook". Bel admonished him for overdoing things and wanted to call the doctor immediately. Sid thought some tea and a lie-down might solve the problem and refused to let her. When Sid was no better the following day, the doctor was called and the Cattle King was confined to his cot. He was there for four days. . . reduced, quiet, reflecting and not complaining, with Bel at his side when he slipped away on 1 September 1935.

Walter remained at home to comfort his mother and the women in the family, while Sid Reid and H. J. Bird attended to matters at the office. The whole world, it seemed to the Kidmans, wanted to say how sorry it was that Sid had gone. He was not gone for the moment, but was borne gently in an expensive but simple coffin into the main room at Eringa where, as the family said, "he lay in state".

The telephone and the front door bell did not stop ringing and, within a day, almost 300 official wreaths were delivered, as well as several hundred telegrams of condolence. Composed, Bel Kidman read every message of sympathy and every card on every wreath but not without a trace of bitterness. Not, it must be said, where most were concerned, but there were those among them who had been hurtful or a hindrance to Sidney, yet sent their condolences just the same because it was the done thing.

There were visitors non-stop at Eringa, with parked cars and chauffeurs pulled up outside. The chauffeurs agreed it was a grim day. Many of them had been calling on and off at the house for years, depositing people at parties. They could always rely on the old boy to emerge during the night and either loll on a car or sit in the gutter and have a good talk about the latest in motor vehicles; he always saw that a spot of tucker found its way out to them, too. It was funny, they said, that if the boot had been on the other foot and they had been giving the parties, they would have been inside enjoying them to the hilt and not giving a care about the chauffeurs outside. But old Kidman genuinely seemed to enjoy giving the inside action a wide berth and hanging around with them, and he wasn't shy about asking questions about fuel consumption and mileages or new models, or telling them about his car exploits and breakdowns in the outback. The chauffeurs watched as an endless trail of people made their way to the house, many without cars, and seemingly people of no account really: women who brought wicker baskets of scones, old men who looked a little worse for wear, young children who brought fresh-cut flowers. For every kind turn Sid had done, there was someone remembering.

His offices in Currie Street resembled a madhouse, as telegrams by the hundred were delivered there by young boys on bicycles wearing suitably solemn faces. The phones did not stop ringing as the Australian press, business colleagues and the world press clamoured for details of Sid's death, some assessment of his life, wealth, holdings and funeral arrangements. Sid Reid and H. J. Bird had their work cut out answering everybody and preparing statements, but Reid saw that all of that was shoved aside until each manager on every station had been notified.

The ultimate sadness was in the bush, where managers' wives took messages for husbands who were out on the run. A sense of total shock rippled throughout the outback. It was unrealistic to think that Sidney Kidman would live forever, but he had not been sick; it was all so sudden, and what would happen to the empire?

The nation's "singing wires" kept the chorus going: "Cattle King dead." Even so, a good number of his men did not know of his death until after his funeral. Where word reached his stations and where there were contingents of Aborigines, particularly in south-western Queensland, there were strange calls of "*aiyeee...*", and the blacks retreated from around the homesteads to a nearby creek to wail and mourn. The "old pfella King of All Adelaide" was dead. He had been, they said, "a good pfella to plenty blackfella".

He had been a good pfella to plenty white fella as well, and in station kitchens, quarters and stock camps, Kidman's bush brotherhood wondered as they heard of his death and funeral arrangements whether it mightn't have been better, more honourable or more fitting for him to have been buried in his swag in the outback somewhere. That would have been a true, good resting home, better than some sort of marble mausoleum in Mitcham in Adelaide. There were older men who shed a quiet tear at his death — the tears stoked to the surface by belts of black rum as they recalled the years and events and achievements — Jack Brooke, of Mundowdna, old Arthur

West, who'd cheated on Sid earlier and been given a second chance, Ernie Kempe, of Macumba, Archie McLean, of The Peake, and his most capable but drunken nephew, Claude Kidman (who had been educated at St Peter's College, Adelaide, before he took to the bush). The old order changeth, but what would the new bring?

While suitably mourning Sid, they could not help but wonder about their own futures. Ted Pratt was the pastoral inspector, a top man, but also a wily, cunning bastard. Pratt was never open and honest with people as Sid was. He made sneak inspections, said little on the spot, and returned to Adelaide and fired people. But there was Sid Reid to contend with as well. He didn't have the knowledge of the bush that Pratt had, but he was a tough, capable businessman who'd run the shop along Kidman lines, perhaps wanting to prune corners more and without the humour or affection that Sid had for his employees. And then there was Walter, a kindly man where employees were concerned, who'd fix you up with a ticket to the races the minute you hit Adelaide, but not a strong man and not sound like his father in bush judgement. In the bush, the Kidman complement of employees could only sit back and grieve and wait and see what happened. Certainly the end of a big pastoral era was over. Elsewhere in the bush, there were some people who accepted his death matter-of-factly and remarked, "Good riddance."

That he was gone was sufficient for the national and world press to trot out handsome headlines and fulsome eulogies, but as to what caused his death, his eldest grandchild, Joan Hopkins, who was 22 at the time, said, "He had only been sick for a matter of days. The doctors said that his heart was strong but that he had pernicious anaemia. There was no proper cure for it then and he used to be given big chunks of raw liver to eat." Whether he had a form of cancer is not known, but anaemia was not known to kill people. He had kept himself amazingly fit throughout his life but the one area he had ignored was a well-balanced diet; this was certainly true of his earlier days when fresh veges and fruit were luxuries and he was grateful for any sort of feed he could get, no matter how humble. Meat was on the menu — sometimes off and sometimes very off. So was damper made from flour thick with weevils...a bit of jam, tea — black as the ace of spades — wild duck eggs. He never complained and was always grateful for any sort of tucker that filled the gap at the end of a hard working day. It is hard to pinpoint why he died. "Natural causes" was the reason given to the family, and pernicious anaemia was believed to be a contributing factor.

OPPOSITE:
In later life Sir Sidney was still keen to put in time behind his desk.

From 1 September to 3 September he lay at home as hundreds called to pay their respects to the family and their last respects to him. In Adelaide, florists virtually ran out of flowers for tributes; oddly enough, no one thought to deliver a floral token made of salt-bush, coolabah or eucalypt.

His daughter-in-law, Muriel Kidman, said, "He lay in state at home. Everyone filed past. I felt too frightened to look — but did. He looked peaceful. Only men went to his funeral. Women didn't go in those days."

His funeral, on the afternoon of 3 September, provided an amazing tribute to his popularity. The cortege was a mile and a half long and Northgate Street, in which he'd lived, was lined with cars on both sides of the street, with many traffic police controlling the large crowds that gathered in silence along the route from his home to the Mitcham cemetery. Many wept openly. Five motor vehicles were laden with hundreds of wreaths, aside from those carried on the hearse. Because of the length of the cortege, cars continued to arrive at the cemetery after the burial service had begun.

The chief mourners were Walter Kidman, Charlie Kidman, Sid's only surviving brother, his sons-in-law, Captain Nelson Clover, Sid Reid and Sidney Ayers, and his grandsons, Robin Clover, John Ayers and Burns Reid. Pallbearers were Nelson Clover, Sid Reid, Sidney Ayers, H. J. Bird (the company secretary), Hugh Davis (managing director of Bennett and Fisher) and Ross Coles (managing director of Coles Bros). Other mourners included representatives from Parliament, charitable institutions, churches, banks, pastoral companies, sporting clubs, racing and hunt clubs, business houses, insurance firms and many outback stations.

The Rev. L. C. Bradbury, of Vardon Memorial Church, King's Park, who conducted the service, said Sir Sidney had been "a powerful and vigorous man who played the game bravely and strenuously and achieved great success which enabled him to give expression to another side of his nature. Apart from his public generosity there had been many quiet gifts of kindness which made him deeply loved.

"His gentle spirit was something to marvel at; he was a man of prayer and deeply religious. He fulfilled his years with honour. He was a great Australian, a noble character and one who had served his fellows well and walked humbly with God."

Newspapers were chock-a-block with tributes. The *New York Times* in a main article described him as "the Commonwealth's most picturesque millionaire", and the London *Times*, in a leader, as "owing much to good fortune but more to his power of seizing opportunity when it came his way and to his courage in facing bad fortune when he encountered it in the shape of drought. It may be

that there are no longer openings in Australia and the other Dominions for careers such as his."

His managers were sought for their tributes. Washington Foulis,
of Corona, said that the news of his death was received with
particular sadness by the older employees, six of whom had been with
him for more than thirty years and at least twenty men for more than
ten years. Few realised the extent of his generosity, Foulis said, and
there were many who were now well established on stations who owed
their success to Sir Sidney.

"He had several hundred employees who worshipped him and
there were few who had not received either help or advice from the
Cattle King. He spoke to his smallest station hand as he spoke to his
most important managers — never instructions, always requests.

"He was extremely proud of his men and every man had the
greatest affection for the boss," Foulis said. "He would talk as readily
to an old drover as to the Governor. In a big deal people had
wonderful confidence in the boss. His word went and whether he
won or lost in the deal, he never quibbled. Everyone who ever dealt
with him knows that."

Foulis added that in the Broken Hill area, where Sir Sidney was
widely known, pastoralists were deeply distressed by his death, and
one of the interesting tributes paid was that by Mr C. Sinclair Wood,
the secretary of the Pastoralists Association of West Darling. This is
interesting, considering Sid's refusal to co-operate with the Western
Lands Commission in carving up his holdings and also because many
people west of the Darling allegedly detested him. Mr Sinclair Wood
said, "There will be many sad hearts outback where the name
Kidman has grown to be synonymous with the greatest industry in
this country; a name around which has been woven the greatest
individual achievement that could be claimed by any man in the
industry.

"That he was of outstanding quality is evidenced by the manner
in which, in the earlier years, he controlled his vast activities
covering wide ranges of country in the four corners of the Continent
with such a limited and unpretentious administration organisation.

"That there was no fluke about his achievement is established by
the fact that his activities covered his whole lifetime. Many were the
confident assertions during the most difficult periods in the pastoral
history of Australia that 'this drought will break Kidman'. But he
always emerged triumphant and always displayed that courage
without which it would have been impossible to succeed. That his
confidence never wavered is proven by the fact that he never left the
industry even when he could have easily rested on his laurels.

"No man achieving this greatness could be without his critics and it has been asserted in different quarters that Sir Sidney held too much country. It must be remembered, however, that he paid for all his acres and there are many who today are living in comfort as a result of selling to Sir Sidney properties which would have ruined them had they remained in ownership."

People were insatiably curious to find out just how much Sid had left, and to whom. His will contained no surprises at all. It was a straightforward document. In it Sid said, "I have, during my lifetime, made suitable provision for my dear wife but as a further mark of the love and affection I bear her I bequeath during her life an annuity of £750 payable half yearly."

Each grandchild received £750, except the four Reid children, who received £500 as Sid had earlier transferred to each of them a block of land at Dry Creek. He left his brother Charlie an annuity of £200 payable half yearly. Each of his children living at his death received £1,000 and his three sons-in-law received £500 each. Muriel Kidman, his daughter-in-law, received £500, and £150 was left to Jean Kidman and May Kidman (his nieces, daughters of his brother George).

For their faithful service, H. J. Bird and Sid's rogue nephew, Claude Kidman, each received £500. His pastoral inspector, Ted Pratt, and Jim Wright (an accountant in his company and a relative of Bel's) received £250. To his managers, W. I. Foulis, of Corona, John Brooke, of Mundowdna, Ernie Kempe, of Macumba, John Horsley, the manager of Fulham Park Stud, Archie McLean, of The Peake, Harry McCullagh, of Diamantina Lakes, and Arthur West, the drover who once cheated him, he left £100.

The South Australian Branch of the Salvation Army headed the list of gifts to charities and institutions with £500; homes for incurables, hospitals, the Deaf and Blind Institution, the Australian Inland Mission, churches, organisations that supported ex-soldiers, orphanages and other homes for children were among the lengthy list of beneficiaries. Sid appointed Bel, Walter, Sid Reid and H. J. Bird as his trustees, giving them the power to make the decision about division of his residuary trust in the event of any dispute arising, and Sid left all of that to Bel, his daughters, Gertie, Elma and Edna, and his son, Walter, in five equal shares. He expressly wished his trustees to carry on the business either alone or in a suitable partnership with others, using the whole or such part of his residuary trust estate as they deemed fit. He finally asked that no mourning should be worn by members of his family after his death. "I appreciate and am grateful to all of them for the love and kindness that has been shown to me by them during my lifetime and I do not wish mourning to be worn by them."

His bequests to charities were noted in newspapers, along with the fact that he had looked after a number of his men (the amounts left to them were not disclosed publicly). But how much had he actually left, everyone wanted to know? If Tyson had left millions of pounds when he died just before the turn of the century, what was Kidman worth? It did amount to something of a shock when it was revealed that he had left a mere £301,689.5.11, with probate levied at £8,888.1.3.

His daughter-in-law, Muriel, said, "There was no doubt he was a millionaire. I thought he would have left £1 million. It certainly didn't seem to be as much as people expected, but trusts had been set up in advance for everyone in the family."

That Sid was no fool was obvious. Why leave millions as mulctings for the tax gatherers? After the introduction of federal income tax in the First World War, Sid was paying both federal and state income tax, as well as Commonwealth land tax. He was also obliged to pay federal and state death duties. Excellent business brains devised ways of leaving as little as possible for the tax men. It had taken years to resolve, but when the figure of £300,000 was revealed, it was thought by many people that the poor old Cattle King couldn't have been all that well off after all.

Bel took his death philosophically, according to granddaughter Joan Hopkins. And Muriel Kidman can recall the time, shortly after Sid's death, late in the afternoon when Bel and her daughters and Muriel were at the house, that Bel announced, "Well, my dear girls, it's time we all had a drink. Here's a glass of sherry."

"We all took a sip and nearly fell out of our chairs, spluttering. It was pure whisky," Muriel said.

Joan Hopkins can also recall Bel handing away those things of Sid's that other people might value or enjoy. They included a box of handsome cigars from his desk drawer. Bel gave them to the Italian gardener who looked after the grounds at Eringa. He was overcome with gratitude — until the first cigar exploded in his face! They were a box of trick cigars that Sid had acquired. "The gardener was terrified," Joan said, "he thought Mussolini was after him."

Bel batted on, endlessly opening fetes and throwing her weight behind charity work. Joan Hopkins said, "At the age of 75 in 1937, she decided she wanted to travel again. She wanted to go to South America; it was one place she had not been. I went with her. We left around Christmas 1937 and I returned a year later, but Grannie came home after war was declared. She stayed on in England for a while with Gertie. I've forgotten how many ships we hopped on and hopped off in that year. She was tireless. We saw it all. She was as lively as a cricket."

Perhaps it was just as well that Bel had her stamina for what was to follow, and that Sid had died when he did and did not live to see his family quarrel lengthily and bitterly and tear apart so quickly the empire it had taken him a lifetime to construct.

If Sid was aware of any lack of harmony within his family it is not disclosed in his will, in which he saw that everyone was treated as equally as possible. If he did have any inkling of discord between Walter and Sid Reid perhaps he sought to avert it by making them both trustees along with Bel and H. J. Bird.

Walter automatically became the head of the company, but it was something of a hollow title when Sid Reid and Bird called the shots and made the decisions. It meant that he was still being treated as an office boy. Walter had protested this treatment to his wife not long before his father died. Muriel had replied, "I'm not going to stand for that. So I went around and saw the old couple. 'It's not fair,' I said.

"Sir Sidney said, 'Oh, Sid has done so much for the company I don't know what to do,' and Lady Kidman said, 'Well, it's time for him to go. They [Sid and Elma] can have their share and that's that.' Sid Reid could be such a kindly man but he shouldn't have treated Walter so badly."

Whether Sid Kidman glossed over this episode or thought it would amount to nothing is not known, but after his death Walter continued to complain to his mother and Muriel of Sid Reid's high-handed manner. "Sid Reid's just got too big for his boots," Muriel told Lady Kidman.

Giving an outsider's account of the growing rift, Charles Smith, who worked for Sid from 1930 to 1934, said, "After old S.K. retired, Reid and Bird were the brains behind the outfit. Reid had no time for Walter. He considered him an imbecile. Reid was more often at S.K.'s side than Walter. We didn't see Walter in the bush a lot. Once around 1930 he went to Norley and Bulloo Downs and P. D. Edwards brought him out to our cattle camp. I was asked to provide a horse for him and recommended Old Caesar — slow, quiet and suitable for a man with only one good arm. Walter had to be helped into the saddle. Caesar decided he was strange and took off across the sandhills on the Caryapundy Plain. Walter only lasted 100 yards before he was tossed. He seemed to be a sort of zombie. He didn't mix much with the men; where the men were concerned, he was bit of a joke. I'm not saying he wasn't a nice cove — he married an able and capable woman but he wasn't a man who could take executive position or exercise any initiative or resource. He wasn't a patch on his dad.

"Old S.K. was disappointed and realised his shortcomings and did try to enable Walter to take over, but Walter couldn't live alongside a man like Reid, his brother-in-law. He used to brush Walter aside as though he was nothing, and it became progressively worse as Walter tried to make decisions within the firm."

Frank Kelly, who worked as a stockman on Naryilco until 1940 when he became manager, said, "Ted Pratt, the travelling manager, was involved in the split. He and Reid were always at one another's throats over the running of the properties, of which Ted Pratt knew more. Reid knew more about the business side of things and office management. I understood there was some big blue at HQ between Pratt and Reid and Reid demanded that Pratt be sacked from the company but he couldn't do much about it because Lady Kidman stepped in and demanded Reid's resignation instead, because under the terms of the late Sir Sidney's will Pratt could not be sacked and his job was there till the day he died if he wanted it. [There is no such reference about Pratt in Sid's will.] When Lady Kidman demanded Reid's resignation he pulled out a cheque book and asked Lady Kidman if she had any idea how much it would cost them for him to take his share and leave. Lady Kidman was most surprised when she was confronted by an enormous sum. Walter and Ted Pratt were all for each other."

Alex Robb, the son of Indian horse exporter J. E. Robb, insisted, "Sid Reid was a careful, astute businessman. His honesty and integrity could not be questioned. It was said that Kidman had a reputation of 'giving' things to people and then not backing it up, saying, 'I only loaned it to you.' To reward Reid for all he'd done for him and the company, he gave him shares in many station properties and Reid, instead of taking it as a gent's agreement, had it legally secured, so if S.K. ever wanted to go back on his word, Reid had it all sewn up. It didn't happen in S.K.'s time and then, with the family bust-up, Reid withdrew, and Walter wanted much of his stake back but Reid had it all sewn up legally."

That matters were more complicated within the family was attested to by Joan Hopkins, Sid Reid's daughter, who said, "Dad started or helped to start the city office in Adelaide when Grandpa and Grannie were still living at Kapunda. It was first in North Terrace and then Currie Street. He was Grandpa's right-hand man and always in the office, and what Dad did in three days in the end used to take three months.

"It was Aunty Edna's interference that was directly responsible for the Reids pulling out of the company. She was a little girl who had a little curl — and when she was nasty she was ghastly.

"Walter had little responsibility in the early days because he wasn't a well man. Within the family you couldn't help but like him. He was a very likeable person. You couldn't help but *not* like Muriel. She wouldn't tread on an ant and squash it but whatever the Kidman girls got, she wanted.

"Edna and Sid Ayers initially lived at Clare but after Grandpa's

death Edna came to Adelaide and lived with Grannie. She was a difficult lady and jealous of Sid Reid and saw the possibility of the company management going to her son, John Ayers, if Dad was out of the way. Walter and Muriel had no sons. Edna and Sid Reid did not get on well and after Grandpa died, Gertie and Elma, my mother, did not care for the way Edna was going about things and influencing Gran. So the Reid family took its share out of the Kidman empire — and it was a very substantial share — and ran its own operation as Kidman Reid and Co. After the split my mother [Elma] never spoke to Edna again. Nor did Gertie. Mum never went to Eringa either because Edna was always there. But it made no difference with the older grandchildren. Neil [Joan's husband] and I went there for dinner and the grandchildren all got on. You couldn't have lived in Adelaide then at our age and gone around avoiding people. You would have been forever diving around corners."

Muriel Kidman, who had no reason to like Sid Reid, also did not like Edna Ayers. "Gert and Nelson were out from England when Sir Sidney died and were staying at Eringa, and soon after that Edna left Sid Ayers and went to stay with her mother, so Gertie and Nelson came to stay with us and Gert would only visit her mother if she knew Edna was out of the house. When Gert left to go back to England, she took my daughter Isabel with her. Isabel said she sobbed the whole way home about how things had turned out.

"Lady Kidman came around to me and cried when the family split up and said, 'I'm to blame. I've ruined Edna. I've spoilt her but I depend on her and she is looking after the house.' Edna's jealousy had much to do with the break-up."

Edna's grandson, John Ayers Jnr, said, "Sid Reid was managing director of the company after old S.K. died and Walter was chairman, and it was mooted that the company go public and it was generally agreed that the idea had merit, but I understand when it was going to be split in equal portions between the Reids, Kidmans, Clovers and Ayers plus a number of shares that had to be put out to enable it to qualify for the Public Companies Act, Sid Reid, who was in charge of it all, tried to get control by getting front men to take up the shares being floated. I don't know how he could have, with the odds stacked against him, but there was a family get-together and the Reids were put out of the company with a quarter interest handed over in shares and property."

If that was the case, Sid Reid's quarter-share plus the especially pledged interests which Sid Kidman had given him amounted to a very substantial interest.

"I understood," John Ayers Jnr said, "that Walter and his wife didn't speak to Sid Reid and his wife ever again."

Walter's youngest daughter, Anne Abel Smith, said, "Sid Reid tried to get everything and he and my father had a big row. As to who was right and who was wrong I don't know. The Reid kids wanted it all. One of them, Burns, wrote bad letters to my father. Dad was smart enough to know they couldn't have it all. The feeling I grew up with was that I shouldn't speak to the Reids. Mum and Dad said that."

Tensions tugged in three directions. Walter, Muriel and Lady Kidman, who refused to tolerate Sid Reid's high-handedness; Sid Reid and Elma, who thought that what Sid did was the right way for the company to continue to be run and that Walter was being petulant; and Edna Ayers, who thought that if she influenced her mother and played her cards right, she would see the company reins passed to her son. And on the pastoral side of things, Ted Pratt, totally loyal to old Sid Kidman, sided with Walter, whom the bush employees saw as weak, inefficient and not a patch on the old man.

A source close to the family, who wished to remain anonymous, said in 1985, "It was like a lot of family concerns. Shareholders multiplied and had diversified views. Jealousy did creep in between Sid Reid and Walter. It grew over a period of time. Sid was a prominent personality in the Kidman company and also a dominant chairman of Coles Bros, which is why old S.K. put Walter on the board of Bennett and Fisher, to even up the score. Walter, who was not in the best of health, was consumed by Sid Reid.

"The split began after S.K.'s death, with quarrelling in the family, and was effected about four years later when the Reids took their share and the Kidmans took theirs. That Edna was very involved with it (with aims and ambitions of her own and for her son) was evidenced by the sisters never speaking again. Gertie never spoke to her again and nor did Elma. I don't know that Walter and Sid Reid ever spoke again. They were both great racing men, and Sid Reid was chairman of the South Australian Jockey Club and Walter, chairman of the Port Adelaide Racing Clubs. I don't think their terms coincided."

Whereas old Sid Kidman had loved talking to the press, this was an extended time when all the Kidmans kept their lips buttoned, no doubt out of the sheer embarrassment of it all, with the Cattle King barely dead and the family at each other's throats over the spoils. But matters don't have to appear in bold announcements in the press to be made known. Rumour, talk and blame abounded and, as the source close to the Kidman family said, "The split was the talk of the

Australian pastoral industry. The Kidman side drew more sympathy. But that was open to dispute. And Edna Ayers' ambitions for her son were not as widely known as the rift between Sid Reid and Walter.

"It would have been interesting if it had remained as one entity with both John Ayers and Reg Reid [Sid's son] in the company. John Ayers was older than Reg Reid by ten years and a very logical fellow; Reg Reid was also remarkably outstanding.

"The 'Kidman' empire grew for a period, even with splinter groups, as both the Kidmans continued to buy up and the Reids also, under the name of Kidman Reid and Co. Perhaps what Sid had put together could have grown even further but our history has a sad story in relation to family companies — one of greed and jealousy. They start off with a tight half dozen and suddenly there are forty-four people, with everyone wanting quick dividends, and jealousy, fights, splits and sales take place."

The split put many people in an awkward position. Where to place their loyalty — and business? Sid Reid resigned as the head of Coles Bros, after issuing the edict that the firm would have to deal either with him or with Walter. Coles Bros stuck to Walter and the Reids dealt with Goldsbrough Mort.

In the bush, managers and employees were not given much option nor told too much of what had gone on. Jack Watt, who as a young boy had slogged for Sid Kidman during the 1926–30 drought and Depression, digging soaks along the Diamantina with camels, later went to Diamantina Lakes as manager and then to Mundowdna with John Brooke, then to Nundora and Momba.

"The split was a pretty bitter one," he said. "I would have preferred to have stayed with S.K.'s estates but was working with Morden, Wonnaminta and Nundora, which were just some of the stations Sid Reid took. Loyal, wasn't I? But I wouldn't have worked for Reid if I hadn't respected him."

With the Depression behind them and another great war confronting them, in 1939 most of Sid's men took the view that they couldn't afford to be fussy about changing sides and it was better to stay put with their old or new boss, as the case may be. They were devastated at what had happened, and they resented, lastingly, what Walter, Sid Reid, Lady Kidman, the daughters and Ted Pratt had done. Indulging in a spot of power play had torn apart the great empire. Their sense of loyalty was so strong that they were embarrassed, less for themselves than for Sid's memory.

The antagonism wasn't only confined to Adelaide, where Walter Kidman would give vent to his feelings over copious amounts of alcohol, but to the management of the stations where mistakes occurred, the like of which would never have happened in Sid's time. Bulloo Downs was one plum station Sid Reid acquired in the split and Jack O'Shea, who was manager there from 1961 to 1981 for the Reid interests (after which it was sold to Stanbrokes), said, "The split hadn't taken place by 1939 when Sid Reid wanted to buy another property, Connemara. Lady Kidman didn't want him to do it, but he went ahead anyway and bought it in the name of his son, Reg Reid. And then he bought a mob of cattle to put on it and they were going through a Kidman place and Walter arranged for the calves to be taken off and branded as Kidman cattle. It added fuel to the family argument and the split was imminent.

"It was wrong of Walter to do that, but he was under the impression the place had been bought for the company, but it had not been.

"When S.K. died Mr Reid could not get on with Lady Kidman, who had had not much say in it while Sir Sidney was alive, but after that she wanted a lot of say and it just didn't work out. It was always referred to as the 'Connemara deal' and many people were pretty sure it was done deliberately; anyway, it led to the splitting up of the empire and Mr Reid and Walter Kidman never spoke again.

"In 1939, Mr Reid got Norley and Bulloo Downs in Queensland and the New South Wales properties Teurika, Delarra, Thurlow, Yantara, Cobham, Gum Creek, Palgamertie, Packsaddle, Nundora and The Selection, and properties in South Australia but I don't know if they were part of the split or acquired afterwards. One was Saddleworth and there was another on the Murray and later on another one he bought in New South Wales, Moroco.

"The Reid interests prospered and Mr Reid was said to be the fifth wealthiest man in Adelaide (which meant the whole of South Australia). Under Walter, the Kidman interests seemed to flounder along for a number of years, and it wasn't until John Ayers took over (and he was a most capable man) that he was able to stop the rot, the slide.

"The Kidmans got the area bulk in the split and still own many of those properties, but they've never acquired much more, as Mr Reid would have aimed for. The Kidman empire would have flourished further if the split hadn't happened."

It is all a matter of conjecture. But that the rift was both bitter and nasty, there is no doubt. Sid Reid and Walter never spoke again, and Edna did not speak to either Gertie or Elma. Edna's husband (from whom she appeared to be living apart) died in 1941, and in 1948 Lady Kidman died at the age of 86.

Muriel Kidman recalled, "With her father dead, her husband and mother, Edna turned to me in loneliness like a long, lost friend. They're all dead now. Gertie later on in England and then Elma while Walter was still alive. I went to the service and Sid Reid came over and gave me a kiss and thanked me for coming. Then Walter died in 1970. Edna came to the service that was held in our house.

After thirty years there wasn't anything left for her to fight about."

That the fighting went on within the immediate family in such a nasty way showed in Lady Kidman's will, when she died thirteen years after Sid.

Her will was not straightforward and she changed it several times where her son and three daughters were concerned. She left the bulk of her estate to Gertie, Edna and Walter, and as Elma did not share in this (being a partner in the breakaway group of Kidman Reid), Lady Kidman bequeathed her 1,000 shares in the Adelaide Steamship Company. This in itself is straightforward enough and evidence of the break, but Lady Kidman changed her will repeatedly where her goods and chattels were concerned.

Every single thing she owned — right down to the blinds on the windows and carpet and linoleum on the floors — was specifically willed to certain people in order that no misunderstanding could arise. At one stage, her son, Walter, was to receive the cocktail cabinet (the presentation piece that the men of the outback stations gave to Sir Sidney when he retired) and all the wines and liquors, except the whisky. It may have been as a result of Walter's growing reliance on drinking (or some other whim, pressure or infighting) that she changed the matter so that all the wines and liquors — except whisky — went to Edna.

Elma came out of Bel's will somewhat thinly where material goods were concerned, as did Gertie. Valuables, easily transportable, went to Gertie in England: expensive pearl necklaces and the main silver tea service, to which Lady Kidman later added a threefold tapestry screen, which she had worked herself.

Elma received Lady Kidman's writing bureau, afternoon-tea table, dinner and tea service (white with coloured flowers), a sapphire and diamond bracelet and a wedding ring set with diamonds, and six of her own worked tapestry-seated dining room chairs, to which Lady Kidman later added her bellpull in the drawing room and a tapestry fender stool.

Walter retained the cocktail cabinet, minus the grog, all major glassware and cutlery monogrammed "K". Muriel Kidman scored a diamond and pearl brooch, and the grandchildren received Dresden china, tapestry pictures, handsome clocks, gold handbags and tapestry chairs in various styles. Oil paintings of herself and Sid went to Walter. Oil paintings of Sid's grandparents went to Gertie.

Edna received Lady Kidman's pearl and diamond earrings only among the jewellery, but she was also given three candelabra, a Magenta dinner service, two tea services, a coffee service, Bel's house linen and all of her "old real silver forks and spoons", and all of her wearing apparel to be disposed of as thought fit. Later on Bel added more items to be handed to Edna: a diamond and pearl brooch with two clips (so described so it was not confused with the brooch left to Muriel), the Moreland prints in the drawing room, the blankets and bed coverings, the blue rug in the hall, the grandfather clock, and all pots, pans, kettles, saucepans and other kitchen utensils.

Diamond wristlet watches were given to others, and more worked tapestry stools and screens to close family and friends (each one identified clearly to avoid any dispute), right down to her bridge table.

In a last alteration to her will, Bel made a point of giving her billiard table and cues, and all furniture, fittings and pictures in the billiard room to Walter, along with all carpets, rugs, linoleum and other floor coverings not otherwise mentioned in her will, as well as all the curtains and blinds.

In a further addition, Elma was to receive a mahogany chest of drawers in Bel's bedroom in lieu of the afternoon-tea table bequeathed her earlier (and then taken away), and Edna was to get the "glass and china cupboard sometimes called a book case, in the sitting room" plus the Frigidaire refrigerator in the kitchen *and*, Bel added, she was giving more of her furniture and household effects to Edna than her other children because they all had homes of their own and Edna did not. The big disappointment for Edna was that Walter got the stately home, Eringa, Unley Park, and she did not. So she still didn't have a home of her own. She was livid, according to Muriel Kidman, who would have been appalled if Bel had *not* handed it down to her and Walter. The mystery of Bel's will is who got the cellarful of whisky? Perhaps in the thirteen years following Sid's death, with the family fighting hammer and tongs, she sought a spot of relief in it herself and eventually there was none to bequeath. She could have easily been forgiven had that been the case.

24
The Controversies

ONTROVERSY SURROUNDED Sid's life in matters ranging
from the important to the trivial, and at the trivial end of the
scale was his attitude towards men who smoked, and who were silly
enough to light a cigarette around the campfire with a match rather
than a fire ember. Historian Russel Ward, in *The Australian Legend*,
said, "One firmly and widely believed tale was that Kidman would
instantly dismiss any employee whom he saw lighting his pipe with a
match in the evening instead of using a brand from the camp fire. He
was held to have believed that a man so careless of his own money
would be equally careless of his employer's property." The fact of the
matter was that Sid had sufficient sense *not* to dismiss a good man for
something so paltry. Had there been any truth in this story, old
Kidman men would have been able to cite the names of those so
dismissed and the stations where the events took place.

That Sid was not keen on men who smoked a lot is true. When
Charles Smith sought a job with the Kidman organisation in 1930,
he was interviewed by Sid in his offices in Currie Street, Adelaide.
Smith said, "He asked me if I smoked and I said, 'Yes, a pipe,' and
S.K. replied, 'Well, that's better. Any time you want a hand with a
rope in a yard a lot of fellows are too busy rolling a cigarette.'"

Frank Kelly, who was working at Yandama in 1932, recalled, "I
was on deck when Ernie Spencer, one of his favourite managers,
rolled up one day and lit up a smoke. S.K. said to him, 'You jolly
tinker, you shouldn't be wasting your money like that. You should
buy a little pig and fatten it up and send it to market.'"

Les Gardiner, who was droving for Sid in 1928, said, "I was at the
Booka Booka waterhole on Bulloo Downs when I saw S.K. hand a
young bloke a fire stick to light a smoke, in preference to a match,
saying, 'You'll never earn any money when you do that, young
fellow.'"

Jack O'Shea, a later manager of Bulloo Downs, said, "Sid Reid
always insisted that the yarn about the economical way to light a
smoke around a campfire was not true and had been drummed up by
someone."

Two Broken Hill bushies going by the names of "the Fox" and
"the Ferret" claimed, "Old Sid wouldn't have been silly enough to

say something like that. Commonsense was that if you were within 6 feet of the campfire you reached for it to light a smoke; if you were more than 6 feet away, you wore out more in boot leather getting to it so you used a match. It was an unwritten law, just like getting a 'spoon' for your drink of tea. You always picked your 'spoon' from a tree. You never stirred it with a crooked bit of stick from the ground. Some drover might have wiped his arse with it!"

Despite the claim by "the Fox" and "the Ferret", it seems true that on occasions Sid did use the fire stick admonition as a lesson in thrift, but it is stretching the truth too far to suggest that he sacked men who preferred matches to campfire embers. The story was widely circulated for decades and the thrift connotation lost: it grew to be a prime example of Kidman's meanness.

It is certainly true that Kidman was not tolerant of any waste, and why should he have been when outback freight was so dear and his annual bills for rations and their transport sky-high? He hated to see waste of any type on a station — tins and nails and equipment lying around did aggravate him. Any smart manager avoided this or always had an "emu parade" before Sid arrived at a station on an inspection. He also disliked the misuse of food, or its waste. Frank Kelly remembered, "He came into the camp at Bulloo Downs and saw a young bloke wolfing condensed milk from a tin with a spoon. He said to him, 'You jolly little tinker, you'll make yourself sick and ruin me if you eat food like that.'"

Charles Smith remembers there were often accusations about poor quality food on Kidman stations, accusations that didn't hold water. "We didn't have any tinned jam," he said, speaking of tucker rations he experienced from 1930 to 1934, "but we had 'Kidman's Blood Mixture', which was treacle. It wasn't Golden Syrup, which was more refined. We had rice, flour, dried fruits (apples, apricots and sultanas) and lived on that along with beef.

"I said to S.K. once, 'Don't you reckon it would be more economical if we had tins of Camp Pie?' 'No,' he said, 'I have thousands of cattle and the men can kill for themselves.'

"'What about the waste there?' I asked him. 'When the men kill a beast, it is my experience that they eat it' was his reply.

"We didn't get spuds. Kidman's substitute was Muckhardt potatoes (in 5 gallon tins, dehydrated and granulated). You put two or three tablespoons into a container with some boiling water and you had mashed potato.

"I never heard a complaint in our camp about the tucker but mainly about the cooks, who didn't take a great deal of trouble to prepare the food they had. Bert Carr was managing at Nundora Station when I went through once and I said, 'You're living like bloody abos.' The tucker was dreadful. They had everything there but didn't know how to or wouldn't cook it. They had no permanent cook at the time. I said, 'To hell with this, I'll turn out a decent feed for you,' and it could be done quite easily. You could turn corned beef into Burdekin Duck by putting strips of cold corned beef into batter and puftalooners could be made with balls of pre-mixed damper thrown into hot fat, and damper could be turned into brownies with sultanas and currants. Kidman always saw that his men had the best; the trouble was with the cooks. There were cooks, 'cookoos' and wilful, bloody murderers."

The claim about murderers is not bush hyperbole. Jack Watt, a Kidman man at Cowarie in the 1926–30 drought, said, "When rations arrived at Cordillo Downs [a non-Kidman station] that had been sent on from somewhere else in a wagonette, they found their way to the cook. Some dill had put sheep dip in the Coleman's Curry Powder tin. Mickey Fusedale was the cook; Nat Reice died; I think Louey Fahey did too. That sort of mistake just didn't happen on a Kidman place. In fact, old Lady Kidman was just lovely. She sent us up a heap of eggs from Kapunda to Mundowdna, but Bert Carr and me and John Brooke and Clem Lally had a fight over the eggs in the kitchen. We ended up splattering the walls with eggs. When old S.K. spotted the stains, that was the end of the eggs. . .I dunno what the Kidman station tucker was like earlier, but we always found it satisfactory."

Twenty years after Sid's death, Jim Vickery, later to become the chairman of the South Australian Pastoral Board and director of Outback Management, said, "Accusations of meanness are inaccurate. There was thriftiness, yes. In the 1950s Innamincka Station used to be served by TAA's Channel Country Air Service. Men could have ordered up 10 gallons of icecream airfreighted from Brisbane without a question being asked, but if any of that had been tipped out into the chooks' bucket there would have been real strife."

Sid was called not only a "Cattle King" but also a cattle thief. In the earlier days of big, unfenced areas, when a muster produced plentiful cleanskins (unbranded cattle), it is said that Sid was known to chide any of his managers who weren't in first with a branding iron. Bob Napier, a Kidman horsebreaker in the early 1920s, said, "Monty Winton came down from Darwin — he was as thin as a bloody whipstick — and became one of Kidman's top managers. If something didn't have a brand on it, Monty would put a Kidman brand on quick smart."

Melba Milne, the daughter of Stan Foulis, Kidman's manager at Gnalta in the 1920s, said, "It was alleged that there was only one

OVERLEAF:
A get-together for three former Kidman men in 1983 (from left): Reg Williams, Bert Carr and Charlie Smith (now deceased). (Bill Bennett)

bigger cattle thief in Australia than Sid Kidman and that was his son-in-law Sid Reid. When he married Elma Kidman, he was given (it was said) 1,000 cows and everyone said later that in that first year all those cows must have had ten calves."

Bill Brook, who went to Cordillo Downs to work as a stockman in 1918 (and later ended up buying the station), said, "Many people said if there was a strange bullock that came along, Sid would send it along to market. But he rarely sent anyone along [charged them with stock theft], perhaps because the same charges could have been levelled at him or his managers, never specifically on Sid's orders, perhaps."

Mort Conway, a stockman at both Macumba and Mundowdna and later a Kidman drover, said, "It's a useless argument talking about poddy-dodging. Kidman did it. They all did it. The saying was 'I gotta go to your place to eat my own cattle and you have to come to my place to eat your own'. If you were caught, you'd be pinched on the spot for doing it. It was a generally accepted bush practice, not a gentlemanly one, and there were a lot of fights over it when people got caught. It was said Kidman got a lot more of other people's cattle than they did of his because he had more men to feed."

Norman Gurr, who took over as manager of Clifton Hills on the Diamantina River in South Australia in 1926, agreed. "Managers of all types got together at race meetings and dinners and if they met at a dinner the first question asked would be 'Is this one of mine?'. The answer was invariably 'Yes. You've gotta go to someone else's place to eat your own beef'. It was friendly rivalry. They all did it. When it was all said and done, they were only balancing the ledgers."

"Poddy-dodging? Yes. Christ! Kidman did it. But so did everybody else. You had to keep your books balanced!" Jack Watt said.

Charles Smith said, "There was a lot of criticism of Kidman from outsiders about hijacking cattle or that he was unscrupulous in his cattle dealings or a cattle duffer. I know for a fact that he didn't tolerate it where his managers were concerned; he did not authorise it, instigate it or condone it.

"When the old boy was slandered like that I got upset, because most of it was hearsay and said by people to draw attention to themselves. Old S.K. never went to court on any offence of this nature — ever. And if he had been as dishonest as people claimed he was, his managers wouldn't have put their heads on the chopping block for him. Once you start to commit offences, you lose the respect of the man dictating that policy and conniving at it and sooner or later thieves fall out.

"If the truth is known, it wasn't a case of Kidman duffing cattle himself, but of all the little squatters duffing cattle from him in order to set up. They all started up on him. Tom Toohey took up Pyampa, adjoining Bulloo Downs, in 1928 without a single head of cattle. A few years later it was fully stocked.

"We [the Kidman company] got him on misuse of cattle [meat or hides in your possession you had no right to and were using to your advantage] and the penalty for that was very light compared to cattle stealing. He got six months in Charleville. S.K. said, 'Tom Toohey is only doing what all the others are doing where I am concerned. I don't begrudge them a few cattle, but when they go around boasting about it, it becomes a horse of a different colour.'"

Where cattle were concerned, Kidman, aside from favouring any unbranded ones he could lay his hands on like everyone else, favoured two types, and to anyone asking his advice on stock he would reply, "Herefords if you have a long way to go to market; if you have a short way to go, Shorthorns."

And with cattle he did notch up some impressive records. In 1910–11, 38,176 head of cattle were moved from Warenda Station in eighteen months, a world record for stock movement from any one station. Years before that, in 1904, when the Perth market was over-supplied, Blake Miller brought 1,000 head of Victoria River Downs stock west to east to market, reopening the Murranji Track. Later still, 5,000 bullocks were started from Victoria River Downs to travel east, and 3,360 were delivered at Coongie in north-west South Australia, after travelling 1,700 miles. Some of them were later droved to Muswellbrook in New South Wales, a distance of a further 700 miles.

Mort Conway can recall another big droving epic in the 1930s, when Sid's Western Australian station, Yeeda, was closed down. "It was managed first by Deffy Rodgers and later by young John Brooke when it was closed down and the cattle were walked almost 3,000 miles across the continent. They had the BS7 brand and walked from Western Australia, through the Territory, into South Australia and then into Queensland. They were spelled at Momba, which S.K. had with Sid Reid, and they finished up at Melbourne's Flemington markets after they were trucked from Hillston, New South Wales.

"There were more than 1,000 of them and I took them over at Marree from Jim Murphy. A few would have been dropped along the way and one killed a week for the drovers. There was no market for them in Perth or Darwin — that's why they came east. They had been trained to walk by the time we took them, so well trained that all we had to say at dawn was 'up, boys!' and they'd get up automatically, averaging 10 miles a day. They were spelled here and there — at Macumba for six weeks and then at Durham Downs. They were just like skeletons in the end and their feet were spread out and enormous from walking. When they fattened, they were like elephants. It was a mammoth droving trip.

"Not a lot of people would know where stock was concerned that old S.K. got into a real trimmer of a fight with A. C. McDonald who owned Naryilco Station before S.K. had it. It was in the First World War when S.K. was well into his fifties. They had a row over a bullock at a railway station in Queensland and got into it by grabbing each other's beards.

"It was a real proper show after they'd accused one another of pinching a bullock. Anyone who was there stood and watched. They were both done up in suits. S.K. came out the best. He was a powerful man even then and knocked McDonald about. He was not, by nature, a belligerent man and it was probably one of the few fist fights he had in his life. But he wasn't short on knowing how to handle himself, even at a later age."

Curiously, one of Sid's favourite — if not *the* favourite cattle brand — was the X70 from Eringa (and also Macumba). The Eringa brand was one that appeared on his Kidman company cheque; Sid also named two of his three houses Eringa: Eringa in Kapunda, and Eringa in Unley Park.

Sid was credited with being able to spot his own stock — horses or cattle — anywhere, and from a fair distance, but then he did have some very distinctive brands. Explaining the brand system, Jim Vickery said, "Kidman's brands generally were famous brands. All of his racehorses were branded on the neck under the mane with the diamond tail of Innamincka. He had a lot of old, original brands and the diamond tail was one of them. Then all states of Australia brought in various regulations relating to brands so that stock could be recognised as belonging to different states, particularly those states that were significant cattle states, such as South Australia, Queensland and the Northern Territory. The arrangement was that all South Australian brands would have two numbers and a letter, and that all Queensland brands would have two letters and a number, and that all Northern Territory brands would be characterised by a T, so that RDT was Rockland Downs in the Territory and JD1 was John Drynan of Nockatunga, Queensland. All of those brands registered before the regulations came in were allowed to be retained and there were many Kidman brands among them. They included the diamond tail from Innamincka and the anchor brand of Anna Creek, the X70 from Eringa and Macumba, and COB of Davenport Downs, which S.K. purchased from Freeman Cobb of Cobb and Co. The brand still belonged to Davenport Downs in 1984

OPPOSITE:
Mort Conway, a part-Aboriginal former Kidman stockman and drover, in 1984. (Photographer: Roger Steele)

425

although the Kidmans no longer owned the place. BD1 was Bulloo Downs in Queensland and the open Bible was the Quinyambie brand ▭ and still is today."

No one can say why the X70 remained Sid's favourite brand or why he named two homes after the station in South Australia that brought him little luck or profit. Offering some sort of explanation, R. M. (Reg) Williams, said, "Eringa was first taken by up Treloar in about 1860 and as an indication to the difficult country it was, I can remember it being completely dried out and shut down three times in my life. [Williams was 78 in 1986.] Once in my travels in the area I arrived at one of the waterholes on Eringa to find everything dead, including the donkeys and the camels, which indicates the place was very dry indeed. Yet this was the place after which Kidman chose to name his homes from which he ran his empire. Perhaps Eringa was used as a symbol that Kidman valued drought as an educator." Another explanation was that Eringa was the first piece of larger country Kidman took up on his own and not in partnership with his brother Sackville.

Returning to the subject of accusations, there were milder criticisms that Sid and the Kidman organisation did not get on with the unions. These have been dismissed as being without any foundation at all by the majority of men interviewed for this book, whether they were Kidman men or not. Mort Conway said, "I knew of no disputes with unions. S.K. complied and paid the going rates. If he had not, men would have picked up their swags and walked off," especially, it should be said, where shearing was concerned.

When Sid died, *The Australian Worker*, the official paper of the union movement, recorded his death with the story of his life and the size of his holdings and the comment: "He [Kidman] was rather a rough diamond but popular with his employees whom he paid comparatively well. He also generously treated swagmen and other travellers through his spacious domains."

Had there been any union trouble, it would most likely have erupted in western New South Wales, where his large holdings incorporated many sheep stations, which brought him into regular contact with the shearers who were members of the Australian Workers Union. But the secretary of the Sydney-based New South Wales Branch of the Australian Workers Union in 1984 said, "I've been in the union for thirty-five years and never heard of Kidman being roasted for anything. He was a much-talked-about man when I was a boy. Even old-time union fellows then didn't have a word of complaint against him."

Historian Dr John Merritt, of the Australian National University in Canberra, who is the only person to have read the official records of the Australian Workers Union before they became taboo to all researchers, said, "Kidman was never singled out in relation to any big rural strikes in the Western Division of New South Wales. He missed the big strikes of the 1890s and the early 1900s because he was not a landholder in the area then, and in the 1920s it was fairly peaceful. It was a much quieter period industrially. There was a federal award at the time and to cause industrial upset was to cause unnecessary expense. Kidman appreciated the expense saved by having good industrial relations."

It is not to say that they were perfect. Jim Schmidt, who went to work for Kidman at Corona in 1917 when he was 13, said, "There was some trouble later on Kidman sheep stations. The shearers wanted extra money if the sheep were too daggy, sandy or burry. There was always a bit of a fight to get it, but then shearers were putting excessive demands on bigger places, which they thought could afford to pay, and being more lenient with smaller places, which they felt didn't have the same capacity."

Charlie Flavel, aged 90 in 1984, said, "I shore at all the Kidman stations. I moved into contracting in 1926 operating from Broken Hill when I bought a truck. I charged £18 to travel to a station. The station paid £9 and the shearers slung in the rest. I started with a two-stand plant in 1926 at One Tree Station [a non-Kidman station] but later shore at all of their places. At my peak I employed forty-three men and that year we shore 503,000. There wasn't much trouble with the unions on S.K. places. In fact the Kidman sheds were quite good. They never had any spare parts of any description so I always carried my own. I'd never charge them for them if they were needed...I just let it go.

"There was never any argument with S.K. but I had a few with Sid Reid. He wrote to a client saying they'd got 1 shilling a pound for the wool and tenpence a pound for the skirtings with burr. I replied saying, 'If we hadn't taken it off, the whole lot would have been done for tenpence.' There were so many burrs and they were so thick that the men wore leggings. Anyway, it was a letter of complaint directed against me, so I went to Adelaide and had the wool reclassed. The best of the wool went up twopence a pound and the rest of the wool went down twopence a pound so Reid lost out on the deal and we came out on top.

"I've sheared in bough sheds for the Kidmans, on hessian mats to keep the wool clean and out in the paddocks. They always paid but I always waited until after a sale for the money. Yancannia was always a good Kidman shed to shear in and the manager there, Innes Ker, always looked after us well. I wouldn't take on anyone who wasn't a unionist and before the First World War I never changed a hand for eight years — a shearer, classer or cook. Mick Young worked for me later on.

"I must say the Kidman company treated me fairly and when a car insurance matter cropped up and I needed a reference, H. J. Bird, the company secretary, provided one for me saying, 'very favourably known.'"

It should be noted that all of these men are referring to conditions in Sid's time. What happened *after* Sid's death, when others were in control, is pungently noted by Clyde "Shithouse" Cameron, a former federal member of Parliament who started his working life as a rouseabout in Kidman shearing sheds in 1930:

> In 1939 I became a full-time organiser in the west Darling area of New South Wales for the South Australian Branch of the Australian Workers Union, a job that took me to every pastoral property in that district and I covered the state of South Australia as well.
>
> The kind of reputation the Kidman interests had with the union was then bad, very bad.
>
> Shearers' hut accommodation was primitive, latrines were without doors and there was no fly-wire protection against blowflies; cooking utensils were old, stained and chipped, and ventilation and light were often inadequate or there could be *too* much ventilation and shearers would go down with colds and flu.
>
> Blowflies would breed in the latrine pits and then make their way to the kitchen and dining room and pollute the meals. I used to insist on fly-wire seat covers over every opening on the long, common bench of the toilets. I had to recommend prosecutions against the Kidman stations for failing to meet the requirement of the Shearers Accommodation Act. But not once did the branch secretary act, because Kidman interests would always call at his city office and promise to fix the complaint by "next shearing". Next shearing never came! And always the same excuse would be accepted by the union's boss. That was what prompted me to nominate against the secretary in 1941.
>
> It was the manager of the Kidman Wonnaminta Station in the west Darling who gave me the appellation "Shithouse" Cameron. It was like winning the Victoria Cross! The shearers loved me for winning the Award and my vote jumped to a record 92 per cent in 1941.
>
> It may well be that former 80 and 90-year-olds can't remember any union trouble with Kidman. Well, all I can say is that until I went into the west Darling in 1939, station hands on Kidman properties [and here Clyde Cameron is not referring to shearers but to stockmen] didn't belong to the Australian Workers Union and so the Pastoral Award was observed in the breach.

Station hands were expected to provide their own dogs without reimbursement. They weren't given butter as required by the Award and exorbitant prices were charged for clothing and other requisites bought from the station stores. They were required to work long hours, seven days a week without payment of overtime.

I knew old Charlie Flavel well. He was close to Kidman managers and, in my time, shore the sheep on most of their properties. His complaint that "Kidman sheds never had anything in the way of spare parts" coincides with my own concept of their places. Charlie wouldn't complain. He would simply provide his own spares and not even bother to charge for replacements. That's why he was able to hold the contracts!

Charlie was a fellow who was well liked on both sides of the industrial fence. He would have always known me as "Shithouse" Cameron rather than Clyde.

They are words from Clyde Cameron that do not pay the Kidman outfit a compliment, but what needs to be remembered is that he made these assessments *after* 1939 and into the 1940s, by which time Sid had been dead a number of years and his son, Walter, was in control. Certainly when Cameron is referring to Kidman places, he may also be referring to those operating under the name of Kidman Reid that Sid Reid obtained in the split.

One reason for the unhappy state of affairs, as Clyde Cameron himself suggests, was that the Kidman leases in the west Darling area — whether they were held by Walter Kidman or Sid Reid — were running out because an earlier decision by Sid had refused to allow them to be chopped up for closer settlement. That being the case, they felt little need to pour money into improvements.

And that in itself raises the biggest and most controversial issue about Sid himself and his activities over his own lifetime: did he rape the land and leave it beggared? Tear at it for his own gain and then toss it in? How much can he be blamed for using and abusing or for the lack of improvements? Here again, the matter was one of controversy. To challenge anything Kidman in Sid's time was tantamount to a red rag to a bull where his men were concerned. They thought his ways were the right ways because they were big and because they worked. But others were not convinced, and fifty years after Sid's death allows a reasonable time for a wider assessment to be made.

Seventy per cent of Australia is classified as arid or semi-arid — nearly half of New South Wales and Queensland, almost all of South Australia and Western Australia, and about two-thirds of the Northern Territory. Most of the arid lands have been occupied by

Europeans for a hundred years or less. The major land use has been pastoral and it was the pastoralists, forever probing for usable land and water for their flocks, who opened up the interior and established an industry that carried beyond the short-lived gold-rush fever and into the twentieth century, although the gold rushes in Victoria, New South Wales and later in Western Australia and the far west of New South Wales also played a part in the expansion of the pastoral industry by initially providing a market for meat and, when the minerals petered out, a nucleus of settlers hungry for land.

Until the development of wire fencing and techniques for sinking and developing wells and bores and for excavating earthen tanks in the 1870s, occupation of the arid and semi-arid lands was limited to the country fronting the permanent streams (the Darling, Lachlan, Murrumbidgee and Murray rivers) and the country within walking distance of the longer-lasting waterholes on the semi-permanent streams (the Warrego, Paroo, Bulloo, Diamantina and Georgina rivers and Cooper Creek) and the occasionally flooding creeks that made their way across the heart of Australia.

Livestock were able to move out and graze the backblocks in bountiful seasons, but their retreats to the river frontages in dry times placed a great deal of pressure on these lands. Where the soils of the river and stream frontages were highly erodible sands or where these soils occurred in association with heavy grey clays, as they generally do, catastrophic damage was caused by wind erosion followed by water erosion on the stripped surfaces. In this way the red soil fringes of the Darling floodplain, the western Riverina, and stream frontages in northern South Australia and Central Australia and later in Western Australia were seriously degraded and eroded. The heavy use of the country around the natural waterholes often meant their demise, as wind carried sand into the gullies and drainage lines and the storm rains washed it into creeks to eventually silt up the waterholes. However, bores, descending for hundreds of metres and gushing hot water, and water pumped up by windmills and stored in large, excavated earthen tanks, meant that the back country away from the river and creek frontages could be stocked. Yet in the last century, such waters were few and far between, and the country was stocked to five to ten times its real capacity for the areas actually commanded by water. That background, provided by Dick Condon of the Western Lands Commission of New South Wales, accurately sets the scene *before* the entry of Sidney Kidman, who began his pastoral acquisitions from 1895.

Tickalara was acquired by Sack and Sid in 1897, *before* which pastoral inspector J. Hogarth had given the following report in 1896: "The run is 140 miles south and west from Thargomindah and 60 miles north and east from Tibooburra. In the past little judgement has been shown to putting down water improvements. There is little or no feed. The run is eaten out in many places; rabbits are plentiful on all parts and the run is infested with dogs. It will be many years before any return can be got from the station no matter how economically run."

The same year Hogarth assessed Packsaddle Station, which Sid acquired in the 1920s: "There being nothing but a little saltbush outback from the waters and not within reach of the sheep. The whole area is looking very bad." And of Thurlow Downs (which Sid acquired in 1918 along with Elsinora and Urisino in the west Darling region for £65,000), Hogarth said, "There is no grass on any part of the run. Had sheep been the only stock there would be plenty of feed now but they are greatly outnumbered by rabbits."

These reports give an insight into the nature of places immediately before and twenty years before Kidman took them up. The Royal Commission of 1901 into the state of the west Darling region provides some appalling evidence as to how bad the country was. It was stated that almost one-quarter of the nearly 500,000 acre Teryawynia Station (south of Wilcannia) was "as bare as a floor in spite of the great rain they have just had". In the Mossgiel district, almost the whole of one man's homestead lease had gone. "It is just one bare patch. The soil is all blown away except the clay." Rabbit-proof fences were buried under sand and in one case a "second storey" (one built on top of the old fence) was almost buried. A 7 foot high stockyard on Albermarle Station (east of Menindee) had, within eighteen months of being built, been so completely submerged by sand that a witness drove over it in his buggy. Sheep were also being buried alive in dust storms. It was hardly a bed of roses before Sid arrived on the scene, initially in 1908 and again in the First World War years and into the 1920s.

Owen Williams, a senior principal research scientist in water and land resources at the CSIRO, specialises in the arid and semi-arid lands in Australia under pastoral use and has travelled and inspected most of Kidman's territory. He said, "The frontages had been heavily used by 1880–90, before the arrival of Kidman. He was definitely of the third wave. The first wave were the pioneers and then came the developers like Tyson, who put huge amounts of capital in, and the Desailleys in the 1860s and onwards, and Kidman came in the trough after the developers had either been ruined or removed their capital.

"He picked up the debris — the holdings of those who'd failed. He bought in a trough. He picked up the troubles others had been in. He's a new boy, really — actually in the twentieth century. It disposes, factually, of much of the criticism directed against Kidman. He must have been good to have profited from run-down country in the presence of the rabbit.

431

"Australia has the greatest area of poor soils of any continent. They are poor in nutrients and have poor physical conditions; many of them are transported soils (blown or carried by rivers), leached and reworked many times. Essentially, the Australian land surface has been sitting and baking for millions of years. There are few areas of new soils because of very little volcanic activity. The original parent material is lousy anyway.

"The reality is that we could argue the death penalty for anyone who causes the erosion of high quality soils and Kidman certainly didn't warrant it. The damage had been done. The frontage soils, where he was, are heavy, grey, cracking clays. I'm certain he probably got into the frontage vegetation very thoroughly because of the availability of water and feed but the impact of the earlier settlers was to change the vegetation anyway.

"Kidman's holdings were no better or worse than anyone else's. There is no way you could tell the condition of runs now in relation to when he bought them considering the general depredations of rabbits and droughts from 1896 to the 1940s, and from 1930 onwards he was almost in the worst climatic period in south-east Australia.

"It wasn't just the rabbit but the overstocking of sheep before Kidman's time. Sheep are terrible. They drag their feet. They break the skin of the soil. They make it susceptible to erosion to be blown away. It wasn't only their mouths that did the damage but their feet also.

"I hold the view that in the years of the rabbit and before myxomatosis (from the early 1890s until the early 1950s), research on improvement or rehabilitation of native vegetation used by sheep and cattle was impossible. We couldn't do it.

"You can't talk about what Kidman 'may have done' because you don't know what the condition was of Kidman's purchases, in view of the fact that his management ceased in the 1930s, which was twenty years before myxo and contained a series of the most severe droughts in Australia's short history.

"It makes it impossible to state with any certainty what the condition was when he'd finished with them. He could conceivably have taken pastoral degradation a bit further, but I'm sceptical.

"You'd have to give him the benefit of the doubt. Small peaks of prosperity would have relieved the underlying pressure on him and he must have been a fair sort of an operator — astute enough to be selling fat stock when the economic system and production system were under continuous threat (rainfall, Depression and meat prices)."

Sid took up Bulloo Downs in Queensland in 1903–04 from the Bank of New South Wales. He held it until he died and, after the family split, it was taken by Sid Reid and the Kidman Reid interests, who held it until 1981, when it was sold to Stanbrokes. Jack O'Shea was its manager for twenty years from 1960 to 1981. "Kidman bought it when the bank wanted to off-load it during the turn of the century drought," Jack O'Shea said.

"He mustered 14,000 cattle from it and sold 1,000 heifers to Nockatunga, an adjoining property. There was no way in the world after the 1965 drought that I could muster 1,000 heifers on Bulloo Downs to sell them, and you must bear in mind that we had sixty made-waters (bores, tanks and wells), and when Kidman bought it there was one well, six tanks and nine overshots on the creeks. And they say that he didn't put in improvements.

"The overshots were a bad mistake in earlier days. They silted up. They were a terrible thing. Yet I still saw them being put in elsewhere as late as 1953-54. When they silted up they became useless.

"I'll readily admit that the country won't carry the same stock as it did then and one of the main reasons is the rabbit. In 1893 they had the first council meeting at Thargomindah to erect a rabbit-proof fence. There were four on Bulloo Downs and one was the New South Wales–Queensland border. The wire was 1 inch square and the fence was 3 feet high, with two wires on the top of that, and made in 12 foot panels. It will give you an idea of how much timber was needed and I'm sure a lot of erosion was caused by felling that.

"In 1957 rabbits were still dying 18 inches thick on the border fence, and you could smell them half a mile away. In 1963, shortly after I'd taken over as manager, we had 102 rabbiters on the station taking off £5,000 in rabbits a week.

"I do know from former managers on Bulloo Downs that Sir Sidney's express instructions were that he never wanted to see a lot of tracks on a pad. He would know that meant that water and feed were getting short and cattle should be moved elsewhere. It was one of his specific instructions to managers and drovers. It has been my experience that he did care about the land and that he did improve it, certainly where water was concerned."

Bill Brook, a non-Kidman man who started as a stockman at Cordillo Downs in 1918 and later ended up owning both it and Adria Downs and clocking up the reputation as a noted South Australian pastoralist, accused Kidman in 1984 of not doing enough to improve his places. "He could have improved some properties more by putting more water on them — but he didn't. It's one of the reasons that the Kidmans lost a lot of properties or had parts cut off them because they never made the best use of them. Portions were cut off Glengyle, Durrie, Innamincka and Annandale by the Queensland Lands Department and given as additional areas to adjoining stations to make them viable areas.

"In 1939, when I took over Adria Downs, it had no permanent water on it. Since then I've put down fifty tanks of varying sizes, one flowing bore to nearly 4,000 feet and about sixteen sub-artesians, and I consider it to be the best-watered place in the district by far. In 1939 I paid 4 bob a mile for the leasehold. What's it worth today? Christ! I wouldn't know. A flowing bore cost £25,000 in 1955 and was finished in 1957, so water costs money, but Kidman wasn't interested in putting money into them. And he wasn't on his own. But today the government is making people spend money on places. Water should be compulsory rather· than flash joints for managers. A bloody big house doesn't enable a place to carry another head of stock. Water does.

"The Kidmans still own many big holdings in the area — Glengyle, Sandringham, Durrie, Morney Plains and Innamincka — but they sold or dealt away Diamantina Lakes, Davenport and Monkira after S.K.'s death. They're utilising bores on their places by running plastic pipes further out and present managements are holding any desert encroachment. They're wiser about everything.

"Kidman took over most of his places on account of drought, so he didn't leave the country any worse than he found it, but he could have left it better, but then if he'd had more water he would have had more cattle so you just don't know.

"I don't know whether he was an asset or a liability, but if there had been no Kidman about to buy, a lot of people would have been in dire straits because of drought and not got anything. If there'd been more with his foresight, others would have bought up places where he did. But there were no others. They didn't have the assets or the foresight and, if they had, he wouldn't have been in a position to build up in the way he did."

Bushman businessman R. M. Williams, who started out with a leather goods company making packsaddles for the Kidman empire, said· in 1985, "The question that Kidman raped the country is no more relevant to him than it is to any other owner of land. The fact is that bushes in outback Australia are slow to recover, particularly saltbush, and it will come back if the country is left empty and Kidman was known to spell his country. Over the last few years we have witnessed overstocking due to the cutting up of the Mitchell grass country, and it has, in many cases, ruined the Mitchell grass, so I would say there is more damage being done today by small holdings than was ever done in Kidman's time with his large holdings.

"Many were critical of Kidman because of lack of fencing improvements, but it was not his tradition to worry about expensive yards. He preferred to have cattle broncoed out in the open. I have no doubt that the bronco panel was established before Kidman's time, but nevertheless it became part of the Australian way of working cattle as Kidman bought more and more cattle stations. It became an established way of doing things. Call it 'the Kidman tradition', if you like."

When John Kempe retired in 1985 from the position of travelling manager for the Kidman company, he had clocked up fifty years working with it. His father before him had been one of Sid Kidman's favourite managers and had also had fifty years' service with the Kidmans. Despite some overlapping of years, it represented a century of service by two men. Commenting on the broncoing tradition, John Kempe said, "It's a dying art now. Young people don't stop long enough to learn, but the Kidman camps set up the tradition of broncoing that is still continued today. Elsewhere cattle were mustered to a main yard and then branded.

"With broncoing, they were lassoed from a horse and pulled up to a tree or ramp where the calves were branded and castrated. It was a quicker way. It was a timesaver because you didn't have to bring cattle to main yards. You did them where they were pastured. There was no expense. You didn't *have* to build yards. Kidman had no verandah managers. They were all working managers. Kidman set the pace with broncoing — and the others followed."

Charles Smith said in 1984, "Kidman was a master strategist and did have a love for the land. He hated to see it eaten bare. Stock were always moved around his big chain of stations to avoid it. That's why he disagreed with the Western Lands Commission that wanted to subdivide the west Darling holdings into little lots. He couldn't see little lots surviving.

"His judgement was sound and he could see into the future. Some of those stations are now in a shocking state. The old Selection (all he ran there were his stock horses) went to Harry Hyman, a Hebrew grocer, under the Western Lands carve up. He put thousands of head of sheep and cattle on it and stocked it up beyond the limited agreement and it became a dust bowl. He was out to make money quick — and did — but he killed the country in the process. S.K.'s approach was exactly the opposite."

Jim Schmidt, who went to work for Kidman as a 13-year-old buggy boy when Sid bought Corona in 1917 and who stayed on the station until 1949, becoming its manager in 1944, said, "The Western Lands cut the places up in the 1940s, until some were only as big as horse paddocks or were so small you couldn't even raise a cat on them — and they level charges of mismanagement at Kidman."

John Ayers Jnr, Kidman's great-grandson, who now heads the Kidman holdings (still run from Adelaide), said, "When the western New South Wales leases came up for renewal, they took the lot and said, 'Thank you very much, goodbye,' and split them into smaller holdings, mainly for soldier settlements. Most of these blokes went on just before the wool boom of the fifties and became millionaires overnight.

"The sad thing was that a lot of the people didn't know how to handle so much money in the big money boom and then the bad

seasons came and they were not prepared. They are now substand-ard, overgrazed holdings. Most government bodies admit now that the blocks were too small, and it was too hard on the country because the smaller blocks were stocked at a higher rate to make a living."

Jim Vickery, the chairman of the South Australian Pastoral Board and director of Outback Management, said in 1984, "It is true that Kidman had a reluctance where permanent water and im-proving properties was concerned with fencing, wells and bores, but it *must* be remembered that many of the big properties were in the Channel Country and some were endowed with plenty of natural, permanent waterholes. If you have permanent water in an arid zone you can maintain stock permanently, regardless of the condition of the vegetation, and from the point of view of environmental man-agement, it is very desirable to remove livestock from land that is under drought stress, and if your water is not permanent you have to remove livestock when the water supply is exhausted and that relieves the stress on the vegetation.

"Where he didn't improve water, Kidman had to move stock constantly, which was desirable management strategy in arid zones — neo-nomadic stocking — keeping livestock on the move and only grazing on lands capable of supporting them without causing en-vironmental damage and degradation. Kidman recognised that fact from the word 'go', and it was a good strategy for the lands com-prising his pastoral leases. Accusations of land misuse were made by people jealous of him.

"The situation of the condition of the land outside the Dog Fence was fairly stable throughout the development years because from the 1860s to 1970s it was used for open-range grazing, that is, unfenced. There was hardly a fence in the country until the 1970s.

"Because the lands were unfenced, cattle were able to graze neo-nomadically and move where the feed was and vacate the land subject to drought. It was a very good system and didn't degrade the land seriously (with a few exceptions).

"In the 1970s a program was begun to control bovine TB and brucellosis, which meant all cattle in far-flung lands had to be con-trolled both in their numbers and movements. This meant fencing and an end to neo-nomadism, that is, there were fixed numbers of cattle on fixed fenced areas of land. Once we did that we began to have problems of degradation. The problems are becoming very apparent now in the 1980s and will need proper management by state

---

OPPOSITE:
John Ayers Jnr, Sir Sidney's great-grandson, today the principal of Kidman Holdings in Adelaide. (John Ayers Jnr)

land management authorities and land users to prevent future degradation.

"This has been attended by good seasons, which have given us some leeway and time to think, 'What is the future?' And I like to think that, having time to think, we'll be able to prepare ourselves to bring adequate management controls to the land in the future. It's also given us time to get the message to landowners and warn them.

"The facts do not support the allegations that Kidman raped the land. It is handling the truth very carelessly. More degradation has occurred in the last twenty years outside the Dog Fence than in the fifty years before that because of changes in technology. In 1959, 80 per cent of cattle that moved outside the Dog Fence in Australia moved on the hoof. They walked with drovers and 20 per cent went on road trains and transport. In 1960 those figures were reversed with 80 per cent in transport and 20 per cent on the hoof.

"It was dramatic and motivated by the application of vast sums of Commonwealth money into beef roads. The system whereby cattle moved on the hoof was compatible with neo-nomadic grazing and the long-term nature of cycles in the arid zones, but road transport introduced sudden change. It meant that people could hang on until death knock and then shift cattle in a few days, so it brought total change to management strategy, enabling land users to hang on to livestock on drought-stressed pastures long after they should have been destocked. Road transport provided this facility and users maintained the stress on drought-stressed vegetation. Too many are still guilty of doing it, but they'll deny it until they're black in the face.

"To look at Kidman eighty years ago and onwards is to see a man who believed his stations should be run by capable cattle men and horsemen who kept the brand in the fire and wore out saddles and not motor cars. Most of them did not have many literate skills and were not broad-horizon administration managers who knew a lot about improvements, nor tacticians beyond the herds they managed. And Kidman's business embraced an entire chain of properties.

"Ultimately, what Kidman did was to select two strategists who had the capability, one to manage money and the economic side of the business, who was H. J. Bird, and the other, a travelling manager expert in stock and conditions, Ted Pratt. Pratt was followed by Ernie Spencer and they were the cattle tacticians who moved herds from station to station and who managed the properties as a chain with the local station managers as their lieutenants.

"The local managers moved the drovers, organised trucks and had to know the country very well: the stock routes from Derby in the Kimberleys to Wodonga on the Murray, the trucking centres, the meatworks, the buyers, the agents, the borders of their own properties and their neighbours', as well as a vast knowledge of seasonal conditions.

"They all worked for him with a mysterious, almost savage, loyalty, one never found before or since in pastoral companies. I don't think he was fully appreciated enough in his day as a born administrator and tactician and careful user of the land."

25

The Kidman Achievement

WHEN SID DIED he was unquestionably the best-known Australian — certainly within the Empire and also in the United States. Australia was still regarded as some far-flung outpost, but Sid's frequent overseas travel, his "picturesque style" where press men were concerned, his acquisition of large land holdings, plus the tags "Cattle King" and "King of the Bushmen", had made him a prominent personality. Radio broadcasts of his achievements were relayed overseas for some years before his death, and moving pictures could bring to the screen snippets of the way of life on his outback stations and the chaos and crowds at his big seventy-fifth birthday rodeo.

From the time he was knighted in 1921 until 1935 when he died, it was Kidman, along with Dame Nellie Melba and Don Bradman, who had "Australian achievement" stamped all over them and could stand up and be counted. There seemed to be no one else of their calibre, and Tom Clarke, presumably an Australian writer who was working in London in 1934, wrote angrily to the *Sydney Morning Herald*, saying, "While here writing a chapter I have just received a copy of the *Australian Year Book* with the biographies of 500 prominent Australians and the name of Sidney Kidman was not there. This man, whose life of 77 years is the story of the real Australia in flesh and blood — for he spans so much of its period of development — is not there. Could such an omission happen in any other country? What is the standard of measurement or is it that Australians are so jealous of their Big Men that they wish to hide them from the world's prying eyes? The thing baffles me."

So how big was Sid? The assessment given by his office when he died was that he owned or controlled sixty-eight stations over an area of more than 100,000 square miles. That was no doubt true in itself, but it did not incorporate the financial interest he had in many other places. While not owning or controlling them outright, at least he had a stake in them, and this is true of a number of places, which took his total land interests at his death to around 130,000 square miles spread over more than ninety stations. Throughout his life, since the moment he had started acquiring places (not counting the tiny portion of land, Thule, bordering on the You Can't Lick It run),

440

he controlled, owned or had an interest in about 160,000 square miles of country, which is still a conservative estimate, because not all the area details of the 150 stations the figure represents can be traced accurately.

Anyone wanting an instant insight into 160,000 square miles should see it translated at more than 100 million acres and bear in mind that the average Sydney building block of land plus suburban house represents a quarter of an acre, so there were four of those to every acre. Therefore Sid, at one stage or another through out his life, had property interests equivalent to the area of 400 million Sydney suburban homes. Shaded in on a map of New South Wales, for instance, it would cover any two-thirds of the state.

By 1903 he had been dubbed the "Cattle King". It was a tag that stuck. As time went on he might have been called, more accurately, the "Land Lord", for he certainly seems to have acquired more of it than anyone else in modern history. In the United States, where they had severed any association with royalty, they still enjoyed the use of the word "king" in relation to businessmen who were tops in their field, and there Sid was also known as "the ranch rajah", "the cattle conquistador", "the beef baron" and "the homespun herdsman". "The king of the bushlands" was another tag applied to Kidman, though used less frequently. The emphasis was always on cattle, which he certainly did not lack, but if he is looked at in terms of land holdings, then it is hard to find a private businessman in modern times who has eclipsed him.

In England at the time of Sid's first visit in 1908, when newspapers rapturously carried the stories about his vast estates, American papers picked them up and made comparisons, stating, "It is said that Sidney Kidman controls 32 million acres and so is believed to be the largest landholder in the British Empire. It would be pretty safe to say the world, for Henry Miller, the largest landholder in the United States, falls a long way short of the acreage. Miller, the last of the cattle barons, owned at one period of his life 14,080,000 acres. Some ingenious person then made a calculation showing that Miller could start at the Mexico border travelling by team to British Columbia and camp every night of the journey on his own land. He then owned 80,000 cattle and 100,000 sheep, falling short of Kidman who is credited with 250,000." (When Miller died in 1916 at the age of 88 his land had dwindled to a mere 800,000 acres.)

Not a few people have assessed the Vesteys as being far greater than Kidman. No exact parallel can be struck where the Vesteys are concerned, because they were Englishmen who operated outside their own country, whereas Sid was an Australian operating entirely within his own country. But unquestionably the Vesteys had considerable land holdings in South America for their beef and meat export trade before moving into the Northern Territory just before the First World War, where, within two years, they had acquired 36,000 square miles of pastoral land.

The Vesteys put paid to the adage that two things are inevitable: death and taxes. For the super-rich Vesteys, only one of these applied — death. The family found that, by some ingenious schemes, taxes could be delayed by sixty years or more. Total secrecy of their business operations was one aspect of the scheme of the gilt-edged tax dodgers. The Vesteys did not believe that any publicity was good publicity. They thought no publicity was far, far better, and trying to extract information from them is like trying to take Fort Knox with a jemmy and few firecrackers. A request to the company to state its land holdings and cattle numbers at its zenith produced the following reply: "We note you are particularly interested in our total land holdings for purposes of the publication of a book on Sir Sidney Kidman and we regret we are unable to provide the figures you request," said C. H. Carrell, secretary to Sam, Lord Vestey, Dame Nellie Melba's grandson. "Details of pastoral and other holdings going back a number of years are not readily available and for both private and competitive reasons, together with company policy, we prefer not to contribute."

Martin Summons, a skilled Australian journalist working in London in 1985, diplomatically pressed the company for a more specific answer and received the following reply from Carrell: "I am asked to state that the Vestey family have no interest in disputing any allegation that Sir Sidney Kidman was, in his time, the largest pastoral landholder. On the other hand, Lord Vestey is not willing to allocate staff for the purpose of establishing the total size of land holdings or cattle numbers in any particular part of the world at any particular time. He has no wish to be uncooperative in these matters but the information is not readily available."

The veil of secrecy is in direct contrast with Sid's frank and open attitude to his business. At any time during the forty years of his life that he was buying and selling properties, he could answer any enquiry as to how much land he had but less readily the number of cattle. He never avoided any questions on cattle numbers, saying repeatedly that it was hard to know within 25,000 or so if the figure was correct. In any event, the Vesteys do not dispute the fact that Sid was the larger landholder, while being extremely shy about stating their own acquisitions.

Tom Cole, who worked at some of the Northern Territory's major station stock-camps from 1928 onwards and later became Australia's foremost buffalo and crocodile shooter, said, "Vesteys got hold of some big places. In the Kimberleys in Western Australia they had Margaret River, Flora Valley, Lower Sturt, Gordon Downs,

Nicholson and Ord River, and in the Northern Territory, Mistake Creek, Limbunya, Waterloo, Birrindudu, Wave Hill, Delamere, Willeroo, Manbulloo, Glencoe, Burnside, Mount Litchfield and Marrakoi, but some of these may have been taken up in the 1930s after Kidman had died."

Other Australians also held large slices of pastoral land, but they were before Kidman's time. By 1882, C. B. Fisher and J. M. Lyons had amassed holdings in the Territory of 38,890 square miles, while their biggest run, Victoria River Downs, was no smaller than the Kingdom of Denmark: 15,885 square miles. And certainly the name of James Tyson cannot be overlooked.

Kidman and Tyson were the two giants who dominated the Australian pastoral scene for seven decades. Because of certain parallels, their lives deserve a general comparison.

When research for this book was being done, a terse suggestion was made by a distant member of the Tyson family that the "Cattle King" title should not be given to Kidman and that the only true claimant to the title was James Tyson. It was also claimed that Kidman did not devise the "chain-of-supply" theory — that of owning a series of grazing properties extending from breeding country through fattening country to holding areas close to the desired market — and that Tyson had such a scheme working well for him years before Kidman was ever on the scene. Nearly a hundred years after Tyson's death and fifty years after Kidman's death, the issue still tends to smart.

What can be said of the "Cattle King" tag is that it stuck like glue to Sid Kidman for thirty-five years of his life, from the turn of the century until his death in 1935. The term was never applied so zealously to Tyson. From the mid-1880s until his death in 1898, there are some press references to Tyson in terms of his being "a cattle king"; more often he was referred to as "well-known pastoralist, Mr Jas Tyson" and often in conversation as Jim "Hungry" Tyson or "Hungry" Jim Tyson. It was the Australian press who saw Kidman as taking over where Tyson had left off and who dubbed Sid the "Cattle King". These words said it all. It was a description the world press was happy to apply, too.

As for the "chain-of-supply" originator, it is of little import whether Kidman was the first or not. Chains of supply may have operated successfully for others before his day — lesser chains in safer country and those so insignificant as to escape attention. Tyson, it must be said, did have a chain of supply working for him, but it was a much smaller chain of stations in far superior country than Kidman ever occupied, mainly in New South Wales and Queensland. It certainly did not have the risk factor attached to it that Sid's operation did.

Whenever the words "chain of supply" are used, they will always be associated instantly with Kidman, because his was the most daring chain of supply ever envisaged and then put into practice and was, in fact, not only one chain but two, his north–south chain and Central Australian chain. The north–south chain saw stock moved from the Gulf Country or western Queensland down the "three rivers" to his holding depot, Mundowdna, in South Australia, before being trucked at Farina. The Central Australian chain existed for staging stock from Western Australian and Northern Territory holdings into the north of South Australia and to Mundowdna, and then trucking them at Farina. Some Queensland and New South Wales stock were also moved via the chain of properties in remote western New South Wales to Broken Hill and to the depot station, Forders, before trucking at either Cockburn or Broken Hill.

Kidman's properties were from coast to coast: Yeeda, Western Australia, to Dotswood, Queensland, Vanrook in the Gulf Country to Yambacoona on King Island. It was the vastness of the Kidman chain of supply that took people's breath away; it was certainly the biggest, boldest chain of supply ever contemplated and undertaken in Australia, if not the world.

Unquestionably Kidman was the first person to see the potential of the "three rivers" (the Cooper, Diamantina and Georgina) for a chain of supply. Tyson, on the scene for decades before Kidman, either did not see their potential or else ignored the possibility because of the high risk involved and opted to set up a less extensive chain in safer grazing and more reliably watered country.

It has been said that Tyson held more stock than Kidman, something that could not be clarified for the purposes of this book. He certainly died a wealthier man than Sid, with his estate in three colonies probated at £2.27 million, a figure that was reduced from an estimated £4 million in 1893 by the long series of bad seasons that had prevailed throughout the 1890s.

Tyson was born in 1819 near Campbelltown, New South Wales. Like Kidman, he received little in the way of schooling and before he was 20 was working as a station hand in western New South Wales. In 1852 gold provided a launch pad for the Tyson brothers, just as silver at Broken Hill had for the Kidman brothers. James Tyson and his three brothers started a butchering business and an abattoir at Bendigo, about 200 miles by a good stock route from the large runs Tupra and Juanbung that they had pioneered in the lower Lachlan area of New South Wales. They sold their own stock direct to the miners on a first-come-first-served basis. It was almost a licence to print money. They butchering business was bought out three years later and how the money was divided between the brothers is uncertain, but in any event the sale left Jim Tyson with the incredibly large sum of £200,000, which staked him for what was to follow.

After Bendigo, Tyson bought out his brother from Tupra and Juanbung and began lending money with a vengeance and often without any legal security. There seemed to be some sort of hoodoo in accepting Tyson money. Luck seemed to desert a property: bad seasons set in, and station after station fell into Tyson's hands in this way, earning him little in the way of popularity, just as Kidman was detested when hard times forced people to the wall and he acquired stations at rock-bottom prices.

By 1865 Tyson owned 2.4 million acres of property in Queensland, New South Wales and Victoria. He later added to his holdings with other Queensland runs. The period of the largest extent of Tyson's land holdings was from 1880 onwards. From that time until his death in 1898, his lands remained fairly constant at about 9.6 million acres; Kidman had surpassed him five times over as early as 1908, when he owned, controlled or had an interest in 50 million acres and had not yet started with his considerable western New South Wales holdings, and those in the Gulf Country and the Northern Territory were also yet to come.

It does appear that in modern times there was not another person to rival Sid Kidman either in Australia or elsewhere in the world, one who rose from scratch and bought up huge tracts of a continent. Most of them were bought with a deliberate purpose: to add to either one or the other of his chains of stations that were geared to move stock in a streamlined way to market. Each station did have a purpose in the link — either breeding, fattening or trucking — with numerous stations in between providing links for feed and water. At their best, the chains produced great results, bringing stock in an even flow to markets; at their worst, under severe stress in times of drought when losses were great, expert drovers could still get through with stock in reduced numbers, and the chains held.

Until there is evidence to the contrary, Sid can be considered the greatest pastoral landholder in modern history and be given full credit for the gamble with his chains of stations in remote country. It is unlikely that such a chain will ever be established anywhere in the world again. The sadness, if not the disgrace, of the matter was that so soon after his death, and through jealousy and avarice, his family split the lot.

There were other interesting similarities in the lives and natures of Kidman and Tyson.

Both were middle-aged before they moved towards success in a big way (Tyson was 46 and Kidman 38). Kidman was the more rash of the two men and Tyson the more cautious; it is strange, therefore, that despite the tremendous amount of wealth he did accumulate Tyson left no will. He avoided every form of indulgence and luxury.

The bush was his chosen home and out of this environment he was unhappy. Kidman also was happiest when he was roughing it in the bush. Kidman was more outgoing, affable and popular; Tyson was more austere, dour and reserved, often seeking anonymity when he travelled, using either the name Smith or Shiels.

Both men were intensely patriotic. Kidman did his utmost to help the First World War effort. Love of country had prompted Tyson to offer the Queensland government a loan of £500,000 to relieve that state of the obligation to grant an Anglo-French-Jewish syndicate 12 million acres in Queensland as payment for laying a railway line from Charleville to the Gulf Country. Later, in the financial depression of 1892, Tyson took up £250,000 of Queensland Treasury bills and in gratitude Premier McIlwraith appointed him to the Legislative Council. He sat in the chamber for several weeks but made only one speech, on the nesting habits of kangaroo rats and paddymelons, and when a bewildered Hansard reporter wrongly recorded the names of the animals, Tyson was so disgusted he never addressed the House again. "It was my only speech," he said sadly, "and they spoiled it." He went back to the bush.

Tyson avoided women with an eccentric fear. He never married, and it is said he counselled young men against marriage and chided married men for being married. His philosophy relating to women was confided at least to stock agent Harry H. Peck. It was a philosophy that Hitler was expounding decades later. "He thought that at the time of full development all women should be medically examined and those that did not come up to the standard in development and constitution should be sterilised and the race thereby improved," Peck said. "His argument was 'We cull our breeders to improve our stock, why not improve the human race along the same lines?'. To him it was logical and also a system civilisation might one day have to apply."

Like Kidman, Tyson was a fanatical tea drinker and at Felton on the Darling Downs, where he lived for the last twenty years of his life, he had his tea served in a billy on the sideboard. Tyson said, "My housekeeper used to serve my tea in a teapot covered with a nightcap [the way he referred to a tea cosy] and several times I burnt my mouth from the over-hot tea. I asked her to cut out the nightcap but as she persisted I eventually threw teapot and nightcap out the window and have had the billy ever since and the tea as it should be."

Kidman also didn't care for tea from teapots or fine china, and on the many trips he made by railway he would ignore the buffet car, saving any thirst until the train pulled into a station, where he also ignored the refreshment kiosks, preferring to scratch together a few handfuls of kindling and boil the billy on the platform. Stories such as this don't necessarily indicate meanness on his part, but like Tyson, a preference for the old billy as the only way to enjoy a good drink of tea.

Neither Kidman nor Tyson was ever known to swear in his life. On his first visit to Heyfield, in the Gippsland district, Tyson was taken on an inspection by the manager who asked him what he thought of the various paddocks of Victorian-bred stock. "Well, mister," Tyson said, "I think them a lot of 3 Bs." In cattle terminology "3 Bs" meant "browns, brindles and bastards".

Tyson was a life abstainer from alcohol (this is partially true in Kidman's case) and a non-smoker (Kidman also abstained from smoking for most of his life). Both men later in life suffered from deafness and both were similar in their desire to weave as many members of their families as possible into their pastoral businesses. Tyson detested personal publicity (the main reason that he travelled incognito); Kidman was not averse to it.

Tales of Tyson's meanness have circulated, just as they have about Kidman. When a new church was being built on the Darling Downs, Tyson was approached for a donation to head the list. He asked the amount of the estimated cost, got his cheque book and, to the surprise of the people who had called on him, gave a cheque for the lot. When the church was nearly finished it was found the architect had omitted to allow for a lightning rod and the church committee returned to Tyson asking if he would like to complete his gift by paying for the lightning rod. "No," he replied. "If God thinks proper to strike the church with lightning I am not going to attempt to interfere."

One thing Kidman but not Tyson was accused of was lack of improvements on properties. Tinnenburra at the time of Tyson's death was the most expensively and best artificially watered property in Queensland, and it had more artesian bores on it than any other property in Australia. Some of the bores were of great depth, with bore drains running water out to otherwise waterless country. Any improvements he made on his stations were always substantial and made to last for generations. He did not begrudge spending money on yards, fences and dams.

Kidman knew that Tyson had a fine stamp of a man working for him, and after Tyson's death when his holdings were sold, Kidman encouraged Tyson men to join his outfit. Among those who did, and later became Kidman managers, were John Brooke (who managed the depot, Mundowdna), Albert Edwards (who managed Glengyle) and his brother Pierce Edwards (who managed Norley). Pierce Edwards started his career on Tinnenburra: "I began there at 15 shillings a week and later as a full-blown stockman equal to any in the country I got 25 shillings a week and worked sixteen hours a day.

In 1894 Mr Tyson sent away from Tinnenburra 10,000 fats and spayed 10,000 cows. The manager, Mr John MacDonald, who spayed them, holds the record for one day's spaying — 427 cows.

"Once I drove Mr Tyson from Tinnenburra through his stations in New South Wales in a buggy drawn by two horses. I landed one night with Mr Tyson at one of his sheep stations. We camped about a mile and a half away from the homestead in the horse paddock. Mr Tyson said to me, 'You need not get up too early. I will take a walk down in the morning.' He got down there at daylight and caught the manager exercising two racehorses around the house. The poor manager was paid off."

Sid Kidman had a few words to say about Tyson himself: "I worked with Jimmie Tyson in the 1870s and travelled with him during the time of the big 1891 strike. In spite of numerous legends of his meanness, I always found him a good man to deal with. His pay wasn't big, but he used to say if he paid a man too much he would get rich too quickly and leave him. A man had to be a top-notcher to stay on Jimmie's payroll.

"He used to wear a beautiful big gold watch-chain," Kidman added with a twinkle in his eye, "a bootlace!"

"I don't care what they say about Tyson, I liked him. He was a very reserved and humble man. He told me that when he was in Sydney he used to get a bag of letters asking for donations and that he would throw them into the fire.

"He had the most extraordinary habits. He used to get around the country like a swaggie and he was worth millions. I remember that fellows use to ask him for a lift on his buggy to some station where they were going to work for him. He used to travel under the name of 'Smith'. Sometimes he would give them a lift and they used to talk about the mean old devil Tyson. Not all his men knew him and sometimes he would drop in on a camp under the name of Smith and switch the conversation around to Tyson. Some used to abuse the name soundly then Tyson would get up and say, 'Here's your cheque. Get out!'

"He hated women. He never married. He wouldn't have them on his stations if he could help it. That was a queer kink in the man.

"He went out to one of his stations once and called at the homestead and asked for the manager. The manager's wife said he was out on the run for a couple of days. Tyson said he would wait and the woman invited him to stay in the house. He said, no, he would camp down by the creek. He wouldn't eat meals in the house but cooked his own. When the manager returned he introduced his wife to Tyson. She nearly swooned. She had no idea he was their millionaire boss.

"On another occasion he called at a property to buy steers. The lady of the house asked him to stay and have a warm wash. But he said, 'No, thanks. I will wash in the creek — the sand there is better than soap to keep a man clean.'

"They used to say Tyson lived on grass. Starting out on a fortnight's drove he would cook a damper big enough to last all the way. Ned Pender who was travelling with him once said he made a damper almost as big as a buggy wheel and he wouldn't use the wood picked up from the ground as there was too much sand on it; he would have it clean off the trees. He never gave his men anything but flour, tea and brown sugar. 'Kill a steer if you're hungry,' he used to say.

"But for all his hard ways he was a great man. He made his own start from nothing and lived as he expected his men to live. He was always first up on the trail. He slept when the cattle slept like a true cowman. When he supplied the Bendigo diggings he bought cattle for £2 and got £20 from them, yet I have seen thousands of his Tinnenburra cattle make only £3 or £4 gross. They would not have netted him more than £2 or £2.10.0. He used to brand his cattle TY1 with a triangle on the jaw as a safeguard. When he died I'd say he was worth five millions. If he'd lived another five years he would have been worth ten millions. He would not employ inspectors to watch his interests but did it all himself. He was always working. He said that if he did not keep a look-out, his managers would have him carrying his swag within a year."

Tyson and Kidman, Kidman and Tyson — the pastoral giants. Just as there were similarities, there were differences. While Tyson lived as a somewhat homeless, lonely wanderer, ever suspicious, trusting few people and acquiring few friends, Kidman married and raised a family and his life approaches nearer than Tyson's to the ideal. Possibly Kidman had a larger capacity for happiness than had Tyson. Whether Tyson, who remains a legendary figure of the bush, was really happy none can say. Though he had great possessions he was content with little, and it is certain that no other life other than the life he chose would have brought happiness to him.

Sid's achievement poses a remaining question: could it all be done again? "No bloody way," said Jack Watt. "No one could ever hope to repeat what he did. All stock walked in his day and what he created was a line from go to whoa in his own country."

Ted Hayes, a Territorian cattle man in the Alice Springs area, said, "It's not possible. It would not be possible because of the conservationists and the disease problems which make it hard to shift cattle from A to B over long distances as Kidman did and always towards the fat market. It's not possible now because of the brucellosis and TB eradication program and in the Northern

Territory the stock routes' water has not been maintained by the government, which also has certain restrictions about the amount of country that can be owned by an individual. Never, ever again will anyone be able to do what Kidman did."

"Done again?" said Bill "Mr Birdsville" Brook, one of South Australia's leading pastoralists. "No. No single man could ever build up as Kidman did and even Kidman himself couldn't do it today. He couldn't have such big holdings because governments wouldn't allow it, even if the stations were fairly well watered to the point of carrying herds better. No. It just couldn't be done."

"Our laws these days wouldn't allow it to happen," said Jack O'Shea, of Queensland, the Kidman manager of Bulloo Downs for two decades from 1961 to 1981. "It's not to say that companies haven't tried. Stanbrokes virtually tried to work along the same lines but didn't have what Sir Sidney had, and that was one single person having total control. Stanbrokes now own Bulloo Downs. They bought it in 1979 for £3 million — a far cry from the £20,000 that Kidman paid for it in 1903. The company has nineteen places [in 1984] and Bulloo Downs is one of them, their biggest holding in Queensland. I think the person who came closest to Kidman was "Hungry" Tyson, and that was before Kidman's time. Tyson had land near Wyandra, 64 miles from Cunnamulla, down to the border and in New South Wales and running into Victoria; a chain if you like, but not a patch on what Kidman had."

"It's out of the question that it could ever be done again," said Charles Smith. "Kidman seized an opportunity at a time when there was a great vacuum. Government legislation blocks any similar build-up today by not granting licences to anyone with too much money for too much land.

"The other fact to be considered is that you'd never get as much pastoral bankruptcy at one particular time again as happened in the Kidman era. Landholders, as such, perhaps were not 'bankrupt' but they did not have sufficient liquidity to carry on and the banks would not grant it. Kidman was an exception and when the Bank of New South Wales was looking for a way out of its troubles, it felt that Kidman with his shrewdness, knowledge of the land and sound reputation was someone who could provide it. He was a logical solution for the bank at the time."

R. M. Williams said, "The Cattle King was held in great awe by Australian cattle men as a legendary figure in his own lifetime. His name stood for something that was big, something unapproachable and something that almost defied imagination. As to whether what he did could be done again, I can only say that in the past few years one man by the name of Peter Sherwin has been buying up repeatedly to the point that he now controls a large amount of territory."

In 1985 Sherwin had a cattle empire of 260,000 and controlled sixteen stations, the plum of which was Victoria River Downs, which he took up late in 1984 after several other buyers had either placed offers in the area of £10 million to £12 million and then withdrawn or not had them acknowledged by the Hooker Corporation, which owned the 12,000 square kilometre station, or by the Northern Territory government. An element of secrecy surrounds the Sherwin family operations, as it has always done with the Vestey concerns. It is said that the Sherwin family now controls 69,446 square kilometres (or 26,800 square miles) of land (about 1 per cent of the Australian continent) with a cattle herd second only to the AMP's Stanbroke Pastoral Company's 300,000. Sherwin started buying in 1958, when he was aged 27 and he drew the remote and wild Wallamunga Station on the Northern Territory–Western Australia border in a Crown Land ballot. Since then, Mungabroom, Birrindudu, Anthony Lagoon, Gordon Downs, Flora Valley, Cluny, Springvale, Diamantina Lakes (a former Kidman place), Keeroongooloo, Marama, Galway Downs, Walhallow, Cresswell Downs, Eva Downs and Victoria River Downs have been added.

In one respect Peter Sherwin is akin to Kidman: a self-made man who started out as stockman as a youth and who, by 1952, was the head stockman on the pick of the Vestey stations, Helen Springs. Just what Sid Kidman may have thought of Sherwin had he lived in his own time is debatable, given that gospel had it that 'a Kidman stockman was a Vesteys manager'. And Sherwin was simply a Vesteys stockman. . .

In almost thirty years since he started acquiring pastoral land, Sherwin has notched up the above figure. He stands out as the only single (or family grouped) Australian to have done so in that time, but in a similar thirty years from either 1895–1925 or from 1900–30, Sid's buying pattern puts Sherwin very much in the shade: he owned, controlled or had an interest in more than 150 stations during his lifetime, land extending over more than 160,000 square miles; and he owned, controlled or had an interest in more than eighty stations and more than 130,000 square miles at his death.

But it will not be possible for anyone — one man or one family, or even a major company — to build up land again in the Kidman manner.

In amassed land area, in 1985 it was a commonly held view that Stanbrokes were first, followed by the AA Company and Sherwin; this top trio of landholders is frequently named, but this underrates the position of the Kidmans in the Australian pastoral hierarchy today.

The not inconsiderable remnants of Sid's empire are still held by the family and, in area, the holdings amount to nearly twice that occupied by Sherwin. It does seem odd that the Kidman holdings can be overlooked in any current assessment of pastoral greatness. The holdings consist of Anna Creek, South Australia, of 30,114 square kilometres (11,627 square miles), which is the largest pastoral property in Australia and almost three times the size of Victoria River Downs, Arcoona, South Australia, 3,460 square kilometres (1,336 square miles), Durham Downs, Queensland, 7,950 square kilometres (3,069 square miles), Durrie, Queensland, 6,710 square kilometres (2,591 square miles), Glengyle, Queensland, 5,500 square kilometres (2,123 square miles), Innamincka, South Australia, 13,817 square kilometres (5,335 square miles), Macumba, South Australia, 18,260 square kilometres (7,050 square miles), Morney Plains, Queensland, 2,130 square kilometres (822 square miles), Naryilco, Queensland, 7,057 square kilometres (2,725 square miles), Quinyambie, South Australia, 12,119 square kilometres (4,679 square miles), Sandringham, Queensland, 5,123 square kilometres (1,980 square miles), Ruby Plains, Western Australia, 3,747 square kilometres (1,447 square miles), Ned's Corner, Victoria, 86,543 hectares (213,687 acres), Netley, New South Wales, 7,454 hectares (18,404 acres), Ned's Corner, Western Australia, 8,912 hectares (22,006 acres), Point Sturt, South Australia, 810 hectares (1,999 acres) and Eringa Park, South Australia, 1,215 hectares (3,000 acres).

After the family split in the late 1930s, when Sid Reid pulled out and set up as Kidman Reid and Co., he received some plum cattle and sheep stations. The sheep stations were mainly in New South Wales and were roped in by the Western Lands Commission as their leases expired. The Kidman Reid company continued to operate as an entity, but in 1983 Reg Reid's family withdrew its interest and began operating on its own. Reg Reid was Sidney Reid's youngest child (born in 1921 and died in 1977), and his son, Philip, a great-grandson of Sir Sidney, assumed authority of the splintered interest.

It was either too hard for, or perhaps not preferred by, Kidman Reid and Co. and the Reg Reid interests to state their holdings while this book was being written. Suffice to say that they have been reduced over the years and it is claimed by some within the Reid–Kidman family that the feud continues today, with Philip Reid "not talking to" John Ayers Jnr, also a great-grandson of Sir Sidney, who captains the Kidman interests today.

Walter Kidman had assumed full control of the company after Bel's death, albeit with the pastoral knowledge and back-up of Ted Pratt until his retirement, in 1940, as the company's pastoral inspector and travelling manager. The job was taken over by Ernie Spencer, a young but highly considered station manager in Sid Kidman's time. Spencer died in harness in 1964, when the position was assumed by John Kempe, son of Ernie Kempe, another favoured old Kidman employee. Between them, the father–son Kempe combination had clocked up 100 years' service when John Kempe retired in 1985. It meant that, for most of the years Walter Kidman operated as chief of the holdings, he had Spencer and then Kempe Jnr as his main consultants.

Sid Reid was still running his own breakaway show and ought not to be dismissed as insignificant. He was host to the Duke and Duchess of Gloucester when they stayed at Norley during their Australian tour in the 1960s and also sat next to the Queen as her form adviser and racing tipster during her visit to Australia in 1963, when he was chairman of the South Australian Jockey Club and the Queen attended an Adelaide race meeting. Sid Reid died in 1971 aged 83.

Walter, on a visit to England in 1951, received an invitation to a Buckingham Palace garden party along with his eldest daughter, Isabel, and his wife, Muriel. He remained the head of the Kidman holdings until 1970, when he died just before Christmas. Muriel Kidman recorded, "Walter kept up his father's tradition of supporting the Salvation Army, which came with a band on the back of a lorry and played in our garden each year at Christmas time. They would ask what carols we wanted and would play them and Walter would give them a handsome cheque. They would say a prayer and bless the house, while our neighbours peered through the gates wondering what was going on."

Walter died on 23 December 1970 at the age of 70. That his health was greatly impaired was attested by Muriel, who said, "Our daughter Isabel had just come home from a hair appointment and announced, 'I'm home,' when she saw Walter walking towards the bathroom. She said, 'Dad, you shouldn't be walking. I'll get you your chair.' 'Yes,' he said, 'I just want to go to the bathroom. I'll be back in five minutes.' In that time he'd fallen from the toilet and hit his head on the floor. There was blood coming from it. He was just about dead and trying to say something that we could not understand. His funeral service was held in our house. I've never seen the house so jammed with people. The flowers stretched from the house to the fence. They don't carry on with flowers like that now. They shouldn't. It's such a waste. They came from all sorts of people including Louie, the head man at the South Australian Hotel. He ran the dining room."

That Walter Kidman's physical disability had magnified over the years is obvious, as had his capacity for alcohol. "He'd embarked on a lot of liquid diets in his younger days," according to a source who knew Walter well, "and had the early reputation of a playboy. He tried to live two lives — one, socialising with the toffs, and the other with the bushwhackers. When the bushmen were in town, Muriel, his wife, was always a great asset: 'C'mon you boys,' she'd say, 'hop

up with me out onto the dance floor.' But drink? Walter certainly did so, and towards the end of his days he could be found down at Walsh's (an Adelaide hotel) with a large glass of gin conducting business from mid-morning onwards. It was said that, at his home, he had a cocktail cabinet in the bathroom and also his bedroom. The whole thing was quite tragic. He was, at heart, a very good man but one who didn't have the stamina and wherewithal that his father had."

When Walter died, the Kidman company had to look to another to head the firm. And Edna Ayers, who had always hoped that the company would come to her only son, John Ayers, had her wish fulfilled in the latter days of her life. John Ayers took over the running of the Kidman holdings and held control until his death in 1981 at the age of 66 when his only son, John Ayers Jnr, resumed control at the age of 40. So the not inconsiderable interests of the remaining Kidman family today are still under the control of one of Sid's great-grandsons. The 45,000 square miles (116,550 square kilometres) of country the family still has represents less than half of what Sid had at his death fifty years ago, but almost twice the amount currently held by the Sherwin interests.

Sid's Fulham Park racing stud still exists in the form of the main home with minimal grounds and is occupied by his grand-daughter Anne Abel Smith. In 1985, she said, "It's still a landmark. As a young child, my outing for the week was a trip to Fulham Park with Dad and, if I was lucky, I got a milkshake on the way home.

"Dad gave it to me for my home later on. I was always so pleased that I'd be living there. It had the air of an English country property with its high-gabled roofs. Dad always said, in later times, that he'd never come to grief — either by burglary or foul play with horses — because a 'king of the Underworld', 'Treacle' Fimeri, kept his horses there. Treacle always had a big, black car and bodyguards that got out and Dad would always say, 'Hi, there, Treacle...,' and they'd check out the horses.

"Dad shared all his horses with me. It was really terrific. All I had to do was turn up at the races and he paid the bills! Fulham Park was 700 acres initially and three years after Dad died the bulk was sold to Stokes, the builder, and it was developed into a suburb of Adelaide, Kidman Park."

David Ross Coles, the son of Ross Coles of Coles and Thomas and then Coles Bros, who is now chairman of the South Australian

---

OPPOSITE:
Walter and Muriel Kidman at a social function in the 1950s. (The Kidman family)

Jockey Club, said, "Fulham Park, Adelaide, was sold at the Wool Exchange, Adelaide, to Stokes the building developer for £1,350,000 after an opening bid of £1 million. It drew one of the largest crowds ever at the Wool Exchange and the sale was televised because of the interest in it."

The once-fabulous home Eringa at Kapunda is now the Kapunda High School and has been since 1921, with rarely a student not knowing of the life and achievement of the man who bequeathed it. The equally notable home in Adelaide, Eringa at Unley Park, which once occupied an enormous area (it was hemmed in by streets rather than other houses), was sold off for a vast amount and subdivided in the 1970s after Walter's death. The main home and grounds surrounding it have since been resold in 1984 for $400,000.

Sid's name has been kept up, here and there, and perhaps to no significant degree. Kidman Springs, a small, remote place in the Northern Territory, is named after him as is Kidman Creek. The suburb Kidman Park exists in Adelaide. In 1936, the year after Sid's death, the Master Butchers of Adelaide put up a commemorative plaque at the saleyards to honour him, and the following year, his family provided the impressive entrance gates at Adelaide's Wayville Showgrounds with a handsome plaque to perpetuate his name.

By 1985 the name Kidman had little or no meaning to many Australians, certainly in Sydney, where almost one-quarter of the entire population of Australia (almost 16 million) lived. In a snap opinion poll, hundreds of people were asked, "What does the name Sidney Kidman mean to you and do you have any opinion about him?" One classic reply was "Australian tennis has gone downhill ever since he took the cream of our players in the fifties and turned them into professionals." (The respondent had obviously confused Kidman with the American entrepreneur Jack Kramer.) For the most part, people said the name meant nothing to them. Some people did react to the name immediately: "Oh, the old Cattle King. What do you want to know about him for?" or "I suppose you're asking about Sid Kidman; that's the only Kidman that rings a bell." Such responses were very much in the minority and given by older men.

The question-answer session was undertaken in January 1984 when research for this book was first started, and it seemed a good omen that the major newspapers of Australia carried large headlines saying, "Farmers rejoice at the big wet", "Inland sea hits four states and Northern Territory", "Widespread floods in four states" and "Nation awash; floods in four states". In a simple translation, heavy rain over Central and north-eastern Australia had brought down not only the "three rivers" but other, lesser streams and creeks as well. It was the type of rain occurrence Sid would have liked more often in his life but was not destined to see. Yet he knew the risk he was taking in acquiring such massive land holdings and linking them together in a bid to make them drought resistant.

Such rains in Sid's day would have drawn him to his feet at the Adelaide cattle sales or Kapunda horse sales, bawling, "Knock 'em down. Knock 'em down," and not bothering to wait for the highest bids while his pockets bulged with telegrams of wonderful rain reports. Major rains in Sid's time, while they drew great rejoicing, were not without tragic overtones, as packhorse mailmen, drovers or stockmen were swept to their deaths in the floods. In 1984, the rejoicing was no less among the people who now occupy the far-flung outposts. The greatest drama in the news stories related to stranded outback travellers in their cars and the slick, modern communications and transport — light planes and helicopters that made food drops, took medical supplies and evacuated any sick or injured.

Sid Kidman built up and added to his empire in an age when Australia owned few railways and fewer telegraph lines and when there was no wireless, motor transport nor aircraft. For forty years he guided the activities of numerous stations scattered over the length and breadth of Australia, controlled the movement of great herds hundreds of miles apart and, with the aid of a phenomenal memory, an intensive knowledge of the geography of the bush and a small, scattered army of superb men, sent the products of the arid and semi-arid lands in an evenly flowing stream to the markets of the country. Where others had failed, he succeeded. It brought him wealth and it brought Australia wealth. Asked constantly about the secret of his success, he gave the standard answer: "I have always taken care of the little things and don't think one can go far wrong who does. If the small things are let go amiss, so will the big things."

It goes without saying that, while his name may not be generally known or saluted in big cities, this is not the case in the bush, where it has universal acknowledgement — sometimes laudatory and sometimes not. Indeed, Kidman still lives in the memory of many bush people and, fifty years after his death, there are still quite a few around able to talk of first-hand experiences with him, more often good than the reverse.

A number of them spoke of "the spirit of the man", "the awe in which he was held" or "the loyalty he commanded from his men", not by might or right but given willingly, to the extent that to them he *was* a "king".

Many of the men and women interviewed for this book either pointed to a framed poem — sometimes aged and discoloured and on a station kitchen or suburban lounge-room wall — or retrieved it carefully from memorabilia, almost in tatters from the paper folds, as something that "might be of use" to illustrate the man Kidman and the spirit surrounding him. The poem was written by Les Daley and

broadcast by him from 5CL radio station on 5 September 1932, just
two days after the public rodeo party to commemorate Sir Sidney's
seventy-fifth birthday. It is entitled "Kidman's Boys!" and it reads:

> The old man sat in the grandstand
> And he gazed at the oval below,
> At the boys in blue, at the boys he knew
> Round his heart was a sort of a glow.
> And his thoughts travelled far from the city
> With its hustle and bustle and noise,
> He was riding back on the cattle track
> Riding with Kidman's boys.
>
> Once again with the greenhide and stockwhip,
> He was wheeling the mob on the plain,
> How they baulk and dash as the writhing lash
> Sings its staccato refrain.
> And his eyes they kindle and sparkle
> His head takes a statelier poise,
> The horses' manes toss as they bow to the boss,
> Aren't they ridden by Kidman's boys?
>
> For these are the men of the stations
> Who ride 'neath the Northern stars' light,
> Where the saltbush blows and the mulga grows
> And men must be men in the fight.
> Where they're not yarded up by the tramlines
> And no boundary of brick wall annoys,
> A thousand mile ride they take in their stride,
> 'Tis the day's work for Kidman's boys.
>
> There's Hooper of Diamantina
> And Archie McLean of the Peake,
> Pierce Edwards there with silvering hair
> And Mick who prefers not to speak.
> John Brooke is down from Mundowdna
> And Cusack whom Morney employs,
> Kempe of Macumba and Ferber of Momba,
> And Johnnie, they're all Kidman's boys.
>
> Durham Downs sends us McCullagh
> And Carr's from Nundora, the tinker,
> Gourlay and West are there with the rest
> And Spencer from far Innamincka.
> Riding through good times and bad ones
> Riding through sorrows and joys,

Like Crombie of Glengyle going broke with a smile
'Tis the spirit of Kidman's boys.

And we who sit snug in the city
And rail at the drabness of life,
Rave of depression and have an obsession
That we were just born into strife.
Let's take a cue from these riders
And stop all this gloom that annoys,
Get a stockwhip and rope, put a lasso on hope
And smile, just like Kidman's boys.

Let's ride on the trail of good fortune
And cut out bad luck from the mob,
When there's a muster bring dull care a buster
And stick on like glue to the job.
And tho' drought and ill luck may assail us
Stick your chin out and don't drop that poise,
And tho' tough be the battle
You'll muster fat cattle
And win out — like Kidman's boys.

Bibliography

BOOKS AND PAMPHLETS

Angliss, J. V. *The Life Story of Sir William Angliss*. Premier Printing, Melbourne, 1959.

Australian Pastoral Directory 1897. Twopeny, Pearse & Co., Sydney and Melbourne, 1897.

Barnard, Alan. *The Simple Fleece. Studies in the Australian Wool Industry*. MUP and ANU, Melbourne, 1962.

Bauer, F. H. *Historical Geography of White Settlement in Part of Northern Australia*, pt 2. CSIRO Division of Land Research and Regional Survey, Divisional Report No. 64/1, Canberra, 1964.

Birch, Alan, and MacMillan, David S (eds). *Wealth and Progress: Studies in Australian Business History* (James Tyson, Employer). Angus & Robertson, Sydney, 1967.

Carter, Jeff. *In the Tracks of the Cattle*. Angus & Robertson, Sydney, 1968.

Charlton, Rob. *The History of Kapunda*. Hawthorn Press, Melbourne, 1971.

Coghlan, T. A. *Labour and Industry in Australia*, Vols 3 and 4. Macmillan Company of Australia, Melbourne, 1969.

Duncan, Ross. *The Northern Territory Pastoral Industry 1863–1910*. MUP, Melbourne, 1967.

Duncan-Kemp, A. M. *Where Strange Paths Go Down*. W. R. Smith and Paterson, Brisbane, 1964.

Durack, Mary. *Sons in the Saddle*. Hutchinson Australia, Melbourne, 1983.

Encel, S. *Equality and Authority — A Study of Class, Status and Power in Australia*. Cheshire Publishing, Melbourne, 1970.

Farwell, George. *Land of Mirage*. Rigby Adelaide, 1950.

Foley, J. C. *Droughts in Australia 1857–1955*. Commonwealth Bureau of Meteorology Bulletin No. 43.

Gibbs, W. J. and Maher, J. V. *Rainfall Deciles as Drought Indicators*. Commonwealth Bureau of Meteorology Bulletin No. 48.

Greenwood, Gordon. *Australia — A Social and Political History*. Angus & Robertson, Sydney, 1955.

Hanson, William. *The Pastoral Possessions of NSW*. Gibbs, Shallard and Co., 1889.

Hardy, Bobbie. *West of the Darling*. Jacaranda Press, Brisbane, 1969.

Harrington, G. N., Wilson, A. D., and Young, M. D. *Management of Australia's Rangelands*. CSIRO, Melbourne, 1984.

Hatfield, William. *Australia through the Windscreen*. Angus & Robertson, Sydney, 1936.

Holmes, J. Macdonald. *Australia's Open North*. Angus & Robertson, Sydney, 1966.

Kearns, R. H. B. *Broken Hill 1883–1893*. Broken Hill Historical Society, Broken Hill, 1973.

Kearns, R. H. B. *Broken Hill 1894–1914*. Broken Hill Historical Society, Broken Hill, 1974.

Kearns, R. H. B. *Silverton*. Broken Hill Historical Society, Broken Hill, 1972.

Kelly, J. H. *Struggle for the North*. Australasian Book Society, Sydney, 1966.

Knibbs, G. H. *The Official Year Book: Commonwealth of Australia 1901–16*.

Knightley, Phillip. *The Vestey Affair*. MacDonald Futura, London.

Litchfield, Lois. *Marree and the Tracks Beyond in Black and White*. Gillingham Printers, Adelaide, 1983.

McPheat, W. Scott. *John Flynn — Apostle to the Inland*. Hodder & Stoughton, UK, 1963.

Makin, Jock. *The Big Run*. Rigby, Adelaide, 1970.

Martin, Florence. *Three Families Outback*. Sun City Print, Geraldton, WA, 1980.

Messer, John, and Mosley, Geoff (eds). *What Future for Australia's Arid Lands?* Australian Conservation Foundation, Melbourne, 1983.

The National Handbook of Australia's Industries, (Artesian Bores and Wells in South Australia). Specialty Press, Melbourne, 1934.

Nimmo, W. H. R. *Summary of the Hydrology of Cooper's Creek*. 1947.

Peck, Harry H. *Memoirs of a Stockman*. Stock and Land Publishing Co., Melbourne, 1942.

Roberts, Professor Stephen. *The History of Australian Land Settlement 1788–1920*. Macmillan Company of Australia, Melbourne, 1924 and 1968 edns.

Ronan, Tom. *Deep of the Sky*. Cassell Australia, Melbourne, 1962.

Ronan, Tom. *Moleskin Midas*. Angus & Roberston, Sydney, 1956.

Tarling, Lowell. *Thank God for the Salvos*. Harper & Row (Australasia), Sydney, 1980.

Trengove, A. *The Story of BHP*. Cassell Australia, Sydney, 1975.

Ward, Russel. *Australia Since the Coming of Man*, rev. edn. Lansdowne Press, Sydney, 1982.

White, Myrtle Rose. *No Roads Go By*. Rigby, Adelaide, 1932.

Willey, Keith. *The Drovers*. Macmillan Company of Australia, Melbourne, 1982.

Yeomans, John. *The Scarce Australians*. Penguin, Melbourne, 1969.

Unpublished Manuscripts

Disher, Garry. Before the Age of Hurry-Up: Australian Landscape Writing, 1925–1950. BA thesis, University of Adelaide.

Hungerford, H. K. V. Droving for Kidman — A droving trip from Innamincka to Nandiwapna. Original held in Mitchell Library, Sydney.

Private Manuscripts and Documents

Bootra Pastoral Company. Minutes of the general meetings, 1924–1932.

The Dickson family, of Aramac, Queensland. Family records.

Kidman, Beryl, of South Australia. Memoirs.

Kidman, Isabel Brown. Last Will and Testament, 1948.

Kidman, Sir Sidney. Last Will and Testament, 1935.

Kidman, Walter Sidney Palethorpe. Memoirs.

Government Reports

Royal Commission inquiring into the Condition of Crown Tenants, Western Division of New South Wales, August 1900 (Report and Summary of evidence).

Select Committee inquiring into the Sale of Pastoral Lands and Construction of Railways in the Western Interior, 1902.

Royal Commission on the Meat Export Trade of Australia, 1914–1915.

Royal Commission relating to the Beef Cattle Industry, 1928.

Royal Commission inquiring into matters relating to Livestock and the Meat Industry, 1945.

Newspapers and Periodicals

Adelaide Advertiser: 31 March 1914, 21 May 1914, 18 May 1915, 28 May 1915, 11 August 1918, 11 November 1919, 11 November 1924, 19 March 1927, 21 March 1927, 3 September 1935, 24 December 1970, 2 June 1971, 3 June 1971.

Adelaide Chronicle: 6 November 1930, 11 July 1935.

Adelaide Mail: 3 September 1932.

Adelaide News: 2 September 1935, 3 September 1935.

Adelaide Observer: 2 February 1924, 21 March 1925, 17 July 1926, 23 June 1928, 14 July 1928, 25 August 1928.

Adelaide Register: 1 April 1909, 28 May 1915, 21 March 1927.

Adelaide Stock and Station Journal: 4 September 1935.

Adelaide Truth: 10 September 1932, 12 February 1938.

Australasian: 25 June 1921.

Australian Worker: 11 September 1935.

Barrier Daily Truth: 12 December 1923.

Barrier Miner: 1 April 1908.

Brisbane Courier: 5 November 1919.

Bulletin: 5 August 1918, 15 April 1936, 13 April 1955.

Catholic Press: 12 November 1903.

Daily Express, London: 17 July 1933.

Daily Mail, London: 6 October 1980.

Daily Telegraph, Sydney: 11 October 1915.

Evening Standard and St James's Gazette, London: 14 March 1914.

Kapunda Herald: 31 December 1904, 28 July 1916, 13 May 1943.

Kapunda Herald Illustrated Supplement: 5 January 1905, 3 April 1908.

London Daily Standard: 12 March 1912.

London Daily Telegraph: 30 August 1913, 7 April 1914.

London Times: 16 January 1920, 22 January 1920, 19 May 1959.

Melbourne Age: 16 January 1917.

Melbourne Argus: 14 January 1920, 3 September 1935.

Melbourne Herald: 3 August 1917.

Melbourne Punch: 1 May 1913.

News, Adelaide: 2 September 1932, 19 November 1936.

News Review, Port Adelaide: 1 December 1971.

Observer, London: 4 June 1921, 11 June 1921, 21 March 1925.

Pastoral Review: 15 January 1903, 16 September 1903.

SA Critic: 15 April 1899, 8 July 1899.

St George Standard, UK: May 1894.

Stock Journal: 7 January 1971, 1 August 1985.

St Peter's College Magazine, Adelaide: 1926.

Sunday Times, London: 5 October 1980, 19 October 1980.

Sunday Times, Perth: 24 May 1923.

Sydney Mail: 11 September 1935.

Sydney Morning Herald: 1 January 1916, 7 January 1919, 9 January 1919, 12 September 1919, 2 June 1921, 22 August 1924, 26 August 1924, 24 March 1926, 2 September 1935, 3 September 1935.

Sydney Sun: 7 September 1914.

Town and Country Journal: 22 May 1918.

Western Daily Press: 11 May 1918.

World's News: 5 May 1937.

Yorkshire Post: 25 February 1956.

Hundreds of other extracts from newspapers and periodicals (Australian, English and American) were made available to the author by members of the Kidman family or by former Kidman employees. They cannot be included in this list because their sources were not fully identified.

BIBLIOGRAPHY

ARCHIVAL MATERIAL

Australian National University Archives, Canberra

Australian Mercantile Land and Finance Co. Ltd 1856–1963. Melbourne, Sydney and London offices. Correspondence, financial records, station returns and maps.

Australian Railways' Union. Deposit N5, E256, P1, P104, P123, P125.

Corona Station, Broken Hill, 1883–1920. Corona, Gnalta and Packsaddle. Station records.

Dalgety Australia Ltd 1887–1966. Adelaide, Brisbane, Sydney and Charleville branches. Minutes, correspondence, reports and financial records.

Elder Smith and Co. Ltd 1862–1962. Head Office. Company records.

Goldsbrough Mort and Co. Ltd 1853–1962. Head Office. Company and station records, including the Bagot, Shakes and Lewis papers.

Graziers' Association of NSW 1890–1974. Minutes, correspondence and printed material.

Pitt Son Badgery Ltd, Sydney, 1888–1972. Annual reports and minutes.

Victoria River Downs, Northern Territory, 1900–1970. Station records.

Bank of New South Wales Archives, Pyrmont, Sydney

Bank of New South Wales. Records including board minutes and Sydney manager's diary entries and correspondence relating to Sidney Kidman from 1901 to 1936.

CORRESPONDENCE

Letters sent to the author by members of the Kidman family, by people who knew Sidney Kidman, had met him or worked for him, and by others offering information for this book:

Charles Achilles
Peter J. Bridge
John Cahalan
The Hon. Clyde Cameron
Bert Carr
David R. Coles
Rob Dempster
Garry Disher
Mrs M. L. Donaldson
Jim Fiddaman
Owen Francis

Bill Glasson, Queensland
   Minister for Lands and
   Forestry
Lois Hardy
James Hartmann
Dr Frank C. Hinder
Ross A. Kelly
Banks T. Kidman
Bill Kidman
Ellen Kidman
Ken Kidman

Rex Kidman
Thomas B. Kidman
Tom H. F. Kidman
Jim Laffin
Lois Litchfield
Rod McCarthy
John McMaster
Jock Makin
Florence Martin
John Menzies
Dame Mary Durack Miller

Hayden Murray
Jim Nicholas
Don Peacey
Colin T. Pelham
Gwen Rowe
Sylvia Sennett
Desmond D. Smyth
Errol Tapp
Lord Vestey
Guy Watts
Rita Winter

Letters from Sir Sidney Kidman while in Australia and while overseas to Sidney Ayers, Burns Reid and "Galloping" Jack Watts.

Letters from Sir Sidney Kidman to his pastoral inspector, Ted Pratt, and to several station managers (held in the Dubbo Downs file, Queensland State Archives, Brisbane).

Telegrams to Sir Sidney Kidman (held in the Elder Smith and Co. Ltd records, Australian National University Archives, Canberra).

Letters to Sir Sidney Kidman from within Australia and from overseas, requesting help, financial assistance or proposing marriage (held by Hugh Gooch and made available by Joan Hopkins).

INTERVIEWS

Author interviews with members of the Kidman family, people who knew Sidney Kidman, former Kidman employees and their families, and others (historians and academics).

John Ayers Jnr, of Adelaide
The Barlow family, of Broken
  Hill
Wal Bottom, of Broken Hill
Charlie Bowman, of Bourke
Bill Brook, of Birdsville
Mrs Peter Carboyd, of Roseville,
  Sydney
Tom Cole, of Lindfield, Sydney
David Ross Coles, of Adelaide
Mort Conway, of Alice Springs
Rob Dempster, of Broken Hill
Roy Dunk, of Bourke
Mrs Myrtle Eddy, of Broken Hill
Charlie Flavell, of Broken Hill
Eric Fuller, of Kapunda
Les Gardiner, of Broken Hill
Hughie Gilby, of Broken Hill
Norman Gurr, of Alice Springs

Mrs Kathleen Hart, of Broken
  Hill
Ted Hayes, of Alice Springs
Joan Hopkins, of Adelaide
Frank Kelly, of Adelaide
John Kempe, of Adelaide
Muriel Kidman, of Adelaide
Dr John Merritt, of the
  Australian National University
Damian Miller, of Alice Springs
Mrs Melba Milne, of Broken Hill
Bob Napier, of Broken Hill
Jack O'Shea, of Toowoomba
Jenkin Coles Propsting, of
  Adelaide
Jean Reid, of Adelaide
Alex Robb, of Adelaide
Bob Routledge, of Broken Hill
Jim Schmidt, of Broken Hill

BIBLIOGRAPHY

Anne Abel Smith, of Adelaide
Charles Smith, of Adelaide
Jim Vickery, of Adelaide
Professor Russel Ward, of
  Armidale

Jack Otto Watt, of Broken Hill
Owen Williams, of the
  Australian National University
R. M. Williams, of Toowoomba